GREETINGS, NOBLE SIR!

By
Nigel Flaxton

This edition published in 2015 by
Andrews UK Limited
www.andrewsuk.com

Contents

Foreword

I was fortunate to be born rather late in the twenties and so missed call-up for the Second World War by just one year. When I did register I found that if I wanted to train for teaching I had to apply for deferment, which I did. Call up followed after the two year course, delaying my entry into a permanent post by almost another two years. I finally gave up work in 2006 so I was involved with education in various roles for the entire second half of the twentieth century.

This is an account of some of my experiences with comments upon the considerable changes I saw in teaching and learning over that period. I hope, also, that it conveys something of the enjoyment I experienced during a very satisfying career. To avoid embarrassment, usually my own, I have changed all relevant names. I apologise unreservedly if, in so doing, I have inadvertently selected the name of someone else who was not part of my experience.

NF

GREETINGS, NOBLE SIR!

Chapter 1

'GREETINGS, NOBLE SIR!'

The improbable salutation didn't sound particularly pompous because it was chanted in chorus by forty-six lively ten year olds. What made it so unlikely and added so much to my confusion was that it was directed at me, only seven years their senior. To make matters worse they leapt to their feet to bestow it and embellished it with a kind of salute.

This was the first time I had looked at a class from the front of the room since becoming a student teacher all of three weeks previously. But as I well knew I should certainly not have been at the front; I should have been seated with the other students and a tutor at the back, in safe anonymity.

The class teacher was annoyed, and glared. He was taking a demonstration lesson for our group and was nicely into his stride when my late intrusion disrupted his flow. The tutor turned in my direction from his seat and I flashed what I hoped was an apologetic glance, then nearly collapsed on the spot. He was no ordinary tutor – he was St Andrew's Training College's Vice-Principal. I had really put my foot in it!

As I looked round desperately for a seat an unnerving silence settled upon the class and I felt the steam of embarrassment envelop me. Dimly, through hot clouds of confusion, I could see the children's faces wearing that expectant look characteristic of a group watching from comfortable safety the squirms of an individual in trouble.

I had been stupid enough to be late leaving the college. I knew the school we were to visit was not far and, when I lost sight of other students ahead, thought I knew the way. I took a wrong turning and walked too far. When I back-tracked to St Barnabas

Roman Catholic Junior School I was greeted by an empty playground and silent buildings. My heart sank sickeningly.

I hurried through the large green iron gates flanked at the pavement's edge by the safety crush barrier. As I crossed the playground the metal tips on the heels of my shoes drummed the message of my tardiness loudly and insistently. But the large windows in the red brick walls, divided into many small panes, were set high and mercifully no faces of the inmates could be turned towards me. Thankfully I spotted a pair of solid wooden doors, also painted green. I pushed open one of these, did the same with the heavy brown swing doors immediately inside, which closed with a noisy thump behind me, and found myself at the end of a long empty corridor.

Classrooms were ranged on either side but the doors were firmly closed. I tried peering through the panes of glass in one or two but the view was obscured by notices or pictures strategically placed to discourage unwanted Peeping Toms like me. Once or twice I did gain a glimpse of a class but the children were hard at work and I couldn't bring myself to disturb the peace by entering and confessing my foolishness to complete strangers. Finally I turned a corner at the end of the corridor and in the distance saw a very tall man walking stealthily with head bent forward. He didn't see me immediately and I watched him pause by a classroom door. He seemed to be listening and it suddenly dawned on me that he was the headmaster and was checking for evidence of unruly noise. I considered that singularly unnecessary for, as I knew very well, the place was as quiet as a tomb. He looked up as I walked hesitatingly towards him.

'Excuse me, sir,' I began, then noticing his clerical collar, fumbled for the correct address. I had absolutely no experience of Catholic churches or schools… 'er, Reverend Father…' That came from whence I knew not, but it sounded right.

'Oh, good afternoon, young man. I had no idea you were there,' he replied in a pleasant but firm voice with a hint of Irish. 'What can I do for you?'

'I'm looking for a group of students,' I ventured nervously. 'That is, I should be with a group that were due here this afternoon.'

'Oh dear,' he said, rather heavily, 'you are late, aren't you? They came some time ago. They're with your tutor in Mr McCormick's classroom. Come on, I'll take you there.'

'Oh, thank you so much,' I gasped, relieved the situation was being retrieved at last. I dropped into step with him as he strode down the corridor and across the hall. As we walked I explained why I was late.

'I don't like having lessons interrupted,' he answered, 'and normally you would have to wait until the end. However, as this is your first visit, I'll let you go in.'

My heart sank again. Obviously being late here was a particularly odious crime. I knew already the college's view of such matters because in his first lecture the Vice-Principal had impressed the fact upon us in no uncertain terms.

'Students must maintain the very good name of the college by being punctual, courteous and industrious at all times when visiting or working in schools.'

As he addressed us in the old lecture room, resplendent in both cap and gown as a deliberately impressive introduction, we decided it would never do to cross this imposing authoritarian figure. Little did I realise that I was about to be ushered into his presence, in front of a class with its teacher and a group of students, extremely late – and by the school's headmaster of all people! It was to be a singularly inauspicious beginning to my teaching career.

But I wasn't actually ushered in. No doubt knowing what was about to happen and feeling it would teach me an appropriate lesson, the head stopped short of the door.

'That's the room. I'll leave you to go in and make your apologies. But do try to be on time next week now you know how to find us.'

'Thank you very much, Reverend Father, I certainly will,' I said, laying it on slightly but no less fervently, then moved to open the door.

The eruption of the class turned the beginning from merely inauspicious to positively ghastly. In the event, Greetings, Noble, and Sir were utterly inappropriate in their attribution to me.

Of course, it was simply the school's method of extending courtesy to a visitor. However, it was accorded to each and every person who went into any classroom – all men were Noble Sirs and all women Gracious Ladies whether they were teachers, caretakers, cleaners, or – very rarely -- parents. The exceptions were the headmaster and the headmistress of the attached infants' school. These were accorded 'Greetings and blessings Reverend Father/Mother'. The children were blessed en bloc in reply, but no doubt an individual then hauled out of the room to account or atone for a misdemeanour felt decidedly unblessed.

The classes were large and full of lively personalities bred in the old industrial area surrounding the school. Obviously they enjoyed the chance of enlivening a lesson occasionally by leaping to their feet and chanting their mandatory greeting. No wonder the head let me enter the room on my own. Later, in a more reflective frame of mind, I realised the custom enshrined not only courtesy but also an effective deterrent to classroom interruptions.

The other students were taken aback as well. However, ensconced as they were on chairs around the sides and rear of the room they soon recovered their composure and with forty-five members of the class enjoyed the completion of my discomfiture when I realised there was no chair waiting for me. But there were two vacant places in the rows of double desks containing the children. One was right at the front and consequently unthinkable but the other, mercifully, was near the back well away from where Major Darnley, the Vice-Principal, was sitting.

Quickly, before anyone could be sent on the errand of fetching a chair from another room, I stammered an apology to Mr McCormick at the blackboard and bolted for the back. The forty-sixth member of the class was the girl sitting in the other half of the desk I had spotted, who became highly embarrassed as I attempted the difficult task of fitting my lanky frame into it. I slid on to the wooden seat easily enough, but had a real problem squeezing my long legs and big feet past the cast iron framework and failed to fit my knees under the spacious book compartment with its heavy lid, which I thumped noisily with my contortions. I finished with legs apart and knees poking upwards, giving a tolerable imitation of a grasshopper. My companion blushed furiously at the giggles of children nearby, for not only was she now perforce sitting by a male, she was also being gradually ejected by my right knee.

Finally the class, accepting the show was over, returned its attention to Mr McCormick and his demonstration lesson. As their gaze swung away from me I tried to lapse into obscurity but failed signally due to my transfixed posture. The slightest move I made to ease my limbs punctuated the salient points of the lesson with loud crashes of the desk lid.

The exercise we were beginning was 'Instructional Practice' and we were to look back on it as a particularly helpful element in our training. Obviously the practice of teaching is a fundamental part of all teacher training courses, but frequently students were dispatched to schools and visited only occasionally by their tutors. The less-than-full-year Post Graduate Certificate in Education (PGCE) usually put students into schools for one of the three university terms. The three year Bachelor of Education course, introduced in the late sixties, allows practice to be divided into shorter blocks with a more useful time spread. But inevitably it falls to the individual school to supervise most of the students' efforts as, rich with inexperience, they face classes for the first time simply because it is impossible for tutors to be assigned to them individually. To-day, also, mature students with other qualifications who want to move from other employment can qualify as teachers largely with on-the-job training. Sensibly they will seek out schools with good track records in such guidance. At best, schools and teachers have always given excellent tutorial support. But at worst the fledglings were dropped in at the deep end and sank or swam according to their personalities. Robust ones always made it. It was unfortunate that in the past the less-than-robust nearly always made it as well. The failure rate was extremely low in the immediate post war years as the child population expanded and more teachers were required despite class sizes that would be regarded as horrendous to-day.

In the past some colleges were dynamically involved with the practical aspects of teaching; St Andrew's had possessed its own Practising School on the college site to which tutors and students

5

were regularly assigned as part time teachers. This ceased to function following a direct hit during an air raid so the pupils transferred to neighbouring schools. Instructional Practice was conceived to provide the next best experience for us.

The system involved groups of students each with a tutor visiting schools to take responsibility for lessons of particular classes for half a day each week for a term. After the first demonstration lesson the students each taught lessons in turn. Next day each group held a discussion in college with its tutor to make a critical appraisal and prepare the outline for next week's lessons. Had the work been too difficult or too easy for the pupils? Did the student hold their interest? Had he done sufficient preparation? Were his instructions clear and precise? How had he dealt with the problem when Mary accidentally spilt glue on Robert's new shirt? What changes should be made if the lesson were to be repeated? Each week the lessons were examined increasingly microscopically as the term progressed. Obviously a student whose turn came later was expected to learn by the mistakes of those who had taught earlier so they were challenged more robustly. By the end of the exercise lessons were being torn to shreds with reckless abandon as we seized on every minor *contretemps* - and were stubbornly defended by the embryonic teachers.

Naturally we realised that in the normal routine of day-to-day teaching no lesson is ever subjected to such searching analysis. Even OFSTED team inspections (Office for Standards in Education, Children's Services and Skills) to-day are normally undertaken by one person per class. But the experience certainly made us sensitive to every aspect of planning, presentation, class control, evaluation and later modification. It taught us much and I am sure we all benefitted in later years. Hopefully so did our classes.

As we settled into the routine and got to know one another we decided Instructional Practice at St Barnabas Roman Catholic Junior School needed livening up. We got our chance quite soon when it was Bill Heppleton's turn to teach.

Bill was a stolid north country lad who, unlike most of his breed, didn't possess much of a sense of humour. He was ambitious and determined to become a successful teacher, which was most laudable, but he was prepared to accomplish this at the expense of others, which was not. In our critique seminars he did his utmost to impress the VP with his analytical skills by prodding at every minor blemish on the smooth surface of other lessons. The rest of us formed the impression that he intended making his first lesson something really worth watching. We decide to help him achieve this goal.

It was borne in upon us that the budding teacher had to be in the classroom before the pupils arrived. Accordingly Bill stood in front of the empty desks and checked the pile of papers that were the worksheets he had prepared. It was a History lesson and the topic was 'Monasteries'.

The bell sounded signifying the end of the afternoon break and the children filed in. As was their custom as soon as they were all standing in their places, they began chanting a 'Hail Mary'. The fact that Mr McCormick was not in the room and that we students came from a college supported by the Church of England mattered not a whit. They always said this prayer on entering the room and, having done so, sat down. Momentarily silent they turned their corporate eye on Bill.

He looked at me rather disconcertedly. I was sitting at the back but the chairs flanking mine were unoccupied. Major Darnley also was absent and I was the sole representative of the student body. I assumed what I hoped was a Poker face and sat back as though I could see nothing unusual. But I knew what Bill did not – that Archie Forton was contriving to waylay the VP and Mr Mac as they emerged from the staffroom where, no doubt, they had enjoyed the traditional cup of tea as yet denied to us students. We were supposed to be far too busy during the half day practice to have time for such luxuries. I also knew where the other students were.

'Are you teachin' us to-day, sir?' asked a precocious blonde with ringlets and a pink blouse.

'Course 'e is!' said a tough looking lad with holes in the elbows of his faded brown pullover. ' E's standin' there, ain't 'e?'

Due to its proximity to the college the children were used to having groups of students in their classroom, but it was a rare event to get one on his own and virtually all to themselves.

'What's the lesson about, sir?' asked another voice.

'If no one comes in, will you send us out to play again?' wheedled another.

'Oo, yes,' joined in many more, 'go on, sir, please…'

Bill was wise enough to realise he was lost unless he acted quickly. Though obviously annoyed at having a minimal audience to appreciate his carefully prepared attention-catching opening, nevertheless he plunged in.

'No, I shall not. Never mind where the others are. I'm here and I'm taking the lesson. Now sit still, and watch.'

He seized a suitcase from the floor in front of him, placed it carefully on the high teacher's desk and opened it gradually in true magician's style with the lid towards the class. Slowly he began to take something out. The children naturally became perfectly silent and watched.

Something long began to emerge, a thick, brown, coarse material. Suddenly, with a flourish, he swept it out fully and held it at arm's length.

'There!' he said triumphantly. 'Now, if I were dressed in this, what sort of a person do you think I would be?'

'A monk!' shouted every voice.

Bill looked surprised. He had forgotten the possibility of Catholic children being used to seeing monks' habits.

'You'd 'ave to 'ave the top o' your 'ead shaved,' called out a cheeky but angelic faced lad in the front row who had already troubled two or three of us with disconcerting questions and comments.

'Would you like that, sir?' asked someone else.

'Be quiet,' snapped Bill. 'Now listen. Yes, this is the dress of a monk. Now where do monks usually live?'

Before the assembled company could boom the next obvious answer, Gordon Mersely opened the door.

'GREETINGS, NOBLE SIR!' chanted the class dutifully, standing up with a great clatter as the heavy desk seats crashed back on the iron frames. Gordon nodded at Bill.

'I do apologise, Mr Heppleton,' he said. He rapidly turned away and made for his chair. When he sat the children did likewise, again to the staccato rattle of seats.

From the front Bill watched open mouthed, having been stopped so abruptly. With an effort he collected himself then turned his gaze heavily from Gordon to the class.

'Well, I'm sure you all know that monks live in monasteries,' he said, sensibly scrapping his question. 'Now, you will all need one of the sheets of paper I've duplicated.' He pointed to one pupil in each of the four front desks. 'One, two, three, four – you take these and give them to everyone in your row.' Four piles of proffered sheets were grabbed by the recipients with slightly overdone enthusiasm.

At this point I nodded at Trevor Walfrey who was peering surreptitiously through the door window, just as Gordon had done a few moments earlier. Trevor made his entrance with a commendable flourish.

'GREETINGS…' chorused the class to the familiar noisy accompaniment. Trevor didn't look at Bill as Gordon had done. Instead he strode to his chair wearing a fixed expression and stared intently at the worksheet of the pupil sitting in front of him. I could see the corners of his mouth twitching.

So was Bill. With three students in and seven to go, realisation hit him hard. He was furious. He strode to the door and flung it open. He glared up and down the corridor outside but it was completely empty. We guessed he might do this at some point and had decided the group would wait beyond a corner and that each next entrant would only move up to the door when he guessed the lesson was proceeding. That particular spot also put the conspirators in a better position to hear the approach of the VP and Mr Mac when Archie's list of questions about his forthcoming lesson became exhausted, or they brushed him aside and made for the classroom. In that event the group judged they could manage a combined dash and entry that would be tolerably spectacular.

Bill slammed the door in annoyance. The class watched with mild interest and waited for him to continue. They hadn't twigged yet.

But they got it when Malcolm Ashterleigh entered in similar fashion. The buzz went round as they leapt to their feet and fairly shouted their greetings at him. As he sat down some turned and took stock, pointing to our seats. Four in, six to come! If only Mr McCormick and the other old chap stayed out, their afternoon was made.

But Bill's certainly wasn't. Attention was riveted on the door and he fought to retrieve it.

'Never mind these interruptions, children,' he said tersely. 'Look at the sheet. I've drawn two pictures of monastery buildings and at the side there is a list of names of the rooms. I want you to write each name on the picture where you think it should go. Let's think about the first one…dormitory…'

'GREETINGS, NOBLE SIR!' yelled the class at Berny Wilton.

'Oh, do come in, Mr Wilton,' Bill tried heavily. 'So glad you could join us.'

The class enjoyed the irony. They were with us wholeheartedly; positively glowing with mounting excitement. What a fun afternoon!

We managed two more. After Berny's entrance Bill did the only possible thing. Having told the class what to do he retired to the teacher's desk and waited for them to finish the work. The class, pencils poised, watched the door.

After Jon Kennton and Bob Brinkton made successful home runs Archie's ingenuity faded and with the VP and Mr Mac he walked heavily along the corridor. The last two picked up the sound of footsteps and provided the class with a grand finale as they burst in and sat down hurriedly. Bill guessed from their haste the show was over. He rose heavily to his feet.

'Now perhaps we can get down to work,' he admonished. 'Just finish off that first section of the sheet.'

But there was one more entrance to be made and when it came the children overdid things. There was just too much excitement about their greetings to Archie and the two men and it was accompanied by some giggling that almost gave the game away.

'There's no need to shout so loudly, we are not deaf!' said Mr McCormick sharply. He turned to Bill. 'I'm so sorry for this interruption. We were delayed. I hope we haven't spoilt your lesson.'

I thought Bill was going to have apoplexy. The class, on the other hand, having had a thoroughly satisfying ten minutes of pure entertainment turned their attention quite willingly to monasteries. But a few contrived to flash delightfully conspiratorial glances in our direction.

Dame Fortune does her best to redress the balance of life when possible and I was the recipient of her ministrations on Bill's behalf. At the seminar next morning, when his lesson was to be discussed, the VP surveyed us closely.

'Gentlemen, I missed the beginning of Mr Heppleton's lesson yesterday because I was discussing next week's work with Mr Forton. Would someone be good enough to tell me the relevant points of the lesson prior to my coming in? Do you feel the beginning was sufficiently lively to secure the children's attention?'

The rest managed to keep their mirth silent but involuntarily I chortled aloud, which left me facing the VP's sharply questioning stare alone. I also had to deal with the problem of explaining what I found amusing about the production of a monk's habit from a suitcase. I failed miserably, to Bill's delight. He deserved no less. But the VP's scowl proclaimed eloquently his view of me as a shallow character unlikely to take teaching seriously. I had got firmly on the wrong side of him twice in the space of my first few weeks in college.

It was not at all the kind of beginning I had imagined for myself.

Chapter 2

The college had been built in a pleasant pastoral setting in the middle of the nineteenth century when the need to expand elementary education was being accepted by various religious organisations. It was twenty years old when Forster's Education Act (1870) decreed compulsory education for all and ninety years old when the midland city in which it stood was regularly bombed. Its site was not far from the centre, in twentieth century terms, and for years it had stood cheek by jowl with factories whose wartime production made them worthwhile targets. A number of bombs exploded harmlessly within its perimeter walls, excavating craters in its lawns and cricket field but these did not immediately interrupt the flow of its life. Young men continued to pass through it during the early war years, emerging to go directly into the Armed Forces. Then a direct hit on one of its wings caused a rapid and complete evacuation.

For the remainder of the Second World War its life was completely uneventful. The buildings were unoccupied except the refectory and kitchen which became a 'British Restaurant' for the local populace. These institutions were government sponsored, locally organised replacements for many local cafés 'Closed for the Duration' as the familiar notices announced. Meals were basic but reasonably wholesome. They were a godsend to those families bereft of hearth and home in the sudden night.

In 1945 the college was rapidly reopened to cope with the large wave of students needed for the forthcoming bulge in the child population. With rapid demobilisation of men from the Armed Forces that piece of planning needed no prior investigation into anticipated changes in social activity. Existing facilities had to suffice; there was no time or money to extend buildings or refurbish rooms beyond the necessary minimum to get the production line working again. Every possible room was pressed into service to contain beds.

Training College courses were two years in length. Such was the urgent need for teachers that an Emergency Training Scheme was set up, providing a mere one year course for selected men and women returning from the Forces. Across the country a scattering of empty buildings of widely varied quality was pressed into service as Emergency Colleges which operated until well into the fifties. Typically the scheme provided fertile ground for seeds of class distinction in the education service; years later 'Emergency Men/Women' found promotion harder to come by unless they gained further qualifications. Nevertheless selection was rather more strict than for normal courses; Hansard records an answer given in 1948 by Mr Tomlinson, the Minister for Education, that following a new recruitment drive, of 11,200 women who applied 6,800 had been rejected or had withdrawn; 2,650 had been accepted whilst 1,750 were being processed.

The Reverend D.W.Silton MA (Cantab.) was Principal of St Andrew's. He was an ageing bachelor whose life had been devoted to training students. He had been in post for virtually all the years between the wars and thus experienced the turmoil of the second towards the end of his career. The immediate aftermath was an even greater upheaval for him – quite literally. He relinquished the spacious Principal's house in the college grounds, filled most of its rooms with beds to accommodate even more students, and occupied a single room next to his study in college as a bed sitter. He knew it would be for two years at most. He knew changes were on the way and he wanted none of them. He would be happy to retire once the old place was back in business.

So it happened that I entered the college at a time when the past was still with it but the future was about to descend in true whirlwind fashion. I don't think any of us realised we were to receive a pre-war training for post-war schools. Looking back, on the whole I am grateful this was so, for whilst my teaching experience spanned much of the second half of the century and embraced many changes in education, nevertheless I felt firm on the bedrock of old-fashioned training. I found that especially useful because my nature is to look ahead most of the time and welcome change. Occasionally, though, my roots provided the strength to remain firmly planted when buffeting winds swirled without direction.

I failed Latin at school. I was in an Arts sixth form of eight students, four in each year. Few teachers could be spared to teach such small groups – the Science side faired better, mustering about twenty-five in each year. The whole sixth form totalled just under sixty students in a grammar school of six hundred; a ten per cent ratio that was quite normal at the time. In a forty period week I was taught for only seventeen and even some of these were shared between upper and lower sixth. I had not taken Latin in the lower forms, then found I needed it for university. Course advice was non-existent. I tried to take the subject from scratch with minimal teaching but didn't make it.

The fact that I discovered girls at the same time no doubt contributed to my failure. This happy state was surprisingly enhanced at school in a totally unexpected quarter. Many unlikely teachers were called upon to fill gaps caused by those who had been called up, making teaching standards a patchwork quilt. Youth, inevitably, was singularly lacking in the wartime profession. Call up for military service began at the age of seventeen and a half. Compulsory registration for service actually reached the age of forty-one and many approaching this age were taken. But near the end of the war the call-up of young women was eased; then female teachers of tender years were sometimes employed to fill the gaps in schools for boys.

Six months before higher examinations I found myself, at sixteen plus and growing rapidly, with a most attractive though diminutive twenty-one year old mistress – the teaching sort, that is. During the sunny spring and early summer prior to my examinations we found a pleasant spot amongst the roof gables of the old building which conveniently could be reached via the fire escape. It was an excellent place for sunbathing, being completely sheltered from both wind and prying eyes. If I pleased her in any way it certainly was not with my prowess at Latin. Neither did I tell her of the headmaster's weird obsession that boys and girls should not meet in any way before they reached twenty-one and had concluded their studies, nor how I had discovered the fact!

Quite rightly university places at the end of the war were being made readily available to ex-servicemen and, young though I was, I could not wait another year to retake Latin so I settled for the Head's offer to ask the Principal of St Andrew's to consider me for a place at the last moment.

Thus I arrived for my interview in late August. It was also set, quite literally, late in the day, 8.00 pm in fact. I found that interviews continued at half hour intervals until 9.00 pm each day as they considered extra applicants. Dusk was falling and so was steady rain.

I approached the Victorian gothic façade with a truly sick feeling. I had always wanted to teach; only I knew how much. I had missed university but could alleviate my sense of failure by promising myself an external degree later. Teaching was my goal; I would accept anything which led to that – but what could I do if I were turned down now?

The old blue-grey pavement bricks echoed to my footsteps. Small and patterned, each had two rows of raised knobbles and the lines formed between them produced radiating patterns like stars. These collected and held the rainwater, so that as I walked towards each street gaslight I trod a stellar pathway beckoning me onwards. Though fascinated I could only wonder whether the return journey would be so inviting.

The building straddled the end of the road with its deserted pavements. Tall and narrow windows, grouped in pairs, extended in three orderly rows across the entire front with the exception of the middle section which housed a pair of massive, black doors. These arched away to a point; I imagined times when they must have opened to students of yore arriving in horse-drawn coaches, with luggage and boxes piled on the outside, perhaps with the less wealthy ones sitting there also.

As I reached these solid barriers, firmly shut, I felt a momentary twinge of panic as I envisaged having to knock to gain admittance. My fist would have produced the lightest of taps upon their vast structure. I was relieved to see a small pedestrian door let into the framework of the right hand one. I saw no bell, push or pull, but found it opened to my hesitant touch. I stepped through into a short, lofty passage that opened on to a quadrangle.

This area looked most unprepossessing, especially in the subdued light, and consisted of a very ordinary hexagonal lawn surrounded by worn paving stones. It was the centre of the oldest part of the college and I learnt subsequently was known universally as 'god's acre'. The absence of the capital was to avoid any possible confusion with the Deity. This was important because the individual I now approached through a small door on my right labelled 'Enquiries' was, in fact, 'god'. His official title was Caretaker but that was rarely used.

The unofficial nomenclature asserted his standing in the hierarchy as far as students were concerned. Generations of students returning after lock-up bestowed the title on this college servant who held power over them by reporting them to tutors, or otherwise. Probably he benefited from 'otherwise'. But at that moment I knew nothing of this and merely followed the slight figure walking with a noticeable limp across the quad towards the Principal's study.

This, also, was redolent of age. A large oak desk with inlaid green leather was flanked by two massive bookcases. There were two or three upright chairs, upholstered in leather, and two very large easy chairs similarly covered. I was surprised and confused to be motioned to one of these by the Principal; even more so when I sank into it and had to extend my legs out in front to retain any semblance of an upright posture. No one else was present and I saw only one other person after 'god' during this visit. He was another candidate who took my place in the Principal's study as I left. The place looked and vaguely smelt like a mausoleum.

I was forced to look up to the gowned figure of the Rev. Silton sitting behind the desk. He was tall and large boned, features lined with age, sharp eyes beneath grey bushy eyebrows. From his wide, firm mouth I expected a strident voice and swift, incisive questions. Instead I was surprised to hear a fairly quiet, almost apologetic voice asking me trivia. In the flush of youth I never considered the probability he was tired. Later I was to see the rigid authoritarianism he still practised in the college which belonged to an age soon destined to seem a hundred years away. But his last question was the one that left me groping.

'It's the obvious one,' he said diffidently, 'but it has to be put. Why do you want to teach?'

My mind flashed over my decision which had crystallised in an instant I could well remember. But the process leading to that moment had extended for many years. I knew that, despite my immaturity.

I remembered being a thoroughly bewildered young boy attending my grammar school for the first time on Wednesday, August 30th 1939. I remembered joining all the other boys in the school two days later, September 1st, as we arrived each carrying one suitcase, a gas mask and one day's supply of sandwiches, as officially instructed. We were ushered on to waiting buses and taken to the central railway station where we joined many hundreds more youngsters in subdued queues, also being evacuated. We left home with absolutely no idea where we were going; later we found that the teachers were similarly mystified. Only headteachers held that information, in sealed envelopes they were forbidden to open until their train journeys began. Society was suffering paranoia about spies. The mind boggles at the notion of some clever interloper collecting the vast timetable and journey information of the nation's schoolchildren that day, carefully encoding it and transmitting it to the enemy. I also remembered feeling very lonely in deepest Gloucestershire on Sunday 3rd September when I heard that war was declared.

But the sudden and massive bombing feared by many adults from the scenes of the Spanish Civil War three years earlier did not materialise. A schoolboy cousin and I found time lying on our hands. Our school shared accommodation with another, so we had afternoon lessons only, from 1.00 to 5.00 pm six days a week. As the rich autumn gave way to a biting hard winter we turned to imaginative games. He criss-crossed the gentle hills and tranquil lanes of our lengthy walks with the routes of imaginary buses which we 'drove' and for which he produced detailed timetables. Indoors he assisted me in organising our imaginary school for which I produced timetables of a different kind, but no less detailed. When we left school he went into the city's transport department and I wanted to teach.

The moment my intention crystallised occurred one day when the headmaster walked into the fifth form and asked, unusually diffidently, whether anyone wished to take up teaching as a career. I believe he found it strange that anyone at that level – nowadays year 11 – should be thinking so far ahead. Traditionally, for him, boys went on to university and considered the notion of employment after graduating. But we were approaching the end of the war and government needed to plan ahead. In schools, however, the notion of careers advice for students lay well in the future.

'Your headmaster says he believes you could become a good teacher, Flaxton,' I heard the Principal saying. Applicants were not college members, of course, hence he used my surname as at school.

'It's what I've always wanted to do, sir,' I croaked, 'I think I'm reasonably good at explaining things to children. I've had a little experience at Sunday School,' I finished lamely, woefully aware of the inadequacy of my reply. I wanted him to thrust incisively at me on the topics I had mulled over in preparation – the History of Education in the nineteenth century, a favourite of mine in History exams, or how I thought I would be able to control a class, but he seemed interested only in trifles.

I had learnt something about control from experience as a prefect. Due to being swept into an accelerated stream I entered the sixth at a very young age and found, when the prefects' list of classes was drawn up, that I was assigned to 5C. Prefects had the duty of standing in front of 'their' class at the beginning of each session and keeping control until the teacher arrived. The members of 5C were my age, indeed some were older because they were repeating the year. Some, also, were quite hefty. I suffered from the disadvantage that my growth pattern was slow to begin with but accelerated later when I grew nine inches in three years. I was still fourteen when I faced 5C for the first time and all of five feet three.

To be accurate, I didn't actually face them immediately the first time we met. Having seen from the list who they were getting, they prepared a simple reception. As I walked through the door I was seized from both sides, lifted off my feet, hurried across the room and thrust feet first through the opposite window opened ready for the purpose. Considerately they knew the drop was only four feet and there was a small border of bushes outside to accommodate my fall. The window was then firmly shut.

For a moment I pondered my pride and position; then a sixth sense emerged from somewhere. I strode back into the building, straight to the classroom, flung open the door and walked in very decisively. For a split second 5C stopped their mirthful noise and I eyed as many as I could directly.

'I grant you round one, gentlemen,' I said with as much poise as I could muster, mentally grateful that I enjoyed acting. 'Round two will be mine, however, since you know prefects carry the authority of the Head.'

Some smirks were interchanged, but we all knew the hierarchy was established and I would be in control. Everyone knew perfectly well in what form that authority was dispensed to anyone sent to him on a disciplinary matter. From then on 5C and I enjoyed our relationship and, unusually, the story did not travel around the school. I learnt more in those few moments than I could possibly have imagined at the time.

'Alright, I'll take you,' said the Principal suddenly. 'I will send the formal letter in a day or two. Term starts quite soon, as I'm sure you know.' He stood up and held out a hand.

'Welcome to St Andrew's, Mr Flaxton.'

I bit off the question, 'Who?' and managed to suppress surprise at the form of address. I struggled to my feet, took his hand and muttered some totally forgettable platitude. He turned away, then as I made for the door, asked me to invite in the next candidate. Our eyes met as I held the door open for him and I smiled encouragingly. But when term began I looked for him in vain.

I walked out of the college feeling a strange mixture of anticlimax and elation. The interview had been ridiculously low key; I'd had no opportunity to show what I thought was mettle. But very soon that gave way to thorough excitement because I now had my career, even though I wasn't entering it in the way I had intended.

Looking back many years later, I have no regrets whatsoever. The endless fascination of teaching lies in the fact that it is entirely about people. Different age groups present different problems and satisfactions – a class of seven year olds is different in most respects from a class of adults, but not entirely so! I have taught both, and all ages in between.

It is the same with schools. Each is different and each has its particular problems and successes. In the majority of cases the latter predominate, even though the former are more readily noticed, especially by the public at large through being seized upon by the media. Gradually throughout the second half of the twentieth century society turned its spotlight on to the educational arena which, on balance, has been to the advantage of both. In scrutinising education the discussion, understandably, is conducted in broad terms of policies, organisations, systems, curricula, discipline and so forth. But to the vast majority of children, their parents and their teachers what occupies most of their concern about schools is what sort of people come together in them and what takes place in the day to day interplay of their lives.

That interplay is full of ordinary human stuff, most of which has no attraction for the media and so goes unreported. If you really look into the school world there is much humour, good friendship, and a surprising amount of respect, albeit often hidden beneath a disparaging veneer, balanced by some disagreements, occasional nastiness, some frustrations, and occasional sadness. There are successes and failures amongst both pupils and teachers, just as in any other area of human activity.

Many people assert that teaching to-day is very different from what it used to be. Certainly some things have changed dramatically but I feel its basic elements remain broadly similar to those I experienced in my early days as a teacher. Certainly I have never had cause to regret being successful at that college interview, though I have never had such an easy one since, no matter for what post I applied. As I walked home that wet August night the glistening pavements were strewn with cascades of stars and on the whole they have continued to shine brightly ever since.

And I have found that I don't hate Latin, though for a fortune I still couldn't pass an exam in it.

Chapter 3

The bomb had crashed through the roof and exploded in the middle of the small hall excavating a crater, where the floor had been, into which the remnants of the school had fallen. It was obviously only a small bomb but sufficient nonetheless for the school also was small, very small indeed. Three classrooms had clustered round the hall but their inner walls were demolished and their rubble, intermingled with twisted and shattered desks, now lay in the crater. The door of a fourth, much smaller room, hung precariously over the pit from one rusty hinge. A nameplate proclaimed the title of the former occupant with hollow importance. 'Headmaster' remained remarkably legible. No attempt had been made to clear the site.

Above, charred slateless rafters etched a chequer pattern against the sky. Outside, the walls bore little trace of the internal chaos. They were built of strong stone and had directed the blast upwards, gutting the inside and the roof.

From the little building the high surrounding walls survived smooth and unbroken encircling the college's original playing field, itself now a series of grassy hollows and mounds where other bombs had fallen. The school was the Practising School where many former students had learnt to teach. The pupils who attended from nearby houses had received the best and the worst teaching, with a mixture in between, as novices struggled with their charges. Fortunately, at all times there were the college tutors and the resident teachers to counteract mistakes and moderate blunders. As with the great majority of schools there were successes and one former pupil progressed to become a Fellow of the Royal Society. But its very existence was a nineteenth century concept. It was outmoded but still functioning as the

Second World War began. The bomb brought about its demise, fortunately achieving it without hurting anyone.

Gordon Mersely, Malcolm Ashterleigh and I were exploring the college the day after we arrived.

'I wonder when they'll get around to clearing up this mess,' I said.

'It certainly won't have a high priority,' Gordon asserted. 'They'll never rebuild it, of course.' He kicked a brick into the crater, which echoed noisily.

'What takes its place, I wonder?' mused Malcolm.

'Oh, the senior men have told me that,' replied Gordon. 'We'll still get plenty of practice. It's divided into three kinds, observational, instructional, and block. We start the observational kind quite soon, apparently. They send us to look at schools we won't be doing the other practices in, such as nursery and infants, schools for the deaf and the blind, for delicate kids, and so on.'

'That could be interesting.' I said. 'I've never been into places like those, except when I was an infant myself. We do the other practices in junior and senior schools, right?'

'Right,' said Gordon. 'Instructional practice is half a day a week in schools with a group and a tutor. Everyone takes it in turns to teach whilst everyone else watches. For block practice we go into schools pretty much on own, for four weeks at a time.'

'No tutors?' asked Malcolm.

'You are attached to one, I'm told, and he visits you occasionally. Most of the supervision comes from the staff at the school.'

'You have been genning up, old boy,' said Malcolm. 'Come on, let's get out of this ruin.'

The college staff were trying hard to bring their courses up to date. For this they needed far more than a single practising school. The city had a rich variety of schools caring for children with various problems. It also had a few new nursery schools for two to five year olds, largely experimental. The idea of sending children to school before the traditional age of five was quite innovative.

Educational Psychology was advancing again from strides made before the war. Study of children's play was becoming important to see the role it played in children's learning. As Gordon said, our first experiences at this early stage were to be observation without any practice. So I found myself in a group that was to visit a nursery school containing a very modern facility. This certainly did not extend to its buildings which were solid nineteenth century, but inside a room had been adapted for the special purpose of observing young children's natural play.

A section of one side of this room had been removed and replaced by a screen of stiff, fine, dark green mesh. It was illuminated by artificial light on the classroom side so it appeared quite solid, seemingly a large unadorned board. On the other side of the screen was a small room in which an observer could sit. Its walls were black and there was no internal light. From this viewpoint it was easy to watch children in the classroom through the mesh. But before our visit the tutors impressed upon us the need for absolute silence in the observation room because it would become quite useless if the children knew they were being watched.

The school was in a depressed slum area which had been opened up considerably in recent years with the help of the Luftwaffe. The people who lived there were rough and tough Midlanders whose courage in the blitz had burst forth from their natural resistance to being pushed around by anyone. Hitler had united them as never before and ensured their combined wrath was directed at him personally. The children were natural chips from the parental blocks.

My group happened to be the first to visit the school from our year in the college. We were welcomed by the headmistress, Miss Webster, who spent some time talking to us about pre-war developments in the education of children in Geneva, about which most of us knew absolutely nothing. Then we were directed to the classrooms to move about and talk to the children and get to know something about them.

There were two classes, each containing about twenty children, known respectively as the 'seniors' and the 'juniors'. The former were aged from three and a half to four and a half, the latter covering the tender age of two and a half to three and a half.

There were six teachers, three assigned to each class, but only one had as yet completed her training.

Our group of ten students divided equally. I then entered the first nursery classroom I had ever seen. It comprised the seniors and everyone was active, very active indeed! Some were painting with large brushes on paper pinned to upright easels, some were playing with sand and water using gaudy beach buckets of various sizes and were covering themselves liberally with the mixture. Others were rolling plasticene and making animals and people. One was playing with a large wooden railway engine, sitting astride it and jerking it forwards, dragging coaches behind. The room was furnished with tables, grouped informally, with benches around the room and a sink and tap in one corner. There were some picture books, a few dolls, a motley collection of other toys, and drawing paper, glue, small rounded scissors, powder paint, bits of wood, crayons, in seeming profusion.

Used as we were to extreme austerity in all things and especially in our own wartime classrooms, we couldn't believe our eyes. Gordon Mersely blinked in astonishment.

'Heck, I didn't think I'd be saying I wish I was back in school myself!'

'Too true,' I agreed. 'I remember doing work in my infants' school sitting firmly in a desk and risking a smack if I stood up before being told. This looks like fun!'

We towered over the children, of course, and so crouched down as we talked to them. They seemed very self-possessed and uninhibited and very soon we realised they were used to having visitors because it was, in its way, a 'show school'.

'What's that you're painting?' I asked a mop of mouse-coloured hair hunched over a piece of paper on the floor.

'It's Peter, init?' the mop replied without moving.

'Who's Peter?'

A pink face appeared as the mop turned. 'Me rabbit, course,' its owner emphasised with exaggerated deliberation, disgusted the palpable idiot hadn't instantly recognised her pet.

'Ouch!' I exclaimed as the railway engine hit me provocatively on the ankle. I moved involuntarily and the tough, ill clad driver surmounting it with an impish look in his eye pushed it onwards with very loud 'choo, choos', satisfied the simple ploy had successfully cleared his tracks.

I looked up to see Gordon in conversation with Miss Carstairs, the teacher in charge of the class.

'Yes,' she was saying, 'I have two assistants as you see, so we keep our eyes on about ten children each, when they're all here. Sometimes, of course, we have quieter activities, such as when one of us reads a story. Whenever the weather allows we take it in turns with the junior class to go outside – you probably saw the climbing frames outside as you came in. There's a larger sandpit out there, as well, and of course we have some tennis balls.'

'Can any children come here?' I asked.

'Yes, but priority is given to families whose mothers have to go out to work. Some lost husbands in the war, of course, as you'd expect.'

'How long are the children here each day?'

'We open at half past eight, and the children are brought in between then and half past nine. They're collected between half past three and a quarter to five.'

'That's quite a long day for the very young ones, isn't it?' said Gordon.

'Ah, but they all have a sleep for part of the afternoon,' smiled Miss Carstairs. 'They need the break – and so do we, sometimes!'

'What about food?' I enquired, pen poised over my notebook. We were charged with writing about everything we could see and getting information about anything we could imagine. The notes were to be written up in 'Notebook B'; the equivalent 'A' was for practice lessons we would teach. At that time we were happily unaware of how many editions there would be.

'We're fortunate in having a British Restaurant here, so the children have meals prepared in it, though they eat them in this room. On the whole they're good; certainly it means the children get one balanced meal a day. Oh, yes, the parents pay two shillings a week towards the cost. You need to put that in your notes,' she grinned.

Subsequently those pontificated: 'Because a British Restaurant is attached to the building the school therefore has the advantage of the most modern food preparation machinery. The menu is prepared for the children on a fortnightly basis; they have meat three times in one week and twice the next, fish pie and cheese pie once or twice in alternate weeks. The children also have processed egg, vegetables and of course potatoes, etc.

'A qualified nurse attends the school each day to give treatment to any child who needs it. Children can have a course of sunlight treatment if it is necessary. A doctor visits the school on regular occasions, so the medical needs of the children are also well looked after.'

The government should have signed me up to run an advertising campaign. But Gordon threw the spanner.

'All this seems excellent for these children, but how many nursery schools are there in the city?'

'Ah, that's the problem. At present there are very few, less than five per cent of the under-fives get this opportunity. But those that do are in the poorest areas, so we're starting in the right places. Once the country is through this austerity period that's hitting us all so badly, whilst we pay for winning the war, I hope enough will be built for all children.'

With youthful optimism I ventured, 'How long do you think that will be – ten years?'

'I'd like to think that will be the time scale, but I'll bet it will be nearer twenty,' replied Miss Carstairs with what I considered undue pessimism.

Was there nursery education for all by 1966? No way! By 1970 20.5% of all children aged 3 to 4 were in pre-school education; by 2000 that had risen to 63.8%. I wonder what odds you would get on full provision before 2046.

The other three chaps in the room had buttonholed the other two assistants and were pushing them equally hard to extract note fodder. On the overview of the children's activity mine read with some pomposity but reasonable accuracy:

'The timetable is very flexible, the only rigidly fixed times being for meals and sleeping. The only thing that is actually taught is the Nursery Routine, which consists of washing, elimination, dressing, brushing teeth, and how to use a knife and fork. During the remainder of the day the children have complete freedom, the staff give them the apparatus and endeavour to foster in them the incentive to play and learn.'

It was when our questions turned to the role of play in child development that I gestured to the screen section of one wall. It appeared solid enough; the bottom edge was set three feet off the floor and some low pieces of furniture were placed strategically in front.

'I presume that is the observation room,' I whispered confidentially.

Miss Carstairs gave a half smile. 'Oh yes, that's the famous room. Cupboard would be a more accurate word, though, as you will see.'

Later Miss Webster agreed as she briefed us upon our period of observation. 'You'll find the room is very small. It's only intended for two people really, but since the expectation is that they need to take notes there is usually some elbow room. We can't leave the children totally unsupervised for long, of course, so to give all ten of you the chance to experience it I'll allow you two sessions with five of you watching at a time. I'm afraid it's going to seem like playing sardines!'

We interchanged glances. 'Sardines' was a popular game at teenage parties about which we could hardly imagine Miss Webster knowing anything. Certainly not when played by the most interesting rules…

'Now I can't impress upon you too strongly the need for absolute silence in there,' she refocused our attention. 'You mustn't talk to each other, you mustn't cough, and for heaven's sake don't sneeze or try to blow your nose. There won't be room in any case, but the whole concept of this place will be ruined if the children find out what that room is for. There are two psychologists from the university who are using it regularly and are preparing theses. We mustn't do anything that would compromise their work. So do be careful.'

We promised to be as silent as the grave.

After the 'seniors' had enjoyed an outside session and were back in their classroom and absorbed once more in their activities, Miss Webster gave Miss Carstairs a signal through the window of the door. Shortly afterwards the latter sidled out quietly with one of the assistants.

'I don't think anyone has noticed,' she said.

'Good, in you go then,' came the command. Miss Webster led us into the corridor alongside the classroom and turned a small knob on a neatly concealed door set quite high in the wall. The door opened noiselessly and a bench seat alongside served as a step up. Holding our breath the five of us mounted on tiptoe and slid along a similar seat inside. We felt like Royalist priests evading Cromwell's Roundheads as the door was carefully closed.

The seat was smooth but the floor seemed to be of a rough, black and slightly soft rubber-like material designed to muffle footsteps. The room was indeed a deep cupboard with matt black walls, ceiling and seat. We five could just fit in with hips jammed together and arms extended forward unnaturally straightened. With backs against the wall our knees were about six inches away from the front wall, above which was the mesh panel.

The view into the classroom, though dimmed, was reasonably clear. The light shining outside on to the mesh was shielded inside by a single strip of wood so that it didn't shine directly into the observers' eyes. From this side it seemed remarkable the children couldn't see us. The scheme was a simple adaptation of the revelation scene effect, beloved by pantomime producers, where an apparently solid backcloth melts to reveal hidden depth when the lighting switches from the scene in front to the one behind. The theory was that so long as no sound or light emanated from within, the secret of the observation room would be preserved and educational psychology might be favoured with deeper insights into children's learning. It was crude but effective, I thought, as I held my breath. The notion of two way mirrors and hidden microphones was quite beyond the meagre educational budget of those days, of course.

At first nothing happened. That is to say the children continued to behave exactly as before, quite absorbed in the various activities available to them. We realised this absorption came from the simple fact that, in their lives, they could only play to this extent at the nursery school. Toys were rare at home. Play there consisted of what could be done on the front doorstep, on the pavement and in the gutter, wherever all the other children congregated. Much was achieved there through the vivid imaginations of the brightest but apparatus and materials to enhance games were conspicuously absent.

Gradually some realised Miss Carstairs and her assistants were not in sight. One lad, running near the easels where others were daubing paint to their hearts' content, half tripped and fell against one of his classmates. Incensed the latter turned on the culprit with fist clenched and the lovely large brush held aloft as no mean weapon. We saw the momentary intrusion of a sixth sense as he glanced around. No adults! The brush landed with commendable accuracy on the miscreant's head.

'Yah, din't 'urt!' the fugitive yelled over his shoulder as he set off again. But he was watching the possibility of chase being given and so could not avoid crashing into a girl who wandered rather aimlessly into his path.

'Gerrout me way!' he flung at her, roughly pushing her aside.

The girl stood were she had been pushed, looking the picture of misery. The corners of her mouth turned sharply downwards as only a four year old's can and tears welled in her eyes. She, too, looked for Miss Carstairs, but being unable to see the one person to whom she could confide her woes, sat down abruptly in the middle of a vacant space. She made no sound but her appearance, as she sat with arms clasped tightly around her and lower lip trembling, told all. In the midst of all this happy, noisesome activity she was completely alone.

'Choo choo - choo choo.'

The train hove into sight at the end of something of a cutting between three sand trays and the tables where children were happily bashing plasticene. I now had the opportunity of watching the driver more closely. It was obvious he had a reputation, for anyone who happened to be standing in the path of the train moved aside to facilitate its unchecked progress.

He was adept at the job. With legs astride the engine he rocked forward and half stood up, at the same time pulling it forwards. Then he flopped back into a sitting position and contrived to help its momentum with two or three pushes on the floor with his feet. At the same time he yelled 'Choo choo' loudly and insistently.

It began to dawn on me that his current route was bringing him directly towards our cell. As he steered it into the open space in front of us he came to about five feet. We sat, bolt upright and rigid, not daring to make the slightest movement.

'Whatever happens,' I thought to myself, 'it's not going to me that gives the game away.'

The engine driver turned to his left and tried to steer the train parallel to our seat. As he did so the second of the two coaches he was pulling stuck on the leg of a nearby table. He dismounted and with a practised kick freed it.

As he walked back to the engine he looked directly at our wall. But it was not just a casual glance. He was about to jump aboard again, then changed his mind and walked slowly but purposefully towards us, peering up over the bookcase directly in front until his nose was as close as he could get. He put one arm across his forehead to shield his eyes from the light above.

'Oo, look!' he called slowly and deliberately over his shoulder to no one in particular. 'There's lots of people in the monkey cage to-day!'

Chapter 4

'I expect to hear nightly sounds of self-flagellation.'

Berny Wilton neatly encapsulated several opinions when he looked for the first time at our accommodation in the college. The comparison with austere monastic cells was unavoidable.

He was in what the college quaintly referred to as his 'room', but that was a misnomer. The walls were wooden screens, six and a half feet high, which once had been painted white but now were the colour of antique ivory. The large dormitory had a central narrow corridor with rows of doors on both sides. Each led into a tiny cell about six feet by nine. Facing the door was a slim, vertical window heavily barred, alongside which the inside of half a gable sloped downwards to a point about four feet above the floor. Here a sink was located ensuring that, however irreverent we might be about other matters, at least we had to wash in a praying posture. Against one wall was a bed. A small and completely plain cabinet of drawers and a chair completed the furniture inventory.

This was Upper North, one of four such dormitories each housing twenty students, ten on each side of the passageway. There was a Lower North and two similar Easts. The equivalent Wests had received knockout blows from bombs that had missed the middle of the college.

Access to Upper North was by a winding and completely enclosed staircase of minimal width. It was quite impossible for two people to pass on it without turning sideways. At the top was an equally small, dimly lit landing on which two doors flanked the narrow entrance to the dormitory. Formerly these single rooms had been the exalted abodes of the 'bucks', lordly men from the senior year who took charge of junior year students. Now denuded of furniture, with their tiny iron-fronted grates badly rusted and filled with rubble fallen down their chimneys, they looked utterly decrepit.

In time we came to realise that when the college was built these two rooms were the only private accommodation on the floor. The dormitory was then quite open. Our screen walls had been added as a touch of modernity at some point in the past.

As winter progressed and increased the internal gloom it was darkly rumoured that, years before, one of the rooms had witnessed a hanging. Someone, it seemed, had taken the quick way out. Jon Kennton took his bed into it one wild January night and rose happily the next morning, having seen not a wisp of a ghost, to collect a few bets from us more imaginative mortals.

The senior men soon had us yearning for the passage of our first year because their accommodation was on the opposite side of the playing field in a building completed shortly before the war and fortunately unscathed. This was South Wing which comprised accommodation for most of the year in truly single and commodious study bedrooms. Better still, their overflow was housed in the Principal's house. But for us these were twelve months distant.

Our feeling of monastic seclusion from the outside world was heightened at our second lecture on the morning following our arrival. The first was delivered by the Principal and was innocuously welcoming. The second was flung at us by the Vice-Principal who meant to make his mark upon us. He succeeded.

'I've been involved with this college, student and lecturer, recruit and officer in the Corps, for thirty five years this month. There isn't a stone I don't know, so don't imagine you'll dodge me if you try to get out when you should be in, or come in after your absits have expired.'

Major Darnley didn't look a typical former officer. In fact he had a deceptively smiling, round, boyish face with blue eyes enlarged by his bifocal lenses, framed with neat but not severely cut grey hair. In his cap and gown, which he wore frequently in college, he looked far more academic. His fresh complexion belied his drinking and pipe smoking. We soon discovered the latter but the former lay concealed from us at this early stage.

'I intend to give you an outline of the timetable to-day, gentlemen. The rising bell is at 7.00 am. but breakfast is not served until 7.45. Gone is the time when the day began with study from 6.30 to 7.00. We live in decadent times!' he laughed indulgently. We chuckled politely but mirthlessly. What did remain from the Spartan past, we wondered. We soon discovered.

'Chapel service is at 8.20 am. Attendance is voluntary but, naturally, as you have chosen to come to a church college we hope the majority of you will attend regularly.

'Lectures begin at 9.00 am. and continue until 12.50. Lunch is at 1.00 pm. Afternoon lectures extend from 2.00 until 5.00 pm., although on one afternoon each week you will soon be visiting schools for observational and later instructional practice.

'Tea is served at 5.15 pm, following which you are free until 7.00 pm. At that time you will go to your study area where you will be expected to work until 9.00 pm. Evening study is an institution of long-standing in this college, gentlemen, and I expect you to make good use of it. Because your bedrooms this year are too small for proper study you will be allocated in groups to various larger rooms that we have available, such as the common room, the library, this lecture room, and so on. These have sufficient tables and chairs to enable you to work adequately.

'College is in session each Saturday morning except at the half-term break. Lectures extend from 9.00 am to 12.30 pm that day. After that week-end activities are, regretfully, rather limited at present. You will hear later what sports we can make available. On Sundays, of course, there are Matins and Evensong.'

By now we were feeling mentally battered. Would we ever have any time to ourselves? Apparently not, for the VP continued –

'College weekends are another feature of which we are proud,' he beamed seraphically. 'To foster the corporate spirit of working and studying together it is natural you should want to spend a reasonable time in relaxation with one another. Accordingly, twice each half term there will be weekends during which no absits will be issued. On other weekends,' he conceded regretfully, 'you are allowed to be absent until 10.30 pm on both Saturdays and Sundays.'

He paused, suddenly. There was a moment of complete silence.

'Any questions, gentlemen?'

He wasn't the lecturer in Psychology for nothing. No one dared move, let alone speak.

'Good. I am delighted you are all in accord with our *modus vivendi*. I am sure it will not be long before you are completely at one with St Andrew's and you will soon feel part of its very fabric.'

Grimly I thrust aside the thought as the strictures placed on our freedom became apparent. But the memory was to surface the day I left, when I mooched around the deserted building until after 10.00 pm so unwilling was I to sever the bond that had indeed grown by then. But at the beginning I'd never have believed such a change of attitude possible.

'Now, gentlemen, let me turn your attention to this term's programme of lectures...'

In retrospect I believe our feeling of being cloistered was fully justified, even for those times. The college expected to control almost as much of our lives as did a boarding school. There were gestures to our developing manhood, of course, such as being referred to as gentlemen. Also, from the outset, every lecturer without exception spoke individually of Mr Flaxton, Mr Kennton, Mr Forton. But the regime was still that of the pre-war era.

But I wonder just how much the Vice-Principal and some fellow lecturers, alert to the future, enjoyed something of a final taste of the past with our year. The next intake would be of men returning from up to seven years of life and fighting in the Armed Forces, of years of privation and even torture as prisoners of war. Their frontal attack overwhelmed the cloistered life forever and cleared the ground for modern college life in which one's time is one's own outside lectures and tutorials.

A great deal more has changed. Modern college and university halls have plenty of creature comforts – personal furnished flats with cooking facilities, high quality refectories and kitchens, multimedia lecture theatres, extensive study facilities, attractive buildings and surrounds, student union bars...

The buildings survived for another thirty years. Then, despite modernisation to an extent we couldn't have imagined, the college closed. Quite brilliantly, with support from the local MP who served a term as a government minister, it became an urban village, with small industrial units offering employment. Inside rooms were gutted and remodelled into cosy and attractive self-contained flats. The playing field was kept, enhanced with surrounding well-stocked beds, to become the venue for various sports. Spectators could close their eyes on summer days and listen to the gracious sounds of cricket untroubled by the cacophony of modern County Ground terraces. Beyond the walls, however, lay the contrasting scene of inner city unkempt sprawl and a dash of squalor.

Bars! Even the notion of alcohol on site in our first year was unthinkable, let alone the idea of an internal business venture selling it. Nevertheless we were pioneers in the post war era and were keen to exploit the heady feeling of freedom pervading everyone's thoughts. Surely we could let a little light into the monastic gloom? As Christmas approached we considered organising a Dance. Many of us were members of churches where socials had been welcome distractions during the war years, once air raids subsided. We were sure we could arrange a modest little affair. We were to learn just how tight the monastic grip really was!

The only women who ever appeared within the walls were cleaners and refectory servers whose minimum age of employment seemed to be sixty, or thereabouts. Whenever we managed to escape, especially at weekends, we found a few girls of far more tender years lying in wait for us beyond the college gates. We were sufficiently on the ball to know they were tender only in years, so generally these were left alone. The internal college view of them approached the mediaeval view of hell.

We decided we would invite students of a women's Physical Training College some eight miles away. The only possible room to use was the common room, a bleak affair furnished with heavy round oak tables and similar wooden upright backed chairs. It was rarely used, except during the compulsory evening study period. There wasn't an easy chair or a cushion in sight. Nevertheless we felt we could liven it up with some decorations borrowed from our homes – new ones were a rarity during the extensive post war years of austerity.

Berny Wilton volunteered to request the Principal's permission for us to invite guests into the college.

'To a Dance?' The Reverend Silton seemed bemused by the notion, as though he had never before faced such a question. 'I suppose I have no objection to such a thing, if that is what you men want. I am sure I can rely upon you to bring colleagues of good reputation.'

Berny blinked. 'Colleagues' seemed somewhat out of context applied to dancing partners, because he hadn't yet mentioned our intended source of supply. He felt he had to leave no room for error.

'I am sure all of us will be most careful in that respect, sir,' he said. 'Some men have their own girlfriends for whom they can vouch, but in the main we intend inviting ladies from the PT College at...'

The Principal exploded.

'Girls? Do you seriously imagine...?' He glared furiously at Berny. 'Mr Wilton, you men may have an end of term function if you wish and that function may include dancing if that is an activity in which you wish to indulge with one another. You may bring guests, as well, if you wish. But women they may not be! Unquestionably NOT!'

His retirement at the end of our first year was opportune and effectively marked the end of an era for the college. It had lasted for nearly a hundred years.

Chapter 5

We knew from the brief Prospectus that we were to study Psychology throughout the course as an integral part of 'The Principles and Practice of Teaching' but few of us had more than the haziest idea of what it entailed. Nothing so exotic had appeared on our school timetables and I felt a twinge of anticipation at the thought of embarking upon real job-related study. To be honest I knew I could swank a bit about it amongst my other friends. But there was also a touch of apprehension because I had no idea whether I would be able to cope with the unknown. The opening sentence of the VP's first lecture in the subject confirmed my fear.

'Gentlemen, we shall study the Paidocentric Theory of Learning during this first term,' he announced.

'What the hell's that?' breathed Bill Heppleton, next to me.

I whispered back disparagingly, 'Sounds Greek to me!'

Obligingly the VP concurred. 'The word comes from the Greek, *paidos*, a boy. The boy is at the centre of the learning process...'

Bill stared at me, momentarily dumbstruck at my erudition, but when my eyebrows shot up in surprise he twigged I was as clueless as he. The incident lodged in my memory but I've never heard the theory glorified by that grandiose title since. Child-centred learning is much more recognisable.

Regrettably writers of courses and reference books have too often clothed their work in unfamiliar garments. The reason probably lies in the mistaken notion that more weight attaches to complex language. Perhaps this arises from the definition of a profession as a group of people that use language and have knowledge not easily accessible to the man in the street. Lawyers, doctors and vets qualify under this heading and we ordinary folk wait upon them to avail ourselves of their specialist services. Recently I heard a dermatologist identify a condition which needed treatment as *prurigo nodularis*. 'Itchy lumps' is a fair translation. But generally in recent years specialists have become easier to understand. We can also find explanations via the Internet

But there are others. In the information technology revolution the term 'becoming computer literate' meant more than just learning how to use software. A baggage of terms needed to be unpacked. How many of us frowned uncomprehendingly when first faced with protocols and portals, drivers and domains, RAMS and ROMS and many more terms deployed by the writers of programs as the personal computer became a household as well as a business tool? User-friendly courses were greatly applauded.

Whoever conceived the title 'paidocentric' was guilty of using an unnecessarily strange term, or obfuscation, as well as being politically incorrect. He ignored girls.

'The child learns only through experience...' continued the VP. 'He can only be conscious of his surroundings by experiencing them through use of one or more of his senses. His surroundings also can be shown to impinge upon his consciousness, thus there is a two way process in operation.' He broke off to chalk up a diagram showing a circle (the child) with an arrow proceeding outwards, opposed by another arrow charging towards it. They seemed about to meet head on.

'However, life is not that simple, gentlemen. In reality there are many and continuous interactions between the child and his or her surroundings, which can be conceived as a series of sensations coming in from the environment and being reacted upon.' He embellished the diagram by making the line continuous with a series of little arrow heads going in both directions.

'More accurately, the model should be thus...' He drew concentric circles with arrows flying from all points of the outer stockade towards the beleaguered child in the centre who, to do him (or her) justice, was valiantly trying to repulse one and all with a set of his (or her) own. This image sometimes floats before me when I watch a game show on TV requiring the contestant to parry balls flying at him/her from various directions. Or goalkeepers under training.

'Now, gentlemen, we come to the key issue. The child, as I said, can only learn from these interactions, these experiences. But many of these are fleeting – a glance, a smell, the brush of a hand, a taste. If repeated often enough the experience will be remembered. However, some interactions are much stronger and the learning is more immediate and long lasting...'

He stopped in mid sentence and stared at us challengingly.

'These...' he intoned dramatically, palpably holding one in his cupped and outstretched palm, '...are significant experiences...'

He dropped his arms, stood back erect, still as a statue. His blue eyes magnified by his spectacles flashed as he flicked them around catching many of ours individually. We hadn't a clue where he was leading us.

Then we got it.

'Each and every one of your lessons,' his tone assumed a Churchillian timbre, 'here in practice, out there in your future schools, day in day out, throughout your entire careers, must be significant experiences for your pupils! Nothing less will suffice. That, and that alone, must be your goal. It must be your lifelong touchstone as St Andrew's men.'

We began to realise that teaching practice was not going to be a doddle. Like everyone else my experience of lessons at junior (then called elementary) school was of a teacher explaining, followed by questions, followed by some form of written work. The pattern was the same for English, Arithmetic, Geography, and History; occasionally Nature Study lessons used specimens – I remember taking an apple for the purpose whilst in the infants' school and *not eating it beforehand*, Art was paint-a-picture-a-lesson, whilst Music was either singing or the use of percussion instruments - I was permanently allotted a triangle. Only at grammar school in Science did I experience practical investigation. Woodwork we took in the first year; my mother used the teapot stand for ages for it was quality oak (dream on to-day's technology teachers!), but the subject was deemed insufficiently serious for the remainder of the curriculum.

Dredging my memory I wonder how many lessons were significant experiences for me? In fact I can recall some quite clearly – and the common factor in each is the personality of the teacher involved. Palmerston, the 19th century Prime Minister, has the veneer of a tall, thin, sandy-bearded History teacher who described him as 'a bit of a lad' and revelled in telling us about dispatching gunboats whenever a Brit abroad was treated badly. 'Civis Britannicus sum.' Ah, those were the days.

Then there was an urbane English teacher of solid proportions who really made Shakespeare live for me – he also did pretty well with Chaucer. He seemed to excel as Antony; Richard Burton later filled the role well but somehow never quite supplanted this man for me.

Perhaps you share such memories? Certainly the personality and enthusiasm of teachers comprise the *sine qua non* in the work of schools, but no one can rely on histrionic ability alone for lesson after lesson. Inevitably fatigue sets in for both teacher and student. Finding the supporting interest for lessons is the perpetual challenge, as the VP emphasised to us right at the outset – hence Bill Heppleton's romp with a monk's habit. Like him we often misjudged what would or would not capture the children's interest; the failures provided useful ammunition for our shots as hapless targets stood in the firing line for the subsequent critical appraisals. On our longer practices we fired at ourselves in the follow-up notes we had to write on two lessons each day.

As the first year of our training progressed we drew nearer to the first period of block practice. For this we were to be allocated to particular schools, usually individually though some were large enough to swallow a pair of students without too much damage to children's lessons. During the month's practice we attended throughout each day, returning to college each evening to prepare lessons for the following day. Each of us was assigned to a class teacher whose job it was to let his or her class fall gradually into our awkward and unskilled hands and prevent us from making too much of a hash of things.

The college, for its part, assigned all its lecturers as tutors to the schools on a group basis, one tutor being responsible for about ten students. They then divided their work between travelling around supervising us and continuing to lecture in college to the senior year.

All our studies in the first year were for the junior age range, youngsters aged from seven to eleven years. Our first spell of block practice, therefore, was in schools for that age band. But schools vary considerably - a fact well known to parents and certainly students. There were good schools and bad schools and all sorts between; and there were all sorts of opinions and rumours and counter rumours...

'That one's awful; the Old Man won't even allow students in the staff room.'

'God help anyone who gets landed with that place – the building hasn't been touched since it was built and it says 1870 over the front door!'

'That's a beaut. Super new place, finished in 1939, right on the edge of town in a really gen suburb.'

'If you play your cards right in that place, pal, you're in. Most of the staff are women and there's none over thirty. Mind you the Old Man and the Chief Ass. share 'em most of the time.'

The junior year gradually became desperate for information as the time for block practice drew near and the senior year, with no one to contradict them, were very willing to minister to our needs and gloat as we writhed. The need to land a good school, it seemed, was absolutely vital to us if we were to hold out any hope of a reasonable mark in practical teaching. I quite believe that as the day drew near for the list of our practice schools to be published, St Andrew's saw an above average weight of prayers being offered up and that the subject of good schools figured amongst them to an excessive degree.

In the meantime we were given instructions in various teaching techniques and shown how to prepare lesson notes in the minutest detail. We soon realised that when the tutors were visiting our schools they would put us under the very closest scrutiny.

Our lesson note books, it seemed, had to be models of neatness and presentation because they were to be available in the classrooms at all times for our own and everyone else's use. We were adjured to write only on the right hand pages leaving the left hand ones entirely free for the advice to be poured upon us by class teachers, tutors, heads, or even it was whispered in awestruck tones, by His Majesty's Inspectors. This also provided us the opportunity, they said, to rewrite those parts of our lessons that had not been successful so we would avoid similar pitfalls in the future. Afterwards the notebooks were to be submitted for final marking.

As we very well knew from our half-day-a-week practice, lessons had shape. Each began with an introduction, continued with development and, wonder of wonders, finished with a conclusion. But lessons were given in response to problems which had to be identified first and written about; they also produced results which had to be commented upon afterwards. There also had to be a blackboard summary; this was supposed to show, approximately to scale, the board with exactly whatever would be on the real one at the end of the lesson – words, diagrams and drawings, all in the correct colours if you were going to be that adventurous.

We realised with awful finality that, no matter what our lessons were actually like in the classrooms, our lesson notebooks would have to be masterpieces. So much toil, tears and sweat were put into them that I have never been man enough to throw mine away. Perhaps some archivist in the year 2200 will ponder the problem of the wealth of extant lesson notes from the first half of the twentieth century's educational system, because I'm sure generations of St Andrew's and other ex-students have willed theirs to their descendants in perpetuity.

The wags were quick to poke fun at the rigmarole of lesson plans.

'How the hell do you write the problem for a lesson on writing a letter?' asked Trevor Walfrey during an evening study period.

'Simple,' said Gordon Mersely. 'At present the pupils cannot write adequate letters, therefore it is necessary to teach them basic format and content.'

'Don't be wet,' said Trevor. 'The March Hare will want a hell of a lot more than that.'

The March Hare was the Senior English Lecturer, so called because he had rather prominent front teeth. He also had the mannerism, when inviting you to consider a point, of putting his lower lip under them and gazing at you with his soft brown eyes, raising his eyebrows and murmuring 'Hmm?' The 'March' bit was a deliberate touch of incongruity because he was elderly and very staid.

'Alright, how about this?' countered Gordon. 'It has been discovered that these pupils have inadequate knowledge of accepted methods of setting out and modes of style in writing a variety of letters, such as applications for employment, complaints to Members of Parliament and pleas to income tax inspectors; therefore it is necessary to impart these skills.'

'Super,' said Trevor, 'but you went too fast. I didn't get beyond methods of setting out. What was next?'

'Rot,' yelled Gordon. 'What I said first was plain English. Put that.'

'Ah, but you don't get marks for being direct and simple,' put in Berny Wilton. 'You have to be more subtle, use a bit of psychology jargon, to show you're on the ball.'

'True,' said Archie Forton. 'Take Results for instance. If you have a flaming disaster, as I'm likely to, you can't write, *This lesson finished with thirty pupils jumping through the windows, ten having a fight on the floor whilst the remainder were more acrobatic and swung from the lights.*'

'No, but if you gloss over what exactly happened,' suggested Malcolm Ashterleigh, 'it does give you a chance to spread yourself rewriting the thing. That's bound to impress the powers-that-be.'

'Well, that's probably true up to a point, but you could overdo it,' said Berny. 'My bet is that you have to make just the right amount of rehash – you know, enough to show them you can improve on parts that went wrong but not too much because that suggests your lessons weren't much good in the first place.'

Archie looked thoughtful. 'This is going to be worse than I thought. If you're right we have to be damn cunning writing these notes.'

Sociologists would say, wrapped up in a little jargon, that we were producing a classic response to a social situation where one group organises a *modus operandi* designed to have value for a second group, but the latter responds deviously because the former wields power over it. The format of our lesson notes was laid down by our tutors to help us teach good lessons, but because they marked our books and our performances we tried to work the system to our advantage.

I am sure none of us analysed our actions at the time, but no doubt in our separate careers we all came to know what it was like when the boot was on the other foot. In my case I was on the receiving end in the early seventies when I was giving a series of lessons on education itself as part of a Humanities course. Our pupils visited a number of schools of widely differing kinds; one was Harrow, conveniently arranged through the friendship of one of its staff with one of ours. Another was a so-called 'Free School', one of the experiments of the time, usually founded in the most neglected urban areas. Many people regarded both staff and children as drop-outs. Many years later the term has reappeared as the official designation of schools created by completely independent groups.

Because the one we met was very small, twenty-five on roll, and operated in a tiny old church hall awaiting demolition, we invited them to visit us instead. Certainly they had very different social values from our own, amongst which was total opposition to any form of coercion or conformity. In order to let our pupils experience the difference, those from the Free School were asked to act exactly as they did in their own building. Probably they would have done so in any case – but we made the point when making the prior arrangements.

The event was highly interesting. Many of our pupils were comparative newcomers to local housing estates following clearance of old properties in the very same area the Free School was located. Most of our pupils had readily accepted the rules, regulations and general set-up of our school which, like many others of the time, was brand new, both in organisation and buildings. Most pupils wore school uniform but those who did not were not particularly unco-operative. The Free School pupils (sorry, members, they would object to the subservient role implied by the word 'pupils') wore whatever they liked which varied according to personality and means. Being recently formed they had not reached the stage when the group fixed its own uniform by tacit agreement – or internal coercion. They smoked all the time and we felt slightly churlish in not accepting the eloquent pleas from our pupils who suggested they should do the same because good hosts should always put their guests at ease! But we were six hundred strong; minds boggled at the resulting atmosphere had we agreed. Of course, this was before the time when such an event would keep local and possibly national newspapers in copy for days.

One intelligent fifteen year old lass, packaged colourfully from green and blonde hair to red and black toenails, quizzed me hard about our School Committee. To me it was a means of teaching our youngsters the rudiments of democracy, since all classes elected representatives to it and it enabled anyone to ask questions about the running of the school and participate in the making of some decisions. Of course it was not a democracy and that was stated quite openly, but to the Free School lass the whole thing was an exercise in hidden control. It was a means whereby we produced a false awareness in the minds of our pupils by making them think they were participating with the controlling power in the school, whereas in truth we were subtly keeping them repressed in a way which made them unlikely to be rebellious. No doubt that is how it looked to some youngsters on some school committees or councils, but it isn't what we intended.

I refrained from inquiring into the level of indoctrination which our fair visitor was receiving. From her conversation I doubt whether her own education was intellectually free. But I won't digress further into how on earth any education can be so.

To my chagrin I have to admit that as a student I didn't view my lesson notebook as it was intended either – a means to help me teach well. I saw it as contributing to getting me through the 'Principles and Practice of Teaching' and so I determined it was going to reap for me every available mark. I was in the greatest need of a lesson and, fortunately, that was forthcoming early in my block practice. But in the meantime I continued to worry about other matters.

'How are you lot getting on with blackboard writing?' I asked them. 'Mine's still appalling – I was never very good at handwriting in any case.'

'Ah, you mean the Eleventh Commandment,' said Trevor. He was referring to an exercise recently set us by the VP.

'Gentlemen, you will all practise writing the following statement on a blackboard:

LEGIBILITY IS THE FIRST ESSENTIAL OF GOOD HANDWRITING.

This is to be written in cursive script and practised over and over again until you can write it perfectly. It must appear absolutely level, but you must not draw any lines underneath. All lower case letters must be of identical size. Each of you will be required to produce it when I ask, and I shall judge it by laying a ruler above and below to test your accuracy. I shall also judge its standard from the back of the room, from whence it must not appear too large nor too small. Needless to say I shall also judge the individual letters and their spacing.

'I feel, gentlemen, that if you can be near perfect in this one simple exercise, you will have a standard ever before you to which you should aim when writing on a blackboard. Remember, you have no right to comment upon the standard of a pupil's handwriting unless you can demonstrate yourself the high standard to which he or she should be aiming.

'Therefore, if you ever have any odd moments to spare, pick up a piece of chalk and practise. There are many boards in the various rooms in college, as you will have noticed. Feel at liberty to use them for this purpose at your leisure,' he concluded expansively.

Though we joked about it at first, we came to view matters differently when we tried doing it. No matter how I started, facing a blackboard, I couldn't keep my writing level. I soon realised the solution lay in good footwork, but putting that into effect was easier said than done. If I moved too slowly the line of writing began to describe something of an arc and by the time I reached the end it was plunging floorwards. I tried to speed up, but then the effect was precisely the opposite. My attempts to co-ordinate hands and feet in the exercise produced a lovely switchback effect.

We stood in front of blackboards and sweated away at the job until our upper arms and shoulder muscles ached. The sentence assumed such importance in our lives that we couldn't imagine how it had been omitted from Moses' tablets of stone.

'I take so long over this that if ever I tried writing so well during a lesson the kids would have a ball behind my back,' I complained.

I put this to the VP rather more tactfully when I next saw him at a tutorial meeting.

'If that is so, Mr Flaxton, as I am sure it is, the remedy is obvious as every good teacher knows. You prepare your blackboard notes beforehand, with illustrations whenever possible, and either turn the board away from the class or cover it with a sheet if it is a fixture. Then, at the right moment, you reveal your work dramatically and your class is spurred to do its work by the high standard you have set.'

We exchanged glances. Surely the VP was getting away from day to day reality in the classroom. Trevor tried to hedge him.

'I can see the value in that, sir, but I'm bound to say I have never seen that high a standard of board work amongst the teachers who taught me.'

There was a gentle chorus of 'hear hears' as we felt his rather daring shaft had penetrated. We were wrong.

'Then they weren't St Andrew's men!' beamed the VP with his arms spread wide to emphasise the transparency of the explanation. 'We produce the best here, gentlemen, and therefore I'll brook no excuses. So, carry on with your practising.'

We did, but it seemed that whenever any one of us achieved a level of which he was proud the VP would whirl in with gown trailing, armed with a blackboard ruler, and demolish hopes.

'No, no, no, Mr Flaxton! The letters of FIRST are at least a quarter inch above those of THE and ESSENTIAL. And look at your capital L – cursive script is supposed to be beautiful and flowing, but you have contrived to draw the coils of a boa constrictor.'

I remembered all this some years later when I was living on a new estate in the south. I made the acquaintance of a chap who lived in the house opposite. We helped one another slosh cement around because we both had paths to lay. He was a representative for a medical firm in London. One day he greeted me with a surprising idea.

'Nigel, they're going to introduce a B.Sc.(Econ) course in the evenings at the local Tech. I'm going to enrol – why don't you join me?'

Evenings would be possible, I thought. Nevertheless there was a snag. 'But they'll expect you to have A level Economics, surely; I haven't got that.'

'Neither have I, but they're starting with an A level course – I'm going to do that first. Then next year they're going to get a really top man from a London university.'

I thought for a while. 'Why not? Let's give it a try.' So we enrolled and enjoyed a happy and successful one-evening-a-week first year – I even joined my friend in Economic History because he needed a second subject and it was on the same evening. Then, one year later, we enrolled with a number of other people, mostly teachers, who were looking forward eagerly to what promised to be a lively and stimulating course. It even made the local paper.

Then we met the London lecturer. He was young, personable, and obviously knew his stuff. But as a teacher, alas, he was a disaster. He made just about every mistake in the book and we practitioners simply cringed. But it was his blackboard work that was worst for me. As idea followed idea tumbling from his mouth in spate he would suddenly round on the board and slash notes and diagrams on it as though the chalk was a sword and the hapless board a dragon. By the end of the evening you could have carted the thing away and made a fortune offering it to the world of Art if you had the right contacts.

'Half a mo, let me sort this out,' he would say in answer to a question. Then he would stand at the board with his back completely to us, scratch his head, and say, 'Have a natter amongst yourselves, the answer's here somewhere. Don't worry, I'll find it.'

I have to admit that from somewhere amongst the mass of figures, graphs and notes which he had superimposed upon one another in a heavy scrawl he always did extract what he wanted. But writ large in my consciousness was LEGIBILITY IS THE FIRST ESSENTIAL OF GOOD HANDWRITING and the memory of my efforts under the critical eye of Major Darnley would make me irritable beyond measure. If only this man had been trained in elementary teaching and blackboard techniques, I thought, what a success he could have been. So did everyone else. Sixteen enrolled in September; by Christmas only three of us were left. They closed the class. I was left with much retrospective appreciation of the grind we had undergone at St Andrew's in learning some of the skills of the trade.

'I have the list of schools to which you have been assigned for your first block practice,' announced the VP, almost diffidently, at the beginning of one of his lectures. The atmosphere charged immediately and we waited, breathlessly.

'I'll read this to you in a moment. But first, I want to comment briefly upon your last essays…' He knew how to keep us on the hook. The moment stretched to half an hour. Then, suddenly, he was skimming through it. '…Mr Ashterleigh, Netherly Farm Junior…Mr Flaxton, Spenser Street Junior…Mr Forton, Houghton Road Junior…'

Spenser Street! My heart sank because I knew very well where that was situated. It was in a rough area of back-to-back slums in between two main roads that met further on near the city centre, but on the old and dilapidated side. That was going to be tough!

I let the others drift away after the lecture and sat cursing my luck. But not for long, because I have always tried to look forward and imagine good things ahead; in those days I was perpetually optimistic. After all, I thought, I've lived in this city all my life and though I live in a very pleasant suburb, many of my friends and some of my relations live in the older areas. During the war the people in these areas were marvellously friendly towards one another – and I remembered what I saw of that on VE and VJ days when the nation celebrated victory in Europe and in the Far East. The real spirit of Britain had bubbled up and welled forth there amongst the street parties and the flags and the bunting. I had wandered along streets very similar to Spenser Street just because I knew they were historic days and I wanted to feel the excitement at first hand. The kids would be just as friendly in school, I felt sure.

In any case, I argued with myself, the tutors knew the schools, if you did well in a tough school they'd mark you up more than if you were in an easy one. Wouldn't they?

I stood up and looked around the lecture room. it was long and bare, with rows of narrow, vertical windows heavily leaded on one side, and plain square ones on the other looking out on to the quadrangle. The desks at which we sat were old and worn, and at the end was a low dais with a single lectern of similar antiquity. Across the wall behind this was the old blackboard with a badly pitted surface. On it was someone's recent effort: LEGIBILITY IS THE...

I dashed out, went to my locker, then grabbed Gordon Mersely. 'Gordon, go and stand in there by the board. I want to photograph the lecture room.'

'Whatever for, man, it's not exactly photogenic!'

'Never mind why, I just feel like doing it. In any case, I want to collect some pictures of the place to remind me of it in the future.'

'Well, perhaps you're right,' he said as we went in. He looked at the board. 'We certainly ought to record that for posterity. It's not bad – probably that's why the VP didn't rub it off during his lecture just now. Do me a copy when you print it.'

I know the negative survived a number of house moves as I climbed the promotion ladder in schools, but I haven't seen it for years. It may still be in the massed paraphernalia of boxes I keep meaning to clear out sometime. But I don't need to look at it to remind myself; the mental image is still perfectly clear thanks to the 'Eleventh Commandment'.

Chapter 6

Major Darnley possessed that elusive quality, charisma, and we acknowledged the fact in our kinder moments. He wasn't particularly eccentric but he certainly was unpredictable and we came to suspect that this was deliberate. It added to the sense of awe in which we very young men held him and so enhanced the power he held over us. This he used gently or harshly in varying measures and you were never quite sure which treatment he was about to dispense. He revelled in prowling the twisting staircases and narrow corridors during evening study, flanked by two 'Committee Men' from the senior year who usually looked suitably embarrassed at having to seek out any recalcitrant fellow student trying to dodge this enforced and hated chore. Its compulsory nature was most calculated to make us feel like children and made the attempt to treat us as men phoney. The VP knew this and wallowed in it. Yet we dared not cross him, because as the sole lecturer in the 'Principles and Practice of Education' we knew his would be the decisive voice in awarding our teaching marks. Those, we understood, were vital to our early careers.

'Ah, Mr Flaxton,' he would say, bumping into me in a corridor, 'as you are going down the road in a few moments, you might bring me an ounce of Four Square Green tobacco'.

Even if I had been going out he wouldn't have known, but that was the manner of his giving a kindly instruction. And of course I had sense enough to obey - or to crawl, whichever way you care to look at it.

But he was absolutely committed to the college, its reputation and to the standards of the teachers it trained. He boasted unashamedly that Education Authorities liked receiving applications from St. Andrew's men trained under Billy Darnley.

He had established his standards years before and the measure of his success was that he had followed this with the more difficult process of maintaining the high level over a long period.

'The way you men conduct yourselves in staffrooms and classrooms in future will show whether you deserve the seal of St. Andrew's,' he would say whenever he could swing a lecture round to this one of his store of favourite topics. It might start as a lecture on the theory of intelligence, but it would finish as indoctrination as to how St. Andrew's men were to deport themselves... or else.

'You can really say your prayers if any headmaster reports you to me for unseemly behaviour whilst you are on schools' practice,' he would thunder. 'A gentleman is always known by his behaviour and we only want gentlemen at this college! The way a man behaves to his colleagues will show whether he is a gentleman. If you truly wish to test a gentleman's behaviour...' he would continue and we would slide a fraction lower in our seats and quietly consign our pens to our pockets, for we knew what was coming. Major Darnley worked this particular piece of advice into his lectures at least once a term, ...'watch him when he is in his cups.' A pause. He would look around, with the Churchillian line to his lips.

'It is not wrong for a man, after a hard day's work, to indulge himself on occasions and, if he is in convivial company, he will enjoy being in his cups. But even then he will know how to behave if he is a gentleman.'

Another pause, and he would stare up and down the rows of young faces in the lecture room.

'You will find out ere long whether you are gentlemen. Yes - ere long.' There would be complete silence. Mentally we would be asleep, leaving Major Darnley no doubt musing upon massive binges of his youth about which we could know nothing.

Suddenly the spell break. 'Now, take Spearman's work, for example,' he would say, briskly returning to his lecture, and we would shift in our seats and wake up.

Naturally the first time he said all this he really did hold us in his spell. We thought it marvellous. Here was a man unashamedly recalling old fashioned virtues, allying them with old fashioned indulgence and advocating them to us who had had our early teens mauled by the war, by rationing, shortage and blackout, and were now entering manhood at an even more dismal time of harsh economic austerity.

The notion of being gentlemen in their cups sounded delightfully profligate, so unexpected from the Vice-Principal of a Training College maintained largely by the Church. We felt we were getting a glimpse of another and more human facet of the VP's character. Then one night Jon Kennton was treated to a full performance all to himself.

Despite the college's stringent regulations and its dire efforts to keep us in late at night, he did stay out on occasions. Naturally this posed the problem of getting back in after lights out, which certainly wasn't easy. Knowledge of Colditz was not widespread at the time but had we been party to it we would have felt it almost as difficult to break into St. Andrew's as it was to escape from that other formidable fortress. Jon Kennton had met a newly qualified teacher who taught girls' PT. (in those days it was still Training, not yet Education.) She was rather attractive, with the kind of figure which seemed to be mandatory for young female PT teachers, and she was helping him with his studies in method. Jon was in fact older than most of us, having served in the Navy towards the end of the war. He was demobbed in time to join our year in college. His greater experience made him rather more adventurous than the rest.

He had spotted a section of the outer wall surrounding the college site which had some stones damaged by bomb blast or decay, or both. With a struggle he found sufficient toe and finger holds to enable him to make a grab for the coping stones on top of the wall. He tested this in daylight, with two friends keeping watch for stray pedestrians who might have been understandably suspicious about a student climbing over the wall into the building when the front door was not very far away. He didn't try actually going over the wall, for that might have been spotted, even though his selected position faced an end with few windows and hardly any rooms in regular use. He arranged for a friend to leave one of the windows unlatched just before lights out, after which he judged it most unlikely it would be found and closed again. It was quite impossible for 'god' to check every window every night. Then he tried his first run in deadly earnest.

He said afterwards that almost the worst time was waiting long enough at his girlfriend's to ensure the streets around the college would be deserted. For once he couldn't keep his mind on his studies. However, in due course he arrived at the foot of his short but vertical climb and, as he had hoped, he had the street to himself. At this point there was extensive open ground belonging to a factory on the opposite side to the wall, so there were no houses to harbour prying eyes. All he had to achieve was some nimble footwork, a massive pull on his arms when his hands curved over the top, and he was astride the wall.

The street was well illuminated with gas lamps installed by the Victorian city fathers and Jon felt for Lady Godiva as he momentarily straddled the wall, but no one saw him and seconds later he dropped into the welcoming and complete darkness on the college side. Here, it seemed, no light penetrated and he was glad to sit against the wall in the deepest shadow and let his eyes become accustomed to the gloom.

As soon as they had done so he realised that although the college had no room lights on anywhere, nevertheless a great deal of light was reflected over the wall from the street lamps, so much of the ground between the wall and the building was by no means as dark as he had first thought. Peering round nervously and stooping as low possible he ran quietly across the intervening space to his target window. He pulled at the metal surround to the heavily leaded pane and to his intense relief it swung open. It took a matter of seconds to pull himself up, twist sideways to squeeze through the narrow opening and drop noiselessly on to the dusty floor of an unused office. After listening carefully he closed the window quietly and opened the door.

His progress down the pitch dark corridor was uneventful and he found the narrow doorway in the oak panelling which was the back stairway entrance to Upper East. The stairs creaked abominably and he could feel his heart racing even though he was climbing with the speed of a ninety year old arthritic. He reached a corner where he could see the faint glow from a very small bulb which was left on all night on the small landing at the end of Lower East. Gradually he turned the next corner and could see the light itself.

Here he knew that he had to be extremely careful indeed because leading off to the left at this point, opposite the entrance to Lower East, was a short corridor which led to a staff flat. Jon knew very well that this particular flat housed Major and Mrs Darnley. However, it was protected from the sounds of the college by a very solid but plain oak door and he surmised that it was most unlikely that they were sleeping in the room immediately on the other side of it. Surely, he thought, they would be asleep at midnight, wouldn't they?

He edged his way on to the landing and was about to take the two or three steps necessary to cross it when a sixth sense made him look into the shadows on his left. Staring back at him like a dragon in its cave was the VP!

'Hell', breathed Jon, and waited for the storm to break. He had suddenly become very weak, and couldn't think clearly.

'Who you?' slurred Major Darnley.

'Kennton, sir', said Jon, and waited.

'Humph', said the VP and turned his head away slowly. Jon was incapable of moving even if he had thought to try. He vaguely wondered whether he would be thrown out of college immediately or whether there was some interim punishment that was meted out to first offenders, and if so what it might be. He fervently wished he had done some research into the matter before attempting his escapade.

Jon waited again. The VP remained standing, stock still. Then Jon dared to look at him more closely and realised with a shock that he wasn't standing upright - he was leaning. In fact he was propped up against the wall of his corridor and wasn't moving at all.

He was very drunk!

From being just weak with shock, Jon became paralysed. What on earth could he do? He couldn't just disappear to bed; the VP had seen him and he had stupidly given his name which surely would be remembered. Then he thought that if he offered to help perhaps the VP would be just a tiny bit grateful and might let him off with a rollicking. What had he to lose?

'Sir', said Jon, at last finding the means to move his legs and going towards the Major, 'may I open the door for you?'

The VP sprang into action.

'Don't you come at me, young man,' he growled barely coherently, 'I warn you, I can shtand up for meshelf.'

'No sir, you don't understand', gasped Jon, trying to squeeze past him in the very narrow corridor, 'I'm just going to open this door for you.'

'Leave 't 'lone, thassmydoor - noshyours, goway!'

'Please sir, let me,' said Jon, groping towards the door with his right hand and scuffling desperately as the situation began slipping away from him.

The VP suddenly gave him a mighty push which sent him staggering back on to the landing. 'You can't push me around,' he bellowed. 'No gen'leman takesh that from anyone. C'mon, put up your dooks.'

Thereupon he lifted his fists like an old prizefighter and slowly and most unsteadily circled Jon, who stared back at him with fascinated horror waiting for the cobra's strike. He couldn't believe what was happening to him.

It got worse.

Gerremup. I maybe in my cupsh, but I can shtill fight. Gerremup, or you're a coward, shir.'

The last sentence was delivered with awful finality, as though it must force Jon to defend himself forthwith or seek some quiet corner and blow his brains out in the approved gentlemanly manner.

Jon glanced towards the closed dormitory door. Surely someone must have heard the racket? Couldn't someone come out and help him somehow?

Help did come, but from a totally unexpected quarter.

A chink of light gleamed suddenly in the little corridor, and a face peered out. Jon glimpsed wavy grey hair enclosed in a net, and a gentle but solemn face above a long blue dressing gown. There was a momentary pause, then the door opened fully and Mrs Darnley stepped out.

She put her right arm across her husband's shoulders and after a second or two succeeded in capturing the wildly waving left fist jabbing in exploratory fashion towards Jon's face.

'William', she said quietly but with firm authority, 'you should be in bed. Wish this young man goodnight and come along.'

He turned and she looked him fully in the eyes. There was a fractional pause, then he deflated and turned meekly towards Jon, who could only gaze.

'Shorry, ole man - got to go. Wifesheer. Prappsh have fight 'nother night. Goobye.'

He tottered gently along his corridor and into his flat, guided by his attentive wife. The door closed.

Jon collapsed in a heap on the bottom stair of the flight leading to Upper East. In the fevered turmoil of his mind one question leapt at him. What was going to happen tomorrow when the VP sobered up and realised what had occurred? With stark clarity he realised the VP would be doubly furious – not only had Jon been out after lights out and had broken into college, but he had now seen him in the full glory of his 'cups'.

'Realising he knew I'd seen him completely sloshed,' Jon confided to us afterwards, 'I thought he'd be so angry he'd chuck me out of the place next morning. Hell, I felt absolutely awful: I thought I was going to spew up there and then.'

But further help was at hand.

Light gleamed again as the flat door opened once more and Mrs Darnley slipped out. She glanced behind her, satisfied herself that she was alone, and came to Jon who jumped to his feet blushing his confusion.

'Don't be upset, Mr, er...'

'Kennton', spluttered Jon.

'Mr Kennton', she continued, 'you weren't to know this, but my husband has these nights every now and then. Relic of past Army life, I'm afraid. He'll be fine in the morning and he won't remember a thing. Slip up to bed now and don't worry.'

Jon stared, unbelieving.

'Go on, I mean it,' she said with a suggestion of sharpness in her gentle voice. 'And don't worry - tomorrow he probably won't know you from Adam.'

'Er, well, thanks, ma'am,' stammered Jon. 'Thanks for your help. Goodnight, ma'am.'

He turned and began to climb weakly up the stairs. She watched him, briefly. He turned at the first corner and glanced down at her.

'Next time make sure he doesn't see you,' she said in level tones, then raised a gently admonishing finger and was gone. Jon went weak again.

Next morning as he was making his way to the lecture room Jon spotted the VP crossing the quadrangle. Though there were other students making the same journey he felt the VP had eyes only for him. It was also perfectly obvious their respective speeds and directions were such that they were on a collision course.

Jon turned crimson and became wet with sweat. Surely the VP would know him immediately... and then what?

Slowly they got closer. Jon dared not look at him. His eyes became fascinated by the path on which he was walking and every stone glistened with quite exceptional clarity. Then he heard humming. He looked up sharply. No, he hadn't been mistaken. It was coming from the VP!

'Ah, good morning, Mr Kennton,' he said brightly. 'A very pleasant day, don't you think? How are you finding the work now?'

There wasn't a trace of recognition in the Major's eyes. In fact, Jon was amazed to notice, neither was there the tiniest hint of a hangover. He stammered a reply and lost himself in the crowd.

But a few hours later, when the power of rational thought returned, he realised the VP had addressed him by name whilst during the night both he and his wife had had to ask who he was.

None of us ever did find out whether the VP really had forgotten what he had done and said in his cups, or whether he simply did a superb cover up job. Neither did Jon ever meet him again in the course of his nocturnal rambles, which he continued of course.

After all, he had virtually been encouraged to do so by a most understanding lady!

Chapter 7

Early in the new century it is fascinating to look back over one's experiences in education during half the previous one and try to set them in a broad context. *Plus ça change, plus ça même chose* may be true of some elements, but the last few decades certainly saw real and permanent changes both in organisation and teaching method.

The basic unit of a class of pupils with a single teacher comes from antiquity and may very well continue long into the future. Some of the earliest cuneiform script from the 'Land of the Two Rivers' deciphers as the gripes of students:

'The days of the schoolhouse are long and hard...'

and sketches show lines of benches on which the trainee scribes sat facing a tutor, learning to be literate. Descriptions suggest they were boarders.

I wonder what the pupil/teacher ratio was. Did the tutors, and the scholars' parents, complain of large classes? Were they hamstrung because of the cost of clay tablets? Apart from organisational problems – and I'll bet there were some – the lessons could not have been just exercises in literacy. The people involved were struggling towards the development and use of written language leading to increased complexity of ideas and thence to greater social interaction. Rulers wanted this to increase power; merchants wanted the same for increased trade and wealth, warriors wanted it to enhance the waging of war.

No doubt as they struggled to master the patterns of wedge shapes on their clay tablets the students revealed varying levels of thinking ability. No doubt tutors revelled in teaching the brightest and struggled with the slowest. The basic problem of conveying a mental concept that you possess to someone else who doesn't have it has been the stuff of teaching across the millennia and will remain so throughout whatever is the future for the race. Maybe it will be enhanced through brain implants everyone will have if futuristic science is to be believed – provided individuals can afford them.

Narrowing the focus to the late nineteenth and all of the twentieth centuries, it soon becomes clear that only in very recent years has something appeared that gives both teacher and student an ability to exchange and grasp concepts and information in ways that were virtually impossible before. The computer.

Lessons must be significant experiences... How teachers have striven to achieve that through the ages! It wasn't until after the Second World War that the cinema's developing technology began to be available to schools. Not extensively, of course, due to cost – that perpetual millstone. First the film strip projector, or slide packs, could bring a neatly packaged series of photographs into the classroom with a clarity largely impossible in printed pictures if the room was adequately blacked out. Then came the cine-projector, one available perhaps to a consortium of schools, or more likely borrowed on a rota from a Teachers' Centre. The first Geography film I saw demonstrated (in 1948) gave an excellent explanation of contour lines – hills cut into expanded segments the edges of which comprised the contours. How much more sharply the notion was conveyed than in my description to classes of a man with a football pitch line marker walking round a hill at precisely the same height all the time. Nevertheless I did supplement it with a visual aid – a model cobbled together from a number of shaped pieces of plywood lessening in size and covered with plasticene which could be dissected to reveal the contours of the twin peaked 'Dog Bone Hill'.

Gradually we struggled to possess at least one strip projector per school; later you could expect one cine projector likewise. But both suffered from the need to have a room that could be properly darkened. In modern classrooms with low ceilings this could be achieved, albeit at some cost, so it was usually done in one or two rooms, necessitating the booking of these whenever you wanted to show a film. But in old buildings this was virtually impossible. The Victorians tended to build classrooms on the grand scale – with large windows sensibly divided into many small panes (misdirected balls caused less costly damage) but set high so wandering eyes could not be distracted by street scenes. High ceilings allowed these windows to be of considerable height thus welcoming plenty of daylight. Alas, blacking out these was inordinately expensive.

Nevertheless, when the films had been booked and received through the post, (I genuflect to various now-defunct education film libraries), the projector and room booked, the timetable altered to accommodate the latter and one's displaced colleague placated, how vividly portrayed was that particular lesson. Yes, a significant experience indeed. Interestingly most cine and film strip projector material was in colour from the early fifties.

If you are of the pre-computer generation, for whom educational films were a normal facility, look back and estimate how often you saw one in your particular school. All too often, though a projector was available, it spent too much of its life on a stock room shelf. The reason was this particular teaching aid was not readily to hand. Deploying it was cumbersome.

Radio programmes were available to schools throughout the half century – indeed for considerably longer. I can still remember listening to a programme, in company with the entire complement of my thirties' infants' school assembled in the hall, on the theme of new traffic arrangements heralded in towns by 'Belisha beacons' and the 30 mile an hour limit.

But lessons had to be arranged to fit programme times and centred upon programme content. Much later the tape recorder eased the logistical problem and replaced it with stern warnings about the infringement of copyright in playing (and keeping) the result.

Television followed radio and the cine projector. At first it had all the same problems – one receiver per school which had to be booked and timed for transmitted school programmes. Although blackout was no longer needed, screen size was an early problem, and classes had to be deployed in matey scrums to view adequately. There was usually some prior aerial shifting to get the best reception. But in the early days, of course, by no means all of the country was covered. Schools and homes in less populated areas had to be patient.

Nevertheless it was worth waiting for – especially when colour arrived, followed by the amazing invention of the video-recorder. I can remember my excitement at hearing that this facility would one day be available for widespread use. What range of programmes we would be able to use for our classes! What freedom we would have to show material when it fitted into our programme of lessons rather than the other way round!

But when it came there was the inevitable package of restrictions. Some time ago a school suffered a swingeing fine because a teacher recorded a Shakespeare play at home one evening and showed parts next day to supplement his lesson. One of his pupils commented ingenuously on this at home – to her TV producer father.

Television, however, demonstrated an unsuspected power. It has a magnetic appeal to a class that is stronger than radio or a cine film. I cannot wholly account for this phenomenon, but I realised it one day when, as a headteacher, I took a visitor into a class that I would not normally have chosen to demonstrate close concentration upon work. Indeed its members were usually quick to seize any opportunity to switch attention to a visitor. Some were notorious for exercising their views that History is boring, Geography is boring, Religious Education is ever so boring… The lesson was Biology and the class was watching a television presentation of the internal organs of a rat. I would not rate the material highly as compulsive viewing. Yet not a single head turned towards we two intruders. Indeed I would have loved to experiment by taking in a current pop idol and seeing how long awareness took.

Soon afterwards I had an extraordinary opportunity to use this finding, employing the adage that if you can't beat them you might as well join them. I set up a television network throughout the school so that every classroom had a wired-in receiver. There were transmission points in most departments and a central transmission point in a small 'studio'. The system enabled a number of significant improvements in the life and activities of the school.

First, talks to the whole school became vastly more personal than in the only space available for such communication – the Sports Hall. Once a week nigh on a thousand students flattened their bottoms on the floor to hear me speak like a political candidate on the hustings. But when any of us spoke to camera each person in the school felt they were being spoken to individually.

Second, video recordings could be shown to the whole school or to a department, so visits, skiing trips, work experience, and video diaries on a host of activities were transmitted with ease. Third, visitors were able to put across information through the technique of being interviewed, with slides and video interspersed for illustration. Other variations were possible, limited only by imagination. Some bright sparks emulated TV programmes, such as the then popular Treasure Hunt, for lunch time transmission.

The degree to which this grabbed attention is, perhaps, well illustrated by the speed with which members of a new intake to the school quickly related to anyone who spoke to camera. Three days into the September term, comments to teachers and me that 'Cor, Sir/Miss, you're the one I saw on the box this morning,' revealed an undreamed of rapport development speed. The system conferred many benefits on the school, not least being the media skills many students acquired and put to use in their careers. It was even featured in the national press.

Perhaps you belong to the generation that has known the personal computer since first consciousness. If so, did you realise that its appearance in schools produced a hitherto unknown scenario that inordinately worried teachers and senior managers? Indeed you may have been one of its manifestations. Quite simply roles were reversed. For the first time in history pupils had greater skills than their teachers.

That's a generalisation, of course. However it is the case that many teachers in mid to late career were faced with new technology for which skills had to be learned – and in the early days personal computer programs were not particularly user-friendly. It was embarrassing to find that even five year olds were appearing in schools with some keyboard skills. The first use of a computer for timetabling I experienced used a program written by a member of the fourth form – Year 10 in to-day's nomenclature. I spent some thousands of pounds in purchasing computers for my school before I touched a keyboard myself – and when I did I sought a lesson from one of the students.

I experienced the extent of the sub-surface shock waves when involved in taking a government initiative called the 'Flexible Learning Project' to schools. I saw the complete spectrum from teachers who rapidly and skilfully embraced the new technology to those who strongly resisted it. In one north Norfolk school I saw a History classroom set up with a range of Mac computers around the periphery, with a central store of varied materials, including computer programs produced by the teacher. I watched one that showed a site in Norwich with computerised sketches of buildings at various dates through the centuries – as you clicked on one date the scene dissolved and the appropriate changes appeared. He also produced a range of video recordings of visits to historical sites – often with classes in tow, so making them useful for revision. The true success of his work, as he very well knew, was revealed in the level of historical awareness shown by his students in their written work. Not surprisingly, their examination results were good, too.

I tried to prise him out of his classroom to give talks to teacher groups – perhaps even to run training courses. He refused point blank to leave his students. He did, however, produce yet another video - for my use, explaining in his commentary that he was demonstrating how 'One ole' country boy behind the Norfolk reeds' used modern technology to make students' lessons significant experiences.

The reverse side of the coin was seen on occasions when I showed that video to groups of teachers. Those attending voluntarily were usually sympathetic, albeit staggered by the amount of time the man obviously put into creating his lesson material. But others, attending by dictat, all too often made it very clear they had no use or time for such frills. Books and dictated notes had served them well for years and they saw no reason to jump on this latest bandwagon.

Far from being such a vehicle the computer is a space ship, freeing students, teachers and indeed everyone from the cumbersome limitations of access to information. The technology and the software have increased immensely in quality and quantity; now, in the days of the national curriculum, many programs are commercially available to supplement courses. If teachers want to produce bespoke courses for their particular students they have a range of excellent programs and hardware to help them produce their own CDs and DVDs. In the 'Flexible Learning Project' at the beginning of the nineties, writeable CDs were beyond the resources of schools – machines cost around thirty thousand pounds and the operation was fairly complex. Now they are integral in PC systems.

But, as you will be well aware, computers enable personal learning – anywhere, anytime, with user-friendly courses, user-friendly tests (as much as any test can be), with a vast range of teaching strategies and ease of access to even more vast amounts of information through the world wide web. They also enable easy links with other learners via the Internet – how much homework has been done with emails being interchanged between class members? More likely mobile phones are involved as well whilst two or more pals work on-screen at a particular task. Or they use a chat room. Much more recently Facebook and Twitter have appeared enhancing social interaction much further.

The downside is that software is available in which, as a teacher sets a piece of homework, he/she enters the details for accessing by parents who use a gateway program to the school. Probably students see this as a step backwards because the truth of the time-honoured excuse that Mr Bloggs didn't set any homework can now be checked instantly. It also prods Mr Bloggs into setting the homework in the first place. For the students that's a double whammy!

Social networking now is widespread. On one hand this enables communication across nations undreamt of in the past. Increasingly, however, the criticism is made that physical social interaction is likely to fade. But children are attracted to social network sites quite early in their school years and these extend now for thirteen years. There is no doubt that most of those are spent interacting in the real social world; then soon afterwards the school world gives way to that of higher education or employment. Certainly it is true there is a heightened chance of an individual fading into reclusiveness, but not the great majority. If you are still doubtful whether children interact fully in the real world during their formative years, ask to visit your local school for a day and undertake what is called 'participant observation'.

As widespread social networking alters society with world-wide power shifts, the loosening of political control and widespread availability of knowledge, it is interesting to speculate whether schools, also, will be radically changed. Or is the classroom model from antiquity so formidable that it will remain? The days of the schoolhouse may be far less long or hard but they haven't been scrapped in 5,000 years.

Chapter 8

I left my seat on the top deck of the swaying tram as it sped noisily along its rails in the middle of the road leading into the city. With youthful agility born of long practice I clambered down the steep winding stairs on to the platform. The conductress smiled at me.

'You want Spenser Street, duck?'

I smiled back. 'Yes, please.'

I have no idea where the idea of 'duck' being an acceptable mode of address came from, but it was woven into the everyday speech of midland conductors, conductresses, street traders and shop assistants along with 'luv', 'son', 'Ma', 'Pop', and 'our kid', according to the age and sex of the person addressed. Only once did I hear anyone repulsed using such terms of endearment, when a conductor held the arm of an elderly lady as she stepped up on to the platform of his bus.

'Come on, muther, 'old tight!' he encouraged.

She straightened up, looked him full in the eye, and replied with perfect diction, 'I am not aware of having given birth to you, young man.' Whereupon she walked serenely to a vacant place inside amidst chuckles from her fellow passengers and a rueful grin from him.

The tram ground to a stop with squealing brakes on metal wheelrims and I jumped down the two steps to the road. I dodged a passing grocery errand boy wobbling his delivery bike with the container over the small front wheel full of customer's orders – and remembered riding one myself on Saturday mornings for pocket money. I walked a short distance along the pavement, then turned into Spenser Street. On one side a row of small terraced houses extended almost unbroken for its full length, though there was an open area on the corner with mounds of rubble covered with weeds revealing it as a bombed site. Two large hoardings had been erected on it; beneath the scaffolding was a cement mixer with piles of sand nearby that bore traces of children's feet. The other gaps in the houses were the entries through which one walked to reach other rows of houses that had no street frontage.

On the other side the houses flanked a large space which was the school site. There was the usual low wall surmounted by tall and very solid railings, painted green like every other school in the city. For safety reasons school railings had not been cut down to provide wartime factories with much needed metal, but they were alone in escaping the ubiquitous scythe. There were two gates spaced well apart; in front of these were the equally preserved silver crash barrier railings to prevent crowds of children bursting unchecked out of the playground and on to the road.

Recently an historical television programme revealed the fact that despite railings being removed throughout the length and breadth of the land none of the resulting scrap was ever turned into shells and bombs. At the time, of course, we believed it implicitly. I wonder what mismanagement lay behind that particular exercise which must have involved many thousands of working hours at goodness knows what cost. No doubt it was just another item on the war bill for which we had to borrow from you-know-who on an extended loan, on which we made the last payment early in the twenty-first century.

The two gates led into two playgrounds provided for the inevitable segregation of the sexes. School builders of the time when Spenser Street Junior and Infants was built had a fixation about the orgies that would be rampant amongst seven to eleven year old boys and girls during their playtime if they were allowed to mix in a communal playground. Infants, five to seven years, were allowed to play alongside older girls, but the older, rougher boys were segregated. Both areas were spacious; between them stood a typical late Victorian school with steeply pitched roofs and gables much in evidence. A few plane trees with their distinctive patchy bark around the edge of the playground contributed a welcome splash of green.

I was visiting the school for a day's preparation, prior to beginning my first period of block practice, in order to find out what work the children were doing and what I would be expected to teach. It was a normal day, so all classes were at work as I pushed open the brown inner doors and walked into a large and very lofty hall. Immediately above me an open framework iron staircase spiralled upwards, as did a second one at the other end. These served two complete galleries, one above the other, flanked on their outer sides by more open framework surmounted by a very solid and high handrail. On two sides of the middle and upper galleries, as on the ground floor, doors and windows were visible denoting classrooms. I walked to the centre of the floor, gazing upwards, the whole structure reminding me strongly of pictures I had seen of prisons.

As I watched a diminutive figure emerged from a door on the top floor and furiously waggled a large handbell. He then walked to one staircase, clattered down it to the next level and waggled it again. He continued his descent until he reached my level, then he began walking across the floor holding the bell over his head and waving it with great relish. As he passed me I seized the opportunity for directions.

'Will you show me where Mr Overton's room is, please?'

'Yeah, up 'ere. C'mon, I'll take yer,' and he marched off up the second staircase with the bell slung like a rifle over his shoulder. He stopped on the first landing and indicated a door.

'That's it – that's Mistroverton's room.'

'Thanks,' I said as he continued his climb back to his classroom. By this time streams of children were emerging from rooms on all levels. It became obvious that a strict one-way system was in operation, because all groups were walking in orderly files to one staircase or the other according to whether they were ascending or descending. I could see two teachers posted as traffic cops and I stood and watched for a moment, listening to the heavy tramping of many feet on the gallery floor a few feet above my head.

Mr Overton emerged from his room as I was about to knock on the door. He was a small, bright featured man with thinning hair. I introduced myself and his face broke into a welcoming smile.

'Ah yes, Mr Flaxton. Delighted to see you. You've arrived at an ideal time – playtime. Come and have a cup of coffee with us; you can meet the staff straightaway.'

He led a few steps further along the short end of the gallery and beckoned me into the staffroom. After introductions I tasted my first drink as a quasi-adult amongst a group of teachers. I felt I was crossing a significant threshold. Many thousands of cups later I can still recall the feeling of pride that engulfed me.

I had never seen a school building remotely like that of Spenser Street. I suppose it was whilst I was there that I first realised how varied the nation's stock of school buildings must be because the original nucleus of 1870 had been added to over a period of seventy years. I was to remember Spenser Street particularly in the sixties when I was working in a Village College which was full of children in the daytime and a lively mixture of adults of all ages every evening and weekend. One day one of the adult students, who was an architect, told me that his firm had decided to enter a competition to refurbish an old Victorian school in London. He then asked my wife and me if he could pick our brains. We told him we would be delighted to help, but warned him that in our experience teachers and architects frequently disagree.

'Are the judges from your world or ours?' we asked.

'I'm not sure – probably both, since they mention a selection panel. I'll try to find out more, but I'll bring the plans to-morrow so you can borrow them and look at them at your leisure. I'm not saying we'll use your ideas, of course, but none of us has actually designed a school, so we thought entering would add to our experience. Anything you have to suggest may help us to see problems we might otherwise overlook.'

The next evening he spread the plans before us and there it was – almost a replica of Spenser Street. The same three levels, two spiral staircases, the large central hall, the spacious playgrounds. No doubt there were many other copies in the larger industrial cities throughout the country, built towards the end of the nineteenth century and designed to house two age groups – infants on the ground floor and juniors on the upper floors. Perhaps a very few, like this one, were destined to survive. Most, I am sure, were to go the way of Spenser Street, beneath the bulldozer as its area was cleared for high rise flats.

My wife and I argued for a week about what should go where, then had a session with our architect friend. He was very surprised at one of our suggestions. One of the competition requirements was the conversion of three rooms into a gymnasium, a name soon to change into physical activities studio. Another was that the infants section, the five to seven year olds, should be kept to one floor though the sevens to elevens could be divided.

We insisted the infants should occupy the ground floor, as originally intended, and as they did at Spenser Street, which would force the gymnasium on to the first floor. Our friend was dubious; what about getting equipment into the room via the spiral staircase? These had to remain; anyway they could be made into a most attractive feature with the resurgence of interest in Victoriana. More importantly, what would happen if they wanted to take physical education equipment out into the playground on hot summer days?

We countered by suggesting a small store on the ground floor with duplicate equipment for such eventualities if that was considered an important proviso. Realistically we knew that hardly happens; games are played outdoors; PE indoors. Converting half the rooms on the ground floor would force the infants' classes on to the first floor, leaving the juniors to be divided between the remaining rooms and the complete second floor at the top. Condemning infants to frequent stair climbs throughout the day was quite unacceptable, we asserted. Furthermore the loos were on the ground floor. But most of all it would mean all that lovely hall floor could only be reached via the stairs and, therefore, in the practical situation some classes just would not use this extra space for all the activities so necessary in modern infants' teaching.

We pressed the point hard. In the end the firm went along with us. Later they showed us their entry. The plans, particularly the elevations, made the building look quite elegant and we realised it did have attractive proportions. The playground looked most exciting with climbing frames, sand pits, ball targets and so forth in profusion between trees, bushes and flower islands.

'Spenser Street,' I thought, 'if only...'

'If we win,' our friend said, 'we'll acknowledge you two as Professional Consultants'. We felt ten feet tall.

The result was announced six months later, by which time we had almost forgotten it. Our friend's firm gained a Commendation, and third place. He was quite pleased.

'Did they say why you didn't win?' we asked.

'Oh yes! The winning entry had the gymnasium on the ground floor and the infants above. The critique said this was undoubtedly best in view of the problems of moving PE apparatus.'

We crawled away.

'That panel couldn't have had a teacher on it,' my wife exclaimed. She was teaching five year olds at the time. 'Why don't they make architects teach in the schools they build?'

My mind went back to Spenser Street, of course, where there was no gymnasium and where I was assigned to a class on the top floor. Although I was there for only one month I came to know those spiral staircases very well indeed.

So did the children. They mounted up them for morning registration then came down for assembly. They went back up for lessons, then down for morning playtime, ascending again some fifteen minutes later. They descended again at lunch time, back up for afternoon lessons, down for playtime, up afterwards, down at the end of the day – not to mention down for any games lessons and back up afterwards, similarly for any gratuitous visits to the loos, or with messages, or to collect material for lessons from the stock room (on the ground floor, of course), and the bell monitor performing his office at least four times a day.

But not the infants. Their rooms were on the ground floor where the Victorian architect intended them to be. On-going aerobic exercise, sensibly, was reserved for the post-seven year olds.

Chapter 9

Everyone knows the adage that the best teacher is a born teacher. This is why you certainly don't have to undergo a course of training to be a good teacher, neither can a course of training guarantee to turn an ordinary mortal into an outstanding one. The fact is that virtually all of us do some teaching at some stage of our lives – usually as an older or more skilled person imparting knowledge or skills to a younger or less skilled one.

Parents teach their children to speak a language and manage it within a couple of years or so. People on factory floors, on farms, in shops, teach trades to newcomers – and many such teachers and students regretted the demise in the latter years of the century of the former apprentice system that served well for many hundreds of years. Fortunately it is being resuscitated, though the television programme of that name conveys a false image for true apprenticeships. A lad kicking a ball resolutely towards a convenient bit of road or park or village green finds a six year old scrap of humanity at his elbow – and though he ignores the insistent, 'Please let me play…go on…' for a time, finally he gives in. Then, in exasperation, when the kid wastes the other's time by mis-kicking and falling over he expostulates, 'No, not like that! Come here, I'll show you…' and proceeds to give a first rate lesson in footballing skills. You can transpose that little scenario to back streets in South American towns, or the West Indies and substitute a bat and cricket ball where such teachers and students alike know that top grade skills are very marketable.

Older sisters show younger ones how to use cosmetics and then wish they hadn't because the stuff disappears so rapidly and kid sisters have no morals when it comes to their elders' belongings.

Precocious youngsters lean over fences and loudly ask neighbours, 'What are you doing?' If they are in a good humour the neighbours show them. 'I want to do that – can I?' comes next, equally loudly, and soon the youngsters are being shown anything from lighting a bonfire to making a garden pool. It's always more interesting when the work is being done in someone else's garden. Yes, I know that's frowned upon by Authority which seeks to protect children from any adult who hasn't been checked against a variety of registers, but I daresay the pendulum of common sense will swing back to an extent in due course.

Many born teachers take up careers in demonstrating and become representatives of all kinds. Some excellent ones become well known on television; presenters of informative and documentary programmes need to have the full range of personal teaching skills to be successful and to be recognised as personalities. Of course, they have superb resource facilities at hand, which helps immensely if the subject is lizards in the Galapagos Islands, or the latest development in laser technology, or how to make over your garden in two days flat.

Husbands teach wives how to drive cars and wives teach husbands how to change nappies. But more than this, at home, at work, in sport, in pubs and clubs, at church, on holiday, in hobbies and pastimes, in much of the vast range of computer software, whenever and however we meet one another, people are interacting and so very often that means someone is teaching and someone is learning. How to hang wallpaper, improve your golf swing, kick a football with dipping spin, line dance, sell your firm's product, ease arthritis…and so on…and so on…forever!

It is also blazingly obvious that some people teach others things that would be best left alone – hence crime, drug culture, sexual depravity – and a whole range of attitudes and actions that foster discord in micro and macro societies.

It is because everyone is engaged in teaching in its widest sense to a greater or lesser extent that so many people show interest in schools and education. Schools may fascinate or infuriate you but it's not very likely that you have no opinion at all about them. After all, nearly everyone goes through them at one level or another and emerges satisfied or not according to individual experience. All adults once had plenty of opportunity to appraise or criticise their own teachers and at some stage most try imagining what they would do in the role. I suppose this is most likely to happen when your own children go to school, especially if they don't get on as well as you expected. At such moments all your innate teaching ability asserts itself and you think, 'I could do the job ten times better than Miss Bloggs!'

Then you look hard at hundreds of happy puppies as they gambol, shove and scream their way out of school, and you have reservations.

The fact is that schools only deal with part of the education of society's youngsters and all adults are engaged in the other, more informal part, either as individuals or in their jobs or their leisure. How short the time in school really is, compared to the 'non-school' part, is revealed when you do the arithmetic. For a child, from age 5 to age 18 seems a lifetime. But when I annually greeted newcomers and their parents to an upper school serving the 13 to 18 age group, I used to emphasise that in most subjects they would have about 285 hours teaching from the moment they set foot in the school until GCSE. Put that into context of a working day and night it covers about one and two thirds weeks. Indeed the whole working school time amounts to about 11.5% of life in the thirteen years from 5 to 18. So non-school time and opportunity for influence has by far the greater weight.

Teacher training courses help with the theory of education, practice and technique, and provide some academic extension for the B.Ed. (Bachelor of Education). For the PGCE (Post Graduate Certificate in Education) the prior degree course far outweighs the training element. But neither can turn a naturally poor teacher into a good one, nor is formal training essential to be an outstanding teacher. A good teacher is a good teacher – in or out of the profession.

On one of our weekly half day practice sessions when it was my turn to take a lesson, the VP had me walking on air when he told me that I had 'a good classroom presence'. This made me so obnoxiously big-headed that I thought I was in the 'born teacher' category and therefore only had to open my mouth and the children would hang on my every word. With so many people watching their every move during our half day lessons they were usually very attentive. At Spenser Street I was lucky that they seemed to take to me quite quickly; and they already had three young teachers on the permanent staff. I was assigned to Miss Beaumont's class, 4a, and although she was not of the youngest in age she was certainly young at heart. She was also the Chief Assistant, so most members of the class were good in both work and behaviour.

It contained forty-seven ten and eleven year olds. The reason for the age spread, which I experienced myself at junior school, was due to the Chief Education Officer. He conceived the notion of six monthly promotion for all schools throughout the city, which meant that every class had two sections – juniors and seniors. Halfway through the year the seniors moved up to the next class, and the juniors became the seniors. The ploy helped at both ends of the age spread – then 5 to 14, but it ensured that every class had to be taught in two halves. It was universally unpopular in schools and I have never experienced it elsewhere.

I soon had a seating plan with the names of the children in my lesson notebook, ready to commit to memory. Miss Beaumont gave me a few thumb nail sketches, such as Harry W who, though quiet most of the time, was apt suddenly to kick out at you in a temper when frustrated and the best solution was to dodge quickly. If he made contact there had to be the inevitable report to Mr Overton and subsequent punishment; rather unnecessary, she said, because his temper evaporated just as quickly. But also there was Sheila C, with an IQ of 132, who was soon to move to a well-known grammar school. We were taught a great deal about IQs – intelligence quotients – and how to measure them. At the time it was generally accepted they were fixed, like one's height. Subsequently it has been revealed there was some fixing of the research data that led to the assumption. Nevertheless with a high IQ Sheila stood tall in the crowd of her peers.

Despite its tough area I found my fears were groundless and that Spenser Street was indeed a good school for teaching practice. All I had to do was dig up some good lesson material from somewhere to manifest significant experiences and I would be home and dry. Fortunately I knew I had just the right source at home in some books which I was treasuring for the future. They had been given me by a near neighbour who was headmaster of a junior school and who had been at St Andrew's in the early twenties. They were entitled 'The Practical Senior Teacher'. I knew they would really come into their own during the next year when we were to train for senior teaching but, as Miss Beaumont's class contained the oldest juniors, I felt sure I should find plenty of suitable material, since many would be moving to a senior school in a few weeks' time.

There were six volumes, imposingly bound in red covers with gold lettering and embossed designs. With them was a box file, made to look like a seventh and much thicker volume, which contained an assortment of classroom charts and pictures. The man said that now he was permanently in his junior school he had no further use for them. Actually they were in pristine condition and had I looked carefully I would have realised he had made hardly any use of them at all.

They carried a foreword by Sir Percy Nunn, an educationist whom the VP was wont to quote in his lectures. Naturally they covered all subjects taught in schools, so they seemed to contain everything that anyone could possibly need for any lesson of any kind.

Not for me the harassed search for lesson materials, I thought smugly. Whilst the other chaps were ransacking college and city libraries, and were begging ideas from the senior year or older relatives who were teachers, I smiled patronisingly at their efforts, secure in the knowledge that I possessed it all in the six volumes of 'The Practical Senior Teacher'. The books were published by the New Era Publishing Company and each had highly decorative book plates inside. These, fortunately, had not been pasted in because on the back of each was an explanation that truly summed up the wealth of my treasures so perfectly:

'AN EXPLANATION OF THE PLATE'
'It is a work of great beauty and considerable artistic merit'...it explained, in case you weren't sure. 'It is designed by Mr W.P.Barrett, who has an international reputation and has designed book plates for an imposing

list of kings and queens' (in those days there was still a list) 'as well as for many other distinguished persons. The design represents the Dawning of the New Era of Learning breaking through the mountains and clouds which may be taken to represent ignorance and the many barriers which obstruct progress. The sun is the source of all power and good and represents the power which can be derived by the wisdom and knowledge which you should derive from the possession of the book...'

I was most impressed by this sentiment: the wisdom and knowledge I could derive from the books and felt sure they couldn't fail to put me way ahead of my unfortunate fellow students who were groping in the dark for their lesson material. As if to prove this to me, after some more detailed description of the plate, the blurb concluded,

'The light...represents the power of wisdom and knowledge to develop that which is latent in the unplumbed depths of the possibilities of the individual, if knowledge and wisdom are laid before him clearly and concisely.'

It was heady stuff for a student teacher. In the volumes were lessons and schemes of work for English, Mathematics, Geography, History, Music, Art, Physical Training, Science, Hygiene, Needlework and Handicraft. How could I fail to plumb the depths of the possibilities of the Spenser Street kids when I had all the necessary knowledge and wisdom laid out before me so clearly and concisely? What was even better, none of the other chaps had managed to find copies of these books, I found out discretely. It was hard luck on them, of course, but that's how life went.

In block practice you were expected to start taking some lessons after a couple of days. Our visiting tutors could be expected at any time after that, and you were expected to be coping well at least or carrying a torch at best, especially if you had ambitions to be one of the rare few who would ultimately receive the accolade of an 'A' teaching mark. Actually final teaching marks were strictly confidential, so of course they were subject to universal leaks.

Miss Beaumont suggested that for one set of English lessons, ostentatiously labelled 'Grammar' on the timetable, I should teach punctuation. I realised from reading a number of their compositions that at least half the class were quite confused about this little matter, so I readily agreed to clarify the situation with a couple of lessons or so. I knew perfectly well the matter was dealt with in 'The Practical Senior Teacher' and therefore the matter was as good as solved.

Of course some of the children could punctuate quite adequately, especially anyone like Sheila. However there was only one other grammar school entrant in Miss Beaumont's class, so the total for the school was two, since hers was the top one. In the city as a whole one-eighth of the children went to grammar schools, a figure arrived at each year by the simple method of counting the number of places available and drawing a line at that point on the examination results list. This procedure was mirrored in all local education authority areas, so entry to grammar schools varied according to available accommodation resulting in widely differing ratios. A very persistent rumour had it that in one town in mid-Wales the single grammar school was three times the size of the only other secondary school, so the 11+ pass rate there exceeded 75%. In our city seven-eighths of the children, therefore, went on to the organisationally new secondary modern schools (or a few to the secondary technical schools which had a fairly short existence as such) established under the recent 1944 Education Act. There were no new buildings, of course, and everyone still called them senior schools.

At night I burned the midnight oil preparing lessons on a range of subjects, including punctuation. I was still in the VP's tutorial group and therefore knew he would visit me at some stage. The problem was I didn't know when, so, as he very well intended, I had to prepare each lesson perfectly, just in case. But with my advantage I didn't worry and commiserated in avuncular fashion with other students who were less fortunate.

'Heaven knows what I'll do if the VP comes into my lesson on long multiplication,' groaned Archie. 'You can't make visual aids on a topic like that, so there'll be nothing for the kids to flash around and impress him. In any case, half of them at my school don't know their tables, so I'm stuck from the start.'

'Never mind, old chap,' I gloated, 'write it all up under Problem. Impress him with your analysis. He can't expect you to do wonders in a couple of weeks.'

'I wouldn't mind if he comes to Geography – I'm doing the weather and there's bags of stuff on that. I've managed to get a film strip on it and the school actually has a projector. Trouble is only one room blacks out, so you have to get the classes swapped around and they don't like doing that.'

I blanched. A film strip projector! He was lucky – Spenser Street had no such luxuries. A good lesson with that was bound to be impressive. But never mind, I'd got breadth in 'The Practical Senior Teacher' and I could illustrate anything – even punctuation! I chuckled to myself for I had just prepared handsheets for the pupils on that topic. Lovely illustrations they were, bringing full stops, commas, inverted commas, semi-colons, colons and dashes all to life directly from the pages of my precious volumes. If only the VP would visit me for that lesson!

He did just that.

On the first Thursday of my practice Miss Beaumont hurried into the staffroom which was situated close to Class 4a's room, conveniently at the top of a short and narrow flight of stairs leading from the top gallery. I was catching up with some marking and was due to take the first of the punctuation lessons the next period.

'Your Major Darnley is here – he's with Mr Overton now.'

'Oh good,' I replied coolly, 'I'll be ready for him.'

She glanced at the table upon which a pile of sheets stacked beside the children's exercise books. She picked up one.

'Is this the handsheet you are giving the children for this lesson?'

'That's right.'

'Did you make this up yourself?' she asked in a rather flat tone.

'Oh no,' I replied airily, 'I used a reference book which I was given a short while ago. It's part of a rather fine set, called 'The Practical Senior Teacher'. Most of the lesson material is geared to older pupils, of course, but I thought this would be about the right level for 4a. Brings things to life, doesn't it?'

'Yes, I suppose it does…'

'May I come into the room and prepare my blackboard work? It's here in my lesson notebook – as you see it'll take a few minutes to draw. I'll use the free standing board; I can turn the easel away from the class so they won't see it before the lesson. Major Darnley rather likes that technique – the sudden revelation.'

'Yes, of course, if you're sure you want to.' She sounded a touch distant. Probably thinking about her own lesson, I surmised.

She returned the paper to the table and left hurriedly. I followed shortly afterwards. Inside the room I became absorbed in my work, which I carefully concealed from the children. I drew the outline of a large comma, filled it in with yellow chalk and added arms, legs, a neck and head in 'pin man' style. 'He' was leaning against a wall. I did the same with a full stop, but this time he was shown lying down. Beside these I wrote, very neatly, 'The comma takes a pause' and 'The full stop takes a rest'.

Then I drew a row of commas, with spaces between, all with hands on hips looking at strips of vegetables supposedly in gardens. At the side I wrote, 'Commas divide up a series of different pieces of information'. I added others, drawn in similar cartoon outline. It was all a direct copy of illustrations from a lesson in my prize possession.

So were the drawings on the duplicated handsheets which showed even more ludicrous events – commas holding each other's arms wide to 'shut off extra pieces of information' as the notes said. A semi-colon was turned into 'a lazy fellow', sitting down, who 'always takes a longer rest'. It looked like the side view of a girl in a bikini. A dash was shown 'yoking together' two cartoon heads of oxen, and I drew them looking completely cross-eyed. But that is how they appeared when I traced them from the pages of the PST.

If all my lessons had been as bad as that one I would have burned my notebook years ago despite the hours of toil that went into it, or rather them, for the total of my various periods of practice ran to a little under four hundred pages. I cringe with embarrassment when I look back now at that particular effort.

So did the VP. The lesson lasted twenty minutes and he stuck it out manfully. Then I should have changed to teaching some Geography. Before I could do so he stood up, came from the back of the room where he had been sitting, and beamed at the children. They were on their best behaviour having been threatened earlier by Miss Beaumont with death or worse if they put a foot wrong with this important visitor.

'I think you all have some reading books in your desks, haven't you?'

'Yes sir,' came the general but subdued reply.

'Good. You take them out and read quietly to yourselves for a short while. I want to have a few words with Mr Flaxton.'

Desk lids rose and were put down gently as books were extracted. Silence descended. He turned to me.

'Sit there.' He indicated the teacher's desk and high chair at the front of the room. I did so and he took up a position facing me with his back to the class. Slowly he leant forward and put his hands on either side of the desk top. As his face got nearer to mine he lifted up his head and stared at me through the lower lenses of his bifocals.

'Does the chair you now occupy signify anything to you at all, MISTER Flaxton?' His voice was a sibilant whisper. I swallowed hard.

'Er, yes, I think so.' Mine sounded strangely strangled

'Then tell me about it', he invited.

'Well…' I began, then stopped lamely. But he had no intention of easing my plight, which was entirely of my own making.

'I am waiting.'

I flushed. At least he might have had the grace to tell me off outside the room. 'I suppose you mean if I am sitting in this chair I ought to be able to teach the children in front of me', I rattled quietly, wondering what he really wanted me to say.

'Obviously.' His face remained a few inches from mine and neither it nor his expression wavered. 'And what is the kernel of all our teaching, of every lesson, of everything we produce for these young minds – WHAT ARE WE TRYING TO DO?'

'Make them think, sir.' I knew that one from his lectures.

He beamed his most artificial smile. 'Good, good – and if we are trying to make the children use their powers of thought is it too much to ask that the teacher should demonstrate a modicum of the same process?'

'Yes, of course – I mean, no, it isn't.'

'Then why are you offering them this drivel?'

He whipped my notebook in front of my face open at the page where my stupid drawings mocked me from the red rectangle entitled 'Blackboard Summary'. But I didn't have the sense to give in and admit my denseness. I had to dig myself further into the mess. I tried looking prim.

'I took those directly from a well-known reference book, in fact it's a very detailed work, covers six volumes, and it has a set of charts...'

'What is the name of this tome?' His voice was very flat.

'The Practical Senior Teacher. Of course I realise that this school isn't...'

'Is it in the college library?'

'Er, well, no, but a former student of St Andrew's, now a headmaster and a friend of mine...'

'I have never heard of it.'

'It has an introduction by Sir Percy Nunn...'

'I don't care who introduced it or who wrote it or whether it was presented to you by the Minister of Education – if it contains this kind of nonsense it is useless. And so are you if you are dimwitted enough not to see that. At first I thought you had dreamed this up yourself in a nightmare but now you tell me you did not think about it at all, not even SUBconsciously!'

He straightened up, took my book and turned away. My face felt as though I'd fallen asleep in the tropical sun. I was sure every eye in the class was watching the debacle and that every ear had heard every word. How on earth was I going to become a teacher after this? Visions of my consoling family floated around my head. 'Never mind, old chap,' they said, at least you tried.' Then they wandered away shaking their heads.

'Take your book,' said the VP turning back to me, 'and think about what I have written in it. Good afternoon.'

He turned to the class.

'You were all very well behaved whilst I was talking to Mr Flaxton,' he said in normal tones. 'Well done, I shall tell Miss Beaumont, and I shall come and visit you again next week. Goodbye.'

It was their turn to beam at him. 'Goodbye, sir,' they chanted happily.

Suddenly he was gone and I was left staring at my notes. I was absolutely immobile. I could feel sweat seeping down my spine under my shirt which was clinging damply to me. I felt just as limp and sodden. What on earth would the kids think of me? Should I just rush out of the room and disappear? I stared and stared at the top of the big desk. The room was completely silent.

'Please sir,' said a quiet and respectful voice, 'shall we get out our Geography books?'

Somehow the question penetrated my reeling consciousness and I forced myself to look up. Slowly, very slowly I looked up and down the four double rows. Most of the children were reading, two or three were writing on pieces of paper, a couple looked bored. None appeared any different from usual.

Gradually I relaxed. No one had heard, fortunately. Thank heaven for large classrooms. At least they weren't going to laugh me out of the room in disgrace. I have no idea how I got through the next lesson, nor what I taught. We didn't have to write every lesson in our notebooks so that tells me nothing. But I am positive no one learnt anything at all from it.

As Miss Beaumont came in to teach the last lesson I shot past her without even a glance. I made a beeline for the loo, fittingly the path of a wounded bee because it was on the ground floor, whither I went spiralling downwards.

After the children had gone home I emerged and climbed back up again. I had to collect my books and I knew I had to face Miss Beaumont. I walked along the gallery with the enthusiasm of someone being led in front of a firing squad.

'I wondered where you'd got to.'

'What an abysmal mess!' I groaned.

'What is?' she said, looking round and sounding surprised.

'My lesson – it was ghastly.'

'Do you mean the children misbehaved?' She was on her mettle in a flash.

'No – my notes, my illustrations, the whole silly idea. What on earth did Major Darnley say about it to you afterwards?'

'Oh, not a great deal. He said you needed to be a little more critical in your selection of material. I guessed the children would like your little drawings, but I don't think they'll really apply them to punctuation. He obviously read through your other work and said you weren't doing badly.'

I couldn't believe what she was saying. Later, when I brought myself to look at his comments in my notebook, I realised that I didn't know whether he meant what he said to her or whether he was just being polite – and really had written me off, as he had done with my illustrations. Across the top of the handsheet which I had pasted in my notebook were the words:

'Consider the value of this illustrative extravagance critically.'

I did so. The six volumes of 'The Practical Senior Teacher' were relegated to the lumber-room at home and I joined the other chaps in their harassed search for appropriate lesson material with what I hoped was a more discerning eye.

Chapter 10

'Sir, sir, come quick! Ronnie Bierton's 'ad a nawful fight with Arthur Braggis and 'e's gorrall sand in 'is eyes!'

Brenda Harson burst into the room gaspring her terrible tidings some time after the children had gone home at the end of afternoon school. She was closely followed by three other girls who had lost the race up the spiral staircase.

I was clearing my things away after a lesson and two other teachers had wandered in to enquire how I was getting on. They were Angela Metchley and Dave Penlyn. Their own college days were not all that far in the past but Dave had been in the Army and had not long returned to teaching. A Welshman, he had started to digress about his adventures when Mary shattered his reminiscences. Her shoulders were heaving as she gulped air; she had obviously been running at top speed.

'Where?' Dave shot at her. Both boys were in his class.

'On the bomb site. Arthur gorrim on the ground, then he sarron 'is chest and shoved sand in 'is face. 'E's blinded 'im!'

The other girls were anxious to fill in the details of the attack.

'They 'ad ever such a nargument, sir, and Ronnie frew a brick at Arfur.'

'It din't 'it 'm, but 'e got ever so mad. All the other kids was crowding round and yellin'.'

Dave was on his way through the door closely followed by the girls pouring out their story. Angela and I followed and the procession raced down the stairs. As we reached the hall floor a small knot of boys met us, stopped, and parted. In the middle, with another lad's arm held consolingly across his shoulders, was Ronnie Bierton.

I heard Dave's intake of breath and Angela gasped, 'Oh no!' All the children stood in silent reaction to our shock. Wet sand was plastered in his hair and the upper part of his face. You couldn't see his eyes, both because of the sand and the fact that they were screwed up in pain. Brenda's description wasn't exaggerated in the slightest. The sand hadn't just been thrown at his face, it had been ground in.

'Get the first aid box from the staff room, will you?' Dave asked Angela. Then to Ronnie, 'Hold tight, son. I'm going to lead you into a classroom.' He shepherded the sorry looking figure across the hall and into a room on the ground floor sometimes used by the youngest of the junior classes. Then he lifted Ronnie carefully and sat him on top of one of the front desks which he pulled out so that it faced the light from the window. The other children crowded round.

'Alright, everyone,' said Dave, 'you had all better go home now. Thanks for bringing Ronnie. We'll look after him.'

'Worrabout Arthur Braggis, sir?' asked one of the boys.

'Where is he now?

''E 'opped it when we said we was going ter take Ronnie back to school. We couldn't take 'im 'ome cos 'is Mom and Dad doan gerrin till six o'clock.'

'Never mind, I'll see Arthur in the morning,' Dave said with a grim expression that was not lost on the boys. They slipped out glancing seriously at one other.

'What the hell can you do?' I asked quietly when they had left. 'Surely he ought to go to the Eye Hospital?

'Sure, that's where I'll take him when I've cleaned him up a bit. But we'll have to go on the bus – they won't send an ambulance if the kid can walk.'

Angela arrived with the medical kit and a large new roll of cotton wool.

'There's some Optrex in the box, fortunately, and I got this new roll from the stock cupboard.'

'Is the Old Man still here?' asked Dave quietly as he opened the first aid box.

'No,' replied Angela. 'I checked. Everyone else has gone.'

'Right, it's up to us then. Now, let's see how bad it is, son.'

Gently he took a dry piece of cotton wool and began to clear sand away from Ronnie's eyebrows and forehead. Ronnie remained absolutely still, his shoulders hunched and his face tightly contorted. But he hadn't uttered a sound, nor did he as Dave moistened the cotton wool and began clearing sand from the screwed-up eyelids.

'I think we had better get rid of this sea shore you've got in your hair,' said Dave after a while. 'Can you lean forward, Ronnie, whilst we shake some of it out?'

A suggestion of a twitch at the corner of Ronnie's mouth showed he was responding to Dave's gentle humour. I saw a chance to be useful.

'Let me do that. Come on, old chap, I'll soon have it all out.'

As delicately as I could I flopped my hands to and fro in the mat of tousled hair. Yellow builders' sand dropped on to the floor in a steady flow until there was quite a patch beside the desk. Meanwhile Angela pulled small pieces off the roll of cotton wool and twisted them into small swabs. She poured a liberal quantity of Optrex into a curved medical dish.

'Now then,' said Dave, 'let's have a good look at those eyes. Don't worry, son, I'll try not to hurt you.'

He sat Ronnie upright and putting his thumbs above and below the right eye prized it open against the clamping of the cheek and forehead muscles. Ronnie's hands involuntarily moved towards his face and his body tautened but he didn't touch Dave's hands. Still he uttered no sound. It was obvious he trusted his teacher implicitly.

The three of us peered at the eyeball which didn't want to emerge from under the upper lid and look directly at the light. Grains of sand were everywhere – on the eyeball, welling up from under the lid, encrusted on the eyelashes. Fortunately nature was coming to the rescue because the eye was watering copiously, but Ronnie was not crying.

'Let's squeeze some Optrex into it,' said Angela.

'Good idea,' agreed Dave, 'tip your head back, old son.' Angela soaked a swab in the liquid and gently squeezed it on to the eyeball as Dave forced the lids apart. Ronnie winced but still said nothing.

'Now we might get somewhere,' said Dave as he put Ronnie's head up straight again and moistened a pointed swab. 'Angie, if I hold the eyelids, can you start wiping away the grains?'

As she did so, I began dipping the swabs in the Optrex so she had a supply in readiness.

'Nigel, have a go at clearing the outside of his other eye,' suggested Dave. This was still as tightly shut as the right one had been but Dave had already cleaned the lids to an extent. I took a swab and began to do the job thoroughly. Then when Ronnie relaxed his right eye as Angela wiped more of the sand away, Dave switched his attention to the left eye and they repeated the process.

Gradually the stage was reached where Ronnie could blink both eyes though slowly and obviously with pain. As he did so we could see more grains appear in a thin line at the edge of each lower lid. Now he managed to keep his eyes open as Dave wiped these away. He blinked again, more grains appeared and were removed.

Soon Dave was able to turn the lids back slightly and wipe gains away from the inner surfaces until we could see no more in either eye. By this time Ronnie was much more relaxed and his feet began to swing a little on the desk. But his eyes looked swollen and puffy and the rims were very red where the sharp sand had severely irritated them.

'Good lord, it's a quarter past six,' said Angela in surprise. 'Your parents will be home now, won't they Ronnie? I'd better go and let them know where you are. Where do you live?'

Ronnie spoke for the first time since he had been brought into school nearly an hour before.

'Twenny four Alma Place. Miss.' His voice was slightly husky, but no more.

'Good, that's not far away. I'll be back in a few minutes, Dave, then I'll come with you to the hospital unless his Mum wants to take him. I'd better telephone my landlady before we go, she'll be wondering where I am. Do you think the Caretaker has locked Mr Overton's room?'

'I'll go and find out for you,' I volunteered. I was slightly surprised there wasn't a second telephone in the stock room which was usually the place where staff had access to one. However I knew that getting extra lines so soon after the war was extremely difficult. We had been waiting a long time to have a phone installed at home.

When I returned Ronnie was looking considerably better. Dave had wiped his face and hands and had combed his hair.

'Thank you, sir,' he said quietly.

Dave put his arm round him. 'Alright, old son – you had a rough time.' Ronnie looked down at the floor.

'Serve me right for chuckin' a stone.'

'Why did you?'

''E called me a, a, well, sorry, sir, but 'e called me a bloody liar!'

In those days swearing was serious, especially amongst children.

'And why – oh, never mind now. Come on, let's get you to the Eye Hospital. They'll give you some proper treatment up there to make sure there isn't going to be any lasting damage.'

We met Angela at the school gates.

'Your Mum was in but your Dad isn't home yet,' she said to Ronnie, 'so she can't come. She says you won't mind us taking you instead.'

'That's OK, Miss.'

Dave turned to me. 'Thanks for helping, Nigel – all good experience for you, I suppose. See you in the morning.'

I felt a twinge of disappointment. Having assisted throughout the crisis I felt I was being dismissed as we reached the final phase, but common sense prevailed. Three people taking one nine year old to the hospital would appear excessive.

Next morning I met Dave at the gate again as we approached the school from opposite directions. As we turned into the playground together quite a number of the youngsters who had been yelling and dashing around with their usual happy abandon slowed and quietened. Some turned towards us, others turned to another boy who was looking miserable. Two self-appointed guards flanked him, taking his arms though not firmly for he offered no resistance. The three walked hesitatingly towards Dave as though impelled by an unseen force.

''Ere 'e 'is, sir,' said one.

The lad between them was Arthur Braggis. His mouth was set but the corners were turned down.

'Upstairs, my lad – my room,' snapped Dave.

Arthur looked down, turned immediately and walked into the school. His step was slow but didn't falter. Most of the other boys turned to watch him and fell silent as he passed.

Inside we met Mr Overton in the hall. 'Good morning, Mr Penlyn, Mr Flaxton. I hear you had some trouble last evening. What's the full story?'

Dave told him succinctly. The Head's face wore a very serious expression.

'Shall I deal with him?'

'No,' answered Dave, 'I'll finish the matter if you don't mind. Having dealt with the victim I'll do the same with the culprit.'

Realising what Dave intended made me somewhat embarrassed and we walked up the stairs in silence. He showed no anger but his expression was set. As I glanced at him I saw he was nerving himself to do something he obviously disliked but felt was necessary.

On the top balcony we parted. I walked into 4a's classroom and began organising some papers for my lesson. Dave walked into his room next door. Both doors stayed open and I heard a short but subdued conversation between him and Arthur Braggis. Then there was silence.

Suddenly I heard a fairly sharp 'thwack', followed by another, followed by two more. The third and fourth were punctuated by single soft cries from the boy.

'Go on, my lad,' I heard Dave say more loudly at his door. 'The matter is finished now, but remember you could have blinded Ronnie.'

I looked up. Through the window I saw the disconsolate figure walking slowly down the stairs, both hands clamped firmly under his armpits.

Mr Overton mentioned the matter to the school during assembly. But as I looked at the children I could see that whilst the girls were looking shocked and serious, there wasn't the same tension amongst the boys. I mentioned this to Dave as the children trooped upstairs.

'Well, it was over by then, see. Most would have heard about the fight last night – news travels quickly on the doorsteps around this area. The lads knew what had got to happen. You saw Arthur came this morning and took his punishment – he didn't stay away. Once that happened it was all over. As like as not you'll find Ronnie and Arthur playing together before the week's out. But there'd have been hell to pay if I hadn't caned Arthur.'

'What do you mean?'

'There'd have been gang warfare! Ronnie's pals would have had a go at Arthur, then Arthur's would have fought back. But Authority stepped in and dispensed justice. It just happened to be me on this occasion, though I hated doing it.'

Obviously he meant it.

'I didn't learn any of this at college,' he went on. 'You only pick it up in school. But the kids and most of the parents round here accept us as Authority – though we have to play detective, judge, jury and executioner sometimes. Generally they accept it if they see we are being what they think as fair. That stops matters getting out of hand.'

I sought him out again at morning break. 'I forgot to ask, what did the hospital do to Ronnie last night? Are his eyes OK? I see he's back in school to-day.'

'They didn't do much. They bathed his eyes then looked at them with a big magnifier. Said they could hardly see a grain of sand anywhere. If it hadn't been for the soreness everywhere they said they would have thought we were exaggerating when we told them what he looked like at first.'

He sipped his coffee and smiled. 'Told me I could have a job there anytime I liked!'

That scenario could not be repeated to-day. First, the altercation between the boys took place outside school, both in time and place. Legally, and today much importance is attached to legality, the headteacher, representing the school, is not responsible for nor has jurisdiction over the behaviour of pupils when they are not in school. This is both sensible and a problem.

It is sensible because, as I have pointed out, school children spend the majority of their time outside school unless they are boarders – and these comprise a very small proportion of the total school population. How could school be responsible for misdemeanours, or worse, committed miles away, late at night, in school holidays, abroad – indeed extension of the idea soon becomes ridiculous.

It is a problem because society is prone to think the school does have such a responsibility, albeit in rather vague circumstances. Case law is usually very sensible, despite the occasional judgment which the media seize upon to show the unworldliness of an elderly judge. In this matter there have been judgments accepting that school children going to and from school, especially when in recognisable school uniform, are in a sense representing the school at the time. They can, therefore, be deemed to be 'in school' for the purposes of discipline. After all, if *en route* children dash to help an elderly person who has fallen over, or call a vet to an injured dog via their mobile phones and are recognised as belonging to the local school, grateful adults may call it with congratulations and ask for their thanks to be conveyed to the students concerned. So for the opposite events – alas, probably in the majority for we are more likely to be critical – school can be invoked to investigate and dispense discipline. However the law certainly does not require them to take action – whether they do so depends upon circumstances and judgment.

At one extreme, when children going to the nearby school pass my home and drop litter, if I want to take up the matter generally I am quite correct in approaching the local headteacher. However, realistically, his only recourse is to appeal to the children's 'better' nature. Occasionally if I actually see something being dropped I pick it up, return it to the individual explaining he/she has dropped a possession. In the ensuing dialogue the youngster may get my message about litter, hopefully given with a touch of humour. Otherwise I know very well there may be a significant increase in litter in my front hedge in the next few days. Nevertheless it does help that I served some years as a governor of the school.

At the other extreme a headteacher died by stabbing when he intervened in an altercation involving members of his school outside the gates. There is a long continuum of events between these extremes.

Nowadays no corporal punishment can be used. Any serious matter, therefore, inside school or outside going to and coming from home, has to be a matter for the police. Many people feel this is correct; schools are part of society; therefore they cannot be places where the normal writ does not run. Yet I can remember a Chief Education Officer saying to me in the sixties that a headteacher who calls the police on to the premises has failed.

There are still plenty of people who, remembering their own school days, will regret that schools cannot dispense physical punishment and close a matter in the way they experienced. Certainly it could be seen as middling discipline – serious enough but avoiding outside agencies which all too likely resulted in making records. All a school had to do was record the event in the punishment book. Incidentally these are now historical, and sometimes fascinating, documents.

In the absence of the cane schools attempt many other kinds of sanction to discipline those who misbehave. But behind all arguments about what should or should not be used, it is useful to consider the four categories of purpose behind the whole notion of punishment. Any book about social principles will give them:

As a deterrent - to prevent others offending.

As retribution – society 'pays back' the individual for anti-social behaviour.

To reform the individual - to improve future behaviour.

As a penance – so the individual feels he/she has 'paid the penalty'.

It is salutary to consider which of these underlies laws, regulations and penalties in society at large and in institutions such as schools. Ideally, I suppose, we would go for number three. In church, as a boy, I remember intoning the confession:

'Thou…who desirest not the death of the sinner but rather that he should turn from his wickedness and live…'

I remember it carried on about us 'miserable offenders' though I never classed myself as miserable. For some, also, number four is accepted, especially after personal confession. But I'll bet most of us think in terms of one or two, especially when some appalling crime is reported in the news.

The question is, which should underpin discipline in schools? Should schools emulate society in general or should they treat children differently whilst they are children? You could argue there was a bit of all four in the matter of Arthur Bragiss. I wonder whether it reformed him and made him less likely to lose his temper the next time someone angered him. No doubt people in the locality felt it was dealt with under number two. He got what was coming to him was the likely verdict.

There is the treatment that Dave, Angela, and I to an extent, gave Ronnie. I have no idea whether either of the other two was qualified in first aid; I certainly was not. How would what they did be classified? What would have happened had their treatment not been successful or made matters worse? There is little doubt that to-day everyone would opt for immediate transfer to hospital, which shifts the responsibility, and any criticism reserved for the ambulance service if its response is tardy.

Another element of the scene might well be missing to-day. At various points both Dave and Angela put their sympathetic arms round Ronnie. To me it is a very sad fact that now even touching youngsters can be misconstrued. Yet throughout the second half of the century, indeed for most of it, the law has required teachers to act *in loco parentis* – in the place of a parent. Case law refined that to infer that teachers should act as very reasonable parents. Show me the very reasonable parent who doesn't put an arm round his/her child! The description surely implies the action of love and sympathy. I am sure, also, that in so doing the very reasonable parent has no thought whatsoever of sexual overtones – which is what is implied by our now sex-besotted society expressing concern at teachers behaving thus as reasonable parents.

There were other things I learned at Spenser Street that did not appear in the college course. A cold wind was blowing one morning driving heavy rain directly into my face as I turned towards the school. I put my head down and pulled up the collar of my mackintosh. I sported a trilby (the then equivalent of 'cool') and in such conditions had to hold the brim firmly to keep it on my head. My other hand clutched a case in which I carried varied items for lessons. The stinging downpour caused me to blink rapidly but dimly I could see other, smaller figures battling with the elements, leaning forward into the wind. Then I blinked again and looked harder. A few of the figures took on the form of elderly gnomes.

I was nonplussed. Yet, sure enough, some bent figures wore dark cloaks of some sort with pointed headgear. They were quite different from other children dressed in normal, but sometimes inadequate, coats and macs. Then one overtook me. A face emerged from under the covering and little Barry M's cheeky face smiled up at me.

''Ello, sir. Blimey, ain'titawful?'

His face disappeared again and I was looking down at his strange garb as he hurried on. It looked for all the world like a coal sack.

It was! But it wasn't just thrown over his back. It had been tied diagonally across one corner with a piece of twine. It was being held across his back so that this corner covered his head with the point jutting forward. The tied part was across his neck, two opposite corners more or less covered each shoulder whilst the fourth just about reached the seat of his trousers. He was bending well forward from his waist and both hands clutched the sack round his neck.

I had lived most of my eighteen years within a few miles of Spenser Street and thought I knew the inhabitants of my home town but I had never seen anything like it. Obviously this was the poor child's substitute for a coat or mac. I stared at them, strangely fascinated and rather shocked. They were effective, certainly, so long as the wearer bent forward – but sacks???

Inside the school I watched the children hanging up their coats in the cloakroom where each, like their other garments, reflected variation in home backgrounds. But the sacks were draped over the hot water pipes at the bottom of the coat racks where they dried effectively during the day.

Most were heavy; these obviously were best because little water could penetrate their tough fibres. Most actually had seen use on coal lorries for soon small pools of black water formed beneath them on the floor. But the intriguing feature was that all, without exception, had a corner tied like Barry's - indeed some of the slightly thinner ones had twine stitches gathering the material. I mentioned them to Miss Beaumont when I met her in the staffroom.

'I know, I was very surprised, too, when I saw them. I'd heard before about parents in poor areas giving their children sacks instead of coats – and of course if you throw a sack diagonally across your back it does just as well whether it's tied or not. This idea of tying them seems to be something local because they all do it.'

Probably only one in ten of the boys appeared with sacks; no girls used them. Naturally they were only in evidence in wet weather. At other times these boys wore coats in various stages of disintegration. But even the poorest family in this area didn't want to give their son just a sack. Although it was crude and rather pathetic, something of these people's character was revealed in the touch of fashioning they gave these strange garments.

I learnt something quite different from the girls. Margaret E and Jean B sat in the front row nearest the door of the classroom. They were dressed quite neatly and both usually wore Fair Isle cardigans. Margaret often wore a smart little navy blue skirt supported by cross straps over her shoulders. Her dark hair was swept back into two plaits, setting off her fresh complexion and brown eyes.

I suppose I had heard about pupils having crushes on teachers but I certainly wasn't thinking about that kind of thing at Spenser Street. If I had been challenged on the subject I would have expected it at secondary girls' schools, especially boarding and certainly well-to-do. Although I certainly did not yet classify myself as a teacher – I was only a student and still a very green one – nevertheless I did imagine a wide gulf between me and the pupils. I was now eighteen and quite tall; at ten and eleven they were young and small, the latter condition influenced by their area and diet. Certainly I heard about some of the things girls at the top end of secondary schools tried with students but they were fourteen plus and very different. But juniors? No, I wasn't thinking about it at all.

But Margaret was. When I later mentioned matters to Miss Beaumont she said she had seen the sloppy looks Margaret flashed in my direction, and of course she took Jean along in everything she did. But she said Margaret was like that with any young teacher so didn't imagine it was any different with me.

It hit me first when I was marking some Arithmetic exercises the children had finished. I wasn't expected to teach every lesson so occasionally, when Miss Beaumont was teaching, I had nothing to do in the classroom. In fact, at least once a day, she continued with preparing the class for a mime performance of 'Bluebeard' which she had entered for the city's Annual Drama Festival. She was extremely keen and the children worked their socks off for her.

'These kids may not be very bright when it comes to the three Rs,' she said, 'but they're natural actors. With mime they don't let themselves down with poor diction, so they can do very well.' The commendations received in previous years bore testimony to this, and her enthusiasm.

I, too, like Drama and later also entered children in the festival with other keen teachers, but that was well in the future. Anyway, Drama had no place in the college curriculum, only Art, Craft and Music from which we had to select one. I was Crafty.

'Would you mind if I took individual children out of your rehearsal lessons when they're not acting so I can go over their work?' I asked, and she agreed.

It did not require much research to discover that those not acting much tended to be those who made most mistakes in Arithmetic. Possibly the odd moments of extra individual teaching had some marginal use.

Margaret was slightly below average ability for the class as far as my record of the IQs shows. Over the years I came to distrust such measurements. Now all those people are in their seventies it would be highly interesting to see how well or otherwise those IQs predicted future success. It would be equally interesting to investigate thoroughly the school records of some now famous people. To prevent that one Prime Minister famously had his records classified as secret documents!

In the production Margaret and Jean, who didn't show great miming skills, were 1st and 2nd Fan Slaves respectively, my notes record. Margaret's absence on one occasion was hardly noticed when I went through her Arithmetic in the staffroom – the only place a spare table was available. The work was on proportion and ratio and the children had not found the concepts easy to grasp. No doubt my teaching had not been pitched at the right level and a number had made mistakes. Margaret, I remember, made many.

'Oh, Margaret,' I said staring at a long line of sums. I had put red ticks by the first two but the rest had crosses. 'Look at all these mistakes. You did the first two sums correctly. Why didn't you do the same with the rest?'

She surveyed the page with a puzzled look; suddenly her hand flew to her mouth as she realised her error.

'Ah, now you're using your brain,' I said. 'You must have had your mind on something else when you were doing this work. You're not stupid, Margaret. What are we going to do with you?'

I was rattling on to no purpose and was about to say she had do some corrections. Margaret, however, did not take my question rhetorically.

'You should give me the cane, sir,' she said brightly!

'Oh,' I said with rather a gasp, 'I don't think it's that serious.' Then, equally unthinking, 'In any case I haven't got a cane.'

''But I've got a ruler, sir, you can hit me with that if you like.'

Margaret also taught me that not only will some children do anything for attention, they can also be persistent. Two weeks after my junior practice the college term ended. At home during the first weekend I was helping my father in the garden. This was his one and only pastime and normally the result was immaculate. However we had dutifully dug up the larger of two lawns to grow vegetables in the Dig for Victory campaign. It wasn't obvious what role we had played in the nation's success, so two years later we were trying to return the garden to its former pristine condition.

My father was hoeing with his usual skill, producing a fine tilth as level as a billiard table and I was weeding where I was not likely to make too much of a mess of things. Mother came to the french windows.

'Love, there are two young ladies at the door asking for you,' she called, sounding surprised.

'For me?' My father echoed the surprise.

I was equally puzzled. They were very happily united and the only member of the family who had any connection to young ladies was me, naturally. I had a brother but he was only nine.

My father took off his gardening gloves, scraped his feet carefully on the spade, and went indoors. I stared nonchalantly at my weeds, wondering which to slaughter next and failing to envisage my father with young ladies. Someone from church, I decided, needing advice. He was on the Church Committee.

He returned quite quickly. 'It's not me they want, it's you,' he said, laughing. I forgot the weeds with alacrity. 'Obviously,' I thought to myself. Then another thought struck me.

'But why did mother say they wanted you?'

'Because they asked for Mr Flaxton.'

Inside the house my mother was smiling, too. 'I've put them in the front room, Mr Flaxton!'

She was enjoying a joke at my expense but I couldn't fathom what it was. But I hurried into the room expecting some delectable female company, even if there was an unseen string attached.

They were both sitting bolt upright on the settee, grinning happily.

'Hello, sir. We were ever so sorry you left school so we found out where you lived and walked all the way from Spenser Street to see you!'

Margaret and Jean were gazing at me with very goofy eyes.

Chapter 11

My stars, what might happen to ten year old Margaret and Jean tramping the streets unaccompanied to-day? I grant they would be more streetwise and also could afford bus fare. I also grant that to-day they certainly wouldn't waste their time chasing up a student teacher. But there is no doubt that our streets to-day are nowhere near as safe for young children as they were before and after the Second World War. To that extent life was better then. I can remember in the thirties walking to and from both infants' and junior schools, about a mile away from home, four times a day, alone apart from other children. I had caring parents but they, nor I, nor anyone else thought it unusual for a six year old. In any case, had I been accompanied I couldn't have played marbles along the gutters with the other kids before they reached their homes and I wandered on with pockets bulging with winnings or bemoaning my losses.

But not much else was better in my student days, Rationing was still in force, indeed ration books were in use well into the fifties. Most commodities were subject to restrictions, including domestic fuel. It seemed to snow most winters, not for Christmas but usually in January or February. It was always cold, I remember, though in retrospect that was due to the way we heated houses. Or rather, did not heat them.

Pleasant though our house was, heating was effected by coal fires and occasional use of a small electric fire. The kitchen fireplace was the usual type with a boiler set into the back so it heated water for the house. Later, I remember, my father lashed out on an immersion heater for the hot water tank. They became widely fashionable in the years after the war, like double glazing much later.

We also changed the entire grate. The one installed when the house was built in 1931 had side trivets that you swung over the fire to boil a kettle, whilst above was an oven. These appliances were rarely used because we had a much more efficient gas cooker. But they came into their own during the blitz on the various occasions when both gas and electricity supplies were cut off. The new facility we changed to was the all-night fire. This had a high front allowing a fire to be banked up so it merely smouldered. With luck it went on doing this happily all through the night. Then in the morning you opened up the front, opened the airflow, attacked the remains with a poker and, with more luck, it burst into life again. It gave minimal warmth to the kitchen during the night – perhaps kept the cold at bay would be more accurate. But it did keep the hot water lukewarm so the morning wash was no longer such a livener-upper.

In some circumstances, though, cold was held to be synonymous with health. I record the fact, simply because it was typical, that my father believed anyone sleeping in a heated bedroom would become weak and probably ill. Even more healthy was the open window; only a small one and only with the latch on the first hole so the gap was a mere two inches on the coldest nights. Nevertheless the room had to have direct contact with the 'healthy' outside air irrespective of temperature even on foggy nights. With the amount of coal burnt on city fires some quite spectacular smogs were achieved on occasions.

But at least we had warm bedclothes and plenty of them. Our ordinary clothes were warm as well. They had to last, of course, but we had adequate supplies and they were washed and kept clean. Also, during cold days, the fires in both kitchen and lounge-cum-dining room were certainly kept well made up. I was fortunate.

Spenser Street and its environs, like the area near the college, had many far less fortunate families living in very poor housing where cold was not a matter of choice. This penetrated my awareness one day during the first winter at college when I passed the local gasworks. The by-product, coke, was sold cheaply at the gates and instant news spread the moment a supply was available. The composition of the ensuing queue revealed life in the local houses. Any container was drummed into use – old sacks, tin baths, perambulators (devoid of babies), buckets, often carried on primitive sledges when snow was on the ground.

The people might have stepped out of a Lowry painting. Hunched and huddled, in various stages of undress, without exception they looked pinched and drawn. Most were teenagers, sent on this so necessary chore. The prizes, obtained by those heading the queue, no doubt gave welcome cheer and warmth in the tiny terraced houses whilst the stocks lasted.

Such minimal houses were built in most towns and cities in the nineteenth century to house factory labour. Though small and primitive, nevertheless they were built to last. Many can still be seen in areas not cleared to make way for flats, supermarkets, ring roads and other modern developments. Usually the survivors have been refurbished. These now provide interesting urban fieldwork for History lessons.

When the still video camera appeared (at a very high price, a forerunner of the digital variety) I had access to one loaned by the manufacturer to experiment with for educational purposes. I used it to record a group of fourteen year olds on such an exercise. They were surveying a reasonably well-adapted area of old terraced housing, learning to interpret its history. The narrow roads had traffic calming features, small raised beds had been built and stocked with shrubs, pavements renewed and roads resurfaced. But the main alterations were to the houses and the students were soon copiously writing notes, drawing and photographing the varied refurbishments made by owners.

That camera could be connected, a tad cumbersomely, to a television set and the images on its small disk played immediately. Alternatively they could be transferred to videotape with an explanatory soundtrack. My purpose was to demonstrate possible uses of this new technology for schools. Later I showed this particular fieldwork exercise to groups of teachers, demonstrating how easy it was to make such pictorial records as resources. They could be stored in the library and easily used for research and revision.

I included shots of typical house front alterations. Some showed new windows – were these in keeping with the original architecture, my voice-over asked the students. Painting schemes were highly varied – comments were invited on these, too. Small front gardens had called forth much ingenuity and, with window boxes, were delightful splashes of colour. There were examples of one or two complete mock stone façades – again students were challenged to comment.

I concluded with one shot that always raised an immediate burst of laughter. Each house front had one window alongside the front door – these were two up two down dwellings with one up and down in front and the other two behind. This owner had removed the entire front room for his conversion. The elevation now had the front door immediately flanked by an up and over garage door!

There are still very many houses of the type of the Spenser Street environs in urban areas throughout the country. No doubt, with our greatly improved standard of living the great majority have been thoroughly modernised in many other ingenious ways.

I managed to reach the end of junior practice without falling foul of the VP again. Miss Beaumont said I'd improved as the four weeks progressed which was encouraging. I thoroughly enjoyed teaching the children who were always lively and responsive. They were well behaved without being repressed; Mr Overton and the staff contrived an environment to which most responded with respect in their rough and ready terms. When tempers boiled over, not unusual given some backgrounds, the children knew the reasons would be investigated patiently and fairly.

The teachers, without exception, were enthusiastic in their work. That always was and remains, the *sine qua non* of good teaching. It certainly was the touchstone of Spenser Street Junior Mixed.

We all felt the return to college, albeit only for two weeks before the end of term, was an anti-climax. There was much catching up with commenting on lesson notes and making suggestions for the future, which should have been done during the practice, of course, but there never seemed enough time because preparation was so intense. Returning to lectures was also irksome. There was also one lecturer who viewed us students in the same light.

He taught part time – indeed he gave two lectures a week, on Hygiene, part of the core requirements for the Certificate in Education. He was a local doctor, press ganged I suspect because there was no one else with adequate qualifications.

I, however, did not view his lectures as merely irksome. I hated them because I never knew what was coming. The first term had been fine – he spent the whole of it on rheumatism in childhood. Initially I had been amazed that children had any contact with this condition which hitherto I considered a matter entirely for the elderly. Later when I learned much more about the local children I realised why it assumed such importance in his practice – and thus our course. Anyway I could cope with rheumatism.

It was different with some other topics. To be accurate, one particular group of topics. At the beginning of his lectures I was always apprehensive when he strode in, seized a piece of chalk and wrote the title on the board. A typical *bête noire* was 'Injuries'.

'If a major artery is cut in the thigh a body can lose all its blood in a few minutes. It doesn't just trickle, it spurts with every heart beat, so if that happens to anyone whilst you're on playground duty you must get your skates on. You've got slightly longer if it's an arm artery, but even then one in the upper arm can flow like a cut hose pipe.'

Despite having only one lecture a week devoted to it, the Hygiene course covered a vast range of topics, from school drains to major surgery and then some. When the Doc strode in to give his first lecture we had been instantly silent; assessing this rotund figure with flaccid cheeks beginning to droop a little, sparse grey hair plastered sideways across a shining pate, eyes concealed behind thick rimmed glasses with equally thick lenses through which he rapidly read his notes. He had much to convey.

But it was his voice that so surprised us. We expected deep, resonant tones but there seemed to be a soft pedal effect in operation which also elevated it half an octave. It simply did not match his appearance. This, together with his non-stop reading of notes, allied to the fact that he hardly ever looked directly at his audience, probably because he couldn't see them, meant he lacked presence. Like any group of children or students we exploited the fact. To be frank we gave him hell.

He was such a contrast to the other lecturers who were either authoritarian or engagingly funny. For them we behaved impeccably. For the Doc we were exactly the opposite, just like kids in school. Usually there was general chatter and a certain amount of commenting on what he was saying which he totally ignored. Most of the chaps could listen with half an ear and make enough notes to pass the exam. But I couldn't. I would listen with mesmerized attention in case he mentioned blood, and arteries, and veins, flowing, pumping, oozing, draining… his quiet voice seemed to get louder and louder in my head and merge into a roaring sound which filled my ears.

Crump! I would slide under the desk as far as I could. The others, who always kindly filled in the details for me afterwards, would carol happily:

'Old Nigel's gone again. Stretcher party, at the double – move!' Then with a quite unnecessary amount of fuss and disturbance they would endeavour to extricate me.

'Keep his head down!'

'Two of you, grab his shoulders.'

'Stop his legs flapping – and mind those big feet, they're lethal!'

'Ready everyone – one, two, three, heave!'

'You weak-kneed lot, you couldn't shift a sack of potatoes!'

'Right, open the door someone.'

'All set, right, after three – one, two, three! Dum, dum, dum, dum, de dum, de dum, dee dee. The slow tones of the funeral march would ring out solemnly from the less energetically involved spectators and I would be carried out prone and laid reverently on the corridor floor outside. After a short while I would rise, resuscitated, and after a walk in the quadrangle feel perfectly fit again.

During my teens I fainted with boring regularity whenever I listened to talks or saw films about any vaguely gory aspect of the human body. I could cope with the skeleton; solid bones, their diseases and breakages didn't bother me at all. Neither did infectious diseases, brain surgery, sickness and diarrhoea and associated conditions in children and all matters related to drains. Nor rheumatism. But a hint of a drop or two of blood pumping through any tube-like passage and my head would reel. Then if I didn't get my head between my knees I would be out.

I remember clearly the first time it happened. I was nine at the time and I was listening to two uncles describing their operations for the benefit of my mother. One sketched graphically his experience as the ether anaesthetic took effect:

'I could see the two big lights above me and they seemed to revolve around each other as they moved away from me down a long tunnel.'

It took me in much the same way except that my two uncles did the revolving as I slipped into unconsciousness. Then they were both looking at me with worried expressions as I tried to figure out why I was lying on the floor. Assuming it was a one-off event I later listened to them explaining what each operation had comprised – both involved bloody surgery. My subconcious duly informed my conscious that whenever I heard the latter I should repeat the former.

Fortunately at grammar school not much happened to trouble me. Biology was an obvious snare but it was taught only in the first year, not being viewed as a serious Science meriting study alongside Physics and Chemistry. In any case the syllabus was packed entirely with plant life, so I was safe.

Although I experienced the entire blitz – like many others I returned home after one year as an evacuee following the fall of France - I never once saw an injury. There was not much point in having a split family if we were to be invaded. So I returned to the city just in time for the first air raids and over many months saw plenty of devastation. The nearest bomb missed our house by a hundred metres and the blast flew parallel so neither our house nor our neighbours' houses had any broken windows. True, people died, killed in their cellar by the blast but I didn't see them. Thoughts as to what I would do in an emergency didn't cross my mind. There were air raid wardens and first aid people for that sort of thing.

Then a teacher at school offered to teach first aid as an extra-curricular activity. Foolishly I mentioned this to my father. He was an air raid warden and also took his turn on fire duty at the central council offices where he worked and certainly saw plenty of activity at first hand.

'An excellent idea – you must go to that,' he enthused. 'You never know when you may have to help injured people, even your friends at school.'

'But they won't want me in the class, I shall faint all the time,' I replied not enthusing in the slightest.

'Nonsense, if you persevere you'll get out of this silly habit. Just don't think about it. The more you worry about fainting the more likely you are to do it.'

He was quite right, of course, but I found it impossible to achieve. No doubt to-day someone would advise psychotherapy. But the NHS was still an idea for the future – this was pre-Beveridge Report – and I didn't even know the word 'therapy'. So I went unwillingly to the first aid sessions and coped with the simple things like slinging broken arms with triangular bandages and binding splints on broken legs. | found I could cope with notes on emetics when poison had been swallowed. I was able to pound away at the chests of my pals who were pretending they had inconsiderately fallen into water and been dragged out fairly well drowned. But then:

'We will now consider deep flesh wounds. In such cases it is likely that a main artery has been severed and therefore it's essential to staunch the blood flow. This can be done to an extent at the site of the wound but it is far more preferable to apply pressure to a nearby pressure point by squeezing the artery against a bone, thus restricting the blood flow. This entails knowing… yes, alright Flaxton, go out if you must.' The master would tail off in a tired voice and I would slink out, go for a brisk walk and recover but learn nothing in consequence about pressure point sites.

I staggered through the course somehow. It came in useful on paper when I joined the school's Air Training Corps (ATC) squadron. I was very keen on that and spent much spare time making model aeroplanes. It helped if you had some useful hobbies and interests, so I cheekily put the first aid course. A different master was CO. of the ATC, fortunately.

There was an equivalent OTC. That acronym meant it was for fledgling officers, but because it became highly popular in many schools in the early years of the war it was patently obvious the Army would never need such a vast supply. The chiefs needed rather more indians. So later it was changed to the JTC – for juniors.

Later, when I considered teaching, the subject of my weakness cropped up again at home. 'What would you do with a real emergency to a child if you're like this when listening to a talk?' asked my father. Children do injure themselves, you know. One might do so when you're the only person to help. What would you do then?'

The scenario did concern me to an extent, but I always managed to push it to the back of my mind and hope. Providence seemed to concur for I never became involved in a serious situation involving blood loss where anyone had to rely on me.

I took sensible steps to avoid fainting. I realised the trigger was any situation where I felt trapped, such as in the middle of a row in a lecture room. I started sitting near to the door and slipped out when I experienced the early signs. Interestingly I found this worked quite well and usually was able to slip back in quite quickly. I also found that once this had occurred I could then listen without a recurrence of the symptoms. However, whenever I did nip out I had to make up my notes afterwards.

Doing that on one occasion standing in the college library, using a reference book on the circulatory system, I felt queasy so shut the book and walked outside into the corridor. I was completely alone as I mounted a short flight of steps beyond the library doors. I became aware of a wall pressing against my right cheek and momentarily couldn't understand why I was trying to turn to the right when the corridor went straight ahead. Then I realised it wasn't a wall, it was the floor and I was lying on it. I remember lying there feeling absolutely idiotic, especially because on that occasion I had no inkling I was about to pass out. I was perfectly relaxed, had done myself no injury, and got up and walked on with no lingering ill feelings whatsoever.

But my problem spread embarrassingly to other matters. Human reproduction was conspicuously absent from the Hygiene course; it was confidently asserted we would never have to teach that. Though to-day mention is often made of the chemistry between people, that also was conspicuously missing from our Chemistry lessons. So what knowledge I gleaned came from tutors of the subject who used the loos as their lecture theatres. And the Encyclopaedia Britannica. This was the only source of reference in the school library that gave any information on the subject. Actually there wasn't much else at all in the library; they rather assumed the volumes covered every necessary topic. So I came to know much about the two forms of human anatomy from this source. All relevant parts were given their Latin names. I've sometimes mused that I might have passed Latin had the questions featured human reproduction instead of Caesar's Gallic Wars.

But whilst I was a student the epochal film 'Birth of a Baby' was made and one half of the population went to see it because they had never seen a baby born. Most of the other half were well experienced in the subject and went to see whether anything like the real situation had got past the Board of Censors for public viewing. General opinion suggested it had, though cleaned up a bit because the birth took place in hospital. Birth at home could be different, they said.

I knew very well I ought to see it but guessed, also very accurately, that it would contain sections that would prey on my weakness. There was also the fact that I would be in a cinema, probably with people all around and well away from a door...

Nevertheless I decided to go with Malcolm Ashterligh who well knew my problem and in the queue outside laid bets as to how long I should last. To cheer me up and give me confidence he gave short odds on half an hour at least. I offered even shorter ones on ten minutes. Nobly he didn't accept, thereby throwing away a cert.

Whenever I come across the phrase 'the darkness was palpable' I think of that cinema. As we stumbled in, blinded from the outside sunshine, I felt that darkness as an entity that could be touched and handled. You could carve a chunk and take it home. Then the screen came alive and with elegant sweetness some attractive ladies, drinking tea, started discussing the babies they were going to have in some months' time. So far so good, I thought, sweat only gently trickling down my back.

'But we must start at the beginning,' a voice said. Nearby there were some sniggers, abruptly stifled because the scene shifted to a diagram with someone in a white coat prodding it with a pointer.

'Here we have a diagram of the female reproductive organs. Once a month an ovum is released from the ovaries and attaches itself to the lining of the uterus. If it is not fertilised, blood suffuses the lining and the walls expand. The diagram dutifully did just that, throbbingly red, then the camera shifted to a close-up and I was reeling for the gyrating exit sign. I staggered dangerously against an usherette who had just taken up her position by the door having seen everyone settled in their seats. She couldn't imagine I was leaving so soon and thought I was making a pass at her. Once she got the message she opened the door and I staggered through.

In the corridor outside she looked hard at me. They had had men biting the dust all week when the film reached the gory parts – that much had made the local papers – but here was one going weak at the menstrual diagram. Her look said it all; The stronger sex! Don't make me laugh.

She was so convincing I couldn't bear to try going back in. I would have been beside her if I'd tried standing inside near the door where I'd have felt less confined. I slunk away from her to the bus queue and home, thoroughly annoyed with myself, wondering how on earth I was going to rid myself of the wretched phobia.

Then one day, Kim, my girlfriend, asked me to take some students to a party that Joanne, a friend of hers, was arranging. Being very dutiful in such matters I arrived with Gordon, Berny and Malcolm to meet Kim, Joanne and two other girls. In those days parties were parties; long, full of rumbustious games interspersed with competitions requiring intelligence whilst you got your second wind. This occasion was no exception and I look back on such events with great nostalgia.

I suppose twenty years later I first went to a party where everyone stood around drinking and chatting. I spent the entire time wondering when the fun was going to start – then, suddenly, people were leaving and thanking the hosts for a great time. I left realising I had stepped over the generation gap.

One game Joanne introduced was quite a simple affair. We boys got on the floor on our hands and knees and the girls sat on our backs as jockeys. The object was to race across the room. The fun ensued from two elements - the girls put their hands over our eyes and the room was not very large. Naturally the boys knew the whole idea was to finish in a tangled heap and were happy to oblige; what we did not know was that the girls had plastered their hands with lipstick and as they put them over our eyes our faces were liberally smeared.

The ensuing pile of bodies looked delightfully sanguine with four redskins rolling amongst the girls, causing much laughter. But the heartiest giggling came from Sonia, Joanne's six year old sister, who had been allowed to stay up for the evening. It was a sensible arrangement for she couldn't have slept a wink with all of us careering round the house on varied treasure hunts.

'I want to ride a horse!' she exclaimed loudly when the laughter subsided.

'Come on, then,' volunteered Malcolm. 'Put her on my back, someone.' Berny immediately sprang into the role of jockey's assistant.

'I want some lipstick as well!' No six year old was going to be content with half measures, so Joanne enjoyed herself covering her young sister's hands with a really thick coating.

'Oo, lovely. Now, gee up, gee gee!' She slapped her hands smartly over Malcolm's eyes and dug her heels just as smartly into his ribs. Entering into the spirit of the thing he galloped round the room most energetically on hands and knees whilst Sonia clung on shrieking her delight and gripping his face so tightly he was forced to keep his eyes completely shut. We sat back enjoying the spectacle hugely.

'Hang on, cowgirl, go to it!'

'Make him jump, Sonia, he's a lazy old nag!'

'Pull his head round, he's so stubborn!'

Malcolm certainly didn't see, nor did we until it was too late, that the door to the next room was half open. He wobbled unknowingly to one side of it; Sonia, slipping in the saddle at that moment, wobbled the other way and hit her forehead on the protruding catch. It was hard metal and sharp and struck between the eyebrows, fortunately missing her eyes but puncturing a small artery. This behaved itself precisely as predicted by the Doc, the Master i/c First Aid and all relevant text books. In a couple of seconds Sonia's face was plastered as red as ours were, but with blood.

I grabbed my unused and folded handkerchief from my pocket and slapped it on her face in the same instant she became aware of the blood and screamed. My hands had collected some of the lipstick in the erstwhile melee and so my handkerchief turned red with blood on one side and lipstick on the other. Very soon it was covered with a macabre mixture of both. Sonia's father, alerted by her scream, dashed in from the other room – parents then didn't evacuate premises for parties – blanched when he saw what appeared to be a terrible injury.

He was a chiropodist by profession and a member of the St John's Ambulance Brigade and so was well prepared for emergencies. In a very short while Sonia was cleaned up and transformed from a serious casualty into a bravely smiling young lady, responding to our jokes about the large pad fixed to her forehead with a bandage. When the untoward excitement subsided and we had scrubbed away all traces of blood and lipstick, Joanne looked round the company.

'I think we all need some refreshment after that. Now, we have plenty to go at – savoury meat and fish things, salmon, egg, tomato sandwiches, then there's trifle and cream, meringues and ice cream, chocolate cake…'

I looked at the others in anticipation. I have always been on excellent terms with my inner man and now was no exception. But suddenly I saw something was amiss. Instead of the sparkling eyed reaction I expected I saw rather fixed stares from three male faces, each of which looked strangely washed out. Momentarily I thought they were tired but rapidly dismissed the thought because they had been wildly cavorting steeds only a short while earlier.

'What's up, men? Aren't you hungry yet?' I enquired.

'Er, no. Not just at the moment,' said Gordon

'I think I'll go out and get a blow of fresh air first,' said Berny. I got rather hot in that last game.' He slipped out quickly.

'Nigel!' expostulated Malcolm. 'How on earth can you, of all people, face food so soon after seeing all that blood? It made Berny and Gordon quite queasy. Can't say I feel all that good myself. But you – you helped, got your hands covered in blood even. Blimey, you should be spark out, not thinking of gorging yourself with trifle and cream!' He looked quite astounded.

But I was feeling fine. After the event I realised I had acted instinctively and had been of some use in the crisis. Furthermore, I'd looked at the injury and the blood and hadn't felt like turning a hair. My phobia was entirely founded in the unreal world of the lecture room and my imagination; it had nothing to do with the real thing. The feeling of release gave me a wonderful feeling of relief – and a fantastic appetite!

I mention simply as a matter of fact that I have since dressed many youthful injuries, watched many operations on television and can talk quite happily on these matters. My word, I enjoyed that supper! The other three had such poor appetites, you see, and I have never been able to let trifle and cream go to waste.

But honesty compels me to record that for many years my weakness reasserted itself when my own blood was involved. I am fortunate that I have never suffered serious injury, but at medical examinations over the years I have had to provide blood samples – occasionally large ones. When giving these, if I dared to look, the vision of my own blood seeping into the phial was apt to turn my legs to jelly. So I studied pamphlets on the path. lab walls or gazed fixedly out of the window. The ploy was never lost on the nurses doing the deed but, bless them, they always told me that was a sensible thing to do.

Many years ago, following the birth of my second son, at one such event I was given a card proclaiming my blood group. It is headed 'Blood Donor Service' and I carry it dutifully in my wallet, but what it suggests about me is completely false. But I've always told myself they wouldn't want me fainting all over the place, would they?

Chapter 12

A trawl through my block practice lesson notebook to-day gives glimpses of educational attitudes and assumptions about children at the time, interspersed with embarrassing revelations about my own attitude. It is intriguing to see how my memory has made comfortable adaptations; some comments were written by a person I don't recognise.

One page is devoted to Miss Beaumont's own class records. She had given an intelligence test and a reading test, as was done in most classes of the time. These were standardized, i.e. they had been given to a sufficiently wide population and the scores aggregated to produce a scale of intelligence quotients in which 100 marked the performance of an average student. Reading tests did the same with an extensive list of words, but in these an average score was that of a child's actual age. It was easy to see, therefore, who was above or below average in reading ability. A graph of IQ results produced the familiar bell-shaped curve of distribution across the population, just as height does plotted against numbers of people. IQ results were regarded as nearly such precise measures of ability.

The lists (not their real names) show actual age, reading age, and IQ. Some of these are:

Roger B 11 years 3 months; 10.25 89
William H 11 years 3 months 8.5 85
Benny C 10 years 11 months 10.5 105
Peter M 10 years 10 months 10.75 91

My 'personal impressions' are recorded as 'Roger: neat, reliable, does good work, has a good voice. William: a plodder, very slow. Benny: neat, bright. Peter: very helpful, tries hard, has poor eyesight.'

Sylvia J 11 years 2 months 9.75 91
Betty H 10 years 4 months 9.0 92
Mildred M 10 years 9 months 8.5 113
Shirley A 11 years 1 month 9.75 105

For these girls my notes record, 'Sylvia: English – fair, Arithmetic – weak. Frail, but helpful. Betty: slow and inclined to be dull. Mildred: intelligent and normal child (heaven forfend!). Shirley: work good, intelligent.'

I am pleased to note that my comments on ability as I perceived it didn't always reflect the test scores. By far the highest IQ was that of Sheila C whom I mentioned earlier and had 132 as her measure. 116 was the next highest. There were 20 above 100 and 27 below – no one was spot-on-average. 4A, of course, was supposed to be higher in ability than 4B. Since the range was 132 to 65 no doubt 4B overlapped considerably. .

In my introduction I pontificated:

'Although an A stream class there are forty-seven children of varying abilities in 4A, thus it is not actually of true A stream calibre. However, there are a few outstanding children who have been very beneficial to the class. Thirteen children entered for the entrance examination to grammar schools but unfortunately only two passed. These, however, passed at a sufficiently high standard to gain free places at the top foundation school in the city.'

I wonder how they fared when they moved on. To move daily from Spenser Street environs and class to a very different suburb, buildings and millieux would call forth whatever resilience of character they could summon. Something of that great divide can be gauged from my equally patronising introductory notes to the school:

'Spenser Street is situated in one of the poorer working class areas of the city; thus the children represent all the attendant anomalies of such an area under present day conditions. The home backgrounds of most are poor, the parents have little or no interest in their children's work and activities. On leaving the school buildings at 4.30 pm many children go home to work or to play in the streets or foul backyards until a very late hour. There is, however, a brighter side to the picture for even in a school of this nature one finds better cared for children whose home backgrounds are good.'

Perhaps the breadth of the divide had been lessened by the war. We had become used to people from very different backgrounds being forced together for many reasons – in the Armed Forces, as directed labour in factories, facing widespread bombing at work and at home, as air raid wardens, fire guards, ambulance people, in the Home Guard. Nevertheless the 'free place' or 'scholarship' schemes enabling bright children from poor areas to go to schools for the intellectually very able inevitably loaded the strains of class distinction upon the recipients. The resilient characters not only survived, they gained immeasurably from the experience. As is well known there are some very famous examples. I hope Sheila survived, at least.

Producers of a television quiz series seemed to have been looking over my shoulder by inviting the nation to test IQs. Questions were devised by a single, no doubt very able, psychologist. What were measured, of course, were the IQs of all people interested enough to take part. Whether these constituted a valid sample of the intelligence range of all Brits cannot be determined; possibly not because it is odds on that people took part who had a fair idea they would score reasonably well. The audience panels, drawn from different occupations, usually seemed to be a reasonable sample from the minimal information actually revealed. If the average of all scores in the studio was about 100 then it was indeed a true sample.

Did I take part? Yes, and usually found I scored worse with the kind of questions I used to do well, manipulating shapes, for example. Then I knew why I could no longer cut carpets and tiles well to fit awkward corners. I was usually greatly relieved to be buoyed at the end by the weighting of scores for age.

Many books have been written about intelligence and many attempts made to define it. Sometimes I think politicians assume that good teaching is bound to improve it. But could it be a physical matter, depending on the numbers and qualities of synapses in our brains? Over the years I've enjoyed watching the quiz show 'Countdown' and marvelled at the ability of the lady presenters of the numbers rounds, first Carol Vorderman and now Rachel Riley, Quite often I am successful in getting an answer, but when I can't I am amazed at the ease with which they manipulate figures. Is the disparity between us due to the way we learned number manipulation, in my case by the traditional chanting of tables in junior school, or have they better synapse pathways in their brains? How do you feel when, perhaps, you get with a group who you feel outstrips you in intelligence? Do you try to keep with them or, if you're at home, ask who would like a cup of tea and go to put the kettle on?

There are other quiz programmes in which knowledge and intelligence are regarded as interchangeable. General knowledge and intelligence are linked, but what sets some people apart is the ability to recall facts. Do we actually retain all items of information we ever see or hear but people whose recall is better are regarded as more intelligent? The 18th century Swedish scientist, theologian, nobleman and seer, Emanuel Swedenborg, asserted that not only do we carry such knowledge with us into the next life but also every significant thought as well. The number of such might seem to be astronomical but it isn't. If you produced a completely new thought every five seconds throughout your waking hours for an average lifetime (and no one does that, not even super intelligent people) you get a figure of just over half a billion. In reality far less because some thoughts are active for much longer than five seconds and some are repeated many times. Not a very large number compared with national expenditure and debt!

Chapter 13

As the summer days warmed our thoughts turned to the forthcoming long vacation. As it approached work slackened slightly now our post-practice work had been completed. In addition to the daily self-criticism I had written on some of the left hand pages of my lesson notebook, along with those of tutors and teachers, I also wrote pages of course reconstruction as we were encouraged to do. Looking back with wiser eyes at my suggested drastic alterations I can see these would have been improvements. In that sense, therefore, my practice was successful for me. But I'm sure Miss Beaumont had to clear up many points with the children once I was out of the way. I wonder how they fared with punctuation.

That starts a train of thought that has irritated me for years now – the widespread misuse of the apostrophe. It is a fact that in all schools in my early teaching days children largely ignored the apostrophe denoting missing letters and especially possession, i.e. to show the missing 'e' in the archaic genitive, which remains in German. Gottes Sohn, O wie lacht …if you're into singing 'Stille Nacht'. God's Son, of course. It was a regular gripe of English teachers that kids, their parents and the public at large hadn't a clue about inserting the apostrophe.

It's my contention that teachers, everywhere, drummed the use of the apostrophe into their charges very successfully for a couple of decades. True, the underlying reason for its use still wasn't grasped, so gradually the apostrophe became widespread for plurals as well. Put one in to be on the safe side became the practice, as it still is. So now we get them all over the place, even on fixed public signs. There's one near where I live – a road name thus:

Wendover Crescent, leading to the following road's:
Blaydon Avenue
Walsall Close…

I once saw a calendar with descriptions of scenes on each monthly page. On one I counted twenty-four incorrect apostrophes in ten lines! But then, as I'm sure you very well know, English delights in anomalies. In this case it's its punctuation. Come to think of it, I don't remember a cartoon for that in the Practical Senior Teacher. How would the chap who dreamed up the sketches explain that *its* as a possessive does not have an apostrophe to avoid confusion with *it's* denoting it is? If he came up with anything, I'll bet children would be just as confused as I'm sure Miss Beaumont's class were with my use of his others.

Still, perhaps Sheila understood.

The VP decided there was another area in which we, also, were less than perfect. This was the matter of voice production and control.

'Gentlemen,' he boomed purposefully during one of his concluding lectures, 'on the recent practice I felt many of you showed poor breath control. In question sequences some of you seemed quite out of breath if you received a series of rapid answers from the pupils. In oral table questioning, for example, you must be able to keep going for ten minutes or more firing item after item at the class – seven eights, five sixes, four twelves, how many sevens in sixty-three and so on and so on and so on and breathe perfectly naturally without any suggestion of strain appearing on your faces or in your voices as I am doing at the moment and I could go on and on and on…'

He managed it superbly, of course. Like many good teachers he was a born actor.

'Some of you I visited were speaking as though you were being strangled. It will not do, gentlemen, you must have some tuition and practice.'

No one was going to venture that our reaction was entirely due to nerves because he was in the room. Even after a year he had that effect upon us in the classroom, especially those who were not in his tutorial group.

'All tutors have been asked to deal with this matter with their respective teaching practice groups, so you should check times and locations on the main notice board. Mine will meet me in study room six at 8.00 pm this evening.'

Our group flashed dismayed glances because, as the end of term approached, the evening study period had been relaxed to an extent. This meant that it was possible to escape, certainly on to the field at the rear of the building to pretend one was improving one's physical training work by throwing a javelin or discus around the grassy bomb craters and mounds, but occasionally also to get beyond the walls. The VP's choice of time was quite deliberate.

Study room six was really a long attic high up in one of the wings of the building. It was narrow and had a sloping ceiling into which small vertical windows were set. The evening sun slipped golden fingers through these, painting a row of slanted images of their bars on a dusty grey wall. Whilst we waited for the VP our restriction seemed even more irksome and we longed for the release of the summer vacation.

So we were not in an entirely co-operative frame of mind when he arrived. Not that we would have dreamt of rebellion even for a moment. The days of student revolt were only in the crystal ball and had we glimpsed them we would have estimated a time span of a hundred years at least before their arrival. Not in our lifetime, certainly. Within twenty years? You can not be serious! Our only day of madness was a permitted one, when we joined the local university's Rag Day – and that was allowable only because it was in aid of charity.

No. Dissatisfaction with our enforced incarceration was modified, according to classical psychological theory, to appear in another form. Mirth.

'We will concentrate upon the diaphragm,' said the VP when he had the ten of us standing in a row with our backs to the attic windows, facing him at rather close quarters. 'It is here.' With a dramatic gesture he parted the front of his gown and his dark suit jacket and slapped the palms of his hands on his lower chest. 'See if you can feel yours, gentlemen.'

We fumbled, feeling distinctly idiotic and rather glad we were not looking directly at one another. I could detect ripples of giggling insufficiently suppressed.

'Now breathe in fully, completely inflating your lungs, whilst I count eight. Ready, go! One, two, three, four, five, six,' he intoned in a rising crescendo.

Trevor exploded. He had inhaled too rapidly and consequently reached bursting point well ahead of the rest.

'Don't be silly, Mr Walfrey. Breathe naturally and feel what happens to your hands. Try again, gentlemen. Go. One, two, three…'

Two more pairs of lungs failed before we finally achieved what he wanted. It was very difficult because breathing deeply exacerbates the explosive quality of laughter. Inhaling slowly whilst biting one's quivering lip is agonising. I felt I was doing myself untold internal damage.

But worse was on the way. The VP managed to prove to most of us that muscles around the diaphragm could increase the capacity of the lungs, used correctly. Unfortunately, Bill Heppleton elected to be obstinate because he was podgy around his middle and his diaphragm seemed buried.

'It's there, somewhere,' barked the VP taking up the challenge. Then to Bill's great embarrassment he stood in front of him and prodded with the backs of his fingers.

'Push against that, Mr Heppleton.'

Bill heaved his body forward and the VP staggered slightly.

'No, no, no. Use some sense! I mean push with your muscles there but keep your body still.'

The VP adopted his most belligerent stance, head tilted backwards, glaring at Bill. We contrived sidelong glances which produced further sniggering.

'You must persevere, Mr Heppleton,' snapped the VP as he stepped back to face us again. 'Now, we must proceed to the real work. When you have fully inflated your lungs you should be able to intone a large number of words without a trace of strain, just as choristers do in church services. This is what we will practice.

However, we shall not use typical responses. Perhaps what I have in mind is more in keeping with your present feeling of levity. But it is intended to give you practice in developing clear pronunciation as well as voice control.'

His stare raked along the line. Then he drew himself bolt upright, perched his hands on his midriff, fingers across his diaphragm and pushed his arms and elbows well forward.

'You will soon pick this up, gentlemen. I will go through it a couple of times using one inhalation for each. Then, when you know it, you will each try it in turn.'

He fixed his eyes above the middle of the row, paused, then inhaled with superb grandeur. It was masterly. Then, very slowly and in rich baritone intonation,

'Marmaduke's natural ability and magnificent memory enabled him to master not only the labyrinthine mazes…'

At first lips quivered, then bodies, then came awful strangled gurgles, then inevitable and blessed relief. We simply collapsed, laughing uncontrollably. The performance was so unexpected, so unlike the VP, and so ridiculous. The atmosphere was quite wrong for serious practice and none of us was in the right mood. Anyway, laughter is so contagious.

It is exquisite agony to be in a group howling with laughter, suddenly to spot someone whose expression is so fixed it seems to be a mask. Suddenly a second wave sweeps over you because the serious face appears so unaccountably funny. The fact that its owner is the only one not to be sharing your near paralysis makes it far, far worse and you laugh until it hurts, and beyond…

Major Darnley stood absolutely immobile, staring into space. We rolled about, absolutely hysterical, our feeling of frenzy heightened by the knowledge that for the first time we were challenging his authority. Fear of his reaction was swept aside by splendid fun.

Very slowly, we subsided. We wiped our eyes, returned to our places and simmered down. When we were completely silent, without a word or even a direct glance at any one of us, Major Darnley inhaled precisely as before and began again.

'Marmaduke's natural ability and magnificent memory enabled him to master not only the labyrinthine mazes of philosophical tautology but also to unravel the circumlocutory rhetoric proposed for his erudition by his professional TU-TOR.'

We bit lips, we hugged ourselves, we swallowed hard. Somehow we confined our laughter this time until he reached the last word. In contrast to the monotone of all the rest, tutor was sung on two different notes as in divine worship responses. One word was lacking.

'AMEN', I sang, insufficiently *sotto voce*. Nine convulsions erupted immediately.

This time the VP did not stand silent and immobile. He moved in front of me with splendid ability considering his years and regaled me with information about my lack of maturity of which I was totally ignorant. Mentally I was still in nappies, it seemed.

'I shall not ask Mr Flaxton to contribute further to this tutorial,' he said as he regained his place. 'He seems quite incapable of accepting the spirit behind this period of instruction. Perhaps, Mr Mersely, you will help us. Come and stand beside me and see what you can do.'

Gordon certainly entered into the spirit of the tutorial, but not in the way the VP intended. Like the rest of us he was determined to enjoy it to the end. He strode out purposefully, stood beside Major Darnley, struck his position and winked at us.

'Marmaduke's natural ability and magnificent memory enabled him to master the something something something, lah di dah di dah, and something about circumlocutory rhetoric which I have for-GOT-TEN.'

He got in the two notes at the end and this time Malcolm and Archie chipped in with an AMEN, but the rest were in fits of giggles again.

'I shall try one more of you,' shouted the VP angrily. 'Mr Heppleton, you normally show considerable keenness for work. Let me see whether you can salvage something from this ridiculous farce and show an atom of an adult approach.'

But for once Bill was with us wholeheartedly. He said afterwards the word farce gave him the notion.

'Certainly, sir.' He swept out and gulped in a quick breath.

'Marmaduke's natural ability and magnif...'

We didn't hear any more because we were howling with laughter again. The VP stormed out, leaving us masters of the situation in deed, if not in fact. Bill delivered his performance in a desperately strangled falsetto!

Reversion to childishness is a phenomenon experienced at all times by all groups of students and we were no exception. It happens in the best adult groups as well and continues to ripe old age, though we euphemise it as letting our hair down. Beforehand we would never have believed we would do it in front of the VP. Nevertheless there was a bonus. He did not repeat the exercise after the vacation when the new student intake was markedly different, nor did he ever refer to our behavioural response. We found also that the other group tutorials were cancelled for some reason.

The Doc was a far more likely target for silly behaviour and ours got worse in his lectures as the year progressed. He would walk into the room, write his topic on the board, turn to the lectern and begin speaking in his wee small voice. We would continue chattering amongst ourselves, ignoring him utterly for the first five minutes or so.

'Good lord – look who's here,' a voice might then say from the back.

'Come on, chaps, give the man a chance,' another would say.

'That's right, let's have quiet,' from a third.

'Quiet, quiet, quiet, quite, quiet…' staccato commands would crack from all corners of the room in every tone from high pitched squeaks to basso profundo.

'…and in children the rheumatism can be seen as nodules which may extend the full length of the legs…' Doc would continue serenely in his world, whilst we gradually emerged condescendingly from ours.

It is a fact that we were taught very little about maintaining discipline in the classroom and I remember that later this became a very sore point with us. In my experience the matter has been similarly sore with hundreds of students I have since seen in the course of my work. Given the amount of column inches on the matter I've seen in newspapers over the years I'm sure the public assume it is bound to be part of teacher training schemes. The reason it is not is because it is almost impossible for one person to show another how to maintain discipline amongst a group in their charge. The exception is in the formalised setting of the Armed Forces.

In teaching it is achieved almost entirely through one's personality. It is possible to learn a few tricks, but if strength of personality is lacking, the result usually is disastrous. Perhaps rather surprisingly, a forceful demeanour is by no means necessary. Although usually teachers who have no problems with control are those who are enthusiastic, energetic, with pleasant but firm voices and possess that highly desirable but indefinable quality called 'presence', nevertheless others can be just as successful. I taught in a city secondary modern with a colleague who freely admitted he was henpecked by his wife and living-in mother-in-law and who, in the classroom, spoke in a restrained and quiet manner, yet he had only to open his mouth and any class fell silent. His very rare punishments were of the order of a hundred lines. Others, however, had only to appear at the classroom door and their charges behaved as we did with Doc.

Oddly, however, we in no way despised him. After every lecture he would walk between our seats, perch on a desk and we would surround him, asking all kinds of medical questions in perfectly reasonable and conversational tones. It was from him that I first learnt details of leukaemia, which I heard my former evacuee cousin had suddenly been diagnosed with in an RAF hospital in Egypt. Knowing nothing of it in those days our family, including his parents, thought at first it was rather like anaemia. He looked up sharply and asked why I wanted to know. When I told him he replied simply,

'His number's up.'

Doc's prognosis was correct. A very sympathetic Commanding Officer flew the lowly AC/1 back to Britain in his own plane because the Service wouldn't do so. My cousin died some days later in the RAF hospital in Swindon with his parents at his bedside. There is no way they could have travelled to Egypt in the time.

Spotting the potential ability to control children in another person is one of the great skills in selecting teachers for appointments. It might be thought that when interviewing an applicant for promotion the fact would be plain in his or her reference. That, too often, is a naïve assumption. If a reference hints at poor class control no head is likely to offer the candidate an interview unless the need is desperate. Too often both the writer and reader of references take great care with that which is between the lines. Sensible managers advertising teaching posts in schools ask for specific questions to be answered, one of which is 'How successful is X in maintaining control of students at all times?'

Unfortunately hardly any such selection is attempted in choosing candidates for teacher training, especially in the young majority. How can such an ability be assessed in a sixth former? It's possible to an extent if the school encourages some form of mentorship, or has a prefect system, and allows a degree of personal responsibility to the sixth former in handling younger students. The snag nowadays is that, in such circumstances, if an accident occurs all hell is let loose from all sides demanding to know why supervision by such inexperienced young people was permitted. Was it a device to cover shortage of teachers, or a means of reducing financial burdens, etc, etc? This is one of the rare occasions when I subscribe to the view that matters were better in the past. Then an accident was viewed as precisely that, devoid of the current avaricious blame culture. The upshot is that teacher training always produces a proportion of qualified teachers who can never keep adequate control. Their lot is indeed a heavy one, as it is for the schools unlucky enough to receive them for one reason or another.

Where is the bolt hole for such teachers? Long term absence through illness, early retirement? Both figure to an extent. Others become very thick skinned and simply plough through the daily grind in the face of a barrage of noise. Years later I tried to help one such person whose Music lessons were anything but mellifluous. 'I have no problems whatsoever,' she averred archly. 'I can quote an HMI on that.' Either the Inspector was deaf, or came on a day when half the class was down with 'flu.

One escape route was very surprising, but enterprising. If sufficiently qualified, after one or two years in the classroom, appointment to the staffs of Colleges of Education was a possibility and taken by a few. There one's ability to control children was never questioned – and normally never tested. But I can remember the abject horror which swept through one such establishment when a new Principal decreed that all his staff should refresh such skills with occasional months back in schools. Immediately there was a rush for the local school with the best reputation for the most amenable students in the most favourable neighbourhood. I can attest to this with accuracy because I received the applications.

In the Doc's case, all that was needed was a succinct dressing down to us at the beginning of a lecture, with a threat that anyone who interrupted would be ordered to the VP's office. That would have stifled most of us, knowing the VP would certainly back up Doc with a suitable tongue lashing and probable withdrawal of a couple of weekend absits. Exactly that should occur in a school, but it should be followed by a determination on the part of the teacher to use more positive attempts to exert control by voice, clarity of instruction, enthusiasm and encouragement. But he, like others of his ilk, made no effort whatsoever. In his case he was in the college for only two hours a week, a minor addition to his work which then was an age away from the pressures of modern GPs. The National Health Service baby was on the point of delivery so hadn't yet uttered its first squawk.

Only once in his lectures can I remember a spark of enthusiasm. He was talking about diet and suddenly revealed he loved cooking. He went on to assert that he could cook a Christmas pudding that delivered four thousand calories per slice. Considering his pear shaped body we concluded that was no rash boast. But in his practice in the deprived area surrounding the college I wonder how he coped with the widespread malnourishment that was the lot of a great many children in the area. How could he look them in the eye at the season of goodwill to all men…and their wives and offspring?

On the occasion of the Doc's last lecture of our first year we decided to give him a pointer to a good lesson. They all had to begin with a lively introduction to engage attention, didn't they?

We decided upon a metaphorical demonstration. In the event I remember it was rather a last minute, scratch affair

The usual group got together and pressed ganged one other because we needed seven for this piece of nonsense. We also raided a cleaner's store.

The Doc appeared walking across the quadrangle at precisely two o'clock, when the lecture was due to begin. He walked into the room, closed the door behind him and continued down the left hand aisle towards the dais. He stepped up in his usual ponderous fashion, toyed with a piece of chalk, then wrote 'Rickets' on the board. He laid the chalk in the receptacle, turned, and began.

'This condition used to be prevalent in the nineteenth century and the early part of this one. Due to our knowledge of vitamins...'

We flung the door open with a commendable crash against a nearby cupboard. The students who were dozing duly woke up whilst those who were talking promptly shut up, so we achieved our intention of a both a moment's silence and attention.

'Hi hoooooooooooo,' rang out seven lusty voices.

'Hi hoooooooooooo,' repeated, an octave lower.

All eyes shot round in our direction. In filed six disreputable looking cleaners carrying buckets with long mops and brooms held rifle fashion over shoulders, a few corner knotted handkerchiefs on heads. To the accompaniment of a lively drum beat on the buckets, we sang

'Hi ho, hi ho, it's off to work we go,

We keep on singing all day long, hi ho, hi ho, hi ho,

Hi ho, hi ho, it's off to work we go,

We keep on singing...'

And we did, around the entire room. As we passed the dais, underneath Doc's mournful gaze, we did a snappy eyes left and saluted with just about everything we had.

As we filed up the opposite aisle towards the door again, the seventh dwarf, aka Archie Forton, swished in with a huge coat worn back to front. He flailed the long arms wildly across the cheering but ducking heads of nearby sitters. He also saluted, then caught us up as we made our exit, still singing. He banged the door shut.

From inside we heard an enthusiastic ovation. We threw our equipment back into the store and slipped in as it was subsiding. It broke out again with renewed vigour. Then it concluded.

'...we can now eradicate it entirely. The appropriate one is vitamin D which can be obtained from the following sources...'

Doc hadn't moved a muscle throughout the entire episode and continued precisely from where he had been forced to stop. I'm sure he would have continued to deliver his lecture to the empty room had we all walked out.

The one time I remember Doc obliterating our childishness and achieving full attention at the beginning of a lecture was when he approached the board and for his topic wrote 'HANGING'. Within seconds the room was hushed. Corporal punishment was widespread in schools as we knew from our own experience, but this seemed a new departure.

He looked at us in his usual mournful way.

'I picked up a book the other day entitled A Handbook on Hanging. I thought it was going to be juicy...' For a moment there seemed to be a gleam behind the thick lenses. 'But it wasn't. It was full of medical facts. Nothing really interesting. All I learnt was the drop actually causes a piece of bone at the base of the neck to snap off and be shot with considerable force into the brain. That's what actually kills 'em. But the rest was awfully boring. Now let's carry on with enteritis...'

A year or so after we left college we heard that one day Doc didn't appear for his lecture. Enquiries revealed he had suddenly left his practice, along with his much younger secretary. Obviously there was a side to his personality we never saw.

Chapter 14

The beginning of our second year at St Andrew's marked a watershed in its life. From its beginning in the middle of the nineteenth century to its demise one hundred and thirty years later there is little doubt that the changes we witnessed shook it most. Although we were not aware of it at the time they foreshadowed the considerable ensuing changes in matters of authority, control and participation. These permeated society at large and schools inevitably experienced a reflection of them. So did the college.

Two events prepared St Andrew's for projection into the second half of the twentieth century. The first was the retirement of the Principal. The Reverend D.W.Silton has not been particularly evident in these pages simply because I did not often cross his path. Although Major Darnley had an authoritarian personality and as Vice-Principal wielded considerable power, nevertheless he drew his strength from the attitude and regime of the Principal. There was no doubt to whom the iron fist belonged. But at this juncture it disappeared with its owner.

The Reverend A.F.Pringley was appointed in his place. He returned to England to take up the post after many years in India. We, therefore, when we heard the news, envisaged a fiery, red faced Army padre with a curry temper. We were utterly wrong.

He was mid-forties, fairly tall, with a scholarly face. The academic look was heightened by perfectly round spectacles beneath a high brow and receding, greying hair. He communicated well with all students and soon earned their genuine respect. He had a good sense of humour but was nobody's fool.

We first learnt something about the real man from Jon Kennton. Like the rest of us, Jon was delighted at the relaxation of restrictions upon our evenings and weekends which had been the new Principal's first pronouncement. The main door now was not closed until 11.00 pm on week-nights, and evening study became voluntary. This suited Jon admirably, because he could now visit his girlfriend at will, without either the fear of being missed from his study room or the dangers of his clandestine route into college.

Then, one night, he dallied too long with his PT teacher and found the main doors closed. He regularly left a window unlatched for just such an emergency and so was not unduly worried. Quietly he walked round the outer wall, past the section where the Principal's house stood, and on towards the open space at the rear of the site.

Suddenly he stopped short. The Principal's house! He would have to be ultra careful because the Reverend Pringley, being a family man, had taken possession of the house which formerly had been given over to students. The rear garden projected into the college grounds. In fact it was merely a rectangle surrounded by a beech hedge some four feet high, and everything in it was completely visible from the college field. Jon had to pass it *en route* for his window.

But after due consideration, he relaxed. A couple of the Principal's children were young and quite likely the whole family would be asleep long before this time, which was almost midnight. He would have to crawl near the hedge to avoid the possibility of being seen from the house, but even if by some mischance this occurred, he would hardly be recognised in the gloom at that distance.

He climbed the wall without mishap and quickly dropped into the shadow beneath. He paused, and peered through the darkness at the outline of the house. The back, like the front which Jon had checked a few minutes earlier, showed no light. He breathed more easily, then set off carefully but quickly across the intervening space towards the hedge, crouching as he ran.

His low viewpoint meant that when he did look up objects were silhouetted against the sky. That was how, just as he dived silently alongside the hedge, he spotted the Reverend Pringley! Lying full length on the ground, sweating profusely, he pondered what to do next. The pleasant aroma of tobacco smoke reached him. Cursing his luck he lay doggo hoping the Principal would soon finish his pipe and silent meditation and disappear indoors.

Gradually Jon cooled off and then, because he had been sweating, began to feel cold. The autumn night was still and there was a distinct nip in the air. Damp was rising from the ground on which he was lying. He began to shiver a little. But the Principal showed no signs of being cold, nor of wanting his bed. He stood still for long periods, then walked rather diffidently in something of a circle. He could be seen through odd gaps in the lower stems of the hedge. As Jon said afterwards, he guessed Prinny was composing a sermon - he certainly wasn't looking at the garden because there was nothing in it except the lawn and the hedge.

Finally, Jon decided he had to move if he was not to catch cold or worse. He began wriggling on his elbows, dragging himself along carefully and silently as though stalking a dangerous enemy. He successfully negotiated one corner of the hedge, then continued along the second side which pointed towards the end of the college building, and sanctuary.

By the time he reached the second corner he was warm again, but very dishevelled, dragging himself along in soil because grass grew sparsely under the hedge. Nevertheless he felt it to be in a good cause because the Reverend Pringley was an unknown quantity in matters of individual discipline. His more humane regime concerned the college as a whole, but by no means did it follow that he would not react strictly to a student who broke his very reasonable rules - and worse, broke in at midnight.

He paused. The final problem was how to cross the short remaining space between the corner of the garden and the corner of the college wing, beyond which was his window. He glanced through the hedge and descried the Principal's back towards him. He decided upon a quick, crouching run. He couldn't imagine the Principal vaulting the hedge and giving chase. Anyway, he'd be running away from the man so was sure he couldn't be recognised in the gloom - after all the Principal was new and the college housed two hundred students. He couldn't possibly know many yet by sight even in daylight. Jon thought upon Lady Macbeth's advice, screwed his courage to the sticking place, half rose and bolted. He swore afterwards he didn't make a sound.

He had managed about six steps when the voice broke the silence. But it was calm and serene.

'Good night, Mr Kennton,' said the Principal.

He made no further comment then or later.

The second event was the impact felt by the college in the composition of its next intake of students. With very few exceptions they were ex-service men, some returning after as long as seven years with the Armed Forces. There were ex-officers, ex-NCOs, ex-privates, ratings and airmen. Some had been fighter and bomber pilots, and some had been prisoners of war. Some had been torpedoed, some had been tortured. Most were late twenties, but a few were already in their early thirties. The large majority had seen a great deal of combat Service life in wartime.

Even though they were all used to discipline, it was the discipline of the adult world of the Forces. There was no possibility of their accepting the kind of boarding school regime to which we had been subject. The Principalship certainly changed hands opportunely.

However, one aspect of the college's new life was a problem not easy to solve. We were now the senior year, but our juniors were older by far in both years and experience. The year groups were not numerically equal either. We were seventy strong but the new intake was one hundred and thirty. We were outnumbered by nearly two to one, as we had been by our own senior year. We felt circumstances had pushed our noses out. For two or three months the relationship between the year groups was one of mutual distrust.

Then it boiled over into a furious argument following a disturbed night during which a few of the newcomers' rooms and personal equipment were damaged. We knew the culprits to be rather wild characters who smuggled alcohol into college - a heinous offence to the authorities even under the new enlightenment. Accusations were exchanged heatedly between the grown men to whom such behaviour was childish and therefore obviously perpetrated by us, and we seniors who would never have dared such vandalism as we very well knew. To our astonishment the VP adopted a low profile during these recriminations.

But we were not cheated out of the senior year's accommodation. This was in South Wing, a comparatively new part of the college built between the wars and consisting of single study bedrooms. These were indeed separate and quite spacious, even though the furniture was again Spartan. Each had a solid table and chair standing on a small dais near a fairly high window. A bed and a wardrobe completed the furnishings. The spaciousness of these rooms, and the very considerable relaxation of the restrictions of our first year, gave us a heady feeling of freedom which we were quick to exploit.

As might be imagined, in various ways girls came clearly into the picture.

Chapter 15

Considering the very wide freedom enjoyed by young people today it seems incredible to remember that in our teens many of my friends and I were quite useless on social occasions when groups of men and women got together. Take dances for instance. All ex-service men and women had been attending these for years and dance music was extremely popular on radio and gramophone records, but how did one learn to dance in the environment of a boys' school where any hint of a boy/girl relationship was severely frowned upon because of its disastrous implications for serious study? How severely I found to my cost when I was in the sixth form and the headmaster learnt that I had a girlfriend. I was subjected to an extremely lengthy verbal battering in which he made it perfectly clear that I was trying to combine oil and water. 'You cannot socialise and study', he said. 'In my opinion the sexes should not mix until after university'. His attitude to schoolboys, followed by the monasticism of St. Andrew's, contributed greatly to the problem which worried a number of us.

As wartime teenagers most of us went to the very occasional church social where we danced after a fashion. Some managed to pick things up. 'Just listen to the music and move with it', people said. The snag was that in any partnership the boy was supposed to lead and I for one needed to be far better prepared before I ventured to dance with anyone I didn't know. Dances, I found, held the terrors of Excuse Me dances, and Paul Jones. These inflicted all manner of matrons upon worried individuals like me. It was worse, of course, on the rare occasions a really delectable girl happened to be in front of me when the music halted the revolving circles of the sexes. The curvacious vision was always a good dancer and rapidly assessed me for what I was. Useless.

My heart goes out to those highly courageous celebrities who, as non-dancers, offer themselves as fodder for the judges in the fascinating television programme Strictly Come Dancing. Normally my entertainment viewing taste is for documentaries, nature programmes and some sports. Nevertheless I find this programme riveting because dancing torture is embedded in my psyche.

I tried to solve my problem by studying a text book. It was entitled Modern Ballroom Dancing and in the main it dealt with the Waltz, Quickstep, Foxtrot and Tango. Each page was devoted to a step by step description of a particular figure, with a diagrammatic representation of the moves involved. Two black footprints represented the man's moves, and white ones his partner's.

During the summer vacation before I started college this became my major reference book. I studied it avidly as bedtime reading, then next evening shut myself away and tried out the moves in a practical session. That is, I held the book in my left hand and slid my feet around the floor trying to emulate the diagrams. Occasionally I tied my legs in knots and not infrequently fell over.

One day my mother found me waltzing with my book in complete silence in our front room. I blushed furiously at her amazed laughter.

'It's all very well for you,' I expostulated. 'Dancing was very different when you were young. You didn't have to learn these complicated figures.'

'I should think not indeed! You just picked things up as you went along. If they were dancing the Veleta, or the Military Two Step, your friends soon showed you what to do. Then you just listened to the music, and you'd got it. You didn't really have to think about where you were putting your feet.'

'That's no good for me. You forget I've never danced much and modern dancing is so complicated'.

'I don't know about that but I'm sure you won't learn it without a girl to dance with and some music. They were considered essential in my day.'

The early months at college effectively stopped my studies in this matter and the old Principal's attitude to the notion of a dance in the college kept it at bay for a time, but gradually, despite the country being plunged into far greater austerity than during the war, social life began to spread. In late teens I knew some social accomplishments were necessary and dancing was high on the list. Then during one vacation my girlfriend Kim informed me we were going to a Ball. A businessman uncle of hers was President, or was it Admiral, of a Motor Yachting Club and it was resuscitating its Annual Dinner and Ball at a fairly grand hotel which was also resuscitating itself as well as it could. It seemed, also, that everyone was using the occasion to resuscitate their evening dresses. Cinderella-like we were to be allowed to go to the Ball only. Men, she also informed me, were to be allowed to get away with dinner jackets.

A Ball and Dinner Jackets! And dancing! In a Top Hotel! This was going to be rather close to hell. Of course I didn't have a dinner jacket, my father didn't have a dinner jacket – nor did he ever – so I had to borrow an ill-fitting affair from an uncle of mine who led a small string ensemble. I also found that with a dinner jacket went suitably matching trousers and a stiff winged collar and fronted dress shirt. And studs. And decent cuff links. And a black bow tie. When I fitted myself into the totality I knew what mediaeval armour was.

The hotel was imposing, but even I could see it was tawdrily elegant. It could hardly be otherwise in the post war squeeze that was hard enough to throttle. Kim managed to look beautiful and elegant. I didn't ask how she contrived to get what seemed to be a brand new evening gown. I was just tawdry. Inevitably, so was my dancing. I can still remember the superior eyes stabbing me whenever perforce I had to dance with someone other than Kim. My one success was the number of toes I trod upon.

In vacant moments I brooded over my difficulties. Then, during the long vacation after the first year at college, the answer came upon me like a flash. Well, actually it literally floated before my eyes. I was upstairs on a bus. At a stop some windows above a large shop occupying a corner site came into view and I spotted a modest but well placed sign: Fernley Dance Studio. Dancing Sessions Wednesdays, 2.30pm, Saturdays, 7.30pm. Private lessons by appointment. The conductor rang the bell and the bus pulled away, but my thoughts lingered. Private lessons – that's what I needed! They would be a natural progression from my book work. Then I wondered how much they would cost.

My destination was the Inland Revenue Office in town, but not because I had any tax problems. I was earning vacation pocket money with other students, one of whom was Malcolm Ashterleigh. In fact we had been at school together before going to St. Andrew's and therefore he was in the same boat as I was when it came to social accomplishments. His girlfriend, like Kim, could dance well with a competent partner. Both of us, therefore, posed problems for them as far as dancing was concerned. We had managed to keep the relationships going with walking, cycling and visits to the cinema. But our inability to dance was becoming desperate.

During the lunch hour I nervously telephoned the Fernley Dance Studio and asked about private lessons. A young, engaging female voice answered in most helpful terms, which was encouraging. I'd feared archly superior tones and was ready to drop the receiver in panic.

'We charge twelve shillings and six pence for half an hour, or five guineas for a course of ten lessons'.

'I see,' I said, er…'

'Which dances do you want to learn, sir?'

'Er, well…' My mind fled to my text book. 'I had thought of the Waltz, Quickstep, Foxtrot and Tango.'

There was a fractional pause.

'Well, we can teach all those, sir. I suppose that means you can dance already and want to prepare for medal competitions?'

'Good lord, no. I can't dance at all, well, not much anyway. I mean, I know a few basic steps…'

'Oh, that's alright sir, I quite understand. Sorry for the misunderstanding.'

I was getting hot around my collar, but the voice had an attractive quality which encouraged me to continue. I decided to fling myself upon its mercy.

'I'm afraid l have to admit that so far my knowledge of dancing has come from a book.'

'That's quite a good way to start,' said the voice.

'Bless you!' I thought.

'I suggest you come along and have an introductory lesson, shall we say for five shillings? If you don't take to it we shan't press you to continue. But if it goes well, you can decide then whether you want more lessons, and if so, how many.'

'Oh, that sounds an excellent idea,' I said with considerable relief.

'Right, when would you like to come?'

Date and time were arranged and I emerged from the telephone box feeling very elated. A whole new world as a socialite was opening up before me and I could hardly wait to tell Malcolm. He met me on the office stairs.

'You look disgustingly happy for someone who's got to stick a thousand envelopes - or had you forgotten?' he said.

'I have great news, old boy. I've solved the dancing problem!'

'You've what?'

'I'm going to learn to dance, you know, Waltzes, Quicksteps and things.'

'How, where…?'

'Private lessons. I've just arranged the whole thing!'

'Private…heck, how much is that going to cost you?

'Just over a fiver for a course of ten lessons, half an hour a time. That's a total of five solid hours of teaching. That ought to solve the problem since I've learnt quite a lot already from my book.'

'Where on earth are you going to do all this?'

I told him, and he became thoughtful. 'I wonder what your teacher will be like.'

'The girl on the phone sounded super - quite young, I should imagine.'

'Ah, but dancing teachers have usually been at it for years. She'll probably be middle aged and fat.' Malcolm had an annoying streak of pessimism.

'Oh, l don't agree. This girl sounded great.'

'Probably the telephonist.'

'Oh, chuck it. I'll tell you all about it on Monday. My first lesson's on Friday, after we've finished with this place.'

'Well, don't forget we start college again the week after next. Are you going to get all your ten lessons in before then?'

'Good heavens, no! I'll do them on Saturday afternoons throughout the term.'

'You disreputable character - slinking off with strange women when you ought to be writing up lecture notes. You'll get a D teaching mark!'

I must admit that as I slapped water on each envelope that afternoon Malcolm's warnings nagged me. Middle aged and fat... no, they'd never do any business. Would they?

When I arrived to keep my appointment I felt distinctly nervous. The entrance to the Fernley Dance Studio was a single door at the side of the large chain store shop, behind which was a long flight of stairs. It was eight o'clock in the evening and everywhere was very quiet. I turned a corner at the top and found a door facing me with a notice, Enquiries. Feeling sure no one was about and there must be a mistake in the appointment, I knocked. There was a pause, then I heard a light step. A bolt was pulled, the upper half of the door swung open to reveal a pleasantly attractive girl with smiling eyes and rich brown hair.

'Mr Flaxton?' she asked.

'Yes, I'm due...'

'...for a trial dancing lesson,' she interrupted. She opened the lower part of the door. 'Do come in - the studio's through here. Did you have far to come?'

'Not really.'

'Oh, good. Now, here we are. It's quite a pleasant room - the corner site helps because it gives us a wide curve of windows. Now, I'll just put a record on quietly as a background and you can tell me what you know.'

She crossed to a gramophone and soon the unmistakable sounds of a Victor Sylvester record drifted round the room. Even I could recognize that. As she came back towards me, wearing a plain but attractive red dress, I couldn't help noticing the quality of her figure matched her face. She was probably a couple of years older than me. Middle aged and fat, indeed! What crowned the experience for me was that, in addition to her appearance, she was also a superb teacher. She put me at my ease from the very beginning and was soon inviting me to hold her in the normal dancing pose.

'Come on, get rid of that stiffness. I'm not going to dance with a guardsman on duty. Put your arm further round me. Go on, no one's watching,' she laughed gently.

'Er, how's that?' I asked, moving at least an inch.

'We-ell, if you've been learning from a book, I'll bet it tells you that in the correct dancing position the man's right hip should be in contact with the lady's left. Just bend your head, nothing else, and look where yours is.'

I did so and realised my stance was tolerable for the arch in Oranges and Lemons.

'Ah,' I said, 'I see the problem.'

'So - put it right.' She looked straight into my eyes. She really had a most engaging smile. I shuffled closer. I could feel her left hand slipping down my back and encouraging my right hip.

'Now, just let yourself sway a little to the music. Just turn a little from your hips. Listen to the distinct beat in every three, ONE two, three, ONE, two three - there, you hear it?'

Who could miss it in a strict tempo Victor Sylvester waltz?

At this point the record stopped, but with practised speed she set it going again and slid easily back into my arms. Without giving me time to think she gently edged me forward and to one side, forward and to the other side, and we were away. Seconds later we were in danger of hitting the chairs ranged around the edge of the room, but with a most gentle movement she altered my direction.

'There you are - you're dancing the Modern Waltz, and you could carry on doing this around the room.'

'We're doing Forward Changes, I believe,' I said.

She laughed. 'You have been swotting your text book!'

It was quite delightful. As I gained confidence and fitted movements to the rhythm, with a distinct lunge forward on the main beat, she simply melted ahead of me.

'Now we'll try a turn. Just start as we did before, lead off with your right foot, but move it to point to your right. Ready, right. ONE, two, three.'

She swept me round so that I had to put my left foot in the correct position, and with her left arm she gave my shoulder a slight push which made me close my feet together.

'Wonderful - you've done half a natural turn already. Now, go back with your left foot, but start turning me to your right. Ready - go. FOUR, five, six.'

With equal ease she turned me throughout the second part, and I had negotiated my first waltz figure with a girl in my arms. But she gave me no time to savour the moment.

'Once again, Mr Flaxton. Ready, now - ONE, two, three, FOUR, five, six.'

I was successful again and tried to stop, but she tugged me on firmly.

'Oh no, you don't. You're here to work, my lad. Just keep on turning.'

Minutes later she had me doing a reverse turn, then I was dancing round the room using both figures, with changes between them. It was a marvellous sensation.

'Well, that's a good half hour,' she said suddenly. I stared at my watch in disbelief. She laughed. 'Yes, it goes quickly when you're doing something well.'

'I don't know about doing it well. I certainly enjoyed it, but that was very much due to you, I think.'

'No, I'm serious. Some people take far longer to pick it up. You're still rather stiff, but you could soon learn to dance quite well.'

'Well, frankly I'm amazed. If you knew how much I've worried about learning!'

'Now, this isn't just sales talk. My sister tells me that she suggested you might consider a course of lessons. I think you'd find them quite useful.'

'Your sister - she spoke to me when I rang the other day?'

'That's right. There's three of us here - my sister, her husband, and me. I tell you what. Try arranging some lessons, then come to one of the dancing sessions, we get a pleasant crowd and most are at different stages of learning. They would make you very welcome. Wednesday afternoons would be best - not so many come then as on Saturdays.'

'Ah, Wednesdays might be a problem. I'm at college, you see, and though we don't usually have lectures on a Wednesday afternoon, I'm not sure I could get away. I'll have to find out as soon as term begins.'

But I booked my second lesson a few days ahead and soon was on my way home feeling extremely pleased with myself. To be able to dance at last - the prospect filled me with great excitement and considerable relief. I crowed over Malcolm the next week.

'Man, you don't know what you're missing. The lessons are absolutely great.'

'Seriously?'

'Sure – and my teacher. Oh boy! Fat and forty indeed!'

'You're really taken with it aren't you, Nigel? Perhaps I'd better put it to the test.'

'That's great. I'm sure you'd enjoy it. She really knows her stuff. Not just the dancing, she's superb at that, of course, but she's such an excellent teacher. Puts you at your ease, gives you confidence, makes you feel successful. Makes you work hard as well.'

'Sounds a teaching paragon. The VP would be proud of her.'

Very shortly afterwards Malcolm told me he'd signed up for a course. I said I was going to charge commission. Then we discovered how much more relaxed the college regime was going to be under the new Principal, so I put it to Malcolm that we might try attending the Wednesday afternoon sessions at Fernley Dance Studio. He agreed and as soon as we had covered half our course of lessons we made our first serious foray into the dancing world.

We arrived early on the first occasion, climbed the long flight of stairs, entered the studio and sat in splendid isolation in the middle of the vacant chairs arranged in a crescent beside the windows. Our teacher appeared shortly afterwards, looking as radiant as ever, and introduced us to two people with her as her older sister and brother-in-law. These were, in fact, the joint proprietors.

'Glad to see you're well on time,' said our teacher. 'The others will be coming in a few minutes, I expect. There'll be about twenty, you'll find everyone very friendly, so don't look so worried!'

We laughed, but our fears remained. What was bothering us, in addition to the ,possibility of making fools of ourselves with mistakes in dancing, was the kind of dancing partners we were likely to get. My girlfriend, Kim, was at work and so was Malcolm's, so neither could accompany us. It was not difficult to calculate that out of twenty clients attending the session, ten or twelve at least were likely to be female.

'That's five or six apiece,' I said. 'Surely it's odds on there'll be a young one for each of us.'

'I wouldn't bank on it. Don't forget, Wednesday afternoons, how many girls are likely to be free to go dancing at this time?'

I thought desperately. 'Shop assistants - it's early closing day. This is a large shopping area, there must be plenty who'd be bored stiff without this place.'

'Optimist - then why isn't it going to be crowded?'

Our argument was cut short by the first arrivals and I had to admit the matter appeared settled firmly in Malcolm's favour, if not his desire. The clients, whilst not exactly elderly, were mature to say the least. As they arrived in ones and twos our eyes shot to the door each time, only to meet as we silently commented on the degree of middle aged spread evident in the women as well as the men.

'I don't think I'll be making this a regular thing after all,' I whispered. 'I wonder if I could persuade Kim to come on Saturday evenings instead.'

'Ah, now that's better,' said Malcolm looking at the latest arrivals.' These were two girls about eighteen who were interesting enough to revive our flagging spirits. They sat down together and started animated conversation.

'Good afternoon, everyone. Let's begin, shall we? All take your partners for a Quickstep.'

The male proprietor's voice was pleasant but definite. He was issuing an instruction, not asking a question. Malcolm and I looked briefly at each other and nodded. We rose simultaneously, crossed the room and I asked the girl on the left and he asked the one on the right. Both rewarded us with welcoming smiles and that was that.

We acted with courage born of desperation. With our background neither of us was inclined to be quick off the mark in such affairs. Fate smiled on us because we automatically went for the girl of our choice. It would have been acutely embarrassing had we both made a beeline for the same girl.

We soon found the girl I was dancing with was named Pat and Malcolm's was Sheila. They were indeed shop assistants; they served in one of the suburbs. Pat was fairly tall, Sheila slightly shorter; both were brunettes. They had been to the studio twice before and danced with each other most of the time, which wasn't difficult because the women outnumbered the men. But looking round at the representatives of our sex we appreciated they had a similar problem to ours.

The girls could certainly dance better than either of us but they also were learning. Half way through the session the proprietor and his wife taught a new figure of the Foxtrot, the dance which was being taught weekly to the group. Neither Malcolm nor I had got on to that in our lessons and we were very grateful for the help that Pat and Sheila gave us but, of course, neither was as skilled as our personal tutor who took it in turns to dance with us on occasions during the session. When the end came we both left thoroughly pleased and made firm dates with the girls for each Wednesday throughout the term.

From then onwards our dancing education proceeded smoothly, albeit to a modest level. It was very enjoyable and soon we were taking our regular girlfriends to occasional dances of various kinds, trying out our new skills on them with reasonable success.

Then I let the whole dancing business go completely to my head. In a moment of monumental crass stupidity I arranged to take two girls to the same dance!

It happened so innocuously. Gordon Mersely announced one day that he had a small number of spare tickets for a dance at a church hall on the south side of the city, where he lived, to which he was taking his girl Wendy. These were snapped up quickly,

Malcolm and I being two of the takers. Naturally he would be taking Melanie, his girl, and I intended taking Kim. Gordon was delighted.

'We'll have a super group. I prefer that sometimes as a change from going just as a pair.'

I suppose it was the notion of a group that penetrated my brain. On my next visit to the Wednesday session at Fernley I mentioned the matter to Pat in casual conversation.

'I'm going to get in more practice on Saturday. One of the chaps at college had some spare tickets for a dance, so a group of us are going.'

'You are doing well. Where's it to be?'

St. Saviour's Church Hall. I don't expect you know it.'

'What a coincidence: I live not far from there. In fact when I attend church, that's where I go usually. I heard about the dance, a friend of mine offered me a ticket as well.'

'That's amazing,' I said. Then, unthinkingly, 'Why don't you go?'

'Alright, I will. Thanks. I'll get the ticket tonight.'

Afterwards I told Malcolm of Pat's link with St. Saviour's and my suggestion. 'Why don't you ask Sheila to join the party?'

'But I'm taking Melanie, you chump.'

'So what? I'm taking Kim. But we'll all be in a crowd, so it won't matter.'

'Of course it will. Everyone will pair off. Who'd dance with Sheila whilst I'm dancing with Melanie and who'd dance with Pat when you're dancing with Kim? You've given yourself quite a problem.'

'Nonsense, it won't be like that at all. She knows other people there - one of them offered her a ticket only this week. Obviously she'll go with him, but she won't dance with him the whole time.'

'You're sure her friend is a bloke?'

'Of course…well…yes, I'm almost sure from the way she said it.'

'You should have checked, you twerp.'

Slowly it dawned on me that I couldn't check my facts now, even if I'd dared to do so, because I had no idea of Pat's address. Neither did I know where either she or Sheila worked. As

Malcolm's words sank in and caused more nagging doubts, I telephoned Fernley with my problem.

'Yes, I do see your difficulty,' said the male proprietor. 'However, it's our firm rule that we never disclose clients' addresses to anyone, not even to other clients. It preserves our confidential service, you see. Normally I could pass on a message for you but the person you mention is not on the telephone.'

'But don't you know where she works? You could telephone her there.'

'No, we certainly do not ask clients for business addresses. I'm sorry Mr Flaxton, there's nothing I can do.'

I put the phone down and decided to pin my hopes on this being another example of Malcom's pessimism. I pondered whether I should tell Kim, then took the further decision to await the Fates' smile again. Perhaps, though, they'd need to grin expansively to rescue me from this piece of idiocy. When Saturday came I met Kim in town as arranged and together we boarded a bus for St. Saviour's Hall. As we sat on the top deck I felt rather subdued.

'You're unusually quiet, Nigel. Aren't you feeling too well?' Kim asked.

'No, I'm fine, really. I was thinking.'

'I suppose you've got your mind on your next school practice. For goodness' sake, forget it for a while. Tell me about this dance. So far you've only told me where it's being held.'

'Well, I don't know too much about it myself. Gordon got the tickets and quite a number of us are going. We thought it would be rather fun to go in a bit of a crowd for a change.'

Kim gave me a slightly odd look. 'That's not like you at all. Usually you have to be dragged on the floor if you think there's a chance you'll have to dance with someone you don't know.'

'Ah, this'll be different. I know most of the other chaps' girlfriends. It'll help to widen my experience and you'll be quite happy dancing with the lads because you can dance with anyone.'

It was Kim's turn to be quiet. I noticed she was looking out of the window with a rather cold stare. I decided to drop a hint about Pat.

'Er, rather a coincidence happened last Wednesday. You know I've told you about Pat, the girl I sometimes dance with at the Studio…well, she lives quite near St. Saviour's Hall. She's going as well. Some friends of hers offered her a ticket.'

Kim's glance now was arctic but still she said nothing. Shortly afterwards when we stood up to get off the bus she was frowning deeply. As we walked the short distance to the hall I joined her in silence because I was beginning to feel that perhaps, after all, Malcolm was right. We parted just inside the hall and made our way to our respective cloakrooms where we left our coats. I went back into the small entrance vestibule to wait for Kim. It was becoming crowded.

'Hello, Nigel, you found the place, then?' called a voice in the crush. Gordon pushed his way towards me followed closely by Wendy. 'Two or three of the others are here already. They've gone in. Where's Kim?'

'She's just coming,' I replied as Kim emerged from the cloakroom.

"Let's go in, the others will join us in a moment.'

He opened up a path through the throng with his left shoulder and guided Wendy along behind him towards double doors which led into the hall.

'Come on, Nigel, get me out of this,' said a voice under my elbow. Kim, rather small, was having a rough time in the crowd. Quickly I held her arm and followed Gordon's lead. We emerged in the hall to welcome breathing space. Gordon and Wendy walked ahead to join the other St. Andrew's chaps and their girls, so Kim and I followed. Four musicians played in desultory fashion on the small stage, knowing perfectly well no one would start dancing yet. We introduced our girls to those students they didn't already know and then sat down. The chairs, as usual at such events, were arranged in a single line all the way round the edge of the room. As I sat by Kim it became perfectly obvious that our group comprised paired units so if Pat arrived unaccompanied I was going to have a whale of a problem on my hands. I tried glancing at the door as nonchalantly as I could to see whether she had arrived yet. Kim sensed what I was doing.

'Nigel.' she said, with mock sweetness. 'You've put your foot in it, haven't you?'

'Er…no…I don't think so. That is, I'm sure Pat meant she was coming with some other people and I simply said that it would be nice to see her here. At least, that's what I meant.'

'But you're not sure, are you?'

'Well…er…to be honest, no. You see she mentioned being offered a ticket by a friend and I assumed she meant a boyfriend. I didn't give it a second thought until Malcolm…'

My excuses were cut short as the tall figure of Pat appeared framed in the doorway. She was looking round the room, now almost full with groups of people sitting or standing and talking to each other. She was obviously looking for someone. Desperately I scanned the company, urging some unseen figure to detach himself from one.of the knots of people and cross the floor to welcome her. But no one took the slightest notice. Then she saw me. Immediately she smiled, waved and came towards me. I stood up.

'Hello Nigel, I couldn't see you at first. I thought perhaps you were even later than me.'

'Er, no, we've been here a few minutes. Er, you know Malcolm, of course. This is Melanie, and Gordon, and Wendy.' I quickly performed the necessary introductions.

'And this is Kim,' I concluded.

Kim rose, and faced her. Their difference in height didn't help the moment one little bit, neither did the awkward silence which settled on our group as its members watched in fascination, all fully apprised of my stupidity.

'Kim…your girl…?' Pat's expression changed to one of amazed incredulity.

'Hello, Pat.' said Kim. 'Yes, you may have heard about me. I think I'd better ask the direct question. Were you expecting to be at this dance with Nigel?'

'Yes, I was. He said a group of students were coming from St. Andrew's, and then he invited me.' She paused. 'At least, that's what I thought he did.'

'Oh, I'm sure he did - in a vague way. But he does have some remarkably blank moments, sometimes. You see, he invited me the day he got the tickets.'

'Now look...I'm awfully sorry...I didn't think it would be...' I tried.

'No, my sweet,' said Kim in her deliberately prim voice, 'you don't think, do you? Come on, Pat, let's sit down, shall we?'

'No, maybe I made a mistake as well. It'll be simpler if I go. I don't want to...'

'Oh no, don't go - that would let Nigel off far too lightly.' She took Pat by the arm and sat her down. Then she looked up at me. 'He's mad keen to practise his dancing, so let's take it in turns to make him work at it, shall we?'

The rest of the group sat back and relaxed. They thoroughly approved of Kim's handling of the matter and were happy to see me get my deserts.

'Good evening, ladies and gentlemen. Welcome to St. Saviour's. We're very pleased there's been such an excellent response to this event which has been arranged in aid of the Church Restoration Fund.' The MC's announcement brought a hush to the room. 'I hope you'll all have a most enjoyable evening. Now, let's begin the way we mean to continue, shall we? Let's see you all on the floor for the opening Quickstep. Thank you.'

The quartet on the stage struck up in lively fashion and within seconds the floor was filled with couples, leaving the chairs almost completely empty. Our group responded to the MC's instruction in exemplary fashion, with the sole exception of me. I was still standing, staring down at Kim and Pat.

'Well,' challenged Kim, 'which of us is going to be honoured first, Nigel?'

'Er...'

'Oh, go on, you idiot. Take Pat. I'll watch, and give you marks out of ten on your progress.'

What else could I do? I stumbled round the room with a very straightfaced Pat, desperately trying to apologise whilst simultaneously wrestling with quarter turns, natural turns and reverse turns. My shirt became distinctly sticky. Suddenly the music stopped. I dropped my arms from Pat far too rapidly and we walked back in silence to Kim.

'I'll only give you three for that, Nigel. You have a rest, Pat, while I put him through his paces in the Waltz.'

The MC really hadn't given people time to sit down. Delighted with a good initial response he wanted to keep up the momentum. Within seconds Kim was swinging me out of trouble's way as much as she could as I tried to make further excuses to her, getting thoroughly bumped in the process. My mind became a whirl of black feet on white feet and simply refused to slot into the melting movements of dance with my Fernley teacher. We circumnavigated the room like dodgems at a fair.

A Paul Jones was announced. For once I joined in with alacrity because, even in my bemused state, I could work out the arithmetical fact that this obliterated ordinary pairing and both Pat and Kim would keep getting partners. It was worth braving my fear of dances I didn't know with strange partners of disparate ages with holds ranging from weak and droopy to judo attacks. This time was no exception and I was pushed and mauled by matronly hands in the Veleta, Gay Gordons and Military Two Step, whilst I struggled hopelessly to guide unknown feet in the other dances. Each time partners tried to make light conversation with me but failed as abysmally as I did with the dancing. By the time everyone was performing hilariously in a Knees Up, I was as miserable as sin.

'Well done indeed, everyone,' said the MC wiping his brow. 'You are entering into the spirit of things. Do keep it up. Now let's give the ladies a chance to sort out the men, shall we? The next dance is a ladies' excuse me.'

I flopped on to a chair, already feeling physically as well as mentally exhausted even though the night was still in its infancy. I assumed I would now have an enforced rest because I couldn't imagine Kim or Pat wanting to dance with me by choice.

But I was wrong. Kim started off, and then, in what I soon realised was a neat bit of quick planning, Pat took over, followed by Wendy, and Melanie, then a couple of the other girls in our group, then Kim again. They all had a great time - not from their experiences with the Great Dancer, rather from the amusement they derived by putting me through the mill. Fortunately for me the musicians stopped the second round from getting very far by ending that particular dance.

But, of course, my troubles continued throughout the entire evening. A group spirit certainly did develop, entirely at my expense. The other chaps occasionally took it in turns to dance with Kim and Pat, which meant I had to choose one of whichever two girls was left. When this happened they pulled my leg hard about taking one out of turn, and what they were going to do to me in revenge.

When the end of the evening drew near I felt absolutely shattered - which was no more then I deserved - whilst the group, including Pat, had enjoyed a great deal of fun. But then the Last Waltz was announced and I realised suddenly that the evening might yet have a nasty sting left.

'It's alright,' said Kim. 'She's gone. She said she felt rather tired. It's fortunate she doesn't live far away, isn't it?'

I shuffled around to the music feeling the memory of the evening would be burned into my memory for many a long year. How right I was!

I simply couldn't face returning to the Fernley Dance Studios, so that was the last I ever saw of Pat. It was also the end of my ballroom dancing instruction, except for what a large number of female colleagues and students have taught me through the years at all kinds of school socials, dances and discos.

One at a time, of course. Or thoroughly enmeshed in a group when partners were totally irrelevant.

To have suggested that Dance should appear in secondary school curricula in the late forties would have attracted opprobrium from academics and ridicule from students. Occasionally infants and juniors were taught motley forms. I remember there being a brass plate in the middle of the hall floor at my infants' school, the top of which was removed once a year and into the revealed orifice a large pole was inserted from which hung alternate long red and white streamers. Each year on May Day we hopped and skipped in various rotations to gramophone music celebrating we knew not what. The object, as we soon spotted, was to tie ourselves in knots which we usually accomplished successfully, an attainment largely unappreciated by our teachers. But once in the rarified atmosphere of the Big School, i.e. the Junior Department, such frolics were regarded as stupid and cissy; which proves that our teachers had not adequately taught us the bucolic derivation of the Maypole and its revelry. Or perhaps, in those days of innocence, seven to eleven year olds were insufficiently mature.

Yet Dance has a history as long as the human race. Cave paintings in France and Spain dating back 30,000 years show examples of this form of expression. It is interesting to conjecture what music accompanied such scenes. Surely it was never a silent activity? So Art and Music are essentially basic to human creative expression, as is Drama. Whether early humans indulged in dramatic representation also has to be conjectural, but it was certainly well established in ancient Greece. So Music, Art and Drama are rightly included in modern educational curricula.

But societies have different cultures, so these have many forms. So does Dance. The question examined one way or another by education pundits in Britain during the immediate post war decades was what Dance, if any, should be taught or encouraged in schools. As with other forms of creative expression it has both formal and informal elements.

My late teenage textural studies were concerned with the attempts to add weight to Ballroom Dancing. There was a dichotomy between modern and old time. The latter certainly had shape, but it was the shape of repetition. It also had a lengthy tradition of being the means of getting men and women together in controlled public display. It allowed couples to start off together and then, usually, provided schemes of exchange within a group, an eightsome reel for example, or even greater progression through a succession of partners. However, as my mother pointed out, all you had to do was learn the basic steps of each dance. Once you had those off pat you could concentrate on other matters. The excellent costume dramas seen regularly on television usually show the main purpose very well indeed.

Modern ballroom dancing, however, was deliberately intimate, hence its development with the rather decadent ennui of the twenty-one years between the two World Wars when so many people shut out the horrors of the first. Later its intimacy was wholeheartedly grasped by men and women in deliberately carefree moments which could be, and sometimes were, close to their last. In the Second World War that applied to civilians as well as those in the Armed Forces, depending on where you happened to live.

So, generally throughout the forties and fifties, dancing of the ballroom kind in schools was reserved for after-school clubs and socials. Definitely ex-curricular. But ideas about dance in schools gradually changed. We didn't know we were entering the swinging sixties as that decade began, though both wartime and austerity teenagers and the next generation who had no such memories felt it was time to loosen social shackles and have a bit of fun.

The sixties came long before the prescriptive national curriculum so schools were responsible for what was taught. Of course, in the main, they all taught the same subjects, but reflecting changes in societal attitudes a degree of experimentation crept in. Drama began to appear on the timetable, rather than being the school play largely rehearsed at the end of the day. At the beginning of that decade I was involved with an English department and to find out what was what in Drama development, I enrolled on a university vacation course entitled 'Drama in the Secondary School'. The prospectus assured me it was about teaching, so there was no *double entendre*. During an enlightening and revealing week I met the most dynamic lady I ever came across, before or since. One of the tutors, she was passionate about Dance. We learned she was battering universities to develop degree courses in it, head teachers to put it firmly in their Drama syllabi, Inspectors to demand that this was done, and anyone else who ever crossed her path - as we unsuspecting temporary students were doing.

So I discovered there were other dimensions to Dance. Particularly, in this case, Creative Dance. Before I went on the course I might have assumed that referred to new figures devised by skilled practitioners for the Waltz, the Quickstep, et al. I knew differently by the end of the course.

Had I known beforehand that I would, at one point, be dressed in very loose clothing, prancing about a room imagining it was the ocean, that we were all fish, that I was a shark and was stalking smoothly - because that's how sharks stalk - a small and sinuous mackerel (well, I think she said she would be a mackerel; anyway, she wanted me finally to lunge and devour), I would have driven home at great speed despite the fact that I had come a long way. But such was the force of personality our teacher could muster that not only did I do just that, like the rest I did many other equally weird things as well. I contented myself with writing letters home detailing the larks we got up to in these sessions, overlaid with a heavy veneer of ridicule. But by the end of the course the dynamic lady had been successful with her most recalcitrant student. I have for years practised her highly successful relaxation techniques, to my advantage I believe. I certainly added Dance to the curricula of schools for which I later had responsibility. I've even had the audacity to sit on judging panels for Creative Dance Competitions in schools. I never followed the lady's subsequent career, but Dance has been available as a degree course for many years.

She was brilliant. What a teacher! I have also since been astounded by the brilliance of students in their creative choreographing of expressive dance to all kinds of music. I've also marvelled at the difference between their experiences of the many creatively stimulating aspects of Music, Art and Drama and my own educational experience. In the matter of Dance they were poles apart – and I'm not referring to Maypoles or similar props.

Chapter 16

At college, as Kim said, my mind was very much on our second and final period of school practice. This was going to be crucial to all our final teaching marks as well as whether a lucky few would gain the rare and coveted 'Distinction' level in the 'Principles and Practice of Teaching' with an 'A' teaching mark. A good performance in one was expected to accompany a similar level in the other.

Our second year was devoted to practice in senior schools, which under the recent Education Act had become secondary grammar, secondary technical and secondary modern. It was ushered in as the tripartite system, but in the next decade or so the technical schools largely disappeared and the system became bipartite. Most college students were sent to secondary modern schools because there were far more of them, and in this city as I explained earlier they educated seven eighths of the pupils over the age of eleven.

Our final year coincided with the raising of the school leaving age from fourteen to fifteen. So when we went into the senior schools, on both instructional and block practice, we found a rather reluctant group present comprised of those pupils who had expected to leave but who now had to stay on for part or all of their fourth year. As they reached their fifteenth birthdays they were allowed to leave at the end that term, so the year group diminished by one third at Christmas, Easter and Midsummer respectively. To-day that is Year 10. I wonder how keen employers would be to recruit from that age group now? Yet fourteen had been the traditional school leaving age since just after the First World War, when it had been raised from thirteen.

Most of us were placed with classes below this age group, as I was at Marsden Road Secondary Modern Boys' School. It was located in the middle of a large estate of houses built between the wars by the city Corporation. I was delighted to be sent there because it had a very good reputation amongst the students, largely because the headmaster, Mr Appleton, organised matters to give them the maximum insight into the operation of the school, as well as the greatest possible number of opportunities for all kinds of relevant teaching experience. So I knew I was in for a busy month.

I was assigned to Form 3A, whose teacher was Mr Painter. At that time secondary teaching was still largely a matter of one teacher teaching general subjects, with perhaps one or two specializing in Music, Woodwork with boys, and Cookery with girls. Sometimes Science also was taught by one person, if the school was fortunate enough to have a laboratory. All teachers were qualified to teach Physical Training, but in practice this was usually taken by the younger and more active ones. So when I taught on my practice many of my lessons were with 3A.

I was absolutely blessed in being with Mr Painter. He helped me tremendously and certainly contributed considerably to my final success in this part of my training. I hope in the succeeding years I was able to do half as much for the students who were with me.

Mr Appleton saw to it that students undertook other work with different forms wherever possible to give us experience of various age groups. I joined a fourth year class on weekly visits to various places of work, designed to make the pupils' extra year more meaningful. The summer leavers actually saw about thirty five varied places, factories, businesses and offices, which no doubt helped them in their choice of a job. Part of the rest of each week was spent in follow-up lessons upon each visit.

The head's policy also resulted in my learning another salutary lesson myself. This time the subject matter was football.

For much of the time during training, teaching practice has an aspect of unreality. Either there is another teacher in the classroom with you, or there is one near at hand The youngsters know full well you are teaching them on behalf of someone else.

There is a tremendous thrill to be experienced when you first face a class which is entirely dependent upon you and when both you and the pupils know this. How will they respond? Will you be able to control them? What will they do if you make a mistake? Questions such as these are in the forefront of every new teacher's consciousness when he or she faces a class truly alone for the first time. The thrill, of course, may not be enthralling!

Many do not experience this until they begin their first job. In the seventies I did some research into the probationary year. You may have passed your initial teacher training with flying colours, but you weren't properly qualified until the end of your first year and a confirmatory visit from one of Her Majesty's Inspectors, though when I did so it was His, not Her. I interviewed a hundred probationers in various schools. One question I asked was:

'How well do you feel your training practice prepared you for your first classroom experience here?'

I recorded most interviews and frequently at this point the microphone was in danger of blowing. Respondents answered variously with outbursts of laughter, shrieks of ridicule and the occasional rude noise. It was very evident a chasm yawned between practice and the real thing. To be fair, however, many of my sample were in schools that had recently changed to comprehensive intakes under the hotch potch of schemes local education authorities were forced to invent due to the spending restrictions on the change imposed by central government. Those particular embryonic teachers were indeed born into the school world with a hefty slap to get them going.

Sometimes, however, during training you do get unaided control of a class unexpectedly, as I did when Mr Appleton asked me to referee a second year football match during a games lesson. Fortunately the days of massive legal restrictions lay well in the future.

The problem was that I had never refereed a match in my life and my knowledge of and skill at football was minimal. My own junior school taught only a form of handball. We walked to one of the many sports fields provided by the city and played on a marked out football pitch, used properly by all other schools many of which travelled by provided transport. Then my grammar school used another part of the same field, but by the time I returned from my year's evacuation most of it was a barrage balloon site and the rest was ploughed for crops. We did actually get to kick a few balls each week, but that was all. The college field was still green and pleasant rolling minihills laid out by the Luftwaffe.

Because Physical Training was a compulsory subject for all students it was legitimate for Mr Appleton to assume this included an elementary knowledge of games. He was not to know it did not extend to football in my case, and I wasn't going to tell him. After all, he would be writing a report on me at the end of my practice, and people said that your final teaching mark stayed on your file forever...

On the field twenty-two twelve year olds crowded round me. This was a half class fortuitously providing the exact number required, though it was quite usual to have matches with illegal numbers. The boys knew exactly what they expected from me. Decisions.

'Who'll be captains, sir?'

'I will,' chorused fifteen volunteers.

'Er...' I said.

'ME, ME!' shrieked the remainder of the form.

It was not a time for prevarication. I looked around, spotted two boys who were actually wearing football boots and promptly appointed them. With amazing speed and surprisingly little argument they each grabbed eight other boys, leaving four standing awkwardly in a sort of no man's land between the two camps. One was fat, one was tall and very ungainly, whilst the other two wore washed out expressions which betokened no stamina whatsoever.

'Ah,' I said brightly, 'you each need two more. Who's having these lads?'

Immediately I realised what a slave market was like at the end of a day when business had been brisk. The clients were well satisfied with what they had and they were not going to give the dealer any help by taking the dregs off his hands.

The captains owed me something, so I used the fact. I had to end the torture the dejected four were undergoing. It's never so lonely as when you're in a crowd, but unwanted. I divided them arbitrarily, glared at each captain in turn, and gave them a pair. They accepted without obvious demur but their henchmen were inclined to be rebellious.

'Don't pass to Fatso, he's bound to lose it,' breathed an unidentifiable voice. 'That'll do.' I snapped, 'I want to see a proper game with everyone joining in and doing his best. It's the game that matters, not the result,' I added piously. In those days that was still true...in isolated social pockets.

The sports fields generally were well cared for but by contrast the boys were badly turned out. For the most part they played in their everyday clothes, taking off coats, pullovers and ties if they wore them. Sometimes they brought football boots. It depended upon whether parents could afford such items, or whether their sons were in the first team. If a lad reached those exalted heights, boots had to be supplied. The school provided shorts and shirts, having organised money-raising efforts to purchase them, but boots were a personal matter.

The teams I had been given to supervise contained only two first team boys, identified as such by their footwear. I had unwittingly solved my first major problem by making them captains. A workable authority system was formed immediately; the team members accepted the captains because they were the best players, whilst the captains would respect me because I had chosen them correctly. All I needed to do was referee properly.

At least you can look the part, even if you are useless at the game was the admonition given by a games master to a motley bunch of lads, of which I was one, making up our house team when I had been at school. I determined to put that advice into action now.

'Captains, place your teams,' I said firmly. Then to one, 'You give out bands to your team.' This was the normal method of distinguishing players. One side wore braids slung over one shoulder and became colours, the other side were whites, albeit incongruously in this instance for neither faces nor clothes would have done much for any soap advertisement.

With a certain amount of argument two sets of forwards, half backs and backs were directed to their positions by the captains who, of course, were the centre forwards. Much more reluctantly went two goalkeepers. Because no one in this group possessed adequate skill, the role of goalie was to be avoided at all costs because it was the one position in which mistakes couldn't pass unnoticed.

I placed the ball on the centre spot, told one captain to call, flipped a coin and settled the kick off. I conveniently ignored choice of ends; to have allowed a change-over would have finished the first half of the lesson. I gave what I hoped was a professional look around the field, and blew the whistle.

One boy kicked the ball sideways, the boy on his left tapped it forward and all hell broke loose. Twenty dervishes surrounded the ball determined to kick it to death. The ball, having little choice in the matter, remained trapped. I blew the whistle again and everyone stopped momentarily. Before I could speak, one boy picked up the ball, placed it in front of his foot, said 'Our free kick, warn't it, sir?' and kicked it hard towards goal before I could contradict him. Nineteen boys hared after it. I decided to let that one pass.

As misfortune would have it, the fat boy had been ordered to defend the goal towards which the ball was flying. He stood transfixed between the posts, arms held sideways in a supplicating gesture.

'Come out to it, Fatso,' yelled his entire team.

He did, mistiming his move as the ball bounced in front of him. His robot arms closed on thin air and the ball sailed unimpeded over his head between the posts. Nets were non-existent, so it was a chore forced upon the luckless goalkeeper missing an accurate shot that he had to run into the far distance to retrieve the ball. At least this allowed him to keep his red face away from the glares of his disgruntled team mates. The fat boy set off on his errand at a fast amble. By the time he returned with the ball the teams were in position for the second kick off. I seized the opportunity.

'Boys,' I announced, 'you must try to keep thinking about your positions. If you crowd round the ball, all trying to kick it at the same time, you'll never learn the skills of the game. Backs, for instance,' I said pointing, 'on the whole you should stay within reach of your goal area. If you two had done that a few minutes ago you might have stopped that goal being scored. It was your job to try to stop it. As it was you left it all to your goalie. Now, come on, let's see some passing this time.'

I detected the merest glance exchanged between the two captains who faced each other across the centre circle. There was a hint they thought I might know my stuff. I began to feel a little more confident. I blew the whistle and this time the ball moved between six or seven players before the *melée* developed again. I ran over to it, pleased to see that five players had declined to join this time and were hovering, torn between a longing to plunge in and the positions they were supposed to be guarding.

The captains were in the crush, though even I could see they were trying to use their skill to clear the ball. One tapped it neatly to his right, very near to the touchline. Two of the pack, oblivious to everything but the magnetic fascination of the football, pounced after it. They stumbled, blocking my view momentarily. Colours captain sidestepped one of them, made an obvious kick at the ball, which went over the line.

I blew sharply. 'White's ball,' I called.

Shocked faces turned towards me. Their owners all wore bands. Had I looked more carefully I might have noticed whites were surprised as well.

'Come on, don't waste time,' I called authoritatively. 'Whites' ball.'

'Sir,' ventured a voice, 'Cooper din't kick it out.' Cooper was captain of the colours. But before I could open my mouth, Cooper swung round on the boy who had spoken, who was one of his team.

'Play to the ref,' he said, through gritted teeth, staring hard at the boy. Immediately colours dropped back; one of the whites picked up the ball and took the throw-in. There was no semblance of an argument, nor rancour. I released my clenched fingers. Obviously I'd gaffed and the ball had bounced off one of the other two boys when Cooper tried to kick it clear, but I hadn't seen this. I resolved to take more care. Nevertheless I felt pleased the boys were such good sports.

Play continued in much the same way for about five minutes with the ball usually caught amongst a crowd of players.

Occasionally one with some pretensions to skill managed to break clear and either kicked it or dribbled it towards the opposition's goal area. On one such foray towards colour's goal Cooper resorted to desperate measures to stop a shot. He raced back into defence, slid along the ground and took away the player's legs and the ball in spectacular fashion. I blew immediately.

'Free kick.' I shouted.

Three of the colours players turned amazed faces towards me. 'But he got the ball first, sir,' one expostulated. Cooper got to his feet.

'I told you, play to the ref,' he said in heavy, explosive tones. In complete silence someone placed the ball. But I had missed something else as well.

'I reckon that oughta be a penalty,' said a quiet voice behind me. Everyone looked, including me. Heck,I didn't look at the lines, I thought. I was standing just inside the penalty area. Again there was silence. But before I could decide whether ignominiously to change my mind, Cooper said, 'Get on with it.' He picked up the ball and placed it just outside the area. One of the whites looked around, prepared to run, then looked at me. I took a cue from Cooper.

'Well, what are you waiting for?' I -said, sharply.

'You ain't blown the whistle, sir.'

I began to feel very fragile and blew hurriedly. He kicked towards the goal; another player shot but not accurately and I blew again for a goal kick. As play swung back to the middle of the field I knew I was letting these lads down. Their game, such as it was, was being marred by my errors.

Watch it, you fool, I admonished myself.

Somehow I got by without further problems until the second half. Then suddenly there was a confused rumpus on one touchline which, when I reached it, degenerated into a tug of war between two boys, each yelling, 'Our throw', ably and vociferously supported by team members, colours and white. From where I'd been, completely out of position, I hadn't seen. I decided I couldn't brazen this one out.

'I'm sorry I didn't see that closely enough, lads. I'll settle it with a dropped ball just inside the touchline.'

I had no idea whether this was correct procedure, but felt no one would report me to the Football Association. I held the ball and the two contenders waited. I dropped it; they lunged. One caught it with his shin, knocked it up and it bounced off the other's midriff, decked with a bright red band, and went out.

I blew sharply on the whistle, pointed firmly in the wrong direction indicating the throw-in.

This time all the players gasped and turned towards me in questioning but silent horror. What is he thinking about? was the mute cry of every expression. What I was thinking about was the previous half when they had been playing in the opposite direction.

'Oh, my mis…' I began, but before I could finish a voice rasped behind me.

'Play to the bloody ref. or I'll thump the lot on yer.' It was Cooper, of course.

The bloody ref. shudders at the reaction there would be to-day in the face of such incompetence. I am thankful I made my mistakes at a time when the old values of authority in sport were strong amongst twelve year olds.

Chapter 17

Finals and farewells followed in quick succession. In fact the whole of our second year at college seemed to pass very swiftly, due in no small measure to the enjoyment we gained from the new social life permitted us. Certainly when we came to leave we took with us a glow of satisfaction and nostalgia which has lasted throughout the ensuing years.

After a couple of weeks I was amazed to receive a letter from the Principal enclosing a cheque for £10. He explained that a fund had been restored which rewarded outstanding performances in practical teaching and final examinations, and the staff had decided to award me that sum. It was all the more welcome because it came completely out of the blue.

Loyalty is one of the most endearing human qualities, whether to an individual or an organisation. It is to his eternal credit that the VP served the new Principal as loyally as the old, even though they were so different. When we parted from Major Darnley we were genuinely sorry, for despite his minor eccentricities he was a great teacher of practitioners; I venture to suggest his skills would be just as outstanding in teacher training today.

He retired a few years after we left and everyone felt he richly deserved his Devonshire cottage. But his reward was tarnished by tragedy, for his quiet, understanding and so loyal wife died within twelve months.

`Were we adequately prepared to launch into our role as teachers? On the whole I believe we were – for schools of those days. The great majority of us expected to teach the junior age, 7 to 11, or the secondary, 11 to 15. No man expected to teach infants; such schools were staffed entirely by women as is still largely the case. Very few expected to teach in grammar schools, although Gordon Mersely did so – at the one Malcolm Ashterleigh and I formerly attended.

The curriculum was laid down by each headteacher. In practice this was in no sense a free choice because all schools taught the three Rs and were expected to do so successfully. Physical Training was also expected, as was some Art and Music. Secondary schools taught Science and practical subjects; Cooking for girls and Woodwork for boys sometimes involved a walk to a nearby school that had adequately equipped rooms. Beyond these heads could be flexible and might introduce other experiences if they had the staff; hence drama festivals.

The only examination was the 11+, then usually referred to as the Grammar School Entrance Exam, previously known generally as the Scholarship Exam. Very few expected to sit it. A large proportion didn't want to do so and certainly their parents wouldn't allow them. Attitudes varied across the country, however. Areas that had suffered in the depression of the thirties were far more likely to have parents who wanted their children to get out of the slough of unemployment and saw education as the means to do so. But during the war employment was full – either in the Forces or due to directed labour at home, when the government took powers to send anyone anywhere to work. In the midlands we had a woman placed with us because we had three bedrooms for only four people, my brother and I being children could share. The woman, in her forties, who had been brought up in a Dr Barnardo's Home and had subsequently entered domestic service, came from London and was directed to a local munitions factory where she inspected percussion caps for bullets eight hours a day on shifts throughout the twenty-four.

Having experienced the war years, followed by the drive to produce at home and not import from abroad because the country couldn't afford to do so, the majority of parents wanted their children out at work as soon as possible. Many did not rate the raising of the school leaving age to 15 a good idea.

There was a chasm between education of the masses and the middle and upper classes. The class system was very evident, providing a ready source of material for authors of both fiction and sociological studies. Some of the latter showed that a great many working class people did not want their children to be educated out of their class. Some children who were felt themselves misfits. Strong personalities overcame the magnetic drawback but they were a minority.

It was unnecessary, therefore, for most schools to have academic achievement as an important goal. Skills for work were required – literacy and numeracy, some dexterity, acceptance of control, acceptance of routine. So college courses did not need to be highly academic. The professional subjects were compulsory: Principles and Practice of Teaching, English Language, Physical Training and Hygiene, beyond which four optional subjects were required, though any one taken to main level counted as two and one had to be Art, Music or Craft. We were advised that a main level subject equated with ordinary degree level. That, of course, was way beyond the level required for teaching the subject even to the new fourth year of secondary schooling catering for the 15 year olds, dwindling term by term as they passed their release birthdays. So academically our training was perfectly adequate

Practical teaching experience was excellent in the modes we undertook at St Andrew's. That it was so was also due to the dedication of heads and teachers across the city who guided us in their schools. As we left, Reverend Pringley said to me, 'You'll take a degree, of course?' I believe many of us intended to do so. All my particular colleagues did and two obtained Ph.Ds. Judged from our personal viewpoints we felt teacher training needed more academic extension allied to the good practical experience. It took many years before an attempt was made to achieve that by the introduction of the Bachelor of Education degree (B.Ed.)

But in 1948 our qualifications were sufficient unto the day.

Upon leaving, most of my year faced a strange situation. Wartime regulations concerning conscription were still in force, so after leaving school we had followed the required practice of applying for deferment in order to undertake teacher training. When this was completed we had to await call-up which came to us all within six months.

Most of us took jobs even though we knew they would be short lived. The shortage of teachers was so acute that the authorities took us on even though they knew our service would be for a matter of weeks. In my case it was five. Shortly afterwards the conscription laws were reorganised into National Service and this anomaly was removed.

Between leaving college and my call up in early October I decided to earn some much needed cash, largely because I wanted to spend it on a week's holiday rock climbing in North Wales. Inland Revenue had no more short term jobs, I found, so I took myself off to the local labour exchange and joined a motley queue in which I stood out because I wore a jacket and tie. On making my enquiry at the counter I received an immediate offer – right here, please! Such offices were in need of the skills of ex-students with backgrounds in inserting forms into envelopes and sticking them. I was certainly their man.

Their urgent need had its origins in the Beveridge Report, commissioned during the war, much of which was accepted and put into effect soon afterwards as the National Insurance Scheme. This produced the National Health Service amongst other benefits. Everyone had to be provided with a National Insurance Number and issued with a National Insurance Card. So I assisted in the birth of this highly important social development by sending out the cards…well, some hundreds out of many millions. That year the autumn term began in the city's schools on August 30th, so on Friday 27th I bade farewell to the Labour Exchange. Not all the cards had been dispatched in time because the Scheme began on 5th July and there were still more to go when I left. I hoped the waiting recipients would understand that I wanted to start teaching.

My first five weeks teaching were uneventful. The first two passed without my knowing my call-up date, but the remaining three were spent in the knowledge that life for me was about to change dramatically. But I can remember well the moment I first walked into a classroom as a qualified teacher.

I was sent to a boys' school in a not very pleasant area of the city. Some of the streets nearby had been flattened during the war by a landmine dropped by parachute. I knew this to be so because

I heard it detonate, as did the rest of my school. The thing had inconsiderately stuck in telegraph wires but had considerately failed to explode on contact as it was designed to do after landing softly. That way damage was more widespread. It was in far too precarious a position to be defused so the immediate area was evacuated. People in a wider area were ordered into shelters for 11.00 am when the device was to be detonated. Lacking shelters we went to corridors deemed sufficiently strengthened for such occasional events, because daylight raids so far inland were rare. The explosion was spectacular but all we heard was the noise. It was achieved without loss of life but many houses were totally wrecked as I saw a day or two later when I ghoulishly cycled the streets.

The head welcomed me at 8.50 am on my first morning. Ten minutes later he took me to a classroom containing forty-eight twelve year olds. He ushered me in and they fell silent.

'Boys, you will remember we had three classes last year in the first year, 1A, 1B, and 1C. Well, as you know, the area sending boys to this school has been enlarged, so some of you have had to join us from another one. This means that now we need four classes in the second year. You've been sent to this room because I have made a new class, 2D. All I need to do now is introduce to you your class teacher, Mr Flaxton here. None of you has seen him before, because he's a new teacher. So you are all starting something new today, a new school for some, a new class for others, and a new job for Mr Flaxton. So it will be interesting to see what you all make of it.' He smiled thinly at the rows of silent faces. 'I'll leave you now. Bring them into assembly in five minutes, please, Mr Flaxton.'

He marched out of the room, leaving the boys eyeing me carefully. Certainly he had contrived to unite them. But one point in his explanation had been rather vague and immediately after I had delivered a couple of completely forgettable remarks to the class, I saw two cheeky-faced characters look at one another. A decision was made, then one put up his hand.

'Yes, my lad?' I said briskly.

'Mr Littleton just said yow was a new teacher, din't 'e sir?'

'That's right.'

'Did 'e mean yow've cum from anuther school, or are we yer fust class?'

I certainly hadn't expected the gauntlet to be thrown down so rapidly. I paused momentarily, then decided to pick it up.

'He meant you're my first class. I finished my training just before the holidays.' More looks were interchanged around the room. 'That means I shall be watching very carefully to see how you all behave. If I'm going to be teaching for the next forty years, I want to be able to look back and say that my first class was a very good one.'

It was my turn to look round. I was pleased to see my point of view appeared accepted to an extent. I think they also liked my frankness. I decided to pursue my advantage.

'But it doesn't mean I haven't done any teaching before. I've taught many classes recently, of all ages and sizes and I've met all kinds of boys and girls.' Quietly I offered thanks for the emphasis on practice at St. Andrew's. 'So don't make the mistake of thinking you'll be able to get away with bad behaviour.'

Two days later a couple of boys tried testing that statement and found I was prepared to supply proof with a forthright dressing down. Nearly three years later I was flattered when those two boys, shortly to leave school, saw me at an inter-school sports meeting. They dashed over and introduced themselves, saying they remembered me and the first few weeks in the life of that particular class, 2D. I was very touched and felt more strongly my regret that I never really knew my own first class group.

To me, October 12th 1948 felt remarkably similar to September 1st 1939, when I had walked out of home and on to school to be evacuated I knew not where. But there was a difference on this occasion because I knew precisely where I was going…well, the name of the place, at least, because it was on the rail warrant. RAF Padgate.

On the platform of the cavernous station, still very dingy because its entire glass roof was painted black in accordance with wartime restrictions, there were not a few young men going to the same venue. Standing apart and unusually quiet, we stood out sharply. My feelings were very mixed and no doubt others felt the same. I wasn't averse to joining the RAF; I'd thoroughly enjoyed years in the school squadron of the Air Training Corps, even being elevated to the rank of sergeant. What was irksome, however, was that I'd spent two years training to teach but at the moment of qualification I was being told I'd got to put my career on hold for another two years.

Never good at standing around, I mooched up and down the platform. In so doing I found Alisdair Sington who had been in my year at college. He was destined for the same address, so our journey became much less lonesome as we swopped anecdotes about all and sundry to mitigate our feelings of concern. The moment of walking through the smartly guarded gates of RAF Padgate seemed bizarre; a variously clad group clutching one suitcase apiece ambled along uncertainly. A loose crowd formed in the roadway outside the first building which, a notice proclaimed, was the Guardroom.

A uniformed sergeant walked out smartly and addressed us in level tones.

'I need to have you in a column of threes. Sort yourselves out, please.'

We shuffled into a reasonable semblance of the formation. Some were well acquainted with drill procedure, as I was, others hadn't a clue so were guided by fairly willing hands.

'Do your best to follow my commands, men,' advised the sergeant. 'Right turn, quick march. Left, right, left, right…' and we plodded off with a mixture of marching and walking towards a barrack hut where we halted with some inertia bumping. We were invited inside to see the kind of accommodation we were to live in for the duration of our service. Typically it comprised a bed, devoid of clothes or mattress and an upright steel locker. There were twenty such units in the hut.

Within a short space of time we collected bedclothes and three biscuits. The latter weren't the edible variety, they were squares which, placed side by side, served as mattresses. Solid, tough and very hardwearing, they looked uncomfortable. Nevertheless I never had any problems getting to sleep on them. We also experienced an Airman's Mess for the first time to sample lunch with its inevitable queues for the meal, for the tee urn, for taking plates to the washing section, then back outside to the scalding tank for dipping irons (jargon for knife fork and spoon, which were issue items, as was a mug) to clean, then to form up again and march off to be kitted out with uniform.

The first few days were unreal. What transpired was the conversion of hundreds of entrants per week into uniformed and slightly informed airmen. Elsewhere entrants *en masse* were also being inducted into the Army and, in far lesser numbers, the Royal Navy. Hair was cut in regulation fashion – a local barber benefitted enormously from his regular visits where his work was exceptionally speedy. Our civilian clothes were consigned to our suitcases which were concealed in our lockers and we were issued with all items of uniform. We attended a sort of lecture in which our still quite pleasant sergeant probed us for details of our education. These he recorded on a sheet on his desk. Then he said he had to leave for a few moments. Slightly nonplussed, we waited, then when he did not reappear, we reacted as typical schoolboys. We wandered about…and I wandered to his desk and looked at the sheet. I was intrigued to see the initials 'POM' beside a number of names, including mine. Also beside the names were our occupations if we had any. Beside mine I saw he'd written 'Schoolmarm'.

I grabbed my pencil and added a slight embellishment, the ubiquitous Chad with a note, 'Wot, no bun?'

Our sergeant finally returned and later I saw him laugh slightly when looking at the sheet. But some of us puzzled over 'POM'. Later, realisation dawned that he left the room deliberately to allow a degree of detecting initiative. The letters were finally resolved as Potential Officer Material. No NCO, however, appeared to have the slightest interest in telling us how such potential might be realised.

The one other major event in the week was the Jab. Irrespective of whether we had been vaccinated against smallpox as children, as I had and sported a one inch circular scar demonstrating the fact, everyone was vaccinated. I had no memory of my childhood occurrence, but allied to my tendency to faint in gory lectures I thoroughly disliked injections. I can pinpoint - pun intended – the cause. Aged seven I contracted scarlet fever and without warning found my bedroom invaded by men in uniform who wrapped me in a red blanket, carried me outside and into an ambulance and took me off to isolation in a fever hospital. There, soon after being ensconced in a bed in a large ward, two doctors arrived, seized both arms simultaneously and stuck needles into the underside of each, lifting the skin as they did so, repeating the action five times, ten in total. I had no idea they were doing this to test for allergies and at that age wouldn't have had a clue what an allergy was had they told me. But the memory of those needles stuck. Hence my queasiness when giving blood samples.

So I was worried about the possibility of fainting when we went on the jab parade. I found the event was in no way aimed at soothing the brows of weak characters like me. The complete entry was lined up in single files in a drill shed. This was a covered building open the full length of one side which enabled drill training to proceed uninterrupted by inclement weather. The jab parade procedure was simple and very clear. When all were assembled a command was given and the first file marched off towards a medical hut directly ahead. The company was then ordered to move one pace to the right, thus filling the gap. After some time the second file was ordered to march away...and so on.

There was a considerable number of files, so the time any individual waited depended upon his file's place in the queue. Mine started about two thirds away from the end so I had ample time to fail in allaying my fears.

I inhaled deeply. I wriggled my toes. I flexed my knees. I tried to look up under the roof to the sky and think of happy times rock climbing. Suddenly my mind switched back as there was a sort of scuffle nearby. Someone had indeed fainted. Then another, and another. These were carried out and laid on the grass in front of the company, then on recovery told to get back into line. Mentally I was joining them.

Then, suddenly, my file was near the operational end. A rapid order was given to remove uniform tops and roll up left sleeves, then we were off into the hut. We moved quickly in file to where five people were standing in a row. The first medical orderly swabbed my arm with a piece of wet cotton wool and threw it into a bin. The second dried the place with another swab and threw that away. The third spread a small amount of serum with a brush on the same place. The fourth was a Medical Officer holding a fat needle set in a cork. This he jabbed slightly into my arm. He didn't throw the needle away…he used it on everyone as far as I could see. The fifth orderly stood in front of a very large board on which hung a mass of crossed pieces of sticking plaster each holding a small piece of cotton wool. He slapped one of these on my arm…and I was out through the far door of the hut. I walked away, massively relieved, inwardly laughing at my fears. The next thing I knew I was lying on the grass, totally relaxed and unhurt. I jumped up, glad that no one had seen me, and wandered back to our billet.

The next worrying event was the Schick test, but I managed that despite ribald comments as to what happened at the event. We hadn't seen the name written, only heard it. An orderly met us at the medical hut holding a large chrome ear syringe and explained it was to be used for the injection. Some lads blanched as they fell for it, but I felt very superior having had my ears syringed a couple of times and did my best to reassure them… after a suitable delay. The test is for immunity or otherwise to diphtheria

After these affairs, medical inspection was a doddle. You just undressed to your pants, then got into a single line. An NCO informed us we would be examined by a Medical Officer. He arrived briskly, flanked by two orderlies. He gazed at the first man, pulled down his eyelids, opened his mouth and demanded the aaah sound, then said,

'Drop your pants.'

The lad pushed them down but held on to them.

'I said drop them!' came the sharp admonition. He complied. The MO looked along the line. 'Everyone do as you're told when I examine you.' He returned his gaze to the first victim, stared at his genitals, put two fingers at the side of his scrotum and said 'Cough'. He then walked behind the man, prodded his back, came back to the front and said, 'Passed'. One of the scribes wrote on his clipboard.

So he proceeded along the line. We all passed. No one was diagnosed with VD, which was what it was all about. The fact that I knew about venereal disease had nothing to do with Doc at college and certainly not first aid at school. I'd learned it from detailed notices which were posted throughout all toilets on all RAF stations we went to for camps with the ATC during the war.

After the week's initiation the intake was divided between four camps for basic training lasting eight weeks: West Kirby, Wilmslow, Bridgnorth and Padgate itself, to which I was sent, so my transfer involved nothing more than a march of about a quarter of a mile. It was memorable because for the first time we were in the hands of Drill Instructors, characters who wore flat caps with shining black peaks pulled low over their eyes so you couldn't see what they were thinking. Nevertheless you knew because they told you in one of three tones - loud, very loud and extremely loud. The last was favoured most of the time.

Once there we were assigned to Flights. Nothing to do with flying, of course, merely a description of groupings occupying one hut apiece. I joined 14 Flight as did Alisdair Sington. We found our lives were laid out in a detailed programme, week by week, for the ensuing two months. Although each flight contained a cross section of late teenagers, nevertheless in ours there was a fair sprinkling of qualified teachers. Largely this did not please our DIs, who lived with us day and night. They seemed to feel inferior whenever a conversation extended beyond a barked order. They varied, of course. Ours seemed to adopt the principle that in the matter of Service knowledge, drill and length of career he had a distinct edge which was certainly so. Within a week or so we looked upon him with some respect. Having got a flight with above average potential he was determined it would appear so in the final parade competition and we were happy to support him.

So life became a round of drill, physical training (exercises on the drill square), lectures in RAF procedure (learning to recognise officer rank emblems, followed by aircraft recognition), use of rifles (how to clean, dismantle, reassemble and offer for inspection on parade), cross country running on Wednesday afternoons (which throughout the Service was Sports Afternoon, made up for by working on Saturday mornings until noon). We learnt how to fold bedding for daily inspection, lay out full kit for inspection and clean the hut for inspection. In the latter case there was a competition for the best hut, the winners of which would get a 36 hour pass to be used at a weekend before any of the others. I'd heard ridiculous tales about washing coal in the hut bunker, blacking the stove and freezing because no one dared light the thing, brass polishing the metal round electric light bulbs…then found these weren't ridiculous at all.

We were also taken to the firing range. Not only were we given rifles we were also taught how to fire them. In that I held an advantage because at school our ATC squadron had taken part in inter-squadron competitions on RAF stations. Amongst activities such as drill, PT, aircraft recognition, morse transmitting, there was always shooting. As it happened I appeared to have a natural flair for this and helped our squadron win a cup occasionally. So I was able to demonstrate my prowess once again and collected an RAF marksman's certificate. I still have it, though I've never fired a rifle since. I also collected a dormant hearing problem from never having any form of ear protection either at school or in the RAF. .303 rifles made quite a noise close to one's ear. But in those days protection was dismissed as something for namby pambys. No one asked for ear muffs at Alamein or on D Day, did they? In the fullness of time my problem has become less dormant.

We also learned about, and had experience of, guard duty: the typical sentry box stuff. The system was quite simple. You were on duty from 18.00 to 06.00 hours. You marched out to a sentry box where you stayed for two hours, then you marched back to the guardroom where you relaxed for four hours as much as you could in a place that seemed to have something going on all the time. The only time it was reasonably quiet was in the small hours, so we soon found it was impossible to get more than three and a half hours sleep that night. You actually guarded for two spells of two hours, so it wasn't too bad. Nevertheless it did seem absolutely ridiculous to have to challenge anyone arriving during the night at a rear gate with the classic admonition, 'Halt, who goes there?' and shoving your rifle forward in the appropriate aggressive gesture After receiving an answer you were supposed to ask them to advance and be recognised and to show you their papers.

Officers, of course, chose to use any entrance except the main one after dark, so the hapless guardsman usually found himself challenging a receding shadow as the entrant walked through totally ignoring protocol. Occasionally one was kind enough to wish us good night over his shoulder. Because we guarded in pairs, in the event of a suspicious event one was supposed to remain whilst the other hared off to alert the guardroom and the real guards, the Military Police. This would have taken some time from one gate because it was nearly half a mile away. During this piece of training I found my only worry was recognising the rank of officers. Lower ones were accorded a butt salute; for this you slapped your right arm across your body on to the butt of your rifle carried over your left shoulder. Higher ones merited a present arms, which I'm sure you've seen ranks of guardsmen doing on ceremonial parade, though it has changed somewhat over the years because Lee Enfield rifles have gone out of fashion. I never discovered how you spotted an officer's rank in the dark. In fact, of course, anyone could have walked in with a touch of acting ability.

After three weeks Alisdair Sington asked me whether I'd gained a Proficiency Certificate in the ATC. I said I had. He then told me such qualified people could have their basic training reduced by two weeks. I hadn't heard of this, but he said he was going to apply and implored me to join him. The attraction was that in so doing we would complete our basic training by Christmas when everyone would go on leave. We would not have to return to Padgate because we would then be posted to our next station. That alone swung my view, because once I'd settled in I almost enjoyed 14 Flight. I was even Deputy Senior Man. I came to regret my decision.

We applied. Not having been asked about this the powers-that-be looked at regulations and found it buried somewhere. Alisdair had discovered it from a family member who'd been in the RAF. Having no reason to deny us, we were given permission, so both of us took up our possessions and transferred to the hut of 16 Flight who were two weeks ahead. I have to say they made us welcome. They regarded us as beings from another planet because we had worked around an apparently fixed system of training by dates.

16 Flight was well advanced in drill, but that was no problem to either Alisdair or me. What we hadn't banked on, however, was missing opportunities given on days set into the eight week scheme. One of these was interviews for POMs. Not that any such event was announced, or appeared on a schedule that we trainees could see. We were told each day what we would be doing. In Flight 16 we were informed that day had already passed for them. So Alisdair and I protested and asked to be allowed interviews. I even wrote to the Principal at St Andrew's asking for a reference aimed accordingly because someone said that sort of document helped POMs. We received a curt response that we should have thought what we might miss before we applied to transfer. We decided not to suggest we couldn't think of something we knew nothing about. Nevertheless it rankled and both of us were to do something about it later on.

Irrespective of whatever camp he was posted to Alisdair kept pushing to be considered. Finally he was told he would be given an opportunity. He was to entertain two officers for a weekend based at a London hotel, expenses paid, to assess his fitness for officer training. He did so and spent a very sticky weekend acceding to their varied requests, entertaining them conversationally at mealtimes and generally being their dogsbody. At the conclusion they said he would be informed of the decision. He was turned down. No doubt they enjoyed their free weekend regarded as work. Alisdair relieved his frustration in a letter to me.

What we did get with 16 Flight was the day when decisions had to be made about our postings to other stations. This implied selecting jobs, because the next move would be for trade training. In looking at the list available to conscripts – soon to be National Servicemen – the one we latched on was in the Education Branch. This involved teacher training – again – and becoming sergeants after a mere eight weeks. Obviously this was the thing for all us qualified teachers. I thought at least it would be a good second best for a POM.

Ah, they said, unfortunately the course is full at present. Understandable, we thought, there's a lot of us about, so what do you suggest? Ah, choose another trade, doesn't matter which, then as soon as there are vacancies on the course you'll be sent for. Fair enough, seems reasonable, we said…

How naïve could we be? But at the time we hadn't learnt how Service bureaucracy worked, so Alisdair and I looked for a trade that trained at a station nearest to home. Thus we decided to become Airframe Assistants, training for which was at RAF Cosford. We had both taken Craft at college, so perhaps similar skills would be involved. We'd also made lots of model aeroplanes, hadn't we?

One event in our basic training particularly stands out in my memory because I couldn't believe what I was seeing – or rather not seeing. We were marched out on to a drab field on a wet November morning with distant clinging mist. Patches of long grass flattened by recent rain were overlaid in places with wisps of dead grass left from desultory summer haymaking. Two very shallow channels crossed the space, hardly disturbing the surface, no doubt for drainage. We were informed we were to have training in camouflage.

Smiles spread around. The chances for concealment in this landscape were nil, we felt. It was just another of those events you had to go through because it was all laid down. Six lads were selected, the rest of us, rifles in hand as ever, were lined up across one end of the field and turned away from the open space, and adjured not to look round. Two NCOs ensured we did not. The others, we were told, would conceal the six snipers. We would then turn round, advance slowly in line and challenge at any point where we thought someone was concealed.

I imagined we would soon spot six lumps of disturbed dead grass, rather as one did when playing hide and seek with young children on summer days. We got the order to turn and gazed in raw astonishment. Everything seemed exactly as before. Then we got the order to walk slowly forward.

Absolutely determined to spot at least one concealed body I glared from side to side as I moved. I'm sure most of the others did the same. Yet as we crossed the open ground not a single challenge pierced the dripping air. Finally we were told to halt. I felt sure there was a catch somewhere. Perhaps they hadn't been hidden for some as yet inexplicable reason. Then we were told to turn round. We did so and still the field seemed devoid of human life. After a salutary tirade of ridicule directed at us, the concealed lads were told to stand up. Each did so, shaking off quite small amounts of grass from places over which we had walked. By chance no one had trodden on one, but had that occurred it would have demonstrated even more strongly how inept we were at penetrating the simplest camouflage. What made this all the more amazing was that we were wearing normal beige fatigue overalls, and certainly the snipers had nothing smeared on their faces. I think we all realised that had that been for real we would have been picked off with ease. We marched off duly chastened about the seriousness of some training exercises and with enhanced respect for the skill of our battle hardened NCOs.

Immediately after our passing out parade, at which 16 Flight did rather well, we collected our rail warrants for Christmas leave and paraded for our posting papers. Boringly name after name was called out, papers were taken and the recipients made a dash for the gates and the railway station. Then only a few were left.

'Trust mine to be last,' I thought.

But I was wrong. Mine wasn't there at all. The NCO distributing the documents looked nonplussed as he and I faced one another.

'What's your name, airman?' I gave it, and my full number rather than the usual last three digits. He scanned the list. 'You're not on it.'

It was urgent I also dashed for the train and home. 'What do I do after leave?'

He wanted to get away as well. 'Report back here to Pool Flight.'

'What do I do then?'

'I dunno. Ask someone in Records in Station HQ.' He disappeared rapidly. Kitted up, everything dismantled in our billet, HQ closed, railway warrant in hand, I shrugged my shoulders and dashed off to the train which I caught by the skin of my teeth. On it Alisdair commiserated with me.

'What did he tell you to do?'

'Report back to Pool Flight.'

'Hell, that's awful!'

'I know.' We all did. Pool Flight was an odd assortment of weirdos that did various odd jobs around the camp. Who or what the members were was never openly discussed. 'Never mind, I'll worry about that after Christmas. I wonder how long they'll take to call us for Education Branch training.'

'Only a month, I should think.'

We were still babes in arms in Service know-how!

Christmas was absolutely great that year. The family, church, the weather, civilian clothes again, much better bed, super food despite rationing - which was getting worse, they said. But two things niggled. One was the Berlin Airlift, the other was my impending return to Pool Flight with concern about why I hadn't been posted. I confess the latter loomed larger, though neither I nor anyone else ignored the former.

In the international posturing following the end of the war, Stalin, having been allowed to capture Berlin, decided he wasn't going to put up with the four power division of that city which mirrored the setup in the whole of Germany. Berlin was well inside the Russian sector which meant that supplies to the English, French and American parts of Berlin had to be sent through it by road and rail. So, expecting the other three powers to knuckle under rather than risk armed confrontation, he closed all overland routes to Berlin and awaited the expected outcome; full Russian control of the city.

The only alternative route was the aerial one. Tentatively supplies were flown in using the good old transport workhorse, the DC3. This was successful to an extent and soon a steady flow of these aircraft flew in and out round the clock. However, no matter how many were used it soon became apparent that demand far outstripped the maximum possible supply. Soon the danger of starvation was a very real threat to Berliners of whatever nationality. No doubt Stalin did the arithmetic as well, and sat back awaiting the inevitable.

Much bigger planes were available in large numbers because they had been trundling in and out of Germany with increasingly large bomb loads until very recently. The snag was the size of the runway in Berlin's Tempelhof airport. To enlarge it needed brilliant logistical planning to supply the materials and a massive labour force. Both were forthcoming; the first provided by the Allies, the second by the close-to-starving Berliners. The result was that airlift logistics gradually became weighted on the side of the Allies who then demonstrated they would go on flying in supplies for ever and a day if necessary. So, finally, Stalin blinked. Although forcing him to back down precipitated the Cold War, nevertheless it showed that appeasement wasn't the best way to respond to bullying tactics. If only the powers-that-be had taken the same attitude versus Hitler in the thirties!

But during the Airlift confrontation no one could foresee the outcome and there were many who thought it would beget the Third World War. Had that been so, those of us then in the Forces would have been looking at a much longer time in uniform and, no doubt, far more action. The airlift operated from June 1948 to the end of May 1949, so at home on my first leave for Christmas 1948 I was unsure about how long my time in the RAF would be. Stalin was a long way from blinking.

After the festivities I returned to Pool Flight and saw a different side to RAF planning than my experience of the highly organised basic training. Or rather, I didn't see, because there was absolutely no planning about Pool Flight. I knew the billet where the individuals comprising the Flight lived, so I wandered to it. It was mid afternoon and a few lonely souls were lying on beds. In marked contrast to the spick and span billets I'd been used to, where bull was the order of the day – and night – Pool Flight billet was disgraceful. I asked one lad, about my age, who was in charge.

'No one. We like it that way.'
'What, no NCO?'
'Nope'
'What do you do here?'
'Anything we're told in the morning.'
'Who tells you?

'The Admin WO'

'When does he do that?

'On parade. We go on the square at oh nine hundred.'

'What duties do you get?

'Anything they want. Cookhouse usually.'

'Why are you in the Flight?'

'Medical. They're wondering whether to chuck me out.'

'What's wrong…oh, never mind. Do I just pick any vacant bed?'

'Yeah.'

Feeling very despondent I did so. I then took myself off to the stores to collect bedding. Another lad about my age was on the issue side of the counter. As he slapped biscuits, blankets and sheets on it, I explained why I needed them.

'Pool Flight? Bloody hell, that's the sink.'

'I think you're right.'

'Why are you there, mate?'

'I haven't a clue. When everyone in our Flight was given postings after basic training there wasn't one for me. No one seemed to know about me, and HQ was closed. I'm going to ask them about it all to-morrow.'

'Cor,' came the response. 'If they've lost your papers you could just hop it. Wish they'd do that for me.'

Laughing at the suggestion I walked off clutching my bedding. But as I made up the bed in the dismal and not at all clean barrack hut, the thought returned. It was to resurface a few more times during the next few weeks.

I suppose that night was the worst I spent in the RAF. Looking back it wasn't all that bad, but I was certainly cheesed off. The members of the Flight were a disparate bunch, sent there for one reason or another, mainly medical but some verging on the mental. It was simply a holding Flight for misfits. Whilst the wheels were put in motion – wherever they were hidden – to decide what to do with each individual, everyone was employed on any necessary odd jobs. The cookhouse had regular needs, not for cooking but for washing up. When I joined the single file parade next day, wearing drab fatigue overalls as instructed by everyone else in the hut and collected from the room at the end,

I soon found that was the norm. The Warrant Officer General Duties– WO GD for short – merely counted a number and we were off. He took not the slightest notice of there being a new face in the sparse ranks.

In the cookhouse I'd seen men on the dirty dishes counter grabbing the returned plates, thumping them over a gaping hole to remove uneaten food, then stacking the plates in a large wooden rack and pushing it beyond the heavy leather flap that concealed the automatic washing machine. That was simply a very strong shower bath of very hot water. At the other end the plates were grabbed again, as they cooled they were returned to racks for re-use. I'd wondered who the people were who did this unpleasant chore. Now I found out.

There were two shifts. The first began at 06.00 hours and finished at 14.00, the second overlapped, from 12.00 to 20.00 because midday was the busiest time. After a few shifts clothes and boots became sodden from the washer and the buckets of water we had to slosh over the concrete floor afterwards and mop clean. The only drying facility was the stove in the billet and in January people got near that, not clothes. These were slung over chairs near it when we went to bed, but the fire died down. You weren't allowed to keep it going all night; austerity and all that.

Of course I went to HQ at the earliest opportunity. In the enquiry office I explained my predicament. The orderly clerk told me to wait. I did so and sat down. He was away for a good ten minutes. Then he returned.

'Give me your 1250.' This was your personal document, your ID, which you were supposed to carry at all times. I handed it over. He disappeared again. After another ten minutes he reappeared.

'Mm, this is odd. I can't find your records at all.'

The notion of disappearing through the gate never to return floated in my consciousness, but dissolved rapidly because I'd alerted him to my physical presence even if I didn't exist as far as the RAF knew.

I threw him an explanation and told him about two of us moving between Flights 14 and 16. I also explained that had caused no problem for A/C2 Sington, A.

'Ah, that must be it,' he said, relieved, and disappeared again. After an even longer delay he returned with a fixed expression.

'OK, that's fixed.'

'You mean I'll now get a posting for trade training, then be called for Education Branch training?'

He looked blank. 'Yes, I imagine so.'

Thinking of the cookhouse, I pushed him. 'Please, can you make sure I'm on a list for posting to Cosford?'

'OK.'

'Can you do that now?'

'Oh no, it'll take some time.'

'How long?' I urged.

'Some weeks, but you can come back in a couple of weeks and ask where you are on the posting list.'

I realised my stay in Pool Flight was going to be extended. I could see there was nothing more I could do then and there, but I took him at his word and returned every few days. I was beginning to see how the bureaucracy worked.

Occasionally the motley collection of oddities comprising Pool Flight had to march somewhere and when this rare event occurred a miniscule character took charge. He stood no more than 5'3" but filled his uniform very adequately. He also possessed a most adequate pair of lungs and could shout and bawl every bit as well as the training flights drill instructors. In an idle moment I enquired his reason for being assigned to Pool Flight.

'Awaiting posting for DI Training.'

'Ah,' I said, 'and getting into practice with us lot.'

'Yep, and I get any other job they need doing. Last week I took a bloke to the glasshouse.'

'Where's that?'

'Colchester. The RAF uses the Army place there.'

Surveying the tiny but well proportioned form of AC Ashe I tried to envisage him taking charge of a hefty man who'd fallen foul of Service law to a serious extent all the way from Padgate to Colchester, but couldn't quite conceptualize the scene.

'Didn't he try to escape…?'

The miniature form of AC Ashe exploded. 'Not f***f***likely. No one puts f***anything on me.' His transformation into a dervish was instantaneous and complete. I realised he had more than a streak of venom in his character. Probably someone had been unsure of his ability to exercise self control and so he was drafted to Pool Flight for observation.

But he had an unsuspected vein of humour. One day he came into the barrack hut grinning widely and responded to the obvious question.

'They gave me a bunch of WAAFs for PT. They hadn't got anyone else for some reason. Told me to take 'em out on the drill square.'

I formed a vision of the someone who was indeed testing AC Ashe's self-control. The drill square was the most public space on the camp.

'What did you actually do with them?' I ventured.

'Usual stuff, like we all do. Four lines, jumping together, feet astride, arms out, back in. I just walked round yelling out the time.'

Knowing the kind of yelling we received in training in similar circumstances, I couldn't resist pressing him as to his calls.

'Left titty, right titty, double titty, BOUNCE. They quite enjoyed it...'

I assumed that would be the last I'd ever hear of him, but it was not. Seven years later when I was on the staff of a secondary school a colleague and I reminisced about our days in the RAF. He was two years younger so had joined up that much later. I enquired whether drill training had changed much and found it had not. Then he said,

'We had one absolute devil of a DI, little chap, I'll never forget him. Corporal Ashe. Cor, he was a cruel sod.' Obviously he successfully beat the system to get his desired niche.

One freezing day, clad in my smelly and dirty overalls, I walked past the drill square and watched 14 Flight on their passing out parade. They were brilliant. From the unusual number of officers clustered on the small saluting base in the distance I guessed they were being shown off. I experienced a longing to be with them – everyone enjoys being part of team success. Then I laughed inwardly as a very fussy Warrant Officer marching alongside, barking quite unnecessary urging to improve posture, slipped and fell on the ice. He leapt to his feet too quickly and fell again. He even managed the trick a third time. Mentally I complimented my erstwhile companions on keeping straight faces.

After three weeks my clothes were as sodden from cookhouse chores as were my spirits. Then one day I paraded in a pair of boots that were dry. These were my square bashers – the ones you slaved over to get beautiful shiny toecaps with much spit and polish and anything else you could get away with. Mine weren't at all comfortable, but they were dry. So I appeared on parade in my wet and mildewy overalls beneath which gleaming toecaps shone obtrusively. For once something about me caught the WO's eye. He turned to his orderly.

'There's a man who takes care of his boots. Give him a job in the Wing Office. Parade, dismiss.'

The orderly approached. 'You'll like this, much better than the cookhouse. Any good with paperwork, you know, writing letters and so on?'

'Yes, er, actually I'm a qualified teacher. Did advanced English at college…'

'What the f* * *are you doing in Pool Flight?'

I explained. He was delighted at having someone else in his office with some literate skills. He suggested I got rid of my overalls, which I did with alacrity, and returned wearing my uncomfortable, saviour boots. Never had I loved them more.

The orderly explained he was the Leave Clerk. All applications for leave came through him. Each week he had to organise all the leave request chits for the WO to sign. All permanent staff on the Wing were allowed 36 hour passes every weekend unless they were on guard duty but they all had allowances of a number of 48 hour passes and other leave entitlement each year. His job was to keep all necessary records.

'So it's dead easy for me to slip in a 48 hour pass request of my own into the pile each week. I've been doing it for months. The WO always signs them. The office isn't open on a Saturday and he isn't here either, so no one is any the wiser. I'll put one in for you each week as well.'

I admit this minor piece of nefarious activity appealed. I'd been able to escape Pool Flight most Saturday afternoons and

Sundays because everyone was free then, though we were on a rota for duty weekends, but the charms of post war Manchester in the winter soon palled. I had nowhere to stay outside camp and certainly couldn't afford even a modest guesthouse even if I could find one. I knew what some people got up to each weekend but I had no intention of embarking on those activities.

The world suddenly seemed a happier place. Each morning I went to work in an office. It was clean and didn't smell. Everyone was friendly. The work was amazingly simple. With a weekend 48 hour pass I could leave after work on Friday and get a train home, returning on Sunday evening. Even the Pool Flight billet didn't seem so dirty and unkempt. I can live with this,I thought. Maybe I'll stop chasing up HQ for my posting.

Two days later I saw my posting was on Station Orders. At least I enjoyed one gash weekend at home.

Chapter 18

RAF Cosford was a smart station, as it is to-day where it houses the RAF Museum on an active airfield. I went to be trained as an Airframe Assistant for the reason I've mentioned. I was sure my stay would not be long; I'd spent six weeks in Pool Flight at Padgate whilst they found my records. Surely a vacancy would soon arise for the Education Sergeants course and they would post me again?

Had I given the matter a scrap of thought I could have worked out the logistics. All stations had one Education Officer assisted by one Education Sergeant. Because all stations more or less had their complement, vacancies on stations would occur very gradually. Demand, therefore, would be a very few replacements a month, perhaps slightly more if you took overseas stations into account. But candidates for training were two a penny because of the fact that all teacher training colleges had turned out qualified teachers that year, running well into four figures, virtually all of whom were on deferment. No doubt quite a proportion had opted for the RAF. So the idea of there being a queue from which candidates would be taken in turn was ridiculous. Most were simply side-lined, as I was.

As with basic training, trade training was very well structured over eight weeks. We were taught various aspects of metalwork, especially relating to aluminium. Much of it I've found useful in home DIY over the years for which I'm duly grateful.

We learned other important skills, such as how to stitch tears in fabric covered wings because such planes were still flying, notably the Tiger Moth. I had met this excellent aircraft on previous occasions. The first was on the sands near Rhyl in 1933 when one, or rather its pilot, offered flights along the coast for five shillings a time. My father took me, despite the extremely expensive cost!

We flew along the coast, waved to mother sitting in isolation on the prom at Prestatyn, turned round and flew back.

The second flight was rather more exciting, though I was unprepared for the thrill. On a day's ATC flight experience at Elmdon airfield – much later to enlarge into Birmingham International – we were handed over to a pilot with a Tiger Moth. He told me, as the cadet in charge, to strap a lad into the rear cockpit. Both are completely open, of course. This involved ensuring a strap came up between the legs from its anchor point below the seat and ensuring the two shoulder straps came over tightly, with their chrome rimmed eyelets placed over a strong pin on the leg strap and a large retaining pin inserted to ensure the straps couldn't come away. He didn't supervise me at all because he remained in the front cockpit with the engine running. Nonchalantly I watched the plane take off and do a simple circuit of the airfield. Instead of landing as I expected, it then went into a steep climb, which went up and up, then got even steeper. Finally to my horror it completed a tight loop, dived down, landed and taxied back across the grass to our group.

'Next!' yelled the pilot over the noise of the engine. I extricated a rather pale faced cadet and fitted the next one in, taking an age over the straps.

'Hurry up!' yelled the pilot. Finally I backed away, crossing my fingers and watched the plane repeat the flight and manoeuvre We all asked the first lad what it was like and were assured that, after the first moment of shock, it wasn't too bad because you are wedged in the seat by centrifugal force. I was greatly relieved.

Finally, after everyone had flown, I clambered in, strapped myself in reasonably contentedly, silently blessing Newton and his laws of motion, the first especially. We took off, flew around the field, then the pilot called over the very simple intercom,

'How are you feeling?'

'Fine, thanks.'

'We'll soon alter that,' was his response. I waited for the climb. Then suddenly the plane rolled sideways…and kept rolling until it was inverted. Centrifugal force does not operate in such a circumstance and I hung in the straps. As we rolled I grabbed anything I could and my first fingers of each hand extended along two very thin wooden strips running along the cockpit. As a hold, of course, it was absolutely useless. My cheeks fell upwards towards the earth which I could see above me.

'OK?' asked the pilot. I managed a strangled grunt from somewhere in my throat which was nowhere near its usual place.

'Good,' he replied and continued the inverted flying exercise.

Later an officer asked me how the boys had enjoyed their flying experience. I said it had indeed been an experience.

'I'm pleased about that. That pilot has rather a reputation. We all call him 'Crash' because of the number of kites he's wrecked. He's been reduced to simple flying activities.'

What price Health and Safety Acts? Or supervision of young people? Had any such considerations been operative we would never have had the chance to boast about our experience for the rest of our lives. So I had an affinity of sorts with Tiger Moths and determined I would patch carefully any wounds they might suffer.

The Commanding Officer of the training unit was rather akin to a headteacher. He had a number of officers in charge of sections, like heads of departments, who in their turn had subject teachers. These, we discovered, were civilians and some indeed were qualified teachers. So we had a different teacher each week as we progressed through the subjects. We had both written and practical tests at the end of each week and the results were posted on boards for all to see. Our progress, therefore, was carefully monitored.

The CO also circulated a book and invited anyone who wished to make any comments about any aspect of the course to write notes therein. At first we all ignored it, so a blank book was returned to him. This, he let it be known, was a pity as courses could only improve through responses by those taking part. After the fourth week I noted a fairly obvious point for comment in the marking system. Everyone's marks for that week were much lower than previously, yet we knew that wasn't because we had all performed less well. It was due to the simple fact that the week four teacher marked more stringently than the others. It happens everywhere when marking systems aren't moderated. Popular television shows demonstrate this very well. Strictly Come

Dancing comes to mind, though subjecting the judges to the procedure would lessen the mayhem and hence the programme's appeal.

So after week four I contributed a small essay on mark moderation, suggesting that were the process to be activated, course members would have a better standard with which to assess their week by week process. In the present instance, I pointed out, an individual couldn't accurately assess whether his week four mark meant he really had performed worse in that subject.

After a few days I was asked to review the response in the book. Someone assumed that I was niggled because my week four mark was lower than for those preceding. Because I had reviewed everyone's marks I realised they hadn't got my message, so I wrote a much longer essay in reply, with aggregated marks for each week, demonstrating the drop for week four.

A few days later I was ordered to go to an office in HQ. There I was told by an NCO to wait outside a door, then, with no further explanation, told to go inside. The room was full of officers, seated, caps on their laps, facing the bareheaded CO at his desk. Momentarily caught on a very large hop, I pulled off my cap. The CO was charming and told me to sit on a vacant chair where all eyes were upon me. He then asked me explain the points I'd written, which I did. I was pleased to see he accepted the notion. I agreed it wasn't easy to get a number of people to use the same mark spread on a scale. He thanked me and told me to wait, then dismissed the officers. Each in turn put on his cap, walked smartly to the front of the COs desk, saluted, smartly turned right and walked out of the room. Whether it was an exercise in protocol for me I couldn't guess, but I got the message. When just the CO and I were left he asked me what I did in civilian life. When I told him he threw his arms in the air, laughed, and said he had absolutely no idea I was a teacher. He had no reason to, of course. For a split second I wondered whether to broach the subject of a posting to train for the Education Branch, but chickened out. I did manage to put on my cap, walk smartly to his desk, turn, salute, turn and walk smartly out.

I've no idea whether an attempt was made to moderate marks across the weeks after that, but most of us continued at about the same individual standards for our remaining stay. Then we reached the final practical test which we took individually with an NCO from another part of the station. We understood that based on the results and our performance over the next six months, our ranks – and therefore our pay – would be confirmed at Aircraftsman Second Class (AC2), as we all were, or elevated to AC1 or even Leading Aircraftman (LAC).

The NCO giving me my test seemed to ask a range of questions that had no connection with anything we had done on the course. He took me to a display of tubes and other devices which seemed the kind of things that went into aircraft engines. There was a separate course on the station for Engine Assistants. In a panic I was about to ask him whether he realised I was on the Airframe course. Then he took me to a piece of fabric covered wing and asked me to stitch up a tear and cover it with the regulation dope. At least I managed that well.

Afterwards we exchanged views on the practical. I said mine was awful. A friend said he'd overheard one of our NCOs say to my examiner, 'Grill him.' The result of my grilling was medium; I passed as AC1-to-be. No one became LAC. Cheaper? Or am I being cynical?

I was posted to RAF Brize Norton, another station that has a long and continuing history. To-day it has an excellent website and has been featured in television programmes. Then it was surrounded by pleasant farming country with a small village outside where many of the permanent staff lived. It was part of Transport Command, having been transferred to it from Training Command at the end of 1945. More accurately it was a development unit for the Command and was an interesting place to be during the wonderful summer of 1949. I went there in spring and was delighted to be assigned to quarters in real buildings, constructed just before the war. They were spacious and airy.

I soon made friends with various other young men. I had relinquished my teenage years whilst enjoying my brief spell in the Wing Office at Padgate. There were quite a few in the billet who were intelligent and out to make the best of their conscript years. Occupying the next bed to me was Ken Steerman, almost the same age as me. We became firm friends for the duration of my stay.

Because its *raison d'être* was development, many interesting aerial projects were being tried and tested. The ambience penetrated the entire station, so life became reasonably easy going. Parades were few; duty rotas the same. The working day was 09.00 to 17.00, beyond which time was our own. The working environment was one of the large hangars into which aircraft of various sizes were pulled by tractor, or simply manhandled if they were small enough. Mainly they came for routine inspections. These were undertaken in increasing depth depending upon the number of hours flown. The range was from a short check after each flight to a 1200 hour service when virtually everything was taken to pieces, examined, renewed where necessary, then reassembled.

All aircraft have two main parts, the airframe and the engine(s). The people who worked on these were Airframe or Engine Fitters. They were assisted by the appropriate Assistants, i.e. the recently designated National Servicemen. Us. We couldn't become fitters…unless we signed on permanently and made the RAF a career. So there was obvious class distinction, especially so because many of the career men had been through part or all of the war. They were also older and more mature. We, however, were more numerous – greatly so.

Our trade training had been good so I soon found I could undertake the jobs that came my way – unscrewing panels, screwing them back again, sweeping up, collecting items from stores for the fitters, cleaning up oil spills, helping to open the huge hangar doors by shoving with many other shoulders whilst someone wound a handle…largely our work was a matter of odd jobs with little responsibility. So it came as quite a shock when I first joined in the rota as Duty Crew.

The hangars, obviously, were close to the perimeter track of the airfield. Near our hangar was the control tower and near its base was a very small wooden hut. This was the abode of the two people designated Duty Crew for the day. With remarkably little further instruction beyond what we'd had on trade training, in turn we spent a day on this duty which was interesting, certainly responsible and, at times, quite hairy. On my first day with another tyro I wandered out to the hut and tentatively opened the door.

'If you can hear this, come outside and give a thumbs up sign,' a voice proclaimed. We identified the source as a small tannoy inside. I obliged the voice as requested.

'Put on the yellow jackets,' came the next instruction. These were on hooks, so again we obliged and looked hopefully up at the control tower.

'Now come through the door into the tower, come up the stairs and wait.' Again we followed the instruction and found ourselves looking at a panoramic view of the field, an array of instrument panels and busy operators. For a time we were ignored, then an officer turned and demanded,

'Have you been Duty Crew before?' We assured him we had not.

'That's what I was told. Did you have the duties explained on your training?' We assured him we had.

'Good. The bats are in the hut. Whenever we want you to park a kite we'll call you. Each time give the thumbs up when you've heard the instruction. Off you go.'

He turned back to his desk and we pottered down the stairs and into our small garden shed and waited. We rehearsed to one another the simple bat signals required. Held out side by side horizontally bat faces towards the aircraft, then pulled up and over each side of your head and repeated signified Approach Me. Then, when the pilot of the taxying plane has seen you, go quickly to where you want him to turn the aircraft, point either the left or right bat towards one wheel and wave the other from a widely outstretched arm back over your head and repeat to signal Turn. When the plane has turned sufficiently and you want it to move forwards again, extend the bats in front of you and pull them up over your head. Walk backwards doing this if necessary until the plane is where you want it. Then cross the bats over your head to signal Stop. Then draw one arm across your throat to signal Cut

Engines. All quite simple…in a lecture room. Suddenly we felt the weight of responsibilty. This was no odd job.

Only one crew member was required for each plane, so we tossed to decide who would bat first. I lost. Suddenly the tannoy crackled.

'There's a Lancaster coming in. Park it on the grass to the right of the control tower. Let me see you've heard this.'

I grabbed the bats and shot outside. A sixth sense made me wonder whether he meant right of the control tower from his point of view or from the pilot's when his plane was facing it. So I stuck one thumb in the air and pointed to the right hand side from his view. I was relieved to hear the tannoy crackle,

'You've got it, airman.'

I turned hurriedly but there was no aircraft in sight, nor could I hear one. I gazed skywards, then picked up a very slight drone. We'd been alerted well in advance. In due course the aircraft landed and turned at the end of the runway. Incredibly it seemed to be looking for something…someone…and awareness hit me. Bats, wave, I'm here, here, look… Then even more incredibly the plane seemed to spot me and came trundling in my direction.

I knew Lancasters were large. In the ATC I'd sat in the tail gunner's turret of one on the ground and turned to look at the wide metal road that was the top of the fuselage stretching away into the distance. But the thing bearing down on me at that moment was gigantic and it wanted me to tell it what to do next. I then realised the obvious. You had to judge how far to let the plane move down its track before you indicated a turn because its wingspread seemed much greater face on. So it would be easy to let it over or undershoot. On this first occasion, fortunately, there were no other parked planes, so I had the field to myself. All I had to do was judge when to turn it to finish on the right of the control tower.

I managed it without mishap or bungle. When the engines cut, which seemed to have nothing to do with my signal, I realised I was now quite superfluous, so I wandered back to the hut. I flopped, sweating, on to a chair.

'Seemed OK,' said my pal nonchalantly.

'Phew!' I replied. I've never forgotten the tingling sensation I experienced that first occasion when a vast Lancaster obeyed my signals…well, the pilot anyway. He could have been an Air Chief Marshall… Actually he was a Squadron Leader.

We spent much time servicing two aircraft, a four engined Hastings and a twin engined Valetta that were being prepared for a good will tour of India. One or two such events were organised at the behest of the government. This one was to visit the country a year after Independence. Exactly what it entailed was not explained to we lowly characters, but we did a great deal of maintenance and refitting. To be accurate, the fitters did the fitting and we fetched, held and handed them the tools, and cleaned and swept up.

One evening in the billet Ken asked me if I fancied going to the gym for a spot of exercise. Every station had its gymnasium, usually staffed by one physical training instructor, a corporal PTI. For a few weeks we weren't getting the normal Wednesday sports afternoon due to timetabled work in the hangars, so I agreed. This was well before the time when you went to a gym to use apparatus. That, for us, was wall bars, a beam or two, a medicine ball to lift, or a football to kick around. But on this occasion the PTI greeted us with a suggestion. Would we like to learn to play badminton? Further than that, would we find a few more men who would like to do the same? He'd just received some new kit and he'd like to see it used.

Neither of us had played before, though in my case I had pranced about tennis courts imagining I could play that game. There were public courts in a park near my home which I had used occasionally. Those at college were relaid and marked out three weeks before we left. Then after parting from Kim I had collected another girlfriend who played for the County Junior Team and who, by bashing me all over the court, demonstrated very well that I wasn't much good at the game. But I'd never even seen a badminton court.

We cajoled a few more from our billet to join us and the PTI duly explained the court and the rules, then demonstrated how to play shots using a flick of the wrist rather than a sweep of the arm as in tennis. After a few evenings we began to get the hang of the game and rather enjoyed it, albeit at a very modest level. The PTI then announced we needed practice playing against people who had a touch more experience. He said he'd fix up a match for us. We assumed he would rope in some other men from the station.

Six of us went to the gym on the appointed evening and were pleasantly surprised to be introduced to some attractive civilian ladies. Flattered, Ken and I were invited to play the first doubles match. One of us served, tentatively, and all hell broke loose. We were chased and battered all over the place by our highly skilled opponents who smashed the shuttlecock very hard. Occasionally we won a point, more by luck than skill. At the end of the game, very shamefacedly, we apologised and said we needed more practice, pointing out we'd only learned recently.

'Oh yes, we know. We did rather put you through the mill. But then we are the Oxfordshire County Team. We've been playing for years.'

We rounded on our PTI but he'd disappeared. Some time later, after we had all suffered the same fate, he arrived with some coffee.

'All good practice, men,' was his sole comment. We felt murderous. Nevertheless, he was right and gradually we became quite proficient. Over the years I put the skill to good use in forming school badminton clubs. Early on we couldn't have painted lines on hall floors - far too expensive - so I became adept at chalking out a court with fairly straight lines before each session. Chalk was cheap.

I found I was to be on Duty Crew one Sunday and detailed unusually to be there at 07.00 hours. Enquiries revealed a Wing Commander was taking an Auster on a flight. Due the pilot's eminence, I was informed I would be partnered by a career corporal, so I knew my role was to look smart and salute at the right time and keep quiet. Other ground crew had prepared and fuelled the plane which we found on the grass in front of the control tower. We stood ready for the Winco's appearance. A small red sports car zoomed around the corner of the hangar, pulled up and parked beside the con tower. Clad in civvies the driver got out, lugged a golf bag and clubs from the rear seat, pulled an integral sheet across to the windscreen and fastened it. Shouldering the clubs he strode towards the plane. We saluted.

'Good morning, Corporal,' he answered. It was not done to return salutes when not in uniform, hence the response. 'Put these in the kite.' He handed over the clubs to the corporal who opened a door under the wing of the Auster and put them behind the pilot's seat. The Winco did the usual visual check of the aircraft – waggling the flaps, peering underneath at the wheels, and so forth. Then he stepped up into the pilot's seat.

To start a single engined plane such as an Auster required a simple procedure which we learned during our Cosford course. The corporal followed the rigmarole.

'Switches off, sir? The pilot looked at his instrument panel.

'Switches off.'

'Sucking in, sir,' said the corporal who then seized the screw, aka the propeller, with both hands and rotated it two or three times. The Auster's propeller had two blades. The procedure ensured fuel was drawn into the engine, but it was necessary to ensure the starter switch and others were in the 'off' position otherwise the engine might fire precipitately which would not do the man at the sharp end any good at all. I attempted to smile knowledgeably but actually did no such thing. I knew I wasn't needed until later. When this was done the corporal called,

'Ready to start, sir?'

'Ready to start,' came the reply.

'Switches on, sir.'

'Switches on.'

At this point the corporal correctly moved to a position to swing the propeller. Like other aircraft of its ilk the Auster had no self-starter, so the ground crew man had to swing the propeller just as you did starting a car with a handle when necessary, which was not infrequent in those days. Just as you had to make sure a sudden kick back on the handle didn't damage your thumb or any other part, so you had to swing the prop with one hand, employing a sort of underarm bowling action, moving with it and away rather smartly. Usually this took two or three goes, then the engine coughed and decided to co-operate.

There was one other, vital, point you needed to observe - the direction the propeller would turn when the engine was running. Like fan blades they are shaped to force air backwards. It might be thought that all aircraft propellers would turn in the same direction. Most did, but the Auster was perverse. It's designer decreed it should turn in the opposite direction to most aircraft. This meant that you swung with the opposite hand and arm compared to normal. Actually you tell by looking at the leading edge of the propeller blades because they have to cut into the air.

I expected the corporal to grab one blade with the correct hand, yell 'Contact' and bowl away. Had he swung the propeller with the wrong hand and had it kicked, it would very likely have bashed his arm severely as it swung back. Or even worse.

Fortunately I mentally switched on marginally ahead of the engine.

'Corporal,' I yelled and, equally fortunately he stopped, turned and glared at me.

'What do you...' But I dashed to his side and whispered. 'Auster screw goes in the opposite direction.'

Momentarily he looked hard at the propeller, rolled his eyes, changed hands and swung. The engine burst into life first go despite the fact that its preliminary sucking in routine must have been in reverse. The Winco set off for his round of golf.

'Thanks, lad. I haven't been close to an Auster in years. Completely forgot.'

'Well, I've not been that close to one at all, but it was one of the odd things I remembered from training a few weeks ago.'

Next day in the billet I recounted the episode for the amusement of whoever was around listening. Ken laughed.

'I know all about Austers. I've got one.'

He was rewarded with blank stares.

'You've what?' I ventured.

'Got an Auster. Actually it's my father's – he bought it. But I've got the pilot's licence.'

We clustered around, hardly believing.

'When did you get that?' someone asked.

'A few months before I was called up. It's kept at Southend Flying Club. It's being hired out whilst I'm in the RAF. I go down and fly it some weekends; it's not too far from where I live in London.'

Most of us found there were convenient ways to get home each weekend. In my case someone in Station HQ organised a coach to my city and someone else did the same to London, so on a Saturday we took whatever we needed for home, usually our washing, down to the hangar. At precisely 12.00 noon when someone rang the dismissal bell we sprinted madly for the main gate and the waiting coaches. Ours reached the centre by 14.00 and with luck I was home eating a meal mother kept warm for me by 14.30. Then we reassembled in the centre at 23.00 on Sunday, reached camp by 01.00 and were in bed by 01.30. The London mob didn't make it until 02.30 but I rarely heard them.

There were two elements which contrived not to make it quite as comfortable as it sounds. I mentioned coach but that's far too polite. It was a very ramshackle affair but at least it was reliable. The yawning return journey couldn't be eased by sleep because we were jammed into upright positions on small, hard seats. Occasionally I managed a few moments' doze with my head in my hands, elbows on case on my lap, but frequent lurches – the driver drove at a creditable speed – negated the effort. The other problem was walking round in a daze throughout Monday. One had to be careful not to mess up anything important.

After some weeks Ken and I invited each other to our homes for exchange weekends. So I had the great thrill of being entertained in his large and very well appointed house. His father had a very successful cycle business. He drove us along the A12 to Southend, where Ken duly took him and me for a flight over Southend with its famous long pier in his Auster. Someone else swung the prop for him.

Ken then visited our very pleasant but rather smaller house. Instead of a flight he came to church in the evening with our family which was our normal routine. The only excitement we were able to offer was a totally unexpected four inches of snow on the Sunday morning, despite it being May. But in those tough days four inches was nothing. It didn't stop buses, nor our coach. They didn't clear the roads, either, just fitted chains on wheels. Anyway, that day it soon turned to rain

News of Ken's qualification soon permeated the hangar – and beyond. No doubt intrigued by having an ordinary aircraftman with a pilot's licence in the camp, one of the officers sought him out in the hangar. The permanent NCOs bristled, but said nothing. The officer asked Ken whether he would have a go at flying his Tiger Moth, to which Ken delightedly agreed, saying however that he hadn't flown one very often. Assured that would be no problem as it had dual controls, Ken was kitted out and walked out with the officer and aplomb. The NCOs bristled some more. This wrecked the natural hierarchy. There were the commissioned ranks, the non-commissioned ranks, the ordinary airmen who formed the groundcrew, backbone of every flying station, and the lowest of the low, the conscripts, glorified with the new title of National Servicemen. They were at the bottom of an extensive ladder and were not expected to be very bright. They were certainly not expected to be pilots. The World Turned Upside Down indeed.

To his great annoyance a nasty cross wind chose the wrong moment to blow across the field as Ken came into land and he had to relinquish control to his superior officer. No doubt news of that mollified the permanent men slightly.

Many years later I saw Ken again – on a television news clip. A Boeing Superfortress was flown into Germany for some kind of ceremony, being the first occasion one had done so since the massive daylight air raids visited upon the country by the American Air Force. Briefly I glimpsed the pilot and recognised the older but still familiar figure of Ken. Obviously he had upgraded from Austers and Tiger Moths.

One fine morning with a blue sky dotted with contrasting cumulonimbus clouds building into glistening white towers, a few of us were detailed for an airtest flight. This was considered one of the perks of our work. After every service an aircraft was flown on an airtest to check whether it worked properly. To ensure that those carrying out the service had also worked properly all such personnel were required to go on the airtest flight. It was effective natural discipline. We took off and I enjoyed watching as we weaved in and out of pristine white valleys and over mountain tops glistening in sunlight. The aircraft having survived for an hour following our ministrations upon it, we landed. As another lad and I were walking back to the hangar a sergeant hailed us and invited us to join another flight going to Belfast that afternoon. Some days were like that. They balanced those that were not. We grabbed lunch and ran down having also, as regulations required, grabbed parachutes again and shot into the waiting aircraft.

We learned we were accompanying a Lancaster that had arrived recently with a highly unusual excrescence on its belly. This was a kind of large bright aluminium box fixed to it approximately where the bomb bay is housed, giving the effect of a weird pregnancy. We had no idea what this contained but it contrasted sharply with the camouflage elsewhere. It aroused a degree of notoriety in the camp. It was now being flown to Short Brothers, located in Belfast and we were in the plane detailed to bring back the Lancaster's crew. So I spent the afternoon in the air. I found it particularly appealing because the pilot flew over Snowdonia and I was shortly to go rock climbing there on 'Whitsun Grant' leave. Actually it was really scrambling, but you couldn't climb Tryfan without using your hands occasionally. At least that's what I found when I climbed it first the previous Whitsun during the last term at college. We flew directly above the mountain still in glorious sunshine. It looked very rocky from above but much more dumpy, as George Borrow called it when he walked through Snowdonia to write 'Wild Wales'. I say *through* accurately because he did the forty miles from Cerrig y Druiddion to Bangor in one day, fortified solely by cheese and ale.

We then dropped to about a hundred feet and skimmed the waves at an impressive speed, then climbed again to pass the southern tip of the Isle of Man at a respectable height. Then we skimmed low again over Strangford Lough and landed at Belfast, more or less as you do to-day. Then, however, the facilities were rather less.

We two very ordinary airmen hung about the very ordinary café to which everyone had gone, wondering why we had been asked to join the flight. Actually we never discovered. But whilst I was hovering, holding a cup of tea and a bun, trying to keep out of the way of officers and civilian businessmen animatedly talking, someone half knocked my shoulder as he passed. I looked up to see a broad shouldered back clad in a sports jacket walking steadily away. An officer must have noticed my look.

'Any idea who that man is?' he asked.

'No sir.'

'Douglas Bader.'

He didn't have to explain further. For years afterwards I traded on the fact that I'd rubbed shoulders with Douggie Bader. Many years later I was invited to be a guest at a ceremony where he was to present awards to Craft Apprentices at a research station, some of whom had been to the school of which I was headteacher. I thought about telling him of the time I had almost met him. Alas, he died before the event.

Early on D-Day, 6th June 1944, many personnel travelled to their key zones in large Horsa gliders towed, usually, by the good old workhorse the DC3, universally known as the Dakota. A number had set off from Brize Norton. So it was logical to use the station for further experiments with such gliders. Most airborne landings during the war involved a write-off of the gliders. Someone, somewhere, wondered whether in some circumstances it might be useful to recover any undamaged gliders complete with the troops.

It was comparatively easy to fill gliders with men, attach a towrope to an aircraft and then belt down the runway at full power and wait for the wonderful power of lift to elevate both aircraft and glider. All you needed was a long runway – a mile or more. But gliders going into a war zone don't always land conveniently on airfields, unless such happen to be their targets. What about open grassy spaces? Those are usually favoured for landings. Could gliders be picked up again?

A mechanism was needed for snatching the glider off the ground. As an experiment a Dakota was fitted with a large, exceptionally strong and extremely well attached hook which protruded well below the fuselage. The next requirement was a cable on the glider which could be caught by the hook on the aircraft in flight. Newton's first Law of Motion comes into play at this point, the one about inertia, i.e. a body in motion or at rest tends to stay like that unless operated upon by a sufficiently large force. I doubt he'll object to my paraphrase. The glider would experience a highly significant jerk from its state of rest, whilst the plane would suffer equally when it met the resistance of the stationary glider. The third law, you remember, is the one that says any applied force meets an equal and opposite force.

Some genius worked out an ingenious solution – as he would. The tow-rope from the glider was to be a very large loop. From the glider's nose it was extended forward and outwards, then placed over two poles set a fair distance apart so the cable then extended across the intervening space in a taut line. From above the cable looked like a triangle with the nose of the glider at the point of one angle and the poles at each of the other two.

The aircraft would then zoom in low, hook beneath, hopefully avoid slashing open the glider's roof, then catch the cable extended between the poles. These would fall apart, the cable would quickly close into a double strand and when taut would pull the glider along and into the air behind its abductor.

To mount this operation successfully needs practice; this was undertaken frequently during one fine fortnight at Brize Norton. The position of the posts, the strength and elasticity of the cable, the shape of the triangle, the weight of the glider, all had to be tested. Pilots had to practise aiming to catch the cable without any possibility of being able to see their hook. Some men wittily, if crudely, described it as trying to investigate a certain part of one's anatomy which requires a rear view. Doing something like that at a couple of hundred miles an hour swooping over a stationary glider, ready to slap on full power at a particular split second showed how skilful they had to be.

The effect upon the glider was not acceleration from zero to two hundred in a second or so. As the cable first tightened it was catapulted forward, but momentarily the impetus slackened because the glider partially overtook the stretching force in the cable, thus lessening the strain. Then it shot forward again as the pulling force took over once more. The effect was a quick start, a brief slowdown, then a rapidly increasing pull as it became airborne.

The predatory Dakota circled the airfield day after day as different pilots practised their skills. Occasionally men were detailed to sit in the glider to make things truly realistic. They came back with grins or pale faces having experienced a novel form of funfair ride. Some said the landing was more violent than take off. Neither did much for the state of the airfield grass.

At this point I insert a note that in 2013 I saw an old documentary film which showed an early attempt in 1945 to pick up a glider from a jungle clearing. The glider cables were slung on simple poles designed to collapse when pickup occurred. The Dakota sported a trailing cable on the end of which the hook was attached. The Dakota had to land the cable on the static cross cable, enabling it to slide until the hook connected. So what transpired at Brize Norton was obviously Phase 2.

A Dakota was used for other experiments. Dropping things out of aircraft is sometimes necessary to supply men on the ground where use of parachutes is not recommended, such as jungles. Aiming a parachute at a small clearing is tricky and likely to result in hapless recipients having to shin up trees to rescue stuff from 'chutes caught in branches. Jungle trees tend to be tall and climbing them is best left to monkeys. So many experiments were conducted just dropping things.

Sacks containing various kinds of white powder were favoured. It wasn't revealed exactly what the powders were but they were supposed to represent flour. Because rationing was getting tighter, much worse than during the war, and bread was rationed for some years, I doubt normal flour was used. Probably it was duff stuff that had become contaminated and therefore unfit for human consumption which is what you tried to avoid eating during the rationed years. Strangely, old tyres were another favourite - for dropping, not eating. These tended to fall upright, given a few moments in the air. Then they bounced spectacularly and hopped, skipped and jumped around the airfield. It was not a good idea to get in their way.

A Dakota was adapted for these exercises. Obviously things to be dropped had to be stacked inside and someone had to throw them out. The side door was removed to assist this process which meant air rushed by. Some rushed in as well producing a sucking effect, so it wasn't a good idea to stagger over to the door space holding a heavy sack or a tyre, otherwise the exercise would include testing the dropping effect on a falling airman. To avoid this unintended addition a very clear curved white line was painted on the floor and men were adjured not to cross it on pain of death, obviously. So you held on to bits of the plane's structure and kicked things out. The Dakota didn't have a nice smooth fuselage inside so there were plenty of handholds.

I imagine that someone, somewhere, produced masses of data from these experiments, such as height/strength-of-bag/weight-of-bag/speed-of-aircraft   wind-weather/skill-of-pilot   ratios. I wonder if the results came into their own in the Korean War which was in the pipeline we call history - when we've passed along it.

The easy going ambience of the station no doubt emanated from the Commanding Officer, a Group Captain, though very ordinary airmen such as we didn't meet such eminence. Very rarely there was a parade and we saluted him. If we ever thought about it we were grateful to him for making our lives pleasant. One day we had even greater reason to thank him. The occasion was a Transport Command Sports Day.

I had learned from such events at my schools as well as college that I had no skills in athletics. I enjoyed cross country running so long as there was no competitive element in it. Running across the countryside was pleasant – full stop. But other men had excellent athletic skills so there were a number representing the station at the event which was being held at another one not very far away. The CO decided our people needed support. He could, of course, have called for volunteers who would have the day off and sent them by road. But he did not.

I imagine something of the man could be seen in the varied aerial experiments undertaken at the station. Certainly it was revealed in the way he ensured adequate support for the Brize Norton representatives at the Command Sports. Leaving just the essential minimum, he airlifted the entire station to watch and support. We yelled, hollered and cheered both our team and our CO!

Dakotas played quite a part in our work at BZ. We serviced them and flew on airtests in them and watched them in their experimental antics. But one in particular we came to know very well. By we I mean Ken, me, and two other guys. One day a rather sorry looking Dakota ambled shyly near the control tower giving every indication of being embarrassed by its appearance, just as you wouldn't want to gaze at yourself in the mirror if you had measles. Of course, it didn't have measles but it certainly had a nasty skin condition. Someone had sprayed it but the process had gone wrong. The result was a dull grey film of rough paint, as though sand had got into the mix. Furthermore it was patchy. In places the paint had come off leaving the original metal. But there weren't many clean patches. We looked at it, sympathised and walked away grieving for its plight.

By some strange quirk of telepathy a sergeant picked up these vibes and suggested we try to do something to assist the forlorn kite. Like rubbing off the duff paint. We commiserated but felt that nothing on earth would remove it short of a miracle. We should have realised we were lining ourselves up to supply the miracle.

It so happened there were plenty of very large tins of metal polish in the stores. By big I mean gallon tins. There were dozens of them. Someone had grossly overestimated the number of buttons requiring polishing on the station. Rags, also, were plentiful it seemed, so armed with these necessities we tried rubbing a small part of the Dakota. After an extensive period so engaged, followed by a lesser amount of polishing, the offending rough grey paint disappeared and gleaming, sparkling aluminium was revealed in its pristine glory. I have to say we were impressed. So was the sergeant.

'Great, lads,' he enthused. 'Carry on.'

We did, for many days. The weather was glorious. We stripped to the waist and revelled in it. To be fair, no one pushed us to finish in a particular time. In fact our work attracted quite a lot of attention as various people wandered along to see the gradual emergence of a very sparkling aircraft, the like of which had certainly not been seen before. Despite the effort expended we also became very proud of the result. We certainly followed the sergeant's admonition and carried on right to the end.

I have no idea whether someone, somewhere, planned the *dénoument*. It was so unexpected that I believe it was, though achieving it would have taken real Machiavellian scheming. An Anson of the King's Flight arrived with due ceremony and a duty crew member, no doubt as instructed, parked it near the control tower next to our Dakota. King's Flight aircraft were *au naturelle* and were supposed to have gleaming skin.

Talk about putting something in the shade! That's exactly where the Anson appeared to be, with our Dak vastly outshining it. The King wasn't in it of course. Probably it had called just to pass on a diplomatic bag, or refuel, or some such fiddling reason. In any event it left quite soon – but not before a number of smirking officers had walked past it and its temporary gleaming companion.

Weeks rolled into months that spring and summer as our pleasant, easy going life settled into routine. Five and a half days not very taxing work each week, home for much of the weekend, very few duties, plenty of badminton, even a spot of cricket on the airfield on summer evenings and plenty of intelligent conversation in the billet. Kings' Regulations, which governed every aspect of life in the Forces, stated you could discuss anything except politics and religion, so we discussed religion and politics. Given the result of the 1945 election and the importance of the Forces' vote in that tidal race of change, plenty of men and women discussed politics throughout the Services.

Gradually my impatience waiting for a posting for education training eased. I passed the date when I could expect to be in the RAF for just a year more, given reasonable quiet on the international scene. Simultaneously Stalin blinked so tension generated by the highly successful Berlin airlift eased. I decided I could stick with the life I had.

Suddenly that life changed. Brize Norton bade farewell to Transport Command and welcomed Training Command – or rather the station was welcomed back into it where it had been years before. That meant pilot training in training aircraft; single seater affairs as a step to combat fighters. Quite a number of these were to be flown in with an attendant number of pilots on courses, with associated support personnel and all their equipment…the list of changes entailed was very extensive. Also training meant people had to be kept up to the mark - and that meant bull* * *.

We all knew what that involved. Parades. End of laid back life. We knew the extent of the change-to-come when a new Station Warrant Officer appeared on the scene, set up his office and roamed the station to assess what he saw. It was obvious he didn't like it.

The Station WO was the key man in disciplinary matters. The previous one had taken his cue from the CO. This one didn't. Or perhaps the new CO agreed there had to be changes. However parades at 08.00 hours became the norm. We had to walk smartly wherever we went. Ambling was out. There were billet inspections at random.

Life changed in the hangar as well. In place of varied aircraft of all shapes and sizes there was now a considerable number of small, single engine dual seat trainers. Their arrival had meant to impress and it succeeded. We watched a squadron of nine fly round the airfield in a vee formation, then they crossed it and one slipped sideways, rolled, circled half the field and came into land. It was quickly followed by a second, and third…until they all landed in a close line. As the first reached the end of the runway it turned on to the perimeter track, followed by the others in a tight line. As the first neared the control tower it turned neatly and pulled up facing the hangers, followed by the others in turn which stopped alongside it, all engines still running. Then, simultaneously, all engines stopped. It was an impressive show. There wasn't a duty crewman in sight.

We, of course, were to be involved in servicing the busy bees. It was immediately obvious that schedules would be tight and work would increase exponentially. We then met Sergeant Robinson, W, who was to organize the schedules. Quickly he installed a very large and long blackboard on one wall of the office we had regarded as our lounge where we ate and drank when on tea breaks, or read when there was nothing to do. It remained as such but there were no longer times when there was nothing to do.

Sergeant Robinson was, in fact, most pleasant and courteous, and thoroughly organised. He quickly interviewed all of us. In so doing he found I was a teacher.

'Marvellous, Flaxton. You can keep the board records up-to-date. You should be able to do that neatly.'

The Eleventh Commandment again! I agreed I could, then wondered what else I would be doing. He soon assured me it would be a full time job. We recorded the reference numbers of all the aircraft across the top. In a vertical column down the left hand edge we wrote the names of every possible form of service they could undergo, mostly hours flown. With the help of the largest pieces of straight edged strips of aluminium I could find I carefully painted masses of thin vertical and horizontal dividing lines. As detailed I collected packets of coloured chalk from stores and plenty of clean rags. Sergeant Robinson then inducted me into the arcana of aircraft logbooks and the groundcrew logbooks of services into which everyone who did anything on an aircraft had to record what he'd done and when and sign it. Entries had to be countersigned by whichever NCO was in charge of whatever was done and the matching aircraft logbook had to be updated. The state of what was happening at any one time for that aircraft had to be displayed on the board in whichever colour we decided was to be used for whatever. I soon realised I was going to be busy as there were usually about twenty-five aircraft in action or being attended to.

Once again I was quite content with the work, in fact rather more so because time passed quickly as I was fully occupied. But one evening I went down to the Education Section. This was a single hut with a lecture room where everyone occasionally went for a lecture on whatever was deemed necessary to improve our general knowledge. The staff comprised the single Education Officer and his assistant, the single Educational Sergeant. There were also displays of posters, pamphlets, and a small library. If you wanted a book for study they could get one quite quickly from the main RAF library housed as I knew, but had not been able to visit, at Cosford.

I can't remember how the conversation developed but at one point, when talking casually to the EO, I mentioned I was a teacher and originally hoped to go on the course to become an ES, but it had been full. I said I had naïvely imagined they really would call me when vacancies occurred.

'They've got vacancies now. I heard that recently. The supply of trained teachers has dried up with the introduction of

National Service, because now everyone comes into the Forces immediately after school, if they stay into the sixth form that is. Anyone wanting to teach would have to do that, of course. If you still want to try for a posting I'll enquire whether they would take you.'

Suddenly my dormant ambition resurfaced and I agreed. Given that I now had less than a year to complete if all went to plan, I didn't really expect any result. However, shortly afterwards I was told I had to attend an interview at Command HQ in deepest Lincolnshire. This was to be with a Group Captain and I was suitably impressed. It was booked for a few days ahead so I was further impressed by the speed of the accomplishment.

I rather expected Training Command HQ to be an impressive, modern, spick and span station, so I was taken aback to find it was largely housed in a series of Nissen huts – the kind that had corrugated completely curved roofs and really were scattered deeply throughout a wood. No doubt a result of being on the eastern side of the country during the war when it was useful to remain hidden. I found the hut to which I was summoned, checked the nameplate on the door, knocked politely and heard a warm and very friendly voice say, 'Come in.' Obviously an orderly, I thought. I opened the door to find a man in civvies sitting behind a desk. Ah, they have civvy clerks here, I thought again.

Most senior officers of such a rank, seeing an airman attending for interview, wandering in without saluting would have given a blistering dressing down. But not this man. He smiled benignly and invited me to sit down, which I did.

'AC Flaxton, isn't it?' he enquired equally benignly.

'Er, yes sir, er…' I latched on to the fact that this was the Group Captain and I'm sure reddened at my blunder. A fleeting thought raced through my brain. Forget the sergeants' course, you idiot.

He couldn't have been more pleasant. In fact, when I gave him details of school and college and the reason for my love/hate relationship with Latin, it transpired he had a son almost exactly my age in similar circumstances. So we simply gelled. It was a very pleasant interview at the end of which he said he wouldn't promise anything but he would see what he could do. He told me where I could get a cup of tea and something to eat, then brought matters to a close. I put on my cap, saluted, he wished me well and I left.

Back in the billet at BZ I recounted the day's events to Ken. 'It was a very enjoyable day out. I'm sure they won't do anything but at least I can always say I did chase up the chance.' I also reported back to the EO.

A couple of weeks later whilst on a step ladder inscribing details on the aircraft serviceability board I overheard Sergeant Robinson say to someone, 'You'll have to take over here because Flaxton's posted.' And I was. To RAF Wellesbourne Mountford, hiding in another arboreal setting near Stratford on Avon. It housed a WAAF Photographers' Course and the Education Sergeants' Course; a cosy serendipity.

Chapter 19

The eight week course, typically, was very well organised. For me, also typically, it began inauspiciously. Having found the right billet, collected bedding, bagged a bed and started filling my locker, general chatter spread around all the other newcomers. They had all come from one of the four basic training camps so, with the first week's initiation added in they had nine weeks service behind them. Inevitably I was asked which camp I'd come from and responded, 'Brize Norton'. In a very short time my bed space was surrounded and I was effectively holding court, giving accounts of my experiences as a very ordinary airman on an extraordinary station. It was patently obvious I was an oddity.

Suddenly a furious figure pushed into the group, rounded on a bemused lad and yelled in a broad Scots accent,

'We don't want your sort 'ere. You f***well shut up, d'ye 'ear, f***big 'ead?'

He pushed away equally quickly and disappeared into the NCO's room at the end of the hut. This was our first introduction to Sergeant Forsyth who was our NCO-in-charge.

Everyone looked stunned. I stood up and said, 'I think that was intended for me. I'll go and put it right.' I went to the Sergeant's room, knocked and responded to his yell, 'Come in.'

'I think what you said in there was intended for me, Sergeant. Let me say I've no intention of being bigheaded. I'm both surprised and pleased to be posted to the course. The lads in there were just interested because I've been in the RAF longer than they have.'

He gave me a thorough look from head to toe, turned away and muttered, 'Yeah, well, we've never 'ad anyone 'cept from basic training. I don't like it. Go on.' By which he meant get out which I did. Outside I quietly shrugged my shoulders at my new companions and carried on making up my bed.

Some time later, Sergeant Forsyth emerged from his den and stood facing down the hut and boomed, 'By your beds.' We obliged in the correct manner, standing to attention at the foot of our beds. He wandered up and down, giving a typical NCO's introduction to new recruits which, translated, meant I'm the boss, you depend on me, I can make your life awful hell or marginally less awful hell; which it's to be is up to you. As he strode out he dug me in the ribs and ordered, 'You're wanted at Station HQ. Get down there double quick.'

I complied, wondering who wanted me there so soon. Once there it was apparent the Officer i/c Education Sergeants' Course wanted me. In a remarkably small and narrow office he stated bluntly that Sergeant Forsyth had pointed out where I had come from, that such a posting must have been a mistake, that no one ever came to the course except direct from basic training and, furthermore, he would arrange for me to sent back to Brize Norton asap. Peremptorily dismissed, I pottered back to the hut where I explained that my stay was going to be cut very short and I would be returning whence I came.

Part of me was sorry, part glad. The former grieved over loss of potential status, the latter pleased that I would not have to revert to the overbearing bull that is heaped on all recruits on all courses to keep them in their places. The new training ambience at BZ was tighter but not as bad as I guessed this course would be. *C'est la vie*, I thought.

On parade next morning I was again ordered to the Course CO's office. Farewell, three stripes, I thought. But I was wrong.

'Flaxton,' he said in carefully controlled tones, 'I've been informed your posting came from the Air Ministry and therefore it cannot be rescinded. You have to carry on here. I suggest you don't brag about your previous experience.'

'Sir, I have no intention of bragging. Yesterday the other men in the billet were naturally interested to hear I'd been on an active airfield. I'd hoped to be posted here after basic training and in fact was promised...'

'Alright, never mind your potted history. Just make sure you toe the line here.'

I assured him I would and left his presence. I can't remember ever seeing him again. Sergeant Forsyth didn't appear very often either. Our entry was taken over by another Scot, physically twice his size. Corporal McBride was truly great in every sense and therefore highly popular. Shortly after I returned to the billet the men were invited to elect their Senior Man. I suppose they decided there was no contest. So I collected the job of marching the flight everywhere, a chore I knew well from ATC days and winning drill competitions in inter-squadron rivalries. Because the camp was small and sparsely populated I must have become a fairly familiar figure as our group marched all over it.

So from having my records lost and almost becoming a non-person I moved to being the subject of an Air Ministry posting. My favourite Lincolnshire Group Captain must have carried weight somewhere. The guys that conceal it best are the nicest ones!

The course was very enjoyable. The intake carried a fair depth of intelligence and good education, so discussions were stimulating and courteous. Much reminded me of college and the practice of teaching. Our targets were to be the cross section of men comprising the bulk of personnel on stations here and overseas which, increasingly, were National Servicemen. These would either have left school at fifteen, the new leaving age, and taken jobs for two years prior to call-up at seventeen, or if they were in the small minority that entered grammar and public school sixth forms, they joined up at eighteen. Either way they were teenagers. Given that National Service was fixed at two years from January 1st 1949. most would be demobbed still in their teens.

On most RAF stations it was pretty obvious the Education Sergeant would be a National Serviceman, the Education Officer most likely a career man. However, as in the country at large, education was certainly not the key concern it is to-day. From the government's point of view the education that mattered was that of the small percentage who went to public schools, plus good grammar schools (yes, there was a hierarchy) and on to decent universities, i.e. Oxbridge and the second level of well established redbrick, led by London. From this small section the higher echelons of the Civil Service were populated and members of the government drawn. In the late forties some outstanding exceptions made it to ministerial level, notably Ernest Bevin, the Foreign Secretary, who left school aged nine in 1890, but he was a rarity.

So education was not in the mainstream of activites in the RAF. That was reflected in the comparatively low key ambience of RAF Wellesborne Mountford at the time. On a website to-day its history records its vital wartime activity, then mentions it being home to the School of Photography from 1948. This was where WAAFs were trained as we were well aware. The history then records it being home to the School of Education from 1950 to 1952. In 1949 the courses such as ours weren't dignified by being in such an organisation, but perhaps they were the beginning, because, just as in the whole country, education grew greatly throughout the second half of the century. We may have been one small acorn.

Of the eight weeks, one forever stands out in my memory. As with all stations you took turns in duty rotas of one sort or another – guard duty, cookhouse fatigues, fire picket, etc. On training courses these were emphasized to ensure trainees got the message they were important. This one, though, was ridiculous. It lasted for seven days, or rather nights. Each day you followed the normal training schedule, then from 18.00 to 06.00 the next morning you were based in the guardroom and divided into shifts taking guard for two hours, followed by four hours off. This meant any one person did two shifts exactly as I'd experienced at Padgate. But there was only one break when it was possible to get some sleep no matter which slots you were on. You couldn't make up a bed before 23.00 and you had to strip it by 05.00. So it was only in your one four hour break in the small hours that you could sleep. Realistically this was reduced to three and a half hours.

We started on Monday night. Most coped reasonably for two nights and days, but by Thursday concentration in the classrooms was woozy and by Friday we were zombies. The problem was exacerbated because the duty involved walking about the camp throughout your two hours – and there was a schedule of places where you to had to be at specified times. There was always the danger of being checked upon. Neither dared you sit down lest you nodded off. Our hearts went out to the memory of those poor wretches caught sleeping on duty in the First World War trenches and the death penalty they suffered.

Saturday provided some relief because we were free after noon. The billet became unusually quiet until an alarm roused everyone and we trooped off to the guardroom again at 18.00. The same occurred on Sunday when blissfully we slept throughout the day, but we did need to eat. The torture concluded at 06.00 on Monday, though again we faced a day in the classroom, or practising drills, or PT. For weeks afterwards we felt we never recovered our lost sleep. It was also obvious that, on each course, there was much more sickness following each week's guard duty. It would have been a simple matter to spread the days, or rather the nights, between all courses thus ensuring far better mental and physical well being.

Plodding round about 02.30 one cold black morning, I remembered an anecdote told me by an uncle who had been an officer in the trenches in the 1914-18 war. One night, as the sole Duty Officer, he was inspecting guarded posts and came across one sentry wedged in a standing position but obviously asleep. He couldn't just wake him; the man would then know what he'd done and that a Duty Officer had to report him. Neither would my uncle do that because of the appalling consequences. The man, of course, was wearing the regulation steel helmet, so my uncle went back round a corner of the mud wall, picked up a stone, lobbed it at the man's helmet, ducked out of sight, then walked round to face him.

'All quiet?' he asked.

'All quiet, sir,' came the reply from a very wide awake guard.

My uncle was Mentioned in Dispatches, but not for that piece of humanity. Subsequently he became Principal of a Minister's Training College. Of course he never knew whether the man guessed what had happened, but I bet he never fell asleep on guard duty again.

One element of training caused surprise when it was announced. We were given instructions on keeping bar accounts in the Sergeants' Mess. We knew that's where we were headed but most of us hadn't realised that in most Messes the chore of serving at the bar was subject to a duty rota. There was no facility for ordinary ranks to buy alcoholic drinks on a station. For them a visit to the local pub in the evening, if there was one, was the norm. But for officers and NCOs there were organised Messes where drinks were available at controlled times. They were also social centres with a considerable degree of autonomy. The lot of corporals varied. Some stations had separate Messes for them but they tended to be pale shadows of those of the sergeants. Actually, sergeant was the lowest rank of the members who included Flight Sergeants and Warrant Officers.

Finally the days approached when we met final tests and exams. The marks from these were added to regular assessments made by Corporal McBride and his fellows throughout our training. Before the results were announced we had a group photograph taken. It was a dull November day as the print shows well. I still have it.

One other event took place shortly before the end of our course. The WAAF Photographers Course lasted much longer than ours - eighteen weeks. The members were a pleasant addition to the station scenery but we had little opportunity to meet them. There was no social centre on site and the local village was quite a walk away. We also had a fair amount of evening study. The weather was cold and frequently wet, so social activity with these young girls was almost nil. Some of us found it possible to reach the Shakespeare Memorial Theatre and get standing tickets on the day which we did on a number of evenings. But even when we found WAAFs with shared interest in Shakespeare, a standing ticket has its limitations.

By luck, one WAAF course reached its conclusion simultaneously with ours. They had to celebrate a very long time under training and, we understood, were going to do so as thoroughly as possible. A large empty room became available and they made valiant efforts to decorate it. Cash was pooled, theirs and ours, and refreshments collected. Music was arranged

– a gramophone, of course, and records. Somewhere some alcohol was stashed and distributed surreptitiously on the night. It was a pleasant, totally innocent evening. I try to imagine the comparison between it and a likely similar event to-day, but fail. It was a different age; different even from wartime when inhibitions were flung aside in the knowledge that shortly you might be dead. The tight post war austerity squeeze dampened such occasions in and out of the Forces.

Nevertheless there was one girl, the daughter of a senior Army officer, who was voracious but her appetite was not for food. She got wilder as the evening progressed and whenever she kissed, which she did frequently, she all but swallowed heads. I wonder where she went after the party. Some of us felt we knew why Daddy allowed her to become a lowly WAAF – permanently.

The announcement of our final results was a shock. I had assumed that all seventeen of us would pass but seven did not. They disappeared rapidly from the billet so our euphoria was tempered for a while. They gave results as an order of merit and I'm still amazed, given my original welcome by Sergeant Forsyth and the Course CO that I was first. I have no idea whether my result was reported back to my Lincolnshire Groupy but I felt I'd confirmed his trust in me. But I wonder where my placement would have been had they known I'd inadvertently marched the flight past a man in civvies with his dog early one morning. Too late I realised he was the Station CO and I didn't give the order to salute. Both he and his dog were very understanding so the news didn't get around. He also was a Group Captain. They seemed a pleasant bunch.

The last two days were surreal. The graduates were officially Acting Sergeants, but we were informed our authority was not active on the station. That was to ensure no one tried lording it over any corporal who'd put us through it during training. Our pay increase also coincided with our leaving for our permanent postings. Never since have I ever experienced a rise of over 150%, because four shillings a day shot up to ten shillings and sixpence.

We also had the chore of sewing chevrons on our uniforms; three pairs, for battle dress (that was the tunic with concealed buttons which didn't need polishing), best dress, which did, and greatcoat, which did as well. Another cottage industry was revealed in a civvy lady who undertook the work for a fee, which we could now afford. We all tried our own hands first, saw the resulting odd angles which would never have passed an inspection, then graciously gave in.

Posting! Everyone else went to unknown destinations as expected. I, however, did not. Not because my records had gone AWOL again, they were well known now up to Air Ministry level. So I followed the normal procedure of anyone who was posted to a course from his main station. I was sent back to Brize Norton. I hadn't given the matter a moment's thought, so the embarrassment didn't hit me until I walked through the main gate and reported, as one did, to the guardroom.

I didn't know any of the MPs – technically RAF Police, but we called them MPs as in the Army – but the basic details of assigning me to quarters soon revealed my rapid metamorphosis. An ordinary AC/1 goes away for two months and returns with three *^!*~*# stripes! Unheard of. Old sweats beaver away for years to get two, let alone three. And this bloke's *^!*~*# National Service! The RAF's going to the dogs…I didn't need to be telepathic to know their thoughts. I just kept my head down whilst they looked for accommodation for me. I wondered if it was going to be a cell behind the guardroom, or perhaps a maintenance hut on the outskirts of the airfield, but it seemed the only NCO rooms free were in the permanent building I'd lived in for six months.

Heaving my kit bag I got out rapidly and set off down the familiar main drive to the far side of the drill square. A nice single room in the block I knew well, that'll suit me, I thought. From its number I knew it wasn't on the same level as my former home on the ground floor, so I could slip in quietly before I faced the inevitable ribbing I was expecting from my erstwhile pals.

After I'd thrown my kit into the room I rapidly made for the Education hut to which I knew I had to report, but it was closed. Too late in the afternoon. I walked back more slowly, looking around and experiencing a weird feeling of being in a familiar place but in an unfamiliar time. I was my *alter ego*, a being that lived in a different age. I was estranged and unprepared to be so.

'Hi Flaxton, you're back!' The familiar voice of Sergeant Robinson reorientated my thoughts. 'When did you arrive?'

He was walking back from the hangar having also finished his day's work. He shook my hand warmly. 'Are you fixed up with a room?' I assured him I was and had intended reporting to the Education Office but was too late.

'Have you been to the Mess yet?'

Inwardly I blanched, realizing another trip to arctic climes awaited. I told him I hadn't.

'Come on, I'll take you. I can show you around.' He was too intelligent not to guess my reservation. 'You'll be a five minute wonder, no more.'

I gave waffly thanks and set off beside him. 'Your name's Nigel, isn't it. Mine's Bill. I never answer to William.'

'Ah…er…oh…thanks,' I responded even more waffly.

Of course my reception was frosty. What else could I expect? My posting to the Education Course was, I suspect, unique. National Servicemen were intended to follow the normal programme of basic training followed by trade training whatever that might be. All other men on the Sergeants' Course had done that and then been posted to stations where they were unknown and on which their authority was plain for all to see. Even the very, very few who were selected for commissions went through their secondary training and were then posted. No National Service bod was supposed to do what I did.

When I did report to the Education Office the next morning my reception could not have been more pleasant. The EO was very happy that his attempt had been successful and even more so when he learned of my course placing. The other sergeant was happy to have an assistant and it seemed we might make a good working threesome. But, of course, the powers-that-be, wherever they were, would not tolerate overstaffing and I was posted within a fortnight. Knowing this was to occur, I wondered whether fortune might be with me again and I would get overseas. As a child and wartime teenager such notions were fantasy, but now overseas was quietening down, everyone said. What about the British Sector in Germany? I'd taken the language at school, so it would be an excellent chance to improve my skills which they certainly needed. In the event I was sent to RAF St Athan, in South Wales. Not even near the nice bits I knew from holidays in Fairbourne and climbing in Snowdonia.

That evening, clad in civvies, I searched out Ken and the other guys I knew well. A search was necessary for they were no longer in the permanent building. They had been transferred to the very ordinary and far less spacious huts of which there were still plenty on the station. The new SWO had decreed that groups should interchange to be fair to all. To be fair, he was right. But as I wriggled between the very narrow, tall, mesh sided lockers and beds set very close together, I accepted this was a descent into the slums. Not that they were dirty – the increase in inspections saw to that, they told me.

We had a good natter with absolutely no thought of my new rank intervening. We did go out – to the only place on the station where all non-commissioned ranks could intermix – the Church Army Canteen. It also had a couple of table tennis tables and two snooker tables, so it was popular. Occasionally clients were regaled with the man i/c singing 'The Old Wooden Cross' but he had an excellent tenor voice, so no one minded. As it happened Bill Robinson was also there and we queued together for a coffee and bun. The girl serving us turned to Bill and enquired,

'When are you going away for a few weeks to become an officer?'

My reputation had spread rapidly.

Chapter 20

The RAF Station at St Athan is another that has a long and continuing history. Its website also reveals how active it continues to be. I reached it in November when fog seeps along the Bristol Channel. As if to emphasize the season's dankness a warning foghorn mourned across the water advising ships to steer clear of the shore which, at the nearest point to the station, comprised seaweed draped rocks sluiced by muddy water. The foghorn sounded remarkably close as I lay on my bed, trying to shut out its regular hoot. The feeling of isolation engendered was enhanced by my room being at the end of a totally deserted barrack hut. Indeed there was a whole row of deserted huts, though in each NCO's room there lived a sergeant. Together we comprised the non-commissioned teaching staff of the Administrative Apprentices School, which was one of the units housed on the station.

Apprentices joined straight from secondary school, at fifteen, for three years training after which they continued for twelve years. They then had the option of signing on for further periods. There was an equivalent Technical Apprentices School at RAF Halton. The organisations combined elements of both school and the Forces; of the former the most attractive to staff members were the ordinary school length holidays. Leave, therefore, was not subject to the much less long allowance permitted to other personnel.

I reported to the school's HQ and its CO, Squadron Leader Griffiths, an avuncular man with a very easy going attitude to life. The apprentices regarded him as an affectionate uncle, the staff as a soft touch. He lived in a nearby village. He gave us to understand that the lady with whom he lived was very much in command at home. He never used the term wife so we presumed she wasn't. He seemed very content with whatever arrangement obtained.

Administrative clerks are essential to all RAF offices. Subjects taught in the school, therefore, were those essential to such careers – English, Maths, Shorthand, Typing, History, Geography, etc., to which were added courses in PT, Drill, and other occasional pursuits such as learning to fire rifles. I was sure I would be used to teach English. Everyone at St Andrew's, in company with all student teachers, had to take and pass English Language, but you could also take English Literature which I did as a main subject. I also took History main, so at St Athan I was sure it would be one or the other.

It wasn't. I was totally flabbergasted when Squadron Leader Griffiths informed me I was to take charge of the workshop.

'Er...workshop, sir?'

'That's right, sergeant. Because the boys spend so much time in classrooms I let them have one session a week doing something practical, using their hands as well as their brains. Helps to give them a more rounded education, you understand.'

I did, but didn't feel I had any qualifications for taking charge of any such element of their education. I did my best to explain... gently.

'Oh, I'm sure you can. You're being too modest. It's on your record. You took 'Handwork for Men' at college. You got a Credit in it as well...'

Realisation sank in. The course in Craft, one of the three required choices in the artistic subjects Art , Music, Craft, was pompously titled thus. For the first year we had concentrated on activities useful in junior schools, notably very simple bookbinding, printing pictures cut into pieces of lino, ditto potatoes, whilst in the second year we had made things in perspex and wood and then made one major item. Mine was a largely oak cirular bedside table which, battered over the years, still bravely supports the occasional magazine and cup of coffee in the summer house. But from such gentle pursuits to running a workshop in the RAF for career committed apprentices was quite a leap, I felt. It certainly would be largely in the dark.

Of course I accepted without too much demur, postponing worry until later. Then Sq Ldr Griffiths explained the downside.

'I'm afraid there isn't a great deal of machinery. Can't get it, at present. Materials are also a problem. Still, I've arranged for you to go to Cardiff docks and collect a load of wood. You'll be able to use that for projects for the lads. A lorry will be waiting by the guardroom at 09.00 tomorrow with a couple of men to do the loading for you. You can get them to stack it in the workshop when you return. Any problems, sergeant, do let me know.'

The timetable for all the apprentice flights was published in various locations for all to see. I perused the one in the HQ offices and was surprised to see flights were due in the workshop that day. I'd been with the CO about fifteen minutes. The first flight was due at 10.00 hours. Just about time for me to get…then a thought permeated my obtuse brain that I didn't even know the location. Sheepishly I asked an office clerk and was directed most efficiently. I was also supplied with keys.

I walked into the scene of my forthcoming teaching experience with twenty minutes to spare. It was a typical school woodwork room. Two rows of benches of the type I knew because they were the same everywhere – a vice on each side, a lower section across the middle of the bench, tool cupboards at each end. We even had an identical one at home that my father had acquired when some old ones were sold to people in the Corporation Education Department. Electric power was laid on to a point half way along one wall. I checked the tool cupboards and found the expected saw, plane, mallet, hammer, pliers, chisels, etc. Of other tools there was no sign.

My small bunch of keys included one to the room at the end of the workshop, which was merely an ordinary barrack hut with benches instead of beds. The style was ubiquitous. Tentatively I investigated the office and found a very well-worn easy chair with a wooden frame that allowed the back to be set backwards for reclining. The easy part comprised well-flattened cushions. On the table stood an electric glue pot which I recognised from college where we had its twin, though possibly other siblings were scattered around the country. It contained a solid mass with a battered, transfixed brush. A pile of well thumbed magazines sat on the only other chair, a regulation wooden upright. These were handicraft magazines. Most were two to three years old.

I managed to pause for a moment. Within the last hour I'd had my educational world in the RAF turned on its head. What I now faced was bizarre. The one asset I could muster from my limited skills was that I enjoyed using my hands; I'd done well on the Craft course at St Andrew's; I enjoyed model making and such creative activities. I'd helped making scenery for a church dramatic society, hoping later for acting roles, of course. I was also aware that NCOs were supposed to enjoy responsibility. My stripes were burning my arms.

A clatter of boots broke my thoughts. Perhaps it was fortunate I didn't have more time to think. Assuming the best acting face I could summon, I went outside. Immediately the small crowd of uniformed boys, junior to me by four years, went silent.

'What flight is this?' I demanded of one.

'Five flight, sergeant,' he responded smartly.

'Do you usually make such a clatter when you arrive?'

'No, sergeant.'

'Then don't do so again when you come here.' I looked around the faces. 'Understood?' They nodded.

'I'll try that again. IS THAT UNDERSTOOD?'

'Yes, sergeant,' they chorused.

'Good. Now walk in quietly.'

Eighteen lambs walked into the pen.

I followed, offering thanks for Service discipline. They knew the score perfectly. They had joined voluntarily. They wanted to pass out successfully at the end of their three years. They saw no problem in submitting to discipline. Naturally, however, people who took charge of them differed. Some were stricter than others, so there was a natural tendency to try out any new arrival. In this instance there was another reason as I shortly discovered.

After having them stand to attention, one to a bench – or rather, one to each vice – I let them sit on the benches facing me. I started by being frank and explaining that about an hour and a half previously I had no idea I would be teaching in the workshop and added what I had expected. Slight smiles slithered around as I hinted that very occasionally one meets surprises in the RAF. They certainly knew that score. I then explained I needed to know what they had been doing beforehand in their workshop periods so I could help them to carry on as smoothly as possible.

The smiles broke into laughter. Everyone looked at everyone else.

'Go on,' I ventured, 'tell me why I'm not getting the joke.'

During the next quarter of an hour they regaled me with the previous setup. My predecessor was near the end of his time in the RAF which he'd been in since he left school and, of course, had come through the war. They assured me he was very old, nearly as old as the CO, they felt. I guessed he was late forties, possibly early fifties. Finally his time was up and he left. He lives in a village close to camp, they said. Obviously, therefore, he was still around, albeit outside.

'Right,' I said brightly. 'Now tell me what things you made here. Where do you keep them?'

Inadvertently I again amused the lads. One volunteered an explanation.

'We didn't make anything, not in the last six months at least. We did all kinds of repair jobs around the huts and in the HQ offices.'

By now I had the picture. I was replacing a very experienced old stager, who probably had skills in wood and metalwork, painting and decorating, repairing, building, mixing concrete, brick laying, glazing…a very experienced all round handyman, in fact. Judging from their wistful looks he was a true father figure and was very popular. No wonder they clattered happily on arrival. No doubt they were hoping for a neat fit to the missing piece of their jigsaw. Oh ***, look what we've got! I knew the news would rapidly spread to the other seven flights. I also knew why the CO had detailed me to fetch a supply of wood from Cardiff for the lads to use. They hadn't done any personal craft work for ages. I guessed also that the way my predecessor carried out his role wasn't remotely as the CO intended but the latter wasn't the man to make him toe the line.

I travelled to Cardiff docks next morning on a large empty lorry in the company of one driver, who knew the way, and two airmen. All three were old enough to be my father. None of them relished the thought of being in the charge of an infant unaccountably with three stripes. They were not on the staff of the Apprentices School but it soon became apparent they had been on this visit before, with my predecessor. Surly looks greeted my wish to get back to camp asap. I guessed I was cheating them of a day out.

The contact at the docks also knew them and also knew what I wanted, an unusual feat of telepathy because I hadn't a clue. He pointed to a pile and the men loaded it immediately. It comprised deal planks measuring twelve feet by one foot by two inches. I tried to imagine using this to teach the boys how to make items of furniture such as my oak bedside table, then relinquished the mental effort. I knew it was impossible. This wood, about which I had no choice whatsoever, seemed ideal for house building or something similar.

Back in the workshop, with the planks shoved in rapidly right across the benches, I wondered where to store it but could find nowhere. The next flight told me they'd never seen such a delivery. I wondered whether to ask the CO but decided I'd better not run to him with such a simple problem on only my second day. I compromised by stacking it alongside one wall, moving the benches to keep a gangway open.

It was obviously going to be difficult to cut a plank into manageable pieces using the small handsaws in each tool cupboard, especially because many were not at all sharp. I enquired whether the boys knew of any power tools. Few such items were commonplace in those days, but lathes, drills and circular saws were to be found in some school woodwork rooms. Here, though, they were not.

In the depths of a cupboard in the NCO's office I was directed to an electric drill. This, I was pleased to note, was a robust breast drill, the sort with two handles on each side and a small platform you placed across your chest to supply pressure. There were a number of drill bits as well. The downside was evident at the end of the flex which was devoid of a plug. I expressed regret and asked where plugs were kept. As on the previous day my enquiry added to the view that I was a budding comedian. To my horror it was explained that electric plugs were as difficult to come by as basin and bath plugs in the ablutions, which were always missing. Apparently my predecessor just put the bare wires into the holes in the wall sockets and inserted small chips of wood as individual plugs to keep them in place.

'But that's very dangerous!' I exploded.

'Sure,' rejoined one lad, 'that's why he wouldn't let us do it. He always did it himself. He let us use the drill, though.'

My predecessor had been doing it for a long time, I was told and there had never been an accident. How then could I, a very green newcomer, complain? I didn't. Fortunately whatever Fates cast their protection over such events continued their ministrations and there was no accident during my incumbency either. Health and Safety…?

I soon teamed up with the other NCO members of staff both because our rooms were close together, albeit separated by the distance between any two billet huts. We were also members of the Sergeants Mess on that side of the station. These served various units of which the Apprentices School was only one, so the members were largely career serving men who had been through the war. We young National Servicemen stood out like babes in woods. But on the whole we were well tolerated.

Very soon I became friendly with the man in the next room to mine, Jonny Skyle. An earnest manner and upper class tone of voice suggested a superior attitude at first glance, but this was rapidly dispelled on better acquaintance. He was well educated, had a B.Sc.(Econ) degree and as a POM had been selected for a commission but failed the course. About this he was totally *blasé*. After we knew one another well he laughingly said I would have probably made it for a commission.

'They want people with Service minds, like you, Nigel. I wasn't prepared to go along with all their rigmarole.'

He taught English at the school and, as I found, was passionately concerned to improve the boys' knowledge of both literature and the arts in general. When he was demobbed, however, it was not to take up teaching. He went into his family's law firm to be articled as a solicitor.

He laughed at my enquiries about the role my predecessor had undertaken in the matter of practical workshop experience.

'Rhys was character; law unto himself. He was building his own house – stayed on here until it was finished. Did enough around the camp to be useful, of course, but no one enquired too closely about other times. You couldn't be less like him. The boys will get used to you, though. They have to be adaptable to stay the course. They're going to be in the RAF for many years, remember.'

Both they and I quickly settled into a routine. We couldn't be particularly inventive with the materials available, but the lads seemed to enjoy their brief time away from more formal lessons. As a group my colleagues were always ready to offer wider experiences to them, so I joined in a number of visits to the theatre in Cardiff. The apprentices, of course, had to wear uniform at all times, so when we took them out we did the same. Public eyebrows rose as a flight marched along a main road, halted outside the theatre and entered to watch a visiting ballet company perform Swan Lake and later Coppélia. We were pleased the boys responded well, as they did when we took them see Gwen Ffrangcon-Davies as Lady Macbeth.

With another staff member, Jonny found a local opera training group. This unusual affair was organised by a formidable lady who counted herself a true doyenne of the genre. She readily agreed to bring some of her students to music appreciation meetings the two set up for anyone to visit on occasional evenings. One young woman was particularly striking when she sang arias from Carmen. These events were sufficiently successful for us to attempt a full blown evening at the Astra Cinema. This was capable of seating a couple of thousand people and for popular films it achieved capacity houses. We knew this would be far less attractive, but the Station Commanding Officer, an Air Commodore no less, agreed to attend, which certainly ensured a good attendance of officers. Other ranks were very thinly represented

Performances by various group members were excellent and those present who could appreciate them were well satisfied. The one highly unfortunate moment occurred right at the end when the SCO walked on to the stage to thank the company. The formidable lady marched across the stage, grabbed him by the hand, marched to the centre and gave a lengthy diatribe thanking him for being so cognisant of the arts and opera in particular to sponsor such an event, reminding him how fortunate he was to have such dedicated NCOs supporting him in such endeavours. Finally she released his hand and the curtain descended. We made ourselves scarce until the SCO's driver lured him back into his car.

Fortified by the comparative success of this venture, a small group decided to present Noël Coward's 'Private Lives'. Jonny's friend was Martin Brinks, a Cambridge graduate who had performed with the Footlights. They had discovered a former member of the Bristol Old Vic Repertory Company, Sheila Brownlowe, quietly living in married quarters as the wife of a corporal. He also had an intellectual background, but they had a young daughter who had appeared unexpectedly, so they married and he joined the RAF to offer reasonable security for his responsibilities.

The cast list is small: two couples. The two men were available but another woman was required. Deft searching elicited the name of a Squadron Leader's wife who had amateur dramatic experience. She was tentatively approached and agreed to join the odd and no doubt unique company. I had hammed my way through various plays at school, including Lady Macbeth in falsetto (Gwen Ff-D had a distinct edge on my performance, I admit), and then had continued with a group that, unusually for amateurs, was very good at farce. So I was asked to direct. Seeing the backgrounds of the cast members I felt this would be largely unnecessary. It was. But I feel I added somewhat to the role of dogsbody.

I was also well placed to build the set, due to my role i/c a workshop. This had to be undertaken from square one. Flats – the scenic sort – had to be made from laths, then covered with hessian, which had to be 'organised', then sized, i.e. covered liberally in goo to provide a surface on which to paint. As the hessian dried the laths warped, so they all had to be dismantled, rebuilt, recovered, resized, then covered with three coats of base distemper, which also had to be organised, then painted for the two scenes, the first of which is two adjacent hotel balconies, as I'm sure you know. The second is a straightforward room – well, it was in our production. I excelled at directing everyone on these chores and also supplying youthful assistants for the process as occasion demanded.

The easy going nature of the school's CO came to the fore in all of this. He allowed us time off, he fixed us up with a colleague to be Officer i/c Drama, who was very useful whenever we wanted unobtainable supplies. The Photographic Unit took publicity shots, posters were printed, advertisements were posted all over the place. We confidently expected the Astra Cinema to be fairly well filled. Then, suddenly, there was an international alert and men were sent here, there and everywhere, so were not available to fill the Astra seats. The performance enjoyed a limited audience. Nevertheless it was rated a success by all who saw it.

Within weeks of the final curtain we were on our way back to civilian life. I was required to hand in my uniform on the station, so spent the last weekend on duty in civvies which felt weird. I then set out for a Camp in Blackpool where demobilisation formalities were handled. The quarters assigned to the birds of passage were filthy and I shuddered to use the blankets on the sheetless beds, so with others I walked along the otherwise deserted sands on a warm, moonlit early summer night, returning well after midnight to lie on a bed fervently hoping not to collect any small farewell presents to take home.

Next morning we were summoned to sit on a row of chairs facing a tannoy speaker. This announced that when our names were called we were to move to our left and turn the corner to our right. One by one names issued forth in desultory tones,

'Blackwell…Carstairs…Evans, J…

I had a brief feeling of *déja vu*. Had my records disappeared again? But it was swept aside.

'Flaxton…' the voice called, then briefly, 'er…Sergeant Flaxton…'

I walked along the corridor, turned right, found a desk at which the progenitor of the voice handed me a railway warrant and two weeks' pay. I signed, he nodded and spoke into a microphone,

'Hetherington…' I walked out into civvy street thinking I had just seen the most boring and depressing job in the RAF. My heart went out to him. I hoped he was a National Serviceman and not a career administrative clerk, formerly an apprentice.

Chapter 21

I have to pose the question 'Was it worth it?' By that I mean my national service. That begs the further question, 'Worth to whom?' There were three possible recipients of worth - me, the Royal Air Force and the nation at large. Did I, as a modern phrase popular in education has it, add value? Was value in some way added to me?

The experience provided me with interesting activities and helped my maturity. I was officially an adult on my release having passed my twenty-first birthday a few months before. Eighteen became the requisite age well over twenty years later. But would I have matured just as effectively without going into the Forces? Probably, though not as quickly.

Did I add value to the RAF? Hardly! I spent twenty-five weeks in three forms of training – basic, trade and education. I wonder what the actual cost was? In return I spent six months as an Airframe Assistant when, apart from keeping a very large blackboard up to date for a few weeks, overseen by a senior NCO, I acted as a fetcher and carrier of tools, a cleaner, a wonderful polisher of an aeroplane and, very occasionally, took responsibility to park aircraft. Then I assumed the role for which I was already trained, that of teaching, but found myself with a subject which in any school was undertaken by a specialist. I was only an ordinaryalist in Craft. I assisted to an extent in slightly widening the educational experience of a few flights of apprentices by outside visits, but little else. With that assessment I also have to question whether my experience was markedly different from thousands of other National Servicemen. Probably it was not.

Did my service contribute anything to the nation? It did in the sense that had international tension built up to an extent that war was again likely, I was in the Forces and could be used more productively. Being readily available was of use. Monarchs of old always had the problem of raising the host quickly. My service book, a document we had to keep at all times and never destroy (so I haven't), tells me I never left the RAF – I was transferred to the Reserve, so maybe I'm still available. I wonder whether the stores issue zimmer frames?

In the cold light of judgment by whoever might look at such matters, National Service in peacetime was not cost effective, but in the uncertain years of international shuffling after 1945 it was sensible to keep conscription for a while. The key problem to a short term of service is responsibility. To train a person to undertake a responsible job in which he or she has to take vital decisions or perform vital tasks requires time. It also requires dedicated people prepared to accept such responsibility and that means career minded men and women. To conscript the undifferentiated mass of young people carries basic problems, the most obvious being that many don't wish to be conscripted at all. Training unwilling people is difficult. Politicians still haven't accepted the fact that a proportion of youngsters in schools don't want to be there and don't want to be educated beyond a basic level – and their ideas of basic don't necessarily accord with teachers' or politicians' ideas. Conscription exacerbates that problem.

It is remarkably difficult to educate, train, or discipline a resistant individual in a society that has pretensions to being free. One of my friends at school, who acted in plays with me and occasionally attended the same church, was called up into the Army. His father, reasonably well to do, was a strict disciplinarian in laying down rules as to what his son could or could not do. I visited him at home once and was astonished to hear him call his father 'sir'. Whether his upbringing entrenched his attitude I know not, but he decided no one had a right to issue him with an order. Such an attitude is difficult to uphold in the Forces beyond the first five minutes, so rapidly he found himself on a charge and was sentenced to the inevitable seven days jankers…attending at specified times throughout the day and night outside the guardroom, dressed in full kit suitably bulled up for inspection, then spending the night in the cells. During the first spell, inevitably he received an order, refused to obey, so the process was repeated with further days added…and so on…and on… He, of course, wanted the Army to dismiss him. The Army, realising, refused to co-operate. Friends said he achieved one hundred and thirty four charges before the end of his National Service which had been useless to both the individual and the organisation. He then took a job with the same diligence he showed during his successful time at school where he obtained good School and Higher School Certificates. I sometimes wonder which side considered itself the winner.

To-day's highly technical Forces need to screen their entries for motivation, determination, willingness to accept discipline, ability to accept responsibility, health and intelligence. Certainly there are the humdrum, routine jobs that someone has to do, but each individual has to be capable of accepting a more responsible role when necessary. Short term conscripts are not there long enough to warrant expensive training, are not dedicated to ongoing service, and may be of inadequate intelligence, or anti-establishment, or opposed to armed conflict, or demonstrate any of a host of problems which have to be dealt with.

So people who call for a return of conscription as a matter of disciplining young people should think again. The Forces are not the institutions for that. If Society really does want a means of exposing all its young people to some form of cohesive discipline it needs an alternative. A Community Service with sensible and thoughtful discipline and care might be the answer, but then objections are likely be raised about cheap labour taking away jobs. The scheme, however, certainly would not be cheap. In the last resort the original question would have to be posed, 'Would it be worth it?' Very careful and wide ranging analysis would be needed to provide a trustworthy answer. Then the party of government would have to decide whether to bite the bullet.

Chapter 22

'I realise you want to make your career in secondary education, but at the moment we have very few vacancies in that sector. We urgently need primary teachers to cope with the bulge in the child population which has just reached those schools.'

Mr Bartram, a member of the Chief Education Officer's staff, was advising me upon my application. 'You'd find a period in a primary school very useful in the future if you gain promotion in the secondary field. Often there's a gulf between primary and secondary teachers which is quite artificial. Someone who has experience of both has a useful edge.'

I might have been suspicious about his line of reasoning had it not been for the fact that he was one of my father's colleagues, therefore I felt his advice could be trusted. So, very much against my actual wishes, I agreed to alter my application to one for a primary post. I extracted a promise that he would allow me to transfer to a senior school after a year or two. He agreed readily because the bulge obviously would do the same.

Typically I celebrated my return by starting with a disaster because I was quite unprepared for the interview format. I rashly assumed it was a mere formality. The reason was that I had been interviewed by one of the Authority's inspectors after I had left St. Andrew's when I first applied for a post. This had been a friendly chat - quite private - and he had accepted me. Of course he knew I had to do National Service; I assumed that, on my return, my re-employment would be virtually automatic. When I arrived at the interview room I found three other people waiting. I chatted with them and found each lived outside the city and wanted to join its teaching force.

'Where are you from?' one asked me.

'Oh, I'm a local boy. I've just been demobbed. I was interviewed when I left college a couple of years ago and actually did five weeks teaching here.' The three took a closer interest.

'What was your interview like? They differ so much between Authorities.'

'Oh, it was nothing really. Just one of the local inspectors who chatted to me in his room. We talked generally about the schools I'd done practice in, then he welcomed me to the city's branch of the profession.'

'Do you think your interview to-day will be the same as that?' one asked with a note of surprise.

'Oh, I expect so. I imagine it'll be a routine check to see whether the Forces have left any lasting scars,' I laughed.

'I was expecting a committee interview.'

'A what?'

'You know, when you face a panel, sometimes they're quite large, ten people or more.'

'Ye gods, no. It won't be like that at all. For one thing these rooms couldn't hold that many people. They're all individual offices. I remember that one was where I was interviewed before - look, the chap's name is on the door.'

I pointed to a small plaque, 'E.G. Carstairs'. We looked at all the doors in the corridor which were painted dark blue with cream surrounds. They were identical.

'Now gentlemen,' a voice broke in upon us. It was Mr Bartram. 'I shan't keep you waiting much longer. I just need to check a couple of points with two of you.' He turned to the others and talked in low tones, consulting some papers in his hand. Then he looked up.

'Fine, no problems there, I'm pleased to say. Now, Mr Flaxton, you're first in alphabetical order so will you come this way please?'

'Certainly,' I said, and moved with him. He walked a few paces along the corridor, turned, placed his hand on a large brass doorknob and held the door open for me. I looked at him as I passed and said, 'Thank you'. Then I looked into the room.

It was not a small office with a single person smiling a welcome at me from behind a desk. It was a very long room indeed and the doorway through which I had entered was at one end. What seemed the longest table I had ever seen stretched the full length of one side on my left. Facing me across the end in the dim distance was a much shorter table placed at right angles. Along the sides of both was an imposing line of faces looking at me. Mr Bartram indicated a chair to my right, just level with the near end of the long table. I collapsed into it and gaped across the acres of space which separated me from the others.

Mr Bartram set out on a route march to his seat behind the short table in the distance. I gazed at his diminishing figure. Everyone else gazed at me.

'I suppose I should begin by asking Mr Flaxton whether he enjoyed his long holiday?'

From somewhere on the other side of the long table a gruff voice broke the silence and was immediately followed by laughter. I tried to drag myself out of the panic which gripped me. Somewhere, someone was Chairman and he had just spoken. I searched the laughing faces in vain. He was quite unidentifiable.

'Oh dear, Mr Flaxton doesn't find that funny. Didn't you like your time in the Forces?

This time I spotted him. Ah, now I know who I've got to speak to…oh hell…what did he say?

'Er, I'm sorry, Mr Chairman, I didn't quite catch that.'

'Good heavens, man, you're not deaf are you? I asked whether you didn't like your time in the Forces,' His voice boomed around the vast room.

'Oh, I enjoyed it very much, sir, very much indeed,' I replied heartily, trying to retrieve the situation.

'Didn't you consider staying on then - signing on voluntarily for three or four years and taking a short service commission?' The question came quite unexpectedly from a different quarter, a lady sitting much nearer to me.

'Er, well, yes I did, as a matter of fact.'

Another spasm of panic gripped me. How do you address lady committee members? Marm, madam, mam…?

'Why did you reject the idea?"

Why did I what? For the love of mike listen to the questions… reject…oh yes, the Forces…'I really was very keen to get back to teaching…mm.'

241

'Good, at last I've heard something I want to hear,' said the Chairman loudly.

'We have your college report in front of us, Mr Flaxton.' A quiet but penetrating voice spoke from the smaller table at the far end of the room. I wasn't sure which person had spoken but the table was so far away I could simply gaze in that direction and get away-with it.

'Major Darnley we all know and respect.' The room erupted with growls and squeaks of hyar, hyar and 'ear 'ear.

The VP, I thought, aghast. What on earth did he write about me?

'His report upon you was quite favourable, Mr Flaxton. That, and your results which you know of course, suggest we could do worse than offer you permanent employment here. What have you to say to that?'

'Good heavens, I am surprised, sir. That is, I mean, I didn't think...'

'You don't sound very sure of yourself, Mr Flaxton. Let me put it to you more directly.' The Chairman took up the questioning again. 'Do you feel you can do a good teaching job here in the city if we appoint you?'

'Oh yes, indeed, sir. Yes, I would certainly try very hard to help the pupils in my care.'

'Good, that's better. Now, one final question about those pupils. Perhaps you can explain to the committee why it is that when you left college two years ago you opted for secondary teaching. Now, without any explanation, you suddenly ask to be sent to a primary school. In my experience teachers are usually particular about which age they teach. Can you tell me why you changed your mind so soon?'

There was a sudden silence and I felt all eyes on me. That is, all except Mr Bartram who seemed busy writing. I thought, 'Why on earth doesn't he tell them?' I opened my mouth to give the true reason, that I really wanted secondary work but the person dealing with staffing, Mr Bartram there, had asked me to take a primary post. Then, foolishly, I thought of his links with my father, in a different branch of Education Department. If I say that, I'll let this chap down in front of the whole committee. I can't do that.

'Well, Mr Flaxton, can you tell us?'

'Er, no, I don't think I can,' I stuttered in total confusion.

The members of the committee sat back, moved in their seats, looked at one another, collected their papers together and generally made it quite obvious they were interviewing an idiot. I stared helplessly at Mr Bartram who continued writing, apparently oblivious to the situation.

'Very well, Mr Flaxton. That is all. Good morning,' said the Chairman in very final tones. I stood up, turned and groped for the door. Immediately I was outside the other three candidates pounced.

'What was it like?'

'Who's doing the interviewing?'

'Is it an inspector, or is it a panel?'

I collapsed weakly into a chair beside them. 'Hell, that was really awful,' I began. Then the door opened and Mr Bartram came up to me. He looked down at his papers.

'Well, Mr Flaxton,' he said in a flat tone, still not looking directly at me, 'that was alright. We shall let you know in a few days which school you will be sent to.' I heaved myself to my feet.

'You mean…they're going to appoint me…after that?'

'Oh yes, there was never any question about that. I think the Chairman wanted to see what you were made of. He's got something of a reputation for that sort of thing. Still, it's all good practice. You may have to face quite a number of interviews in your career.' Then he vanished into the room again with the second candidate.

He was absolutely right. That interview, together with my memory of mistaking a Group Captain in civvies for a clerk, taught me valuable lessons and ever afterwards I was prepared for most questions and situations. I managed to escape similar disasters by being open and frank, which is what most people respect. In company with many of my colleagues I collected various experiences at these mild forms of torture, although I never had anything to match the situation which a friend once told me about. He was a candidate for a headship in a small Welsh town. He was ushered through a door into the interview room to find himself in a courtroom. The interviewing panel were ranged along the judges' bench, interested spectators were in the well of the court and he was in the dock!

A few days later I received a letter asking me to join the staff of Dayton Road Junior Mixed School and to report to Mr Brand, the headteacher. I remember looking at the letter with contentment; I now had my first truly permanent appointment as a qualified teacher. Then I took out a map to find Dayton Road for I'd never heard of it. I located it with a twinge of concern because its surroundings were similar to those of Spenser Street with old houses and a conglomeration of factories. I wondered whether I was being given my deserts for an appalling interview.

I couldn't have been more wrong.

Chapter 23

'So that's it,' I said to myself as I cycled along Dayton Road. It was Sunday, the day before I was due to join the staff. I was making sure that I knew where to find the school.

It was similar to many of the city schools, solidly built in red brick. But it differed in one respect from most - its buildings were virtually on the pavement's edge. They were long but divided by a house set incongruously in the middle. This, I was later to learn, housed the Caretaker who literally lived on the job. Access to the school could be gained through various doors, set back slightly from the pavement.

I was able to see it from three sides. The fourth comprised two high walls, painted black, which were the ends of two back-to-back rows of houses set in two roads of which Dayton Road was one. It seemed a gigantic knife had sliced into the house rows to carve out space for the school. The site extended across the space between the roads and obviously had spacious playgrounds. I couldn't see these from outside because they were surrounded by high walls.

The surrounding houses were typically terraced and built, like the school, at the turn of the century. Most were situated on the edge of pavements; their front doors surmounted large single slabs of stone which were either scrubbed or ignored according to the characters of the occupants. A few rows had miniature front gardens, though a single dusty privet hedge hardly merited the title. There was no room for anything else.

The afternoon was warm and sunny so there were plenty of children about, playing in small groups on the pavement or chasing in and out of doorways. Some girls were skipping, two holding a long rope and chanting whilst five or six others joined in one at a time until all were encircled by the rotating rope. Some boys were playing marbles in the gutter, reminding me of my own junior school days when I had done just the same, so long as my parents didn't see me.

The scene was very different next day. There was a general bustle along the pavements as five hundred children between the ages of five and eleven skipped, ran, or dawdled their way into the school. Some two hundred were infants, between five and seven, and these went to a part of the building organisationally separate from my destination, the junior school.

I chose one of the inevitable green doors and walked through to find a very short corridor with another door ahead. This led immediately into the playground which ran the entire length of the building, and more. It was large, though the effect of size was reduced by surface air raid shelters virtually dividing it into two sections.

The playground was rapidly filling with children. I stopped one boy with a bright, friendly face,

'Can you show me where Mr Brand's office is, please?'

'Yes, it's this way,' he replied and set off briskly through the crowd. I followed, failing to dodge the occasional little body which hurled itself into my legs without looking where it was going. Fortunately none felled me in the process. My guide skipped through a door on his left, then turned to me and indicated another door on his right.

'It's in there,' he announced.

I looked through the small glass panes set solidly in the upper half of the door. The room was obviously a cloakroom. I turned to my companion,

'Come on, young man,' I said heavily, 'I asked you to show me the headmaster's room. This is…'

'That's right, in there, and up them stairs.'

He pointed to a small side door almost concealed behind a long row of pegs, on which a few coats were hanging.

'Up there?' I looked, then turned back to him, but he had gone. Hesitatingly I went into the cloakroom and headed towards the door. But just as I reached it a figure appeared framed in its glass. He opened it and greeted me.

'You must be Mr Flaxton. I'm Mr Brand; I'm glad you managed to find us without any difficulty. Perhaps you'd like to leave your things in my room just for now. It's up here.'

He was fairly tall with a rather elderly, smiling face. He carried himself very erectly - indeed throughout the time I was to teach at Dayton Road I never saw him standing or sitting with the slightest hint of slouching. He must have had a board strapped to his back throughout his growing years. Even when he bent, as he did whenever he laughed, he hinged at the hips. He had a luxuriant shock of greying hair and I guessed his age as in the fifties.

This made his next action all the more astounding because he all but disappeared in front of my eyes. He leapt at the stairs and simply fled up them two at a time. I stumbled after him but was still well down the long flight when he reached the top and walked along a corridor to his room.

'I'm afraid this is rather out of the way but there's nowhere else I can use,' he said to thin air assuming I was at his shoulder. I heard him open a door.

'Here we are - oh, I'm sorry, you're still down there are you?' He peered over the bannisters and watched me breathlessly reach the top.

'Ah, you've got a heavy case. Here, give it to me and I'll put in here out of harm's way - oh, it's not as heavy as I thought.' He took it from me and disappeared into his room. I padded after him, panting.

'There we are. You can collect it later when I've shown you the staffroom.' I looked at him in surprise but couldn't detect a trace of exertion. I was to learn his power with stairs was an enigma. He was never seen to hurry, certainly never to run on any other occasion, and his life consisted solely of the school and his garden at home. He seemed to take no other exercise whatsoever. But in dealing with the two flights of stairs in the building - there were about twenty steps in each - he was an absolute champion. Ascending or descending he easily outstripped anyone including young and very active male teachers.

'I'll take you round the classrooms and introduce you to the staff after I've dealt with your details. I have to fill in various forms on all staff, so I might as well get that chore over straight away. Actually, today is rather unusual, because we're not starting with an assembly. Everyone has some lists to complete, so we've had to use assembly time. Never mind, this will be a good way to look around the school.'

He asked me a series of questions about my school and college records and experience of schools' practice, then asked infomally about my time in the RAF. After a while he said we should go and meet the other teachers. We left the room and he calmly turned to the stairs again then hurled himself downwards with such ferocity I was sure he would fall. Watching him left me still standing immobile on the second top stair when he turned at the bottom and casually held the door open for me. I then descended awkwardly under his waiting gaze.

'Didn't you get much sport in the RAF?' he quizzed drily with a gentle lift of his eyebrows. Before I could answer he pottered off in front of me through the cloakroom and out into the playground, whilst I tottered shamefacedly after him.

'I have four women and two men on the staff - oh no - three now. Dear, dear, I'm forgetting my new addition.' he chuckled. 'That won't do, will it?' I managed a vacuous grin. 'The point is there are six classes. You are an extra teacher at the moment, but that won't last long. One of the men has been appointed Chief Assistant at another school and you are his replacement. Fortunately, because you've just been demobbed, the Office sent you a few weeks early so that will help you to get the feel of teaching again.'

I nearly replied that I hadn't yet had a chance to get the feel of teaching at all but decided against it. Instead I turned my thoughts to the four women that Mr Brand had mentioned.

During my time in the RAF opportunities for regular friendship with members of the opposite sex had been rather limited. Kim and I parted company before I left St. Andrew's. I dated the excellent tennis player next but that friendship concluded some months after I joined up. Since then there had been no regular girlfriend on the Flaxton scene. But during the couple of weeks following my exit from HM Forces I had turned my thoughts to this problem.

I knew it to be a fact that junior schools contained more women teachers than men. It was also fact that women students became teachers as soon as they left college, because they hadn't had to do National Service for some years. That meant there was a proportion of young women of twenty years and upwards adding a lively touch to many staffrooms; so it was my fervent hope that the drab building of Dayton Road School would have its due quota. Mr Brand's statement told me the basic odds were in my favour; the crucial question concerned the age brackets into which these four women fell.

'This is Class Five,' Mr Brand was saying as he opened a door. 'Ah, Miss Browning - may I introduce Mr Flaxton to you? He's come to take Mr Pardoe's place when he leaves.'

'Hello, Mr Flaxton. I'm very pleased to meet you, I do hope that you'll be happy here.'

'Well, if he follows you, he certainly will be. How long is it now?'

'Oh, don't Mr Brand! You make me feel so old when you say that.' Miss Browning turned to me. 'I hate to admit it, but for the record I've been here twenty years, and I positively refuse to say how long I'd been teaching before; but I can honestly say I've enjoyed all my years - war included.'

Miss Browning was an extremely pleasant person; dark hair streaked with grey and a smiling face behind very sensible glasses. She was like a mother to her class and, as I was to find, young teachers as well. For years I heard from her each Christmas and she followed my career with interest. I am glad that she enjoyed many happy years of retirement. But at Dayton Road it was quite obvious she was not in the age group I was thinking about at that moment.

Neither was Miss Shenton, nor Miss Rees. Miss Shenton was a great friend of Miss Browning but was slightly older. Miss Rees was the Chief Assistant and although somewhat younger than the other two she was nevertheless just about old enough to be my mother. All three had been teaching since the days when, if a female teacher married, she had to leave. The odds were lengthening considerably.

I was taken into Mr Pardoe's room. He was a tall, thin man with a round, cheerful face.

'It's a case of hail and farewell with me, I'm afraid. Still, I'm sure you'll be happy here. You'll find the staff and children are very friendly. In many ways I'm sorry to be leaving.' I looked at the children. 'Will this be my class when you've left?'

'No, yours will be younger than these. We're making an extra class in one year group because it has so many children in it,' said Mr Brand. 'In fact it won't be long before we take on another new young teacher, ready for the next increase in our roll.'

For a moment I had the feeling I was to be the only representative of my age group male or female on the staff, at least for some weeks. But then I was introduced to Mr Hughes. He was about my age and had emerged from the Army some months previously. He was a short and stocky Welshman.

'Welcome to Dayton Road,' he said shaking my hand as though he meant it.' I hope you're keen on football and cricket - we've got good teams here and they need plenty of encouragement.' Memories of my efforts at football on school practice floated into my consciousness but I didn't like what I saw.

'Er, well...cricket, possibly...'

'You don't need to be good at them yourself, we want anyone with a loud voice to shout at the kids whilst they're playing.'

Better memories from the RAF appeared, cricket on airfields and yelling at the flight as I marched them around Wellesbourne M.

'In that case, I'm your man.' I said.

'Great, see you later,' he replied.

My spirits rose as Mr Brand led me out of Mr Hughes' classroom. 'There's only one more; I expect she'll be in the staffroom now. That's upstairs, but at this end of the building.'

We had been making our way along the length of the building visiting various rooms, having passed the back of the Caretaker's house halfway along the playground. It was devoid of any suggestion of a garden; there was only a yard enclosed by a massive brick wall. Mr Brand gently ushered me through another door leading from the playground. Immediately on the left I saw the stairs. 'It's just at the top here,' he said and was up them in a flash.

They were long, straight, and each stair was covered in a rubberlike substance with extra thick protection on each leading edge. Obviously they offered an excellent grip.

I'll show him, I thought.

I let him reach the top where he turned, very casually, and looked down at me. I put my head down and charged. My mistake was to try them three at a time. My legs just failed near the top and I crashed on to all fours, narrowly missing nudging his feet with my nose.

'Those need a bit of practice,' he said. I looked up in time to catch the faint gleam in his eye. He opened the first of two doors in the upstairs corridor. 'This is the staffroom,' he announced. I looked in and saw a small room, dominated by a table completely covered with a thick faded green material. Round it were set six solid chairs. There was an old grate with a mantelpiece on one side of the table, and tall cupboards on the other. Through glass panes in their upper sections I could see rows of class text books. There were two fireside chairs with solid sides identical to the one in the workshop office at St Athan I so recently vacated. High windows faced the door, giving the room plenty of light but no view. There was no one in the room at the time.

'I've lost Miss Rockliffe. I thought she would be in the staffroom.' Mr Brand looked momentarily perplexed. 'Ah… I know, she'll be using the duplicator. Let's try the kitchen.' He moved to another door on the landing and threw it open.

'Ah, yes, here she is. Last but by no means least. Miss Rockliffe, let me introduce Mr Flaxton to you.'

I followed him into another small room which served as a kitchen by virtue of the fact that it contained a tiny cooker and a sink. Otherwise it looked exactly like the staffroom. On a table in the middle of the room was a small hand duplicating machine. Operating this was Miss Rockliffe.

Dayton Road School suddenly became a much more lively and attractive place. Miss Rockliffe was certainly in the right age bracket. Our eyes met as we formally shook hands.

'Hello,' she said.

' 'Hello,' I replied.

Mr Brand dissolved the ensuing silence. 'Come on, Miss Rockliffe, you'd better show Mr Flaxton how to use this machine. He'll need to know quite soon and you're our expert.'

'Oh, I'm hardly that,' she laughed.

'Well you use it far more than anyone else.' He turned to me. 'She's very good with it. I often find the children using duplicated sheets with coloured drawings and diagrams which Miss Rockliffe has produced for them. You'll do well to let her teach you to use it.'

'Fine, I'd like that,' I said.

I certainly meant it. Miss Rockliffe had lovely eyes and a warm smile. There was rich dark brown hair with a natural look to its gentle curls and waves. There was a slim waist, a trim figure and an air of vitality that made the old room shine.

'It's quite .simple,' she said. 'You make a master copy on a sheet like this - drawing whatever you want with any coloured sheet of carbon underneath. Then you put the copy on to the drum here like this … then turn the handle, and, oh dear…'

She inserted a blank piece of paper into the machine but it emerged equally blank instead of reproducing the squiggles she had put on the master copy by way of demonstration.

'I think our expert put the master copy on the wrong way round,' laughed Mr Brand.

'So I have - there you are, I told you I wasn't all that good with this thing.'

'Nonsense,' said Mr Brand, 'you were just put off by having a nice young man watching you.' He patted her on the shoulder, bent at the waist and laughed heartily again in what seemed to me a most unheadmasterlike fashion. Miss Rockliffe turned a lovely pink colour.

'Poor kid,' I thought. 'I'll bet she'll hate me after this. What an introduction!'

Hurriedly she reversed the master sheet and pushed another blank sheet into the machine. The result was the same.

'Oh no - now what have I done?' The pink colour deepened.

'I seem to have introduced a gremlin,' I said. 'Never mind, I get the idea. I can see what it does from these sheets you've already finished.' I picked one up. It showed a number of examples of dress from the Tudor period. They were beautifully drawn and I stared at them in astonishment.

'Did you draw these?

'Yes, but they were copied from a book.'

'They're super. I hope you won't expect me to draw like this for my class, Mr Brand. I couldn't do this to save my life.'

'Ah well,' he said happily, 'you'll just have to get round Miss Rockliffe to draw things for you. I'm sure she'd be most willing.' He turned to her.

'You'll give Mr Flaxton all the help he needs, won't you, Miss Rockliffe?'

For a brief moment I had the idea that Mr Brand was mindreading and giving substance to my thoughts. Suddenly it was my turn to blush.

Chapter 24

I enjoyed my first day at Dayton Road Junior School but I didn't teach any lessons. Mr Brand assigned me to Miss Rees.

'You'll probably need to adjust yourself to the classroom again after being in the Services. So watch a few lessons, then I'll give you a temporary time table which will enable Miss Rees to have some spare time for administrative work. You can take a few lessons in each of the classes and in that way you'll soon get to know all the children.'

When he left the classroom, Miss Rees set me up with a chair and a low table beside her desk, which was the usual high pattern. When she sat there she was able to look down at me sitting at my small table. I guessed she considered the arrangement relegated me to my proper station on the staff, that of the lowliest newcomer.

'You can spend a couple of days getting to know the names of the children and looking at some of their work,' she said. 'Then you can take some lessons. I'll watch you at first and you'd better write up some lesson notes. I expect you'll be rusty after being away from schools for so long, and, of course, you're only just starting your probationary year, so you'll need some help to begin with.'

Miss Rees had a brisk, forceful voice with a distinct Welsh accent. I guessed that she was rather formidable in her role as Chief Assistant. In those days most junior schools had Arithmetic on their time tables until morning break, and Dayton Road was no exception. By the time I had been deposited in Miss Rees's room her class were hard at work with a list of sums which she had written on the blackboard. They watched with interest the spectacle of my being settled beside their teacher, but whilst she was talking to me the one or two who dared to continue watching caught her eye and their heads shot downwards to their desk work. When she turned her attention to her own desk, I was able to sit back and survey the room and its occupants.

There were the usual forty-eight in the class. They sat at the familiar double desks with iron frames and tip-up seats. The room had a very high ceiling and the usual large windows divided into small panes in two opposite walls. One faced the playground way above the heads of the children. The other was also lofty and wide, but its lowest level enabled people to see into from the hall.

The children in the room were ten and eleven year olds and they looked very much the same as those I had faced at Spenser Street three years previously. One or two started to look up at me surreptitiously, no doubt wondering who I was and what on earth I was doing in their classroom, sitting like that beside Miss Rees. But when any of them caught my eye the look was rapidly changed into an I'm - looking - up - because - I'm - thinking - about - my - Arithmetic look. I wasn't fooled.

'Robinson, the bell.'

Miss Rees's command broke in upon my thoughts. A tall boy stood up at his desk and walked over to the wide window ledge on the hall side of the room, picked up a large bronze handbell and disappeared into the hall where he clanged it vigorously, then set off to perform the same service for the classrooms at the other end of the building.

'Everyone, stand,' said Miss Rees; the class obeyed with alacrity.

'First row - out you go. Second - third - fourth – last.' She watched with sharp eyes for the slightest suggestion of misbehaviour, which I realised was entirely for my benefit. But the children wanted their playtime and they knew when to toe the line. In seconds the room was empty.

'Come and have a cup of coffee,' Miss Rees invited. I followed her to the end classroom nearest to the staff room stairs. She opened the door busily.

'Oh good, it's here. Now, have you all met Mr Flaxton? She swept a glance at the assembled staff. Everyone was there except Mr Brand and Mr Pardoe. There were nods all round.

'Do you take sugar?' The question came from Miss Shenton who seemed to be officiating with a large white jug. We were in her classroom.

'Yes, please,' I said.

Mr Hughes took the cup, and passed it to me.

'Make yourself at home, Mr Flaxton,' Miss Browning said. 'You'll have to stand or sit on a desk, I'm afraid. We don't have time to go to the staffroom during break.'

'Do you know where Mr Brand is, Miss Rees? asked Miss Shenton.

'No - unless he's on the phone. Miss Rockliffe, would you look, please?

Miss Rockliffe was standing near to one of the doors. She opened it, looked across a short corridor to the stockroom, which contained one of the school's two telephones. Though the other was in his room Mr Brand used whichever he was nearer.

'Yes, he's there.'

'Well, I hope he'll not be too long, or his coffee will be cold,' said Miss Shenton. As general conversation developed, I sat down on the front edge of a desk near the door. After a minute or two Mr Hughes came over to me and sat down on the same desk.

'Well, think you'll like it?' His voice carried the unmistakable accent of a south Welsh valley.

'Oh, yes", I said, "I'm sure I will.' I glanced briefly at Miss Rockliffe,

'Look, I don't want to load you up on your first day, but if you meant what you said about cricket, Rocky and I could do with some help.'

'Rocky? You mean...

'Sure, Miss Rockliffe is Rocky to all her pals. Her name's Megan, but no one uses it. And I only answer to Taff.'

'Megan - that's a Welsh name. But she hasn't got an accent - I mean, she's not Welsh as well, is she?'

'Oh, yes - comes from Newport.'

'There are a lot of you around, aren't there?'

'Sure - the city's schools would grind to a halt if it wasn't for the Welsh,' he grinned.

'I hadn't realised it was that bad,' I grinned back. 'Anyway, what were you saying about cricket?'

'Rocky and I are the only two who really do anything for the kids in sport. You can see the others aren't really the type. Bob Pardoe does a bit - he's outside on playground duty at the moment but he's leaving soon, as you know. We were both hoping for someone our age to give us a hand.'

'Fine - I'm game. What does it involve?'

Our conversation was interrupted by the noisy ringing of the bell in the hall. Everyone stood up.

'See you at lunchtime. Get upstairs as soon as you can. We have our meal, then usually Rocky and I have a games practice in the playground with any kids who stay for lunch, or who go home but get back in time.'

'Right, I'll join you.'

I walked back to Miss Rees's room with a comfortable twinge of satisfaction. It was good to feel wanted - and on my first day, too. I also felt I might get a chance to talk to Miss Rockliffe without any of the older members of staff present. I wanted to apologise to her for our introduction earlier. She had avoided me during break, which was hardly surprising.

The remainder of the morning passed quickly. I compiled a seating plan, quietly walking round the class whilst they were working and asking each child's name,. That enabled me to speak to each one separately and acted as a kind of brief personal introduction. It broke the ice for us all. Then I wrote each name in the appropriate box on my plan which served as a simple *aide memoire*.

All the city children called the midday break dinner time and when it came most went home. It began at 12.00 noon at Dayton Road and afternoon school began at 1.50pm. It was, therefore, a relaxing break in the day enabling teachers to eat a meal at leisure as well as to prepare work for the afternoon or to organise activities with children who were available. Dayton Road was typical of most schools of the period. Of the three hundred youngsters it contained at the time I joined only about fifty stayed for a school meal.

The Schools' Meals Service had begun as a wartime necessity and now, a few years later, it was still being used by a comparatively small number of children. Dinner duty for teachers had also been accepted during the war and also had remained. Like playground duty, one teacher supervised the eating of meals each day. The dinners arrived in containers and were dispensed by women servers who came in for the purpose. The pupils sat on long forms at trestle tables in the hall, which were put up and taken down each day.

In the staffroom I discovered seating for lunch was arranged to demonstrate staff hierarchy. Miss Rees, as Chief Assistant, presided by sitting at the head of the small table with her back to the window. Mr Brand, I soon learned, ate his meals in the solitary confinement of his own room at the other end of the building. Miss Browning sat to the immediate right of Miss Rees and beside her, Miss Shenton, both with their backs to the fireplace. Their relative positions reflected their respective periods of service at Dayton Road. The room had a radiator so the fire was normally unnecessary. But their possession of that side of the table closest to it had long been established and emphasized their seniority. On the left of Miss Rees sat Mr Pardoe, followed by Mr Hughes. At the opposite end to Miss Rees sat Miss Rockliffe, senior to Mr Hughes by a few months.

'I think we can manage to squeeze Mr Flaxton in on the corner by Miss Rockliffe,' announced Miss Rees. It wasn't an observation - it was an order. In fact, on this first day, Miss Shenton's place was vacant because she was on dinner duty with the children, but I quickly got the message that her place was not available for me and she would be present shortly. The corner underlined my status as mid-term intruder most successfully. But it suited me fine.

The staff's dinner containers were deposited in the kitchen from whence the contents were carried in by Mr Pardoe and placed in front of Miss Rees. She dispensed the meat and later the sweet. Conversation during that first meal was entirely related to the school and consequently was lost upon me. But as soon as we had drunk a cup of tea, Mr Hughes turned to Miss Rockliffe.

'Are you taking a sports practice, Rocky?'

'Yes, Taff, I'm going now.'

'Excuse us, everyone, we're taking cricket. Come on Mr Flaxton.'

'Perhaps Mr Flaxton doesn't want to go straight back to the children,' interrupted Miss Rees sharply.

'Oh no, I'm keen to help'. I said.

'Oh, very well.'

I felt I'd inadvertently caused offence, but Taff nodded to me. 'Come on, then.' As we went down the stairs the other two seemed to relax.

'Should I have stayed?' I asked.

'No - but our dear Chief Ass will try to own you for the next week or two. You'll have to watch your step'.

'Are you going to the top end, Taff?' Rocky had reached the door.

'Yes - you'll want this end for rounders, won't you?'

'Right. Now, where are the kids?'

We walked into an empty playground, but within seconds were surrounded by twenty or so excited children who materialised from nowhere.

'Can I bat first, sir?

'I want to bowl.'

'Yow 'ad fust gow yesterday, 'smy turn, ain't it, sir?'

'Can I put the bases out, Miss?'

'Can I be captain today, Miss, please let me?'

As the two teachers walked to their respective ends of the playground the youngsters bounced happily alongside them, trying to stake their respective claims. They ignored me. I walked behind the bunch surrounding Taff, and noticed he made no attempt to answer the questions being flung at him. He turned, then took two ancient sets of stumps set in blocks from a boy who was carrying them. He set up one set, turned and strode down the playground. Then he planted the other. His audience stood expectantly between the wickets. 'Who's got the bat?'

'Me, sir,' said a small, round faced lad with curly brown hair, dressed in an old shirt and brown short trousers. It was obvious he thought possession would secure him first knock.

'Let me have it,' ordered Taff.

'Oh, sir,' came the chorus, 'only Martin can get you out an' 'e ain't back yet.'

'I'm not batting first, Mr Flaxton is.' He turned and held out the bat to me. There was sudden and complete silence. I was an unknown quantity at cricket, and a newcomer as well. They were all too polite to object to a stranger.

'I don't want to take a turn away from anyone,' I said. 'Is there some kind of rota?

'Yes, I give everyone a number as they arrive. You're one today, and the rest are two, three, four, five, six…' He counted as he pointed at the boys, one or two of whom tried to dodge into his view to get a lower number. They were unsuccessful.

I decided to conform. I looked at the bat which was very small indeed and also very old. I wondered what the ball would be like. As if in answer, Taff extracted a worn tennis ball from his pocket. He handed it to a short, thick set looking boy.

'You bowl first, Barry.'

The boy walked to the opposite end, strode about six paces beyond, turned and waited. I stood gaping from the other end, feeling quite ridiculous holding the miniature bat. The fact that I was now quite tall made matters worse. I never was a good cricketer. At school cricket suffered in the same way as football, more so because the required space simply was not available between the barrage balloon and the summer crop. However, airfields made interesting wickets; if you managed to connect bat with ball after unpredictable bounces and dispatched the latter with some force you could amass a respectable score quickly because there was no boundary. But I could hardly try that kind of thing with these little children and their tennis ball.

Be gentle - tap it I told myself as I bent over the bat like a croquet hoop. Barry put his head on one side.

'Play,' he said in a flat voice. His set expression didn't alter as he slowly covered the few paces to the wicket, flipped his arm over end bowled. I looped down the wicket as I played forward, nearly overbalancing. The ball shot upwards past my right ear at considerable speed. The bat missed it by miles.

'Pitch them up - you know what you've been told,' shouted Taff.

Another small boy acting as wicket keeper caught the ball neatly above his head. I turned to see him hesitating with an eager expression as he looked at my back foot. Only politeness to a new teacher stopped him stumping me. He looked at me as he threw the ball back to Barry.

'You 'ave to imagine the crease,' he said. I got the message there would be no second chance. I also missed the second ball, which also cleared the stumps, but not by much. The speed seemed incredible. It had nothing to do with his run; the power was entirely in his arm.

'Play,' said Barry. I could see that he had a good over rate. I only had time to lift the bat which somehow stopped the ball and dropped it in front of me. Two figures pounced on it and one flicked it back hard at Barry.

'Play.'

I wasn't at all sure how I should deal with matters. Obviously these children were much more earnest about the game than I'd realised, despite their primitive equipment. Nevertheless, I thought, I must be careful not to hit it hard because, tennis ball or no, I might easily injure someone.

He who hesitates…my stumps went flying backwards with an almighty crash, not being fixed to the ground in any way. They were knocked clean out of the block and one cartwheeled and rolled almost to the playground wall with third man racing to retrieve it.

'Please sir, can I 'ave the bat?'

Before I had time to feel particularly embarrassed number two was at my elbow. I handed it over.

'Play,' said Barry.

I scarcely had time to move away from the wicket before he bowled again. There was a solid thump and batsman number two shot off to the opposite set of stumps and back again. The ball sailed high over the rounders players and bounced off a shelter wall. It was caught neatly on the rebound by a lad who twisted his way amongst the rounders fielders, who totally ignored him. He hurled it back at Barry but the batsman had run four. I caught Taff's eye.

'Not bad, are they?' he smiled.

'Play,' said Barry again.

There were no overs. One boy batted until he was out and one bowled until he was taken off by Taff, who also played, as I saw. Batsman number two hit one off the edge towards him. He bent, fielded the ball, and hurled it ferociously at Barry who caught it perfectly and crashed his hand into the stumps.

'My turn,' yelled number three.

I glanced across at the rounders game, which seemed to be progressing as actively as the cricket. Every now and then someone chased the rounders ball, which was the genuine article, across the wicket. No one objected.

Rocky was standing by a wall, umpiring. I wandered over to her.

'I'm amazed how keen these kids are. Don't they hit the ball hard?' I said.

'Yes, they're tough, aren't they? They may be small, but they're hot stuff at games.'

'Are they as good in the classroom?

'Good lord, no. We have to be the sloggers in there,' she laughed.

'Look, I'm sorry about this morning. Mr Brand seemed to embarrass you, I thought.' She blushed attractively.

'It's so unlike the Boss. He's very staid and proper. I've never known him say anything like that.'

'Well, he certainly made it an introduction to remember,' I said.

'That's for sure,' she replied. Our eyes met and she laughed delightfully. Secretly I felt pleased at landing odds of three to one.

Chapter 25

I quickly settled into the daily routine. My one regret was that I wasn't yet a class teacher, but I was given a full timetable which included one or two lessons with the top class. This was Mr Pardoe's at the time, but Miss Rees was due to take it over when he left. It merited the label 'top' because it contained the oldest and brightest children, five of whom were destined for grammar schools.

During my second week English with this group taught me a salutary lesson. It was the occasion I became involved with Sheba's Breasts. No, there wasn't a girl in the class with such an exotic name, nor was I in danger of professional misconduct. This particular lesson was literature reading, a lesson of noble antiquity which still continues in some schools. A class reads a good book as a corporate exercise, normally the teacher reading it aloud. If he or she has a spark of dramatic ability the lesson is usually very popular even if there are writing exercises to follow. The format is popular on radio. In the face of all-pervasive television children need to be taught how to enjoy books.

I was asked to take over this lesson and found the class part of the way through King Solomon's Mines. I hadn't read the book myself which was a sad gap in my own education. I should have taken it home and adequately prepared by reading it there and then, but foolishly relied upon what I felt was my good reading ability. I was well used to play readings in drama societies, often done on sight and thought I could easily cope in similar fashion with King Solomon's Mines read to these little eleven year olds.

So I was completely unprepared for Sheba's Breasts which, of course, are a pair of mountains in the book. The class were a quarter of the way through and I felt there was an easy way of getting a potted version of finding out a little of what the early part was about.

'Now then,' I began brightly 'let me see what you can remember about what you have read so far.' A forest of hands waved at me.

'Sir - sir.'

'Alright, you tell me, James.'

I selected a bright lad who I guessed would give me the gist quickly. He obliged.

'...and there's a map of the route across the desert and mountains...'

I interrupted the flow. 'Where's the map? Everyone dived back into the book.

'Page fourteen, sir,' came an urgent cry from the back of the room.

'Good, let's have a look at page fourteen and see if you remember it.' I flicked the pages and glanced at it swiftly. It was a simple map showing the heroes' track across the desert, the mountains and Solomon's Road. At the bottom a squiggly line crossed the track - the Kalukawe River. In the middle there was a shaded crescent, broken in the centre. The track passed through this gap on either side of which were two circles. I glanced at the small print beneath these. Sheba's Breasts, I read. I felt my face turning slightly pink. Hardly the thing to comment upon to a mixed class of eleven year olds, I thought.

'Oh yes, I see. Now, how far along this route has the group travelled at the point you've reached in the book?'

'They're in the desert, sir. We've reached chapter six, Water, Water, sir.'

'Right, let's turn to...' My eye strayed to the small print beneath the map. I, José da Silvestra, who am now dying of hunger in the little cave where no snow is on the north side of the nipple of the southernmost of the two mountains I have named Sheba's Breasts. I was genuinely surprised at meeting such brazen description in a book being read to a mixed class of young children and felt glad the class had progressed beyond it. Then a nagging thought had me wondering whether there was more to come. I regretted my folly at not doing my homework.

Looking back today, my sensitivity seems ridiculously quaint. But in view of my own schooling perhaps it was to be expected. Anything sexual was absolutely taboo. I remember being in a third form at grammar school studying the book, Green Mansions by W.H.Hudson. I can recall very little of it except one line for which we had all been waiting for weeks and which had been the subject of double and triple underlinings in each other's copies. A man and a woman had contrived to get lost in a forest, in the dark, in a tropical storm. Clothes became mildly dishevelled for a line or two. Then it came. Our heads went down, expectant glances were flashed around the room and we all held our breath. Calmly the master's voice droned on,

'I touched something soft and wet. It was her breast...'

Strangled gurgles escaped involuntarily from a few throats and we hugged ourselves at hearing this magnificent eroticism. With that in my background I suppose my concern was understandable. Thanks to Wikipedia I've updated my memory of the book, though I see it doesn't refer to the single event I remembered.

'Yes, turn to the beginning of Chapter Six,' I commanded.

This begins with Allan Quatermain's description of their raging thirst in the desert and I threw myself wholeheartedly into the reading. When I reached the dialogue between Sir Henry, Good, Quatermain, and the Hotentot, Ventvogel, and managed to alter my voice according to the characters, I saw appreciative glances flickering on the children's faces and they settled more comfortably in their seats. I felt I was becoming a minor hit with the top class, which would do my reputation no harm at all. Then Quatermain turned to contemplate the prospect of dawn on the mountains.

'There, not more than forty or fifty miles from us, glittering like silver in the early rays of the morning sun, soared Sheba's...'

I'd plunged into the description dramatically and powerfully and consequently found it quite impossible to pull back when I reached what was coming...

'...Breasts,' I boomed and turned scarlet. I buried my face in the book, not daring to look at the class's reaction. I was sure I could guess it. I hurried on.

'…Now…I attempt to describe the extraordinary grandeur and beauty of that sight, language seems to fail me. I am impotent…'

' I know how you feel,' I thought. But worse was to follow. Quatermain has to revel in the scene. 'Before us rose two enormous mountains, the like of which are not, I believe, to be seen in Africa, if indeed there are any to match them in the world…' But the vision conjured up in my mind was not of mountains but of the objects of comparison. My collar was sticking uncomfortably, my face was burning and my throat was getting unpleasantly dry.

'…These mountains, placed thus, like the pillars of a gigantic gateway, are shaped after the fashion of a woman's…' I swallowed hard, '…breasts,' I croaked, 'and at times the mists and shadows beneath them take the form of a recumbent woman…'

Get me out of this, I thought and quickly took a deep breath. As a result I coughed suddenly and loudly and in so doing hurt the back of my throat.

'…Their bases swell gently from the plain…' I wheezed, then stopped and burst into a fit of coughing. I looked up and saw everyone staring at me. I felt I was turning purple. I gulped and tried to struggle on.

'…looking at that distance perfectly round and smooth…' I swallowed again, and wheezed on '…and upon the top of each is a vast hillock covered with snow, exactly corresponding to the…'

'Oh, no,' I groaned inwardly.

'…to the, er, nipple on the female breast,' I gasped hoarsely and dissolved into near apoplexy.

A coughing spasm racked me until tears streamed down my cheeks. My knees turned weak as I thought of the spectacle I was presenting to the class. What price my reputation now?

A quiet and respectful voice penetrated my agony.

'Shall I get you a glass of water, sir?' I gazed inanely at a demure girl standing beside me.

'Oh, yes please,' I gurgled. She slipped out of the room. I calmed my heaving lungs and struggled on.

'To describe the comprehensive grandeur of that view is beyond my powers.' said Allan Quatermain. Nevertheless he struggled on for a few more lines. But I was vastly relieved to see that he had dropped the simile and had fallen back upon a straight forward description of mountains. The glass of water appeared by my side. I drank it eagerly and, not unnaturally, it quickly settled my throat and visibly cooled me.

'Sheba's breasts had scarcely vanished into cloud-clad privacy before our thirst - literally a burning question - reasserted itself,' I continued. Yes - thank heaven for water, I thought. Then I dared to look at the class.

They were all reading again and were obviously perfectly normal and relaxed. There were no glances, no giggles, no embarrassment. Even a very green teacher such as I could spot any surreptitious ripples of feeling whenever they flowed through a group of children for whatever reason. These youngsters had been completely unmoved by anything except my stupid performance which had been entirely of my own making because I hadn't done my homework. What price all my practice at St Andrew's?

In those pre-television-advertising days eleven year olds were quite unprecocious and that day I learned the fact. A few years later I learned that things would have been quite different had they been thirteen year olds. That was when I was reading Elephant Bill to a mixed senior class. It contains a graphic account of the copulation of elephants…but I was older and wiser by then.

Chapter 26

'Pad Monitor - go and put the pads out.'

Marjorie jumped up from her desk, went to a cupboard and took out seven shiny thick brown boards. Then she left the classroom to place them in strategic positions for morning assembly.

Having sent her upon her vital mission I continued with the early morning routine, marking the attendance and 'dinner' registers. The attendance was checked morning and afternoon in the time-honoured way. Each child's name was written against a number in the register and the children called these out in rotation. All I had to do was to start them off.

'Mary Adams...'

Mary dutifully called out one, the next 'two', and so on. Absentees were immediately obvious. It was regimented and impersonal, but no one seemed to mind. Although this was Miss Rees's class I was enjoying being left to deal with it on my own. After the routine administration had been completed, I told the class to stand and watched the children file out into the hall.

The other classes did the same and soon they were standing very quietly in orderly rows in front of Mr Brand's desk. This was set in a slight alcove formed where the middle classroom was offset from the other two which flanked the hall. It was a long low desk, raised on a dais, and dated from the opening of the school. In those days the headteacher was expected to spend most of his or her time at that desk, retiring only occasionally to the 'Private Room' upstairs. As soon as the classes were in position each teacher sat down. This was the moment when we appreciated the pad monitor's vital duty.

Heating the hall was effected by two sets of massive pipes which were situated in front of the two classrooms on each side of the headteacher's desk. There were two rows in each set. They emerged from the floor, curved into a horizontal stretch as long as the classroom wall, and then returned to the building's nether regions. The boiler was in the cellar beneath the hall. The horizontal section was at a convenient height for sitting, and because the only ordinary chairs were upstairs these pipes were used for staff seating. It was either that, or we stood.

Not that we wanted to sit and relax whilst the children stood throughout the assembly. We stood with them during the singing of the hymn, the saying of prayers and the reading from the Bible, but whenever Mr Brand wanted to talk to them at some length they were allowed to sit cross-legged on the floor. That would hardly have suited the female members of staff, who opted for the pipes instead.

In summer the pipes were cold, of course, so the thick pads provided welcome insulation when thin dresses and trousers were worn. But in winter they were vital, because those pipes were sizzling. In fact I learnt to sit remarkably still. The pads were not very large because their normal use was as firm backing for small sheets of paper on the old classroom desks. If you moved into direct contact with the pipes it took a superhuman effort not to wreck the assembly with a sharp yell. This would have amused the children but certainly not Mr Brand. Wrigglers suffered one or two third degree burns in tender places, then learnt to keep still.

Mr Brand dominated assemblies, although he was not especially forceful in manner at other times. His voice had a rich quality with a hint of the West Country in it. His erect stance, his imposing features surmounted by light grey hair gave the impression of Moses exhorting the tribes of Israel clad for some strange reason in a lounge suit. When he spoke to the children they listened intently.

Once or twice whilst I was at Dayton Road a child was foolish enough to whisper whilst Mr Brand was speaking. Without warning he charged into the midst of the assembled company, scattering bodies to either side. He administered a sharp slap on the culprit's face, turned and walked back to his desk. Then he continued where he had left off. No mention was made of the offender or the offence. It was as unexpected as the way he dealt with stairs. It was also highly successful in gaining one hundred per cent attention.

But his *persona* became magnetic when he was reading from the Bible. His mellifluous voice revelled in the language of the Authorised Version, especially the Old Testament. Each day his performance was good, but occasionally he rose to special heights. Undoubtedly his peak was the third chapter of the Book of Daniel. He read it about once a year, apparently not as part of any particular sequence. It came, therefore, quite unexpectedly both to pupils and staff. But whenever he read it he had us hanging on every word just as much as the children.

'Nebuchadnezzar the King made an image of gold, whose height was threescore cubits, and the breadth thereof six cubits; he set it up in the plain of Dura, in the province of Babylon.'

His voice echoed through the lofty hall like a herald. Then, suddenly, in a matter-of-fact voice,

'Who can tell me how long was a cubit?'

A few hands rose slowly as the children tried to remember. 'Yes, Eric,' said Mr Brand.

'About eighteen inches, sir.'

'Good boy - yes, that's correct. It was the distance from a man's elbow to the tip of his middle finger. So that's one foot six inches. Now, how many things are there in a score? Yes, Monica?'

'Twenty, Mr Brand.'

'Right, well done. So how many are there in threescore?' 'Sixty', she continued.

'Well done. Now, sixty times one and a half feet. Who can tell me the total?'

Some of the top class had their hands up very quickly. Mr Brand pointed to one, and agreed the result.

'Just imagine, a huge figure ninety feet high, standing on the plain. However, I don't suppose the measurement is accurate, because it was only six cubits broad, and that would make it nine feet. It would be very tall and thin, wouldn't it? But never mind, the image was obviously very big and coloured gold to make it

seem very important-to the people. Now listen to what happend.'
The herald resumed his function.

'Then Nebuchadnezzar the King sent to gather together the princes, the governors, and the captains, the judges, the treasurers, the counsellors, the sheriffs, and all the rulers of the province to come to the dedication of the image which Nebuchadnezzar the King had set up.'

I think it was the repetition which fascinated the children, as well as words which were only half understood. Sheriffs, for instance, how on earth did such gun-toting Westerners fit into the scene on Babylon's plain? But Mr Brand did not elucidate further.

'Then an herald cried aloud...' and Mr Brand flicked into overdrive...'To you it is commanded, O people, nations, and languages. That at what time ye hear the sound of the cornet, flute, harp, sackbut, psaltery, dulcimer and all kinds of music, ye fall down and worship the golden image that Nebuchadnezzar the King hath set up. And whoso falleth not down and worshipeth shall the same hour be cast into the midst of a burning fiery furnace.'

Heads turned slightly and some children looked at each other with a hint of horror. Sackbuts, psalteries and dulcimers might have been beyond their ken, but a burning fiery furnace certainly was not.

'Therefore at what time, when all the people heard the sound of the cornet, flute, harp, sackbut, psaltery, dulcimer, and all kinds of music...' intoned Mr Brand, 'the people, the nations, and the languages fell down...'

I caught Martin A's eye. He frowned. I could see he was wondering how a language could fall down. He was a bright lad as I found when taking the top class. But Mr Brand swept on regally.

'...and worshipped the image which Nebuchadnezzar the--King had set up.'

But then trouble loomed. There were three servants of the Lord named Shadrack, Meshach and Abednego...the children were as impressed with those superb sounding names as I had been as a child. Years later I was not surprised to hear them become the subject of a particularly lively pop song even though a couple of letters were swopped round in the last one.

Mr Brand didn't have to explain why Shadrach, Meshach and Abednego weren't going to bow down to Nebuchadnezzar's golden image. The children knew the Ten Commandments thoroughly, of course, because these were regularly taught in Scripture lessons. Thou shaft not make unto thee any graven image …thou shall not bow down thyself to them, nor serve them… Many knew the words by heart.

They also knew what happened to the Children of Israel when they disobeyed and worshipped the Golden Calf. So they didn't need to be told that these chaps, Shadrach, Meshach and Abednego had a problem. It came in the guise of some Chaldeans who sneaked to Nebuchadnezzar.

'O king, live for ever. Thee, O king, hast made a decree that every man shall hear the sound of the cornet, flute, harp, sackbut, psaltery and dulcimer, and all kinds of music…'

A pin dropped in the hall would have made everyone jumpy. The children gazed in awed silence at Mr Brand and even we were immobile on our strange seats.

'There are certain Jews whom thou hast set over the affairs of the province of Babylon, Shadrach, Meshach and Abednego; these men, O king, have not regarded thee; they serve-not thy gods nor worship the golden image which thou hast set up.'

Mr Brand pressed on relentlessly. There was to be no escape.

'Then Nebuchadnezzar in his rage and fury commanded to bring Shadrach, Meshach and Abednego…' I could see some of the girls clenching their fists willing the men to give in to the king's last warning.

'Now if ye be ready that at what time ye hear the sound of the cornet, flute, harp, sackbut, psaltery, and dulcimer, and all kinds of music, ye fall down and worship the image which I have made, well: but if ye worship not, ye shall be cast the same hour into the midst of a burning fiery furnace.'

But Shadrach and company were made of sterner stuff - besides, they had a potent Ally.

'…our God, whom we serve is able to deliver us from the burning fiery furnace…' then, to add insult to injury, 'but, if not, be it known unto thee, O king, that we will not serve thy gods, nor worship the golden image which thou hast set up'.

Consternation rippled gently through the young crowd, now standing firmly in Babylon, watching intently for Mr Nebuchadnezzar's reaction to this outrageous challenge to his authority.

'Then was Nebuchadnezzar full of fury and the form of his visage was changed against Shadrach, Meshach, and Abednego...' Plainly it was so, as the children could see!

'Therefore he spake, and commanded that they should heat the furnace seven times more than it was wont to be heated, and he commanded the most mighty men that were in his army to bind Shadrach, Meshach, and Abednego, and to cast them-into the burning fiery furnace. Then these men were bound in their coats, their hosen and their hats, and their other garments, and were cast into the midst of the burning fiery furnace.'

There were quiet gasps from the most sensitive girls and a hint of ghoulish grins from a few boys, just to show they were tough and could take this sort of thing in their stride. Nevertheless, matters looked exceedingly grim.

'Therefore because the king's command was urgent, and the furnace exceeding hot, the flame of the fire slew those that took up Shadrach, Meshach, and Abednego. And these men, Shadrach, Meshach, and Abednego...' Mr Brand paused dramatically, and dropped his voice in despair...' fell down in the midst of the burning...fiery...furnace.'

There was an audible gasp amongst the crowd. The pause seemed endless. Then suddenly Mr Brand raised his bushy eyebrows and his voice became incredulous.

'Then Nebuchadnezzar the King was astonished, and rose up in haste, and spake, and said unto his counsellors, "Did not we cast three men into the midst of the fire?" They answered and said unto the king, "True, O king." He answered and said, "Lo, I see four men loose, and walking - in - the - midst - of - the - fire, and they...have...no...hurt...

Another pause, and more gasps

'...and the form of the fourth is like the Son of God.'

Perfect silence. Then, at last, came the happy ending, to the obvious relief of all the children.

'Then Nebuchadnezzar came near to the mouth of the burning fiery furnace, and spoke and said, "Shadrach, Meshach, and Abednego, ye servants of the most high God, come forth and come hither. Then Nebuchadnezzar spoke, and said, 'Blessed be the God of Shadrach, Meshach, and Abednego, who hath sent his angel, and delivered his servants that trusted in him, and have changed the king's word, and yielded their bodies, that they might not serve nor worship any god except their own God.'

There was no need for Mr Brand to make any explanatory comments. The result was absolutely plain to every child. Do what God wants and all will be well. At their age they were happily unaware of the complication that some person has to decide what he or she thinks that is and tell them about it.

They filed out of the hall in complete silence. Mentally they remained on the plains of Babylon marvelling at the miracle they had just witnessed through Mr Brand's masterly performance.

After that, Arithmetic was an unfair trial for everyone, including the staff.

Chapter 27

I soon began to look forward to lunch time each day and blessed my good fortune that the seating regime at the staff table had fallen out so propitiously for me. Although the table was small and no one could possibly have a private conversation, nevertheless it was natural to talk to the person next to one. That, for me, was Miss Rockliffe, who was very close to my left elbow.

Once or twice when I contrived to get our heads fairly close together in an animated conversation, Miss Rees would do her best to break it up.

'Mr Flaxton, did you manage to finish percentages with Class Two today?' she would ask suddenly, and I would have to jerk myself away from contemplating Miss Rockliffe's schoolgirl complexion and pretend to be intelligent about the teaching of Arithmetic. But Miss Rees didn't follow the school cricket team in its evening and Saturday morning matches, whilst Miss Rockliffe did. So I soon attached myself to it as well, having already been invited to do so by Taff Hughes. After two or three weeks I began to look forward to these matches very much indeed. The boys were extremely keen and often won their matches. It wasn't always through great skill, but rather sheer determination. They slogged, ran, chased and hurled themselves around the field and were encouraged, shouted at, cajoled and sympathised with by Taff and Rocky. I soon realised their personalities were being transmitted to the boys and the latter responded by giving one hundred percent. There was a keen and warm feeling amongst the group in which I was encouraged to share.

Soon, to my great delight, I found that when I arrived at whichever field the match was due to take place the boys waved and dashed over to me as well as to the other two.

'Allo, Mr Flaxton. Are you umpirin' tonight? Michael 'int 'ere yet.and 'e wus bringin' the bag.'

'Whatever'll we do if 'e doan come, sir?'

'Look, there's the St. Thomas's lot. They've got their stuff. Do you fink they'll let us borrer some o' thern?'

I began to enjoy myself by taking charge in such moments and allaying their fears.

'Don't worry lads, Michael will turn up, I'm sure. I expect he missed the bus. There's plenty of time.'

I soon learnt that nine times out of ten the crisis did not materialise. The tenth occasion provided a problem, of course, and solving it was a matter of experience. In the early days I left that sort of thing to Taff and Rocky who had a wealth of experience compared with me. Two and a half terms to be precise.

Rocky's presence also contributed to my interest in these matches. She exuded enthusiasm which made her all the more attractive. I wondered if there was a boy friend in Wales or whether there was anything between her and Taff Hughes.

One evening after the match the sun was still shining and the weather was delightfully warm. We travelled with the boys on a bus which took us back to the school's area, disembarked and saw them all safely on their way home. Taff wasn't with us, because he had gone directly from the playing field to an evening class he taught.

'Are you taking a bus back to your digs?' I asked.

'No, I think I'll walk. There's not much to do when I'm there, and it's such a nice evening'.

'Do you mind if I join you?'

'Not at all.'

Suddenly the evening was positively glowing. I murmured my thanks and we set off along the road. Unaccountably I was lost for words but after a long silence, I struck out.

'Have you always been called Rocky - it seems rather masculine. Don't you object?'

'Not at all. I rather like it. I've two older brothers who were both called Rocky at school and it got passed on to me.'

'I'd never have believed you're Welsh. You haven't a trace of an accent.'

'You mean like Taff? He's from the Valleys, you can't escape it there.'

'Are you glad you're not easily recognised as Welsh?'

'No,' she replied sharply. 'I'm very proud of being Welsh.'

'Sorry. I didn't mean to offend you. I've always loved Wales. My father took me there as a boy, and now I do some hill walking and a spot of rock climbing.'

'Yes, I love the mountains,' she said wistfully.

'You're from Newport aren't you?'

'You have been doing your homework,' she quipped.

I laughed. 'Yes, Taff told me. I've not been there, though I've flown over it from an RAF station near Hereford when I was in the ATC.

'Mm, I'd love to see it from the air. What did it look like?'

'Like most towns, rather dirty and covered in a bluish brown haze. However, I've also flown over this place when I was in the RAF, and I have to admit that it was worse.'

'Were you a pilot?

Good Lord, no. I was groundcrew.'

'Then how did you do much flying?'

'Simple, whenever you did any work on an aircraft they sent you up with it on the air test afterwards. It was a foolproof way of making sure you did your job properly.'

'Were you just an AC plonk?'

'I was for a time then I was retrained as a Sergeant Instructor. I finished up at St. Athan teaching in an RAF School for Apprentices. Found myself in charge of a sort of hobbies hour for all the lads because I did Craft at college. Quite cushy actually because our leave was the equivalent of school holidays.'

'You sound the sort of character who lands on his feet.'

'That's what my mother always says,' I laughed.

We wandered on in the sultry evening air along what was normally a very busy road. There were houses on one side, and a stretch of grass surrounding a small reservoir on the other. Suddenly I jumped. A bicycle shot passed me ridden far too close to the kerb.

'Heck, he nearly hit me.'

I glared at the retreating figure. It was a boy whose age I couldn't guess.

'Oh - it's him again,' said Rocky... 'and with him will be...'

Before she could finish, or before either of us could turn, another cyclist tore by similarly close.

'Allo, Miss Rock Bottom,' the rider called out rudely in mock-posh tones. I turned to her angrily.

'Who are those brats?'

'They're two from the secondary school most of our youngsters go to.'

'Do you know their names?'

'No, they left Dayton Road three years ago, so I've never taught them. But they've done this kind of thing before.'

'Cheeky young wretches,' I said indignantly.

The cyclists turned some distance ahead and sped back past us on the other side of the road.

'You've got another boy friend tonight, then,' yelled one.

'My stars, if I get my hands on him,' I snapped.

'I suppose they think we're good for a lark" said Rocky. 'When they were at Dayton Road there weren't any teachers of our age.'

'No, I can't imagine them doing this to Miss Rees, or any of the others for that matter, which makes it all the more infuriating.'

'Come on, let's forget it. They'll go home now they've had their fun.'

But Rocky was wrong. Unseen by us they turned again for a second run. The first rider zoomed past as before, narrowly missing my shoulder.

'Yah, ole' Rock bum,' he yelled.

Incensed I turned just as the second was riding up to us along the gutter.

'Rocky bott...'

Without thinking, I grabbed the handlebars. He wasn't travelling very quickly so he didn't pull me over and I stopped the bicycle very effectively. But I failed to grab the rider who was flung off the bike and crashed to the ground, sprawling into the road. For a split second I stood absolutely immobile, whilst my thoughts raced like a torrent...

...busy main road...lorries, buses, cars speed along...many accidents, no, road's empty...he's lying still...oh God, skull fractured, hell, what have I done...?

Suddenly the prostrate figure rolled over and leapt to its feet.

'That was a bloody stupid thing to do,' he yelled at me. 'Gimme me bike.'

He wrenched it from my grasp and jumped on to it Relief at the obvious fact that nothing was damaged but his pride flooded over me. The cyclists wheeled round again in front of us, then rode by on the other side with furious looks. Stupidly I tried to salvage my pride.

'Don't try being so rude in future,' I called pompously.

'Yah,' yelled the first boy and spat ineffectively in my direction.

'You could 'ave killed me,' called the other. We watched them ride into the distance.

'I'm afraid he's right,' said Rocky quietly.

'Yes - I know.' I felt cold sweat trickly down my back. 'But he made me so mad. How dare he be so rude and cheeky?'

'But he's still only a boy and you mustn't let temper get the better of you when dealing with kids.' She paused, and looked at me. 'Suppose there'd been a bus behind you... can't you imagine what the newspaper headlines would have said tomorrow?' I turned even colder despite the warmth of the summer evening. Rocky slipped her hand round my arm.

'Put it down to experience. Anyway, thanks for coming to my defence.'

I opened my mouth to reply, but decided against it. I caught her eye and she smiled sympathetically. For the remainder of our walk she considerately managed to stop me feeling embarrassed at my dangerous thoughtlessness. But for a long time afterwards the lesson seared into my consciousness.

After a few weeks the summer holidays came and the staff dispersed. The three older women were going abroad, a comparatively adventurous undertaking so soon after the war. Taff and Rocky returned to South Wales, whilst I visited the Lakeland hills for the first time in my life. Hill walking and rock climbing cast their fascination upon me whilst I was at St. Andrew's and I managed to spend some of my RAF leaves in the hills of North Wales. Then, earlier in the year I had spent my Easter leave on a Beginners Course of the new Mountaineering Association.

This had been a very enjoyable event, only the second they had organised since the war. We had an excellent tutor who, in employment, was a steeplejack. He was rather amused by the teaching manual he'd been supplied with. Obviously the authors felt beginners needed explanations from the very beginning – or were assumed to have very low IQs.

'Students should be instructed in basic rope techniques.' We agreed.

'On a rope with three climbers, the first is known as the leader. Wow', we said.

'The second climber is known as the second, or the middleman. The third is known as last man, or number three. We'd never have guessed', we said.

'There is no rope above the leader…'

'There is no greater strain on the second than the falling leader…'

Fortunately the practical tuition far outstripped the manual. On the last day of term Rocky said, 'Don't forget to send me a postcard,' to which I readily agreed and asked for one in return. I felt elated because I seemed to be getting on well with her, but I was not as enthusiastic about the six weeks holiday as I expected to be. I was going to miss the school and the children. After all, I had only just begun and had taught for only a few weeks. I was impatient to have my own class as well.

When I arrived in the Lake District it was raining and it continued to do so for days on end. The wettest August for thirty-two years, the locals said. I didn't contradict them. I sent a ridiculously sunny card to Rocky and wrote that it wasn't like that at all. Soon one came back showing Newport looking remarkably clean and tidy. It wasn't all like that, wrote Rocky. She also mentioned that she had repaired my tie.

I was highly pleased with this item of news because the repair of this garment seemed to carry some significance. It was, for those early post-war years, a highly flamboyant Paisley design. Opponents objected if I wore it when playing table tennis matches. It put them off their stroke, they said. Kim had given it to me as a birthday present when I was at St. Andrew's. I liked it immensely and wore it frequently. It was silk with an inner lining to stiffen it. Regular use made it dirty and I had washed it myself. The result was a hopelessly twisted lining. Every time I wore it afterwards it dangled from my neck like a corkscrew.

Rocky had seen it one day and asked what the trouble was. I told her its history and my passion for it. She seemed to accept it as a sort of challenge and said she was sure she could fix it. Her interest in the tie and her success with it brought a gleam to the Lakeland mists. The weather cleared almost immediately and the last few days of the holiday were spent amongst wonderful views in glorious sunshine. I walked hard trying to make up for lost time. As a result I gave myself tenosynovitis in the ankle and came home limping. But it cleared up in time for school.

Few children will admit to longing to go back to school at the beginning of a new term and over the years I have heard my colleagues also complain about it very frequently. It seems it simply isn't done to admit one likes one's job and so is happy to go back. However, in that September I knew nothing of protocol in such matters. I cycled to Dayton Road on the first day as though I was training for a sprint race.

'Allo, Mr Flaxton.'

The greeting was shouted at me from all quarters as I rode the last couple of hundred yards. The children's obvious welcome gave me an inward contented glow of pride. In those days teachers had to sign in and sign out when they arrived and left each day, recording the time of day alongside their signatures The book was placed on the staffroom table and usually Miss Rees hovered over it impatiently.

'I hope you've had an enjoyable holiday, Mr Flaxton,' she said as I signed.

'Thank you, I have. It was extremely wet in the Lake District, I'm afraid, though the weather improved considerably just before I left.'

'Oh dear, that's so often the way. Still, I hope you managed to get plenty of relaxation, despite the weather. You'll need it this term with a class of your own.'

'Actually,' I said, standing up, 'I couldn't wait to get back. This is what I've been looking forward to for two years since I left college. At last I'm going to have my own class. I've had all the relaxation I need - I just want to get on with the work.'

She looked at me. 'A very noble sentiment, I'm sure.' There was a pause. 'Mr Brand will give you your register.'

'Right, I'm on my way.'

I bounded down the stairs, no doubt looking extremely boyish in her eyes. But at that moment nothing could have dampened my spirits. The reason was that all junior teaching, and much senior teaching as well, was done in class units. Being a teacher and having a class were virtually synonymous. Conversely, not having a class had made me, as a young teacher, feel incomplete. I was qualified but not yet truly in the job.

'Here you are, Mr Flaxton,' said Mr Brand after I had ascended to his sanctum. 'Your very own class register. At least I shan't have to tell you how to fill it in, or how to do your dinner register. You had some practice last term. You also know most of the children, which will be quite useful.'

I looked at the large, blue, stiff covered register and opened it. Written neatly in Mr Brand's impeccable handwriting were forty-eight names. My class. As if to confirm matters finally I closed it and looked again at the front.

Class Four I read - and then beneath, Class Teacher - Mr N. Flaxton.

I walked out of Mr Brand's study to the top of the stairs. I was about to run down them when a head appeared round the door at the bottom. I didn't recognise the face.

'Excuse me,' said a voice with a strong Welsh accent, 'I was told I would find the headmaster here - is that right?'

'Oh, yes, Mr Brand's room is up here. Come on up and I'll show you.'

A stocky, broad shouldered figure plodded up the long flight of stairs.

Hm,, good for exercise, these,' he said with a grin as he reached the top.

'That's very true. Here's Mr Brand's room.' I walked the few paces along the landing, knocked and opened the door again as Mr Brand called, 'Come in.'

'There's someone enquiring for you, Mr Brand.'

'Ah, you must be Mr Brown,' he said to the newcomer.

'That's right, sir.

'Well, I can introduce you to one of the staff straight away - Mr Flaxton, this is Mr Brown, the new teacher who is joining us today.'

'Of course, I'd quite forgotten. I'm very pleased to meet you. Is this your first appointment?'

'Oh yes, I'm a new boy. Just finished my National Service in the Army.'

A further gleam of satisfaction was born inside me. I was no longer the newest member of staff. I was fully six weeks this man's senior. '

'I hope you won't mind my saying so, but you're obviously Welsh, yet Brown is such an English name.'

'I know,' he laughed, 'and my Christian name's Wilfred. My mother said she wanted to be different and married someone with an English surname though my father is as Welsh as she is. His family has been in the Valleys for generations.'

'That divides the staff evenly,' said Mr Brand. 'Not quite a take-over by the Welsh but not far off it, eh, Mr Flaxton?' He chuckled loudly.

'Well, I must get away to my class,' I said importantly. 'I'll see you later in the staffroom.'

Minutes later I walked through the playground to where I could see two lines of chattering children facing a door which led into Class Four's room. As I neared them I caught the insufficiently quiet warnings that were being flashed to the heads of the queues, which were out of my sight at that moment.

'Shurrup, you lot - 'ere 'e is. It's Mr Flaxton.'

They fell silent as I walked between the rows. At the door I turned, and looked at their faces. They were quiet, respectful, and expectant. It looked as though they were pleased to have me as their teacher. What they couldn't possibly know was how delighted I was to have them. My own class at last. What would we make of each other?

In loco parentis the law said. Since that first day with my own class I have remained aware that what is fundamental in education is the relationship between pupil and teacher. It always was and always will be. To be an effective teacher the relationship has to be right and that relationship has to be an extension of the parental role.

I used to find it amazing to hear some teachers complaining about children in school. Of course they are mischievous, unpredictable, lovable, naughty, angry, jealous, hardworking, lazy, good humoured bundles of energy just like the vast majority of parents' children because they are the same beings. That's obvious. So if you choose to teach that's what you're going to spend your working life with - and if you're going to be a parent, as the great majority of us are, that's what you're going to spend eighteen years or so with. Teachers, parents, many of us are both. That day, as I faced Class Four for the first time, I knew what had attracted me to teaching. *In loco parentis* to forty-eight of them.

Since then I have taught them, organised them, helped them at sport and in their work; I have cycled with them, climbed mountains with them, camped with them and lived with them. I have seen them succeed, I have seen them fail, I have seen them in tragedy and I have attended their funerals. I have acted with them, I have swum with them, been abroad with them, appeared in court for them. I have grown older with them and they have brought their children to me. Some could easily have brought their grandchildren to me but by moving around the country I've dodged that eventuality. Above all, I have been happy with them.

I called the register, collected the dinner money and took them into assembly. There Mr Brand welcomed everyone back and introduced Mr Brown. Then the lines of children trooped out with their teachers and Class Four and I took our turn to do the same. We entered the room, they sat down and I closed the door. I, picked up the time table, though I knew what it said for this period. Arithmetic. I put it down.

'Let's forget Arithmetic...' I said. Every eye in the room looked at me. 'Well, for a few minutes, at least,' I continued with a twinkle. The eyes twinkled back. 'You all know me from last term, when I used to teach you occasionally when you were in Miss Rockliffe's and Miss Browning's classes. Well, now you're in my class - Class Four.' I looked around. 'Now, you were good in your last classes, of course, but I want Class Four to be the best in the school. It's going to be - ISN'T IT?' I socked it to them.

'Yesmizzaflaxon,' they mumbled, just audibly.

I threw my head to the ceiling and spun round on the spot in a show of mock annoyance.

'I'll try again - THIS IS GOING TO BE THE BEST CLASS IN THE SCHOOL, ISN'T IT?;

This time they roared, 'YES, MR FLAXTON.'

'Great, that's better. That's the spirit I want. I want us to do the best work, have the best teams, the best classroom room display work...yes, Jean, what do you want?'

'Please sir, Miss Rockliffe had the best classroom displays last year. Mr Brand often said how lovely the room looked.' Jean wasn't going to switch her loyalty from Rocky to me that easily.

'Yes,' piped up another voice, 'and she can draw ever so well. Her pictures are super.'

'Well, we shall just have to do better,' I continued, though inwardly worried because I was only too well aware of my complete inadequacy in artistic matters.

'I know,' I said brightly, 'we can make models. Did you do that last year?'

'No sir,' came the chorus with much shaking of heads.

'There we are then, we can do that.' I thought back to my efforts in Handwork for Men and where they had landed me at St Athan. I felt I might dredge up something from the experiences for a junior classroom to counter Rocky's artistic ability.

'Please sir, Miss Rockliffe made our room look marvlous last Chrissmas.'

'Oo yes, she 'ad a super frieze all round the room, an' we all painted Farver Chrissmassis an' snowflakes.'

The children struck a warning note even though it was early September.

'Very well, we shall just have to think of something different,' I said simply. 'At least we've got plenty of time to prepare.'

'Sir, what if Miss Rockliffe's class does the same sort of thing as us?' This was Lorraine B, who was quick to spot problems. I realised that she had a point. If I was encouraging an inter-class competitive spirit, it was my duty to make sure that we started well ahead.

'I know - I'll appoint you 'Spy-in-Chief', Lorraine. Just listen quietly and I expect you'll find out during the term what Miss Rockliffe's class are doing for their Christmas display.'

There were beams all round. Obviously I had hit upon a novel idea which would produce a group spirit in the class. I soon realised that Lorraine was to be guaranteed the service of forty-seven ordinary spies. So began a lively rivalry between Rocky and me which I think was to the advantage of both our classes.

I appointed one or two more children to various jobs - pencil sharpener, blackboard rubber cleaner. But I kept back the most important and most coveted position, that of Class Monitor.

'I shall wait a few days and then make up my mind as to who is the best person for this job. I want someone who works hard and behaves very well. So if you want the job, you must just show me that you're the best.'

For a week all forty-eight tried hard at their varied levels to show me just how good they were. It was not long before some of them showed me other aspects of behaviour which taught me much. One boy was subject to epileptic fits and on occasions would suddenly slide sideways from his desk and sprawl in convulsions in the gangway. I soon learnt to look for his tongue and to flip it forward if he seemed in danger of swallowing it. However, the children allayed my fears.

'There's nuffin to worry about, sir, 'e often does it. Jus' grab 'is tung an' shove a pencil between 'is teef.'

Vague memories of lectures with the Doc. at St. Andrew's confirmed this procedure and it was reinforced by the other members of staff. Gradually dealing with his fits became routine. But what a difference between then and now! I didn't even have a conversation about the boy with Mr Brand, nor his parents. He had fits, he got over them, life went on. No medical reports, no monitoring, no health visitors. Certainly no forms to complete!

There was also a girl who frequently asked permission to wash her hands. At first I thought this was a euphemism for going to the lavatory but soon found she went to the cloakroom to do exactly what she said. I asked Miss Browning about her, since she had had the girl the previous year. But there had been nothing untoward in her behaviour in that class. The girl just smiled rather vacuously when I asked her about it and said she didn't like handling dirty books, and that her desk was dusty. But obviously there was more to it than that.

I asked to speak to her mother, who immediately solved the problem. I was the fly in the ointment, or rather the dirt in the classroom. I had an unwitting habit of putting my hand to my face and, apparently, to my mouth when thinking. Then, when going round the class marking books, I sometimes touched this girl or her exercise book. Immediately she felt contaminated and had to wash her hands to be cleansed.

'Good lord,' I said, genuinely amazed, 'Does she do this with everyone?'

'Oh no, it's only you that bothers her,' said her mother smugly. I felt like crawling away under the nearest stone.

Then there was Penelope L. She was an active, pleasant girl with coal black hair. She also had a temper which she displayed loudly whenever annoyed or frustrated. If she felt I had admonished her unfairly she would suddenly yell, 'I'm gonna tell me Mom,' and race through the classroom door. From there it was two yards to a door leading into Dayton Road and she was away. I soon learned that when parents came the last person they could find was Mr Brand. He was well and truly hidden in his room on the landing at the top of the stairs through the cloakroom, but the classrooms were very conveniently placed for visitors. Shortly after Penelope's first disappearance, she was back, with mother.

'What have you been doin' to our Penny?' she snapped at me across the front of the classroom. She had a full audience.

'Nothing much, I assure you, Penny was talking and I told her to be quiet. Then shortly afterwards I saw her talking again, so I told her she would stay in at playtime. She jumped up and…'

'Did you tell that lad Bobby sittin' next to her to stay in as well, eh?'

'No, because…'

'Well, 'e was talking as well, wasn't you, Bobby?' She called directly to him across the class. Everyone turned to look at Bobby, who turned red.

'Bobby, were you talking as well?' I asked.

'Yes, Mr Flaxton.'

'There y'ar, see. You wanner open them eyes o' yorn before you jump, Mr Schoolteacher.'

With a toss of her head she was gone, banging the door to emphasize her point. Penelope walked back to her seat, looking pleased, whilst I felt acutely embarrassed. However, I did learn to open my eyes and try not to punish children, however lightly, unless I was absolutely sure I was being fair. This is extremely important to young children. But after Penelope had performed the trick a couple of times, I learned to beat her to the classroom door. Then I found she calmed down as quickly as she exploded. When I saw her mother on Parent's Day, later in the year, I felt she was relieved at not having to rush to her daughter's defence any more.

One way and another the members of Class Four taught me a great deal during my probationary year. In fact, by the end of it, our interchange of teaching left me heavily in their debt.

Chapter 28

Within a few days Wilfred Brown was firm member of the younger branch of Mr Brand's staff. Rocky, Taff, Wilf and I thoroughly enjoyed each other's company. We were keen to organise activities beyond the classroom for the youngsters and these they enjoyed considerably because there wasn't much else to put sparkle into their lives. During that autumn term the activities centred largely around football.

Dayton Road had an obvious connection with the game because the school was literally a stone's throw from the Rovers' football ground. The Rovers were in the First Division, now the Premiership. Even in those far off days, before the world of football had mushroomed into big business with its carefully fostered hero adulation, the youngsters in the school had their idols who played every Saturday. I well remember the newspaper headlines when one player became the first in the country to be paid the exceptional wage of £20 per week!

Occasionally the Rovers also played on Wednesday afternoons. On one of them I called the afternoon register in blissful ignorance.

'Girls…' I said. 'One, two, three, four, five…' The voices chirped away and there were only two gaps as there had been in the morning. I pushed the girls' register to one side and flipped open the boys'. 'Carry on, boys,' I said. There was silence. I looked up.

'Come on,' I said, 'what's the matter? Where's…?'

I broke off suddenly. I looked round the class to find very obviously an unusual number of boys missing. I counted quickly. There were ten empty places when there had been only one that morning.

'Can anyone tell me why so many boys are late this afternoon?' I enquired of no one in particular - and no one answered. The class seemed unusually attentive to their library books which they were supposed to read as an aid to silence whilst the register was being called. Avoid putting a question to a group - you will be answered either by silence or a babble. The VP's voice echoed faintly from his lectures on classroom method. I selected an individual.

'Michael - where is Barry? He was sitting beside you this morning. Where is he now, do you know?'

'Er, no sir,' Michael replied, hesitatingly, and looked uncomfortable. I sensed there was a barrier of reserve between me and the class which hadn't been there that morning. But I wasn't yet sufficiently skilled to probe for the reason. Puzzled, I turned back to the register and went through it calling the missing numbers myself as the gaps were revealed. Then I looked up and glanced questioningly at the class again. All I could see were the tops of heads facing me from every desk as each child bent forward apparently in deep study. I shuffled some papers around on my desk, then looked hopefully at the door expecting some latecomers - and some answers. But the door remained firmly shut.

I knew I had to begin the lesson. As soon as I made an obvious move to do so, the class leapt into life. Reading books were exchanged for Geography books with quite unusual speed and not a little clatter, and the tension relaxed. The children faced me expectantly from their seats in complete contrast to their demeanour a few minutes earlier. I launched into a chapter on coal with a show of confidence I didn't feel inside.

As soon as I could I gave them some written questions to answer. When they were happily working, I spoke loudly to Barbara S, whom I had recently elevated to the role of Class Monitor.

'I'm going out of the room for a few moments and I am putting you in charge. Let me know the names of anyone who speaks whilst I am away,' I said importantly. I strode quickly to Rocky's classroom. She was moving expertly around the desks, checking work. Not for the first time I felt a twinge of envy at the way the children responded to her assured manner. Added to which she looked engagingly attractive as she leant easily over the desks with her lovely brown hair falling just slightly towards the youngster below. She looked up and moved towards me.

'No, you can't have any more of my sugar paper.' She smiled impishly. This was a reference to the fact that I was finding it difficult to plan adequately my weekly needs of stock - paper, glue, etc., which we drew once a week from the stockroom under the sharp eye of Miss Rees. It was like getting gold out of Fort Knox, so I found it easier to sponge off Rocky.

'No, for once I'm not cadging. There's something odd about my class - quite a lot of the boys are missing and I feel that the rest of the kids know where they are, but won't tell me.'

'Oh, I know where they are - and there's a few missing from mine as well. Look.' Sure enough there were gaps in Rocky's class which I hadn't noticed because my eyes had been on her.

'There'll be some missing from most classes .this afternoon, I'll bet. It always happens when the Rovers have a weekday match at home.'

'You mean they've skived off to see the game?'

'Oh no, they'll be car minding.'

'Car minding - where?'

I must have looked indignant, because Rocky laughed. 'It's a local, tradition, gone on for years. School has to turn a blind eye. There's not room for many cars in the Rovers' ground, of course, so anyone who comes by car has to park it in the streets around here. So the kids work a system looking after cars while the owners are at the match. They do quite well out of it.'

'But what about all the absences?' I asked sharply. My mind turned to the very official looking absence slips which we filled in each week for the Attendance Officer to collect every Friday. 'Surely the kids and their parents risk prosecutions, don't they?'

'Yes, theoretically. But you'll find they'll all bring absence notes tomorrow, but you'll also find no one will inquire too closely into their accuracy. Don't forget, the kids do this every Saturday when there's a home match - and since the Rovers have been a vital part of the local scene for seventy years or more, the custom is rather well established.

'I'm still surprised the Education Authority doesn't take action. They could easily send the attendance wallah around the streets on a Wednesday afternoon.'

'I thought you were a Rovers' supporter?' Rocky seemed determined to deflate my righteous indignation.

'That's nothing to do with it.'

'Go on - that football team is life and breath to these kids. You live in a posh area of the city. You don't know what football fervour is. You ought to see what happens when Newport play a rugby match in midweek. The town practically comes to a standstill.'

'That's all very well but. I'm still surprised that the Education Committee doesn't…'

'Go on - some of them were kids in this area once, no doubt, and others will be Rovers' directors. Just turn a blind eye like everyone else does. That's why your class was acting strangely. They're wondering whether you'll be sensible about it, or whether you'll be one of the awkward ones.'

'Ah, so some teachers don't go along with the deception, then?'

Rocky sighed. 'True, but I'm bound to say they don't get very far – and they are certainly in a minority in the schools around here.'

'Which side is Mr Brand on?'

'The kids'. Oh, he'll go through the motions in assembly tomorrow, saying how some children have knocked the school's attendance figures - but that'll be for Miss Rees's benefit. He won't actually do anything about it. And if you'll take my advice - neither will you.'

Suddenly the door opened, and Mr Brand walked in.

'Ah, there you are, Mr Flaxton. Your class was making rather a noise, I'm afraid. I've had a look at a few of their books. They seem rather confused about the locations of British coalfields, it seems.'

He raised his bushy eyebrows questioningly. His gentle manner was far more devastating as a rebuke than any sharp reminder about leaving my class unattended. I blushed deeply, murmured incoherent apologies and shot through the doorway. As I sped along the playground a sudden great roar engulfed me. For a fraction of a second I paused, then hurried on as its implication penetrated. The Rovers had scored.

There wasn't exactly a roar as I threw open my classroom door but there was a considerable cacophony of chatter, banging and excitement.

'ONE - NIL!

An unidentifiable voice shrieked this delightful news before sudden silence descended as I burst into the room. At least half the children were on their feet. They fled to their places like bolting rabbits. I was furious.

'How dare you behave like that whilst I was out of the room. You all had work to do! We've read the chapter together and you should all be able to answer the questions. Now I find Mr Brand has been in here because you were misbehaving, and worse still, he tells me that some of you are doing your work badly. I'm ashamed of you, Barbara.' I turned upon the unfortunate girl. 'Where's your list?' I glowered at her angrily. I knew the class had not seen me in a temper before and primly felt it might do them good to see that I had a sharp side. Barbara looked very uncomfortable. Clearly she had been doing her job under very trying conditions. She held up a page of writing.

'I couldn't get everybody who was talking. Some people spoke lots of times and I tried to put their names down every time they spoke, but I didn't get them every time, I know.'

I stared at the paper. There were twenty names at least. It was covered in scrawl on both sides, with extras added in between lines and vertically at the edges where she had fought to find more writing space as the tide of chaos had swept over her.

My conscience got the better of me at this point. Why should I slate the kids for a situation which had been my fault? My error stared at me from the pathetic piece of paper in my hand. The ridiculousness of it swept aside my anger and, involuntarily, I grinned. Immediately the class relaxed, audibly. I guess they'd all been holding their breath. Suddenly, a thought hit me.

'Who shouted 'ONE - NIL?'

Naturally no one volunteered this information.

'I mean…how do you know the other side hasn't scored yet? I heard the cheer for the Rovers but you wouldn't get a yell like that for the other side. So how do you know it isn't one all - or even worse?'

Looks were exchanged all round the room. Expressions changed, smiles broke out and a buzz of delight swept the class. Two boys at the front nodded hard at each other, then one made a hint of putting his hand up.

'Well, George?'

'The crowd groans if the other side scores,sir, - an' if the winder is open, like that, we can 'ear it in 'ere.'

He glanced at the open window which was high up on the playground side of the room. A section, operated by cords which hung to the high window ledge, was fully open. It had certainly been closed earlier.

'Ah - I see.'

There is no doubt that the pupil-teacher relationship improved further at that moment, because in the same second another great roar burst in upon the silent classroom. Eyes widened with delight, mouths opened, male fists shot upwards, but all in mime. There was no noise at all, because they were still not sure about my attitude.

'TWO - NIL, it seems,' I said loudly. Another bust of cheering enveloped me, this time from the class. Worried that Mr Brand might be nearby again, I quietened them quickly and returned their attention to their books. But as I moved around the room, explaining their mistakes due to my inadequate lesson, I decided to emphasize that my standpoint in this football business was going to be in line. Having got over my initial indignation, I was taking Rocky's advice. Anyway, I had no wish to quarrel with her.

'Who are the Rovers playing today, anyway?'

'Everton, sir,' came the prompt reply from most of the boys. 'They beat us three-two last time, so we're out for revenge.'

'It sounds as though we're on the way to getting it,' I said. The boys rewarded me with happy, knowing smiles.

At registration next morning I was hard put to it to keep down the buzz of conversation. After dealing with the registers, I turned to the question of the previous day's absences.

'I hope all you lads who were missing yesterday afternoon have brought notes.'

'Ere's mine, sir,' said Leslie W, almost aggressively. He was a tough, thick set, red headed lad who acted as goalkeeper for the school football team despite being the youngest player. Following his lead, the other nine waved letters at me from their seats.

'Alright, bring :them to my desk.'

The lads dashed forward excitedly, plonked the letters in a pile in front of me and returned to their places. I realised the word had gone round after school yesterday that probably I was not going to be difficult about the absences. But now was the final test as far as the lads were concerned.

'Thank you. I'll read them later. I'll just mark the fact that I've received notes on all your absence slips.'

As I did so, I glanced around the room surreptitiously with my head lowered. I caught Leslie giving the thumbs up sign to someone at the back of the room. He had got the message. When I did read the messages I was not surprised to learn that most of the boys had been suddenly sick at home during the midday break. To-day a sudden virus would be the cause.

It was my turn for playground duty at break and as I wandered around sipping my coffee, dutifully brought to me from Miss Shenton's classroom by a monitor, I found that I was being followed by most of yesterday's absentees from my class. They wanted to chat, it seemed, but were reticent about making the first move. I decided to help them.

'What was the final score yesterday?'

'Three-one to us,' beamed Leslie.

'Ah, good. Revenge is sweet, eh?

'You bet, sir.'

'Tell me,' I said after a short pause, 'do you make much pocket money doing, you know, er, with the cars?'

They nearly mobbed me. I was not only with them, I was even talking to them openly about it.

'Coo, yeah,sir, you can get threepence or even sixpence a time.'

'We work in pairs'- an' if yow're good yow can get eight or ten cars to look after between yer.'

'But why work in pairs - doesn't that halve the takings? I asked.

'That's to get places. One of us finds a space an' keeps it, an' 'is pal runs round the streets till 'e finds a car lookin` for somewhere to park. Then it follers 'im. Then when the driver gets out, 'e asks us to look after 'is car till the match is over.'

'But why should he want you to do that? Why doesn't he just give you a penny or twopence for helping him find a parking space?'

'Ah, well, summat might 'appen to 'is car whilst e's at the match,' said someone rather mysteriously.

'That's not very likely, surely? After all, the streets around here are full of cars when there's a match on. I can't imagine that much could happen to them.'

There was another pause and the boys looked at each other. Then Leslie spoke.

'Ah, but some of 'em ain't bein' looked after, yer see, sir. An' them wot ain't, well, they can easily get scratched by somefink or uther and the drivers don't want that, do they sir?'

I stared into his wide blue unblinking eyes. The conspirators' defences were completely down as they stood behind their leader facing me. I had gone too far along the road of co-operation to turn back now.

'You little tykes!'

'Well, they don't seem to mind, sir,' said Leslie attempting to soothe my trampled conscience, 'an' anyway we never charge 'em so much when Rovers lose, an' when they win the drivers are so pleased they'll pay us anyfink.'

The lads dashed off and merged into the general melee of the playground. I grimaced as I found my coffee was cold.

Over forty years later my sons bought very good tickets as a birthday present for me for a Rovers home match and I drove nostalgically back to the area I hadn't visited for much of that time. I parked at some distance from the ground. I was delighted to be accosted by two hard faced boys demanding payment for looking after the car. I was amused to find they wanted a pound each and paid willingly.

'There's been inflation,' I said to my sons, answering their quizzical looks.

Chapter 29

Football occupied the thoughts and actions of many of the Dayton Road boys. The school team was usually at the top of its league or thereabouts. Its performance depended upon the boys' natural skills, nurtured in time-honoured fashion in the nearby streets and the very real training given them by Taff and Rocky. Despite his background Taff was an excellent teacher of soccer, though he propitiated the wrath of his Welsh gods on Saturday afternoons by playing himself with the odd-shaped ball.

Rocky took games with her own class and also those of the three older women teachers. She taught a range of skills which securely underpinned Taff's work with the teams. In each of her lessons she had the boys hard at work dribbling, passing and heading to one another, or shooting at targets painted on the air raid shelter walls in the playground. She drove the girls equally hard learning netball and rounders skills. She had played netball for her very successful college team. Most of the children loved it because success in ball control gave them considerable satisfaction. But they were in the seventh heaven if they were selected for places in the school teams.

Neither Wilf Brown nor I could pretend to any such abilities in sports teaching. However we copied Taff and Rocky as best we could, trying to make up in enthusiasm what we lacked in skill. We followed the teams in all their matches, which were usually on Saturday mornings. Most schools entered teams in the various area leagues in the city, each with a devoted teacher organising and training it according to his ability. But not many schools had four lively young teachers to follow their teams and it was extremely rare for a woman to be on the touchline. In Rocky the Dayton Road boys had a most knowledgeable female, which they seemed to realise added much to their distinction. They responded by playing their guts out and, as a result, achieved considerable success.

I was able to contribute one personal skill to the corporate effort - that of photography. As well as taking team photographs, which pleased the children, I also took many action shots. These delighted them even more, but they were also used by Taff and Rocky to illustrate points of the game. Woe betide the unfortunate player caught on the fringe of the action without his eye on the ball; In fact I soon realised that I had an added power on the touchlines. If yelling myself hoarse failed, I waved my camera about ostentatiously. It was amazing what reserves of energy it could summon in leaden legs.

Occasionally shots of individual boys showed how good they were. A leap in the air to head a ball; balanced poise at the moment of impact in crossing a ball; the split second contact in a successful sliding tackle - some lads were years ahead of their age group in skills and sometimes also in mastery of the game as a whole.

Yet in later years I looked in vain for a single name from the Dayton Road boys in the Rovers' teams. This saddened me because it meant that the early talent which flourished so close at hand was not developed. We had no links with the secondary school to which most of our juniors went so I have no idea how well or otherwise they fostered football talent. That lack of liaison between education phases was all too common. In the early nineties, when in-service training of teachers was funded directly from central government, I was involved with carrying that into schools. The first event began with all the secondary teachers being introduced to their colleagues from their feeder primary schools because very few had ever met! Liaison about the curriculum was non-existent. Only with the introduction of the national curriculum and requirements of testing across the age range were those barriers broken to an extent.

This sort of thing has been common in sport. Too often promising youngsters have needed a committed adult to find and push them - a teacher, parent, club scout, another sportsperson - and quite a lot of luck as well. There hasn't been a systematic search of schools for likely skills and therefore over the years potential growths have been left high and dry on the shoreline because the wave of sporting interest was not strong enough to reach them.

To-day, the position is better due mainly to the interest in competitive sport fostered by television. Talented youngsters are sought more actively. But schools are still the only places where the majority of people receive sports training, even though that is not evenly distributed. Some schools are fortunately situated on sites with their own sports fields, but others can no longer rely on fields provided by the local authority which, most likely, have been sold for housing. There is also the continued class distinction in some sports. I am sure, even now, we still miss some possible champions.

But even teachers are guilty of ignoring skill when they see it as Rocky learnt when she entered teams for a Grand Rounders Tournament. Someone in the city Schools' Sports Association had proposed the event and advertised it amongst the junior schools. There were to be separate sections for boys' and girls' teams; it was also suggested that if the event proved successful leagues might be formed and a regular competition organised on the lines of those existing in football, cricket, athletics and swimming.

I knew that the Dayton Road children were good at rounders due mainly to Rocky, but aided by Taff. These two not only taught the game but played as well, one on each side, and neither in any way pulled their punches, or rather their batting and throwing. Instead of being intimidated by the adults' efforts the children accepted the challenge readily, and matched effort with effort and skill with skill. Wilf and I were pressed into service and soon were able to acquit ourselves adequately. Then we formed a staff team with the addition of a few eleven year olds. This was quite formidable, but everyone wanted to be in a team which could beat it. Playground battles raged in the lunch time breaks and gradually the staff found the opposition getting stronger and tougher. Finally, Rocky pronounced the Dayton Road rounders teams ready for the Grand Tournament.

The four of us met the team members outside school on the appointed Saturday and shepherded them to the bus stop. The venue was a large sports field on the southern side of the city that we found pleasant and very spacious. Other teams were much in evidence when we arrived and for an instant our team members looked dismayed. Many others were dressed in smart strip in marked contrast to their own motley mixture of clothes. They turned worried and appealing faces to us.

'Never mind,' said Rocky, 'this isn't a fashion parade. What matters is winning.'

'You never worry about how you look when you're playing rounders at school or at our fields,' said Taff, 'so don't start now. Just show them all what Dayton Road kids are made of.'

Leslie, who was the boys' backstop where his prowess at goal and wicket keeping was fully maintained, sensed our attempts at psychological support. He turned his cheeky freckled face towards his pals and squared his thick shoulders.

'Yeah, let's belt the pants off the lot on 'em.'

Taff rolled his eyes but eschewed comment. After all, Leslie did epitomize the spirit we tried to instill into their game. Rocky sought out the tournament organiser, Miss Brahms.

'Ah, Miss Rockliffe, so good of you to enter your teams. Dayton Road, aren't you? I must say I admire your enthusiasm; you've come such a long way, haven't you? There isn't another team from the north of the city.'

'Well, the children are keen and they seem quite good at the game. It'll be worth our journey if we get the chance of competition on a regular basis, if a league is formed.'

The two men and I were standing with the children a short distance from Rocky, waiting to be given instructions. Miss Brahms saw us and reacted slightly.

'Some of your players look rather small. You do realise that most teams are made up of eleven year olds, don't you?'

'Oh yes - and most of ours are eleven as well. One or two especially good ones come from younger classes. But don't be misled by their size. Some may be small, but they're tough.'

Rocky's face began to show that delicate pink shade which made her so attractive. She would brook no criticism of her warriors today whatever their appearance.

'Well, I am sure you know their capabilities,' said Miss Brahms in a tone which left us in no doubt she expected our forces to be massacred. 'The morning matches are being played on a points basis. The teams have been divided into four sections, and each team plays all others in their section. You will find which section yours are in on that board over there. The winners of sections A and B will than play each other this afternoon in the semi-finals, and so will C and D - then the winners of those matches will contest the final.'

'Good. I'll find out who we play first,' said Rocky.

'We should like teams which are eliminated in the morning to stay and watch the afternoon matches, if you can manage it,' Miss Brahms called. Rocky's mouth was set in a firm line as she reached us.

'Pooh, she doesn't think much of us, does she Miss?' said Pauline M who acted as Rocky's games monitor and as such felt she was privileged.

'That'll do. It's up to us to prove her wrong. Come on, everyone, let's get going.'

Rocky seized a rounders bat from Pauline and strode off twirling it like a truncheon. We all fell in behind our undoubted leader. It transpired that each section comprised four teams and therefore each had to play three games in the morning session. The boys' and girls' competitions were identical but quite separate. Rocky naturally attached herself to our girls' team and Taff to the boys. In the ensuing toss between Wilf and me, he won. 'I'm going with the girls as there are two from my class in the team,' he said.

It was a clear sunny day and the neatly cut grass shone in the sunlight. A giant hand had doodled a series of neat, white diamonds over the surface each with a little square at one apex. Taff and I led our team to one marked for our section where another group was already in occupation. The boys were neatly dressed in white open-necked shirts and white shorts. They were nonchalantly throwing a rounders ball to one another whilst a grey haired man watched them,

'Good morning, we're Dayton Road - are you in Section C as well?' Taff enquired.

'Yes, we're Seaton Crescent. My name's Chadderton. 'Hughes,' returned Taff, and this is my colleague, Mr Flaxton.' I shook hands with Mr Chadderton, then looked more closely at his boys. They looked very smart indeed and most certainly were taller than ours. Obviously Seaton Crescent was located in a much more favoured neighbourhood than Dayton Road.

'I believe we should begin straight away,' said Mr Chadderton. 'When the other two schools in our section arrive they play each other on the pitch next to this one.'

'Right,' agreed Taff. 'Shall we toss? Captains.'

A smart lad emerged from the Seaton Crescent group and stood near to Taff as Martin A thrust forward from ours. Apart from being good at most ball games Martin was a fortunate choice as Boys' Rounders Captain in the circumstances. He stood head and shoulders above the rest of our lads, had strikingly blond hair and came from a reasonably well-to-do home. He was also intelligent and knew it. At school it was sometimes necessary to curb his big-headedness but today I took much satisfaction from the way he looked the opposing boy steadily in the eye as Taff flicked the coin.

'You call,' he invited the Seaton Crescent lad.

'Heads.'

The coin fell. Taff looked at it and so did the caller. 'Tails - er, Martin?' Martin was still staring at his opponent like a boxer listening to the referee's strictures before the first bell.

'We'll bat,' he boomed. Then he turned sharply away. 'Come on lads - get stuck in.' Our boys seized their favourite weapons from the stock we'd brought. They lined up grimly well to one side of the batting square. Meanwhile the Seaton Crescent boys moved to their fielding positions. It was decided Mr Chadderton would umpire during our innings and Taff during theirs. I retired to a spot half way between the two pitches allocated to Section C and prepared to act as cheer leader.

Martin faced up to the first ball. 'Play,' called Mr Chadderton. The pitcher bowled a reasonably fast ball. Martin took an almighty swipe at it and missed. The backstop stooped but missed the ball, so had to chase after it. Martin swung round wildly, contemplating a run to first base.

'Stay, stay,' hissed the entire Dayton Road team.

'Alright, keep your voices down,' commanded Taff. The ball was retrieved and thrown to the pitcher. Martin faced him again and this time I saw him focus on the ball instead of the far distance where he intended to hit it. The pitcher bowled and Martin hit it hard. It cracked out of the diamond like a bullet, well between two of the three deep fielders.

'Run, run, run,' yelled our boys at the top of their voices without a thought for Taff.

'RUN,' I yelled, equally oblivious of decorum. Martin needed not the slightest admonition to hurtle round the field, thumping each base pole as he passed. It wasn't necessary to do this, you only had to touch a base when you were going to stop at it, and Rocky would have been furious had she been watching. But in this instance the aggressive act boosted our boys' morale.

Martin's dive at fourth base and home was entirely unnecessary as the ball was in the air well outside the pitch, having been thrown by a scampering deep fielder. The Dayton Road boys exploded into raucous cheering.

Batting order went according to fielding positions, so Leslie was next. His short stocky frame seemed dwarfed in the square, but I knew that if he connected the ball could disappear into the far distance. For his size he had considerable strength. He missed the first ball, and the second was called 'no ball'. On the repeat throw, he thrashed at it so wildly that he spun himself round and nearly left the square, which would have forced him to run. His pugnacious determination was completely stumping his ability.

'Keep your eye on the ball, Leslie,' I shouted.

Fortunately my words penetrated, for on the final bowl he hit it cleanly away to his left and sped round the pitch to complete our second rounder. During the ensuing yells I looked at the Seaton Crescent boys. They were looking at each other none too comfortably. They also looked closely at the next member of our team as he entered the batting square. It was Geoffrey H, who with his twin brother George was a firm member of both football and cricket teams. They were tousle headed tots whose dreamy air was exasperating in the classroom where their inadequacy at any form of written work was only too apparent. But they were highly skilled at ball games.

Geoffrey whacked the ball hard but it was fielded and he only made second base. The Seaton Crescent boys looked relieved. Then George ambled in and slowly looked round from the square. The pitcher bowled. George's figure exploded and the ball soared into the deep well out of range of the fielders. He caught up his brother at fourth base as the latter shuffled in, having not the slightest intention of over-exerting himself unnecessarily.

'Thought you could run,' he quipped as he flashed past his brother. The team screamed and leapt in a wild dance of delight in which I joined with complete abandon. But suddenly I became aware of an audience behind me. The other teams in our section had arrived and were preparing to do battle. Momentarily I caught the eyes of two teachers who were watching my antics rather than our match and I subsided. However a fourth rounder from the sixth member of our team had me whooping again.

The Seaton Crescent boys were visibly shaken at what to them were the totally unexpected skills and determination of our lads. But to their credit they didn't fall apart and gradually began to capture scalps. Martin was caught by the backstop, two others fell at first base, and George was caught in the deep. Finally we were all out with our score standing at ten rounders which was a healthy but certainly not unbeatable total. As the opposing team lined up to bat I couldn't repress the thought that with their obvious size and stamina a few good hits would soon redress the balance and restore their confidence. Little Geoffrey at first base seemed ridiculously diminutive as he guarded his post. I knew Leslie was a marvellous catcher at backstop, but his throws, though hard, could be wild. If the batter missed and Leslie was off target with his throws to Geoffrey the ball would speed into the distance enabling the batsman to score a half rounder off a no-hit with ease.

But I needn't have worried: Their tails were up and when the first Seaton Crescent boy cracked his first shot back hard at Martin who was pitching, and who held it in a fine catch, they really turned on the pressure. Geoffrey was in no way intimidated at first base. After all he was quite used to seeing my six foot frame hurtling at him in our playground matches and taking a ball cleanly from Leslie to dismiss me, so why should he be worried by lads who could give him only a few inches? Three fell to him in quick succession and it was only due to the skill of one boy that Seaton Crescent notched three rounders before Leslie gleefully caught the last ball and smashed it into the ground in the empty batting square to dismiss the last two who were running between bases, but alas for them, not to home.

'Warrabout that, sir? Leslie's chest expanded an extra two inches as he strutted over to me with his coxcomb of red hair standing as erect as its owner.

'Very good, very good indeed. Now you've got to do the same to the other two teams in our section then you'll have something to be really proud of.'

'Your boys really are very good, Mr Hughes,' Mr Chadderton said to Taff. 'Do you get plenty of opposition on the northern side of town?'

'No,' said Taff drily, 'they have to put up with us.' The other man laughed. 'So that's your secret. Are all your staff young and active?'

'No, but the four of us manage to chase them about the playground.'

'Well, good luck to you in your other matches. From what I know of the other teams here, you should do well. We usually win most of ours.'

The ears of adults and boys alike were alerted by this revealing comment and our attention swung towards the other match which was still in progress nearby. After a few minutes it became obvious that Mr Chadderton was right. This match was a very poor affair indeed. The boys glanced at Taff and me with ill-concealed glee, and sat down to await their next combat.

'I'll nip over to Rocky and see how the girls are getting on, and let them have our news,' I said. I made my way across the level grass, weaving in between other matches which were being played by a motley of children. It was a rewarding sight, young supple bodies revelling in physical activity in the wide open space bathed in golden sunshine under a delicate blue sky. The squeals and strident shouts from many games emphasised the total commitment of young minds. I felt again the thrill of satisfaction I'd experienced many times since beginning work at Dayton Road in the early summer. I found the girls' team involved in a game which Rocky was watching, not umpiring.

'Is this still your first?' I enquired.

'No, the second. We won the first eight-one.' Rocky sounded incredulous, but she was beaming.

'Great. The boys did the same, ten – three, and from what I've seen of one other opposition, we ought to win our section.'

Rocky became confidential. 'That's what I think. Look at this one.'

I watched the girls who were batting. Few even held the bat sideways with their left shoulders facing the bowler, if they were right handed, to give them maximum thrust to their strokes. They stood facing the bowler with the bat held up like a truncheon. When hits were achieved they often went straight to the ground which made a score impossible. If no hit was made after three pitches the batter had to run and was stumped with ease at first base.

'Well - keep it up! I'll see you at lunch time. The kids will need their sandwiches, I think.'

I returned to Taff with the good news to find our team fielding in their second match and skittling their opponents out with embarrassing ease. Their teacher, who was umpiring, looked distinctly uncomfortable. Taff sidled closer to me.

'We're sorting this lot out Nigel. Have you looked at some of the other teams? They haven't got much idea compared with ours. I reckon the Seaton Crescent team was the best here. I'm sure they expected to win the tournament, but we've upset their calculations. We should win this section easily.'

He was proved correct Our boys won their other two games without difficulty and when we joined forces with the girls at the side of the field for a composite picnic, we found that they had done the same. The children were ecstatic and showed it, whilst we teachers were quite indistinguishable from them in glee.

I stood up and surveyed the scene. Groups were dotted about, mostly tightly knit and identifiable as separate units. Some children were dashing about as is their wont, but they were in a minority. Slowly it dawned upon me that none of these groups was near to us. In fact we seemed to be set apart from the rest. I mentioned this fact to Rocky.

'Yes - I rather think we've shaken things up. You know I'm not given to boasting and we must watch that the kids don't get big-headed and throw the matches away, but I feel we might even sweep the board. One thing's certain we shall certainly be staying for the afternoon and I rather want to see that Brahms' woman's face when she realises.' I felt Rocky was entitled to gloat a little.

In the event the afternoon was almost an anti-climax. Both our teams won their semi-finals and the boys won the final with comparative ease. The girls had more of a fight in theirs, winning an exciting match against a much larger school than Dayton Road by five and half to four. As the various team members and their teachers gathered for the presentations it became obvious to us that not many had fulfilled Miss Brahm's hopes for a good audience to see the completion of the day's events. Indeed the final attendance could only be described as very thin. Fortunately this fact was entirely lost upon our children.

'We must congratulate the Dayton Road teams on their truly excellent performances,' Miss Brahms announced to the intimate gathering. 'I don't mind admitting they have given us quite a surprise with the standard of their play. So, if their captains will come forward, I will present them with their well-deserved trophies. They are not very large, I'm afraid, but as this was a single event, Dayton Road will be able to keep them permanently.'

Pauline and Martin duly stepped forward and amid thoroughly overdone cheering from their own teams which made the four of us wince, they received two miniature shields. Rocky, who did not enjoy public speaking, murmured our thanks, turning crimson as she did so. Then, as leaves blown by the four winds, the audience disappeared leaving our children and ourselves alone - a victorious and vociferously happy bunch as we crossed the wide empty field towards the surrounding suburban houses and our bus stop.

In the weeks that followed, despite various telephone calls and a couple of letters from Mr Brand, we heard nothing further of the projected Rounders League, This didn't bother our teams much. The boys and girls were quite content to return to their playground .matches but it niggled us, especially Rocky, who not unnaturally felt her teaching had been wasted to an extent.

Leslie summarized the day more than he knew when he announced in a loud voice for the benefit of various travellers eyeing us questioningly on the top of the homeward bound bus,

'Cor, we showed 'em, din 't we sir?'

We certainly had shown them but the fact was not appreciated by the organisers of the intended Rounders League. Too much talent emerged from a totally unexpected quarter and, moreover, one which was socially unacceptable to them. Instead of welcoming our high standard of play and using it to develop similar skills in other teams, it was rejected. The wrong school won and that was the end of the matter.

I venture the opinion that class distinction still exists in recruiting youngsters for some of our national sports.

Chapter 30

We are all prone to generalise. It's so easy to read an item about youths misbehaving in a city centre, then tell your neighbour how awful young people are to-day, or find an unhelpful assistant in a large store and complain that everyone in X & Y Stores is rude. It's not unknown for teachers to do the same and I'm even doing it in saying so! Nevertheless it is easy to say that a particular class is brilliant, or cheeky, noisy, thick as two planks…because one or two individuals manifest the attribute. Many look the same outwardly, have similar physical characteristics at a glance, similar clothes – especially if they are in uniform. However, at the time I was at Dayton Road the notion of school uniform was ridiculous, as it was for virtually all junior and secondary modern schools during the post-war austerity period. The style of clothes most children wore was make do and mend, and some mothers were great stylists in the mode, to their great credit. So there was a degree of generalisation in the way the children were dressed.

It took me a very few weeks to recognise that all, however, had distinct personalities. There was a mixture of happy traits and frustrations, of abilities and blind spots, likes and dislikes. Some were outstanding because certain aspects were accentuated - especially friendly, or particularly neat and tidy, or awkward and sullen, or, as in the case of Jimmy R, because he often seemed to be on his own.

I soon noticed that no other child ever sat by him if it could be avoided. At the beginning I allowed the children to sit in their double desks with their particular friends and this produced twenty-four pairs, if attendance was 100%. But it rarely was because genuine illness was common. So whenever there were spaces Jimmy would be alone. But if I ever tried parting two who were chattering excessively when I expected them to be working quietly and put one in the seat next to Master R, the move was made under obvious protest. Within minutes there was a plaintive plea to be allowed to return accompanied by a fervent promise to be quiet. To my amazement the first time I gave in to this cajoling, the promise was kept faithfully.

I realised why this was so the first time I sat beside Jimmy to mark his work. If body odour was visible he would have appeared perpetually enveloped in a clinging, foggy aura. It had an affinity for any other body, for when you got close to him some of it oozed away and wrapped itself firmly around you to take with you wherever you went for the next half hour or so.

Of course there were other children in the school who would have been nicer to know had they had a bath more often. Perhaps they came from the few families that were known to put their baths to novel uses rather than for personal hygiene. They made useful fish tanks as long as you fixed the plug, or they kept the coal dry if there was nowhere to keep it outside so long as you didn't turn on the taps.

But many houses had no baths at all. In fact whilst I was at St. Andrew's some chaps did a survey of homes in the area near to the college and estimated there were ten thousand people in houses with no internal water supply. The back to back rows shared outside taps from pipes laid between them. They also shared outside toilets which were certainly flush operated but you had to take your own bucket of water in with you to achieve this. I experienced the same when I was evacuated. The three storey house and its associated ironmongery shop shared an outside pump near the back door. Its toilet was across a yard to which you took a bucket filled from the pump. There was a bath on the first floor, devoid of taps, to which we took water warmed by a fire under the copper boiler in the kitchen, but it had no waste pipe and so had to be emptied by bucket again. Though the arrangements were a great surprise to my cousin and me we soon became used to them and in no way did they prevent us from being extremely happy with the lovely people who accommodated us.

But there were only a few children at Dayton Road in Jimmy's category. I doubt if he had ever had a bath in his life, and even washing his face and hands only occurred if he was made to do so in the thick brown earthenware sinks in the school cloakroom. When he did he used the standard school supply of Lifebuoy soap, but it couldn't get into contact with enough of him to perform the feat proclaimed in its advertising slogan, 'Conquers BO'. But bathing Jimmy would have been a monumental challenge for the product.

I met another of Jimmy's attributes all unsuspectingly one November morning. I cycled to. school through freezing fog, skidding dangerously in the tram lines set in the old cobble stones in the road which ran past the Rovers' ground. In the playground hundreds of little steam engines were chugging around on disorganised tracks which crossed and recrossed each other as they avoided crashes by inches. Beneath the puffs of steam rising into the icy air were pairs of cheeky red fireboxes set above rapidly oscillating pistons.

The engines were rescued from chaos by the sound of the stationmaster's whistle which happened to be mine that day as I was on playground duty. Two reasonably orderly lines of engines chugged into the classroom pulling carriages full of girl passengers refusing to take an active part in such childish games.

It was warm in the classroom and coats and scarves were supposed to be left in the cloakroom. But when I looked up to count the children as a check to my attendance register total, I spotted Jimmy wearing a faded piece of flannel around his neck. Years before it might have been described as yellow.

'No scarves on in the classroom, Jimmy,' I said briskly. 'Go and hang it on your peg, please.'

Jimmy's normally pinched features became furtive. The slant of his eyebrows gave him a quizzical expression but it was always hard; his rare smiles never reached his eyes. He looked as though he expected the world to deal harshly with him which it usually did. In this instance his problem was me.

'Come on, Jimmy, do what you're told,' I said with an edge to my tone. A few children turned in their seats. One or two looked at Jimmy and then turned back to me. A sixth sense told me the audience was not just reacting to someone trying a simple challenge to authority. They were not sitting back in safety watching some daredevil going out on a limb. I knew there was something amiss but had no clue as to what it was. I moved down the row towards Jimmy's desk near the back.

There was complete silence except for some shuffling in the seats. Jimmy's face dropped slowly towards the desk and he hunched his shoulders.

'Jimmy, why don't you do what I've told you…?' I stood still near to him. There was a long silence. In the end it was too much for Mavis C, rather a busybody but she had an underlying sympathy with people in distress.

'Please sir, his Mom's sewn him in for the winter.'

I was slow on the uptake. 'She's done what?'

'She's sewn him into his clothes.'

Jimmy lifted his head and faced me with a pathetically defiant look to corroborate this statement. I stared back at him and put a disbelieving hand on the piece of material I had earlier referred to as a scarf. Jimmy swayed away from me, though the movement contained no fear that I might be about to divest him forcefully. But I was near enough to see the strands of thread which zigzagged broadly between the scarf and his ragged shirt. There was no doubt that his neck was effectively swathed until someone took action with a pair of scissors.

My face obviously advertised my sense of shock for all members of the class were now sitting in absolute silence, gazing fixedly at me to gauge my reaction. For my part I was wrestling with a dilemma which I was to find is so common in teaching; how do you counter an individual variation to a rule for everyone when to do so invades personal privacy? Over half a century later high profile attempts have tested the question in courts, so it still hasn't been entirely resolved. I was tempted to tear off the scarf and issue an admonition on the need to wash necks daily, but a wiser voice within me suggested that in view of the evidence before me, neck washing was not in Jimmy's sphere of experience. It also said more firmly that if Jimmy's mother had taken this course of action I had no authority to tear up her handiwork, despite my revulsion. But what clinched matters was the fact, which was becoming more blatant as every embarrassed second passed, that to do anything at that moment would put Jimmy even more firmly into the wedge between the opposing forces of his home life and school. I had to retreat.

'Well, my lad, I've never seen this kind of thing before, I can tell you. I shall have to speak to Mr Brand about it later. Now, take your reading books, we mustn't waste any more time.'

Some time later, when everyone was engrossed in silent reading, I secretly surveyed as many necks as I could from my desk. To my relief, I could see no more scarves and thus no further possibility of winter needlework. In the playground at break I saw Taff and took the chance to unburden my problem.

'Oh, that's started again, has it?' He didn't seem as surprised as I'd anticipated. 'I expect there'll be a few more. But you were right not to take it off. Miss Rees did that last year and there was hell to pay. One mother came up and complained to the Boss that one of his teachers had assaulted her son.'

Rocky and Wilf joined us.

'Nigel's just found someone sewn into his clothes. Sure sign its winter.'

'I've got one too, Kitty W,' said Rocky. 'The buttons at the back of her dress are sewn up.'

'Duw,' Wilf said with feeling. Like me he was meeting this phenomenon for the first time. 'I can't believe it. This is the middle of the twentieth century, not the nineteenth.'

'Well, you'll have to live with it,' replied Taff, 'there's only a few and the rest don't like them because really they think it's as dirty a habit as we do. And of course they can't change for PT. which makes them stand out all the more. But don't touch them - that's my advice.'

'What does the Boss think we should do?' asked Wilf.

It was cold in the playground and the other three walked on to seek their coffee in the warm which deprived me of a reply on the subject for the time being. But during the lunch hour I went to Mr Brand's room and asked him directly.

'Believe me, I appreciate your feelings, Mr Flaxton. I haven't seen much of this kind of thing in my career and, as you know, I'm no chicken!' He laughed as usual. 'But I've always found that each school I've taught in has a small but hard core of children whose families retain some practices which were far more common decades ago. They've become even fewer in number since the war, I'm glad to say, but nevertheless they are still with us.'

His comment jogged my memory of the use to which a few families put coal sacks on wet days at Spenser Street. Nevertheless now I had a responsibility to my class I disliked the incongruity.

'But how can you try to have any standards of cleanliness in a class which contains a child from such a background? It's quite unfair for me to emphasize this to everyone else if they know that there is one who simply will not co-operate.'

'Ah, now that's an idea which is frequently put forward by young teachers, if you don't mind my saying so. If you followed that argument to its logical conclusion you would have to give up trying to improve any standards with anyone. Just because you can't achieve one hundred percent success shouldn't mean you ought not to try for ninety-five.'

'Well, yes, I can see that,' I replied realising my standpoint was defeatist, so wished to relinquish it quickly. 'But don't the children see that as being unfair?'

'Yes, they probably do, and I know many of their complaints are about actions being unfair. But usually those concern comparatively childish matters. Outside they know perfectly well life isn't fair, that families are not equal, nor are the homes they live in. They have their own way of coping with the Jimmy Rs of the world. You notice that he hasn't many friends.'

'But I should like to alter that. Surely if we could make him rather more like the rest, clean him up and get him better clothes, they would accept him more than they do.'

'But how different can we make him from his parents before we alienate him? We might, you know, if we had him in a residential school away from them. But is it right for authority to take such steps?'

'What about trying to alter his parent's attitudes?' I countered, searching for the positive action I longed to take.

'Yes, that's a better way. But would they listen if we went round and told them how to look after Jimmy? I expect they'd give us a short sharp answer: But people like them have been changing gradually, that's why there aren't many of them left. They respond to others around them in the end. But it's a slow process and you'll have to be patient.'

I didn't like what I'd been told but I could feel the force of the argument. I thanked Mr Brand and walked slowly and thoughtfully down his staircase.

Jimmy remained on my mind for some days. Although I had known some men from very different home conditions to my own in the RAF, certainly so during my short stay in Pool Flight, nevertheless I was still mentally shuddering at the thought of what it must be like living in his household. Then an event occurred which provided me with a vivid demonstration.

Because Jimmy was an isolate in the playground, every now and then a small group would form and enliven playtime activities by taunting him. Usually the children crept up behind him and yelled unfriendly comments such as Muck Bag, Stinker, or Pongo. Depending upon his mood Jimmy would either suffer these slings and arrows of outrageous fortune, to quote Hamlet, till the teacher on duty rescued him, or he would give way to his fury and chase the miscreants. Usually he was thwarted by numbers. A moment's indecision on his part meant that the group could scatter with ease to the corners of the playground, so keeping plenty of distance between them and him no matter how hard he ran.

On this occasion he took up his solitary stance near to the corner of one of the air raid shelters By an unhappy coincidence the taunters came up to him alongside one wall. With hands pressed against it in readiness they propelled themselves away into-the wide open spaces to avoid his blind rush at them. Jimmy, having committed himself, couldn't stop or turn to take avoiding action. With head down like a charging bull he hit the corner of the wall and reeled sideways, clutching his scalp.

Leslie, who had seen it all, fled into our classroom where he knew I was.

'Sir, it's Jimmy. 'E bashed 'is 'ead and it ain't 'alf bleedin.''

I dropped my pen and shot into the playground. Jimmy, claspring his head, was being pushed towards me by a group of

315

anxious faced children. Blood was oozing through his fingers and had begun to trickle down his face.

'Miss Rockliffe - first aid kit.' I snapped at Leslie. 'Mind how you go…!' I yelled ineffectively at his retreating figure. Leslie was the sort of boy who would have run with alacrity into Nebuchadnezzar's furnace if he had been entrusted with an urgent message for Shadrach and Co.

I guided Jimmy inside and sat him down on the top of a desk amidst a chorus of explanations as to what had happened. But I cut it short and shooed everyone outside with no ceremony whatsoever. Then I turned to Jimmy who was silently rocking himself forwards and backwards on the desk, still hugging his head. I grabbed a large roll of cotton wool from the cupboard where it was kept for a multitude of purposes ranging from Christmas snow on models to first aid. I tore off a huge chunk and faced Jimmy.

'Come on, old chap, let's see if I can clean you up a bit before Miss Rockliffe gets here. Will you move your hands and let me see what you've done?'

The hands faltered and edged away slightly from the middle of his head. What I could see appeared to be a river of blood between them. Absolutely no memory of queasiness surfaced. Quickly, but as gently as I could, I covered it with the cotton wool intending that it should soak up the blood so that I could see the extent of the damage.

At this point Rocky came in with the school's full medical kit. With blood covering his hands, trickling down to mingle with the dirt on his face, and seeping through the large piece of cotton wool I was holding on his head, Jimmy looked a really serious casualty.

'He'll need stitches, I'll bet,' she whispered quietly to me. 'It's a miracle he didn't knock himself out.'

Carefully I removed the cotton wool as Rocky sprinkled a large swab with TCP.

'Now then, Jimmy, 'I'll try not to hurt you. Let's see if I can clean you up.' Her voice sounded easy and comforting. Jimmy looked up and for a moment I detected a fleeting look of trust in his hard eyes. He lowered his hands to his lap where I started to wipe them to remove some of the ubiquitous blood. Rocky plunged her left hand into the tangled mop of dirty blood-stained hair at the back of his head to hold it steady and began swabbing with the other. Suddenly I felt her stiffen. I looked up at Jimmy' face, and then at hers.

'What's up?' I whispered

My God, Nigel – look,' she whispered back.

I looked at the cut. It was nasty and looked deep. But vaguely I felt that it might have been worse.

Hm, it's probably quite deep, but…'

'Not the cut - his hair.' She grimaced and shuddered but kept her hands working. I peered closely. The reaction was thoroughly unusual for Rocky who normally seemed unmoved by blood, urine and vomit which the young children in her class contrived to present her with from time to time. It was some seconds before my mind registered what she meant. At root level the whole surface seemed to be moving. Jimmy's scalp was alive with head lice.

Chapter 31

'Nigel, you're coming to a stag evening on Friday.'

Taff made this announcement almost belligerently in the staffroom one day whilst we were having lunch. Miss Rees was presiding, as usual. She looked up, disapprovingly.

'Oh, am I? Who says so?' I asked.

'I do - all the MEN involved in school football are going. But no women allowed, you see,' he grinned at Rocky. She rolled her eyes.

'Oh, you mean the Annual Dinner. You won't make me jealous. I hate beer. Anyway the whole thing is only an excuse for getting drunk.'

'You men think far too much of yourselves,' snapped Miss Rees. 'If it weren't for women primary education would collapse. On top of that we have to suffer iniquitous unequal pay. You men ought to be doing more work than women to make up for that, not wasting time going out pub crawling!'

'It's not a pub crawl.' Taff assumed a shocked tone. I could see he was enjoying himself. He liked to stir the men v. women argument every now and then. Recently he had been having fun quoting an article asserting that men's brains weighed on average two ounces more than women's. Needless to say the female members of staff were not impressed with the deductions he drew from the fact.

'Well, what is it in aid of and where is it?' I asked.

'It's the Annual Football Dinner and it's organised by Mike O'Leary, the Secretary of the city's Schools Football Association - and a very respected headmaster.' The last point was directed in pseudo reverence at Miss Rees who chose to ignore it. 'It's an annual institution and nearly everyone goes. Wilf is coming so you must come as well.'

Wilf was not in the room because he was doing dinner duty. I looked at Rocky.

'I think it's most unfair Rocky can't go. I know there aren't many women who help with football to the extent that she does but that shouldn't mean the majority should exclude them.'

'You needn't worry about me, Nigel, I'm not interested. I might be if it was just a dinner, but from what Taff told me about last year it's a competition to see who can drink the most beer - and it's well known the record holder is Mike O'Leary himself. You've only got to look at his shape to see that.'

I had seen Mr O'Leary at Saturday morning matches. He was absolutely unmistakable. A caricaturist would have drawn a gigantic pear with short arms and legs.

'True, I'm not in the same league as our respected Secretary,' said Taff. 'But Wilf and I, being ex-Army, reckon we ought to have our own little competition with Nigel here, who of course was one of the Brylcreme boys and as such doesn't really know what beer drinking is about.'

'There you are,' Rocky said quickly. 'Be warned Nigel, those two will have you drunk in no time.'

'Oh, will they? I'm not so sure about that.' Then I paused, realising I'd jumped in with both feet. Taff grinned victoriously

'Right then, you're on. Army v. RAF. We'll show you.'

It happens to be a fact that at the time I had no real taste for beer. I enjoyed wine and at someone's demob party shortly before leaving the RAF I had tried to create something of a record in the consumption of port. The result was a day lost in my life for which I have no memory at all - fortunately it was a Sunday - followed by a day on duty with a hangover which is utterly impossible to forget.

So I didn't really expect to match Taff and Wilf at their chosen sport. I was prepared to go along with them to an extent and then bow out as gracefully as I could. I was quite prepared to submit to Taff's chaffing which I knew would ensue in the staffroom on the Monday following. Nor was I worried the Royal Air Force would suffer materially as a result of my defeat.

The hotel was on the northern side of the city which meant a comparatively short bus ride from my home. I met the other two in the bar before the meal. They had been there some time and were luxuriating in the *bonhomie* which exuded from Mr O'Leary on these occasions. Judging by the crush of young teachers in that bar I imagined he was spending a small fortune. Taff steered me towards him.

'Here he is,sir, this is Nigel Flaxton, he joined Dayton Road last summer.'

Mr O'Leary looked at me hard with his small bright eyes. 'Got you. Seen quite a bit of you on Saturday mornings but couldn't put a face to the name when young Hughes here was talking to me earlier. Well, how do you like teaching in a big city?'

'Oh, fine, Mr O'Leary, thank you. Actually I know it well, I've lived here practically all my life.'

A questioning look spread across his face.

'Flaxton, I've heard that name before. Now, where …?'

'Probably my father, sir. He's in the Education Office. Deals with our salaries, actually.'

'Of course, Bernard Flaxton. So he's your old man is he? First rate chap. Always a gentleman on the telephone.' I stood awkwardly finding it difficult to answer his praises.

'Barman, another pint. Bitter is it?'

I realised he'd put the question to me. 'Oh, yes, thank you, but really, I'd prefer a half, if you don't mind.'

The big man stiffened and gave me the sort of look a teacher lavishes on a child who has given a really stupid answer.

'If you're thinking in halves you'd better go home again. This do is for men. Good God, Flaxton, what would your father think of you?'

I opened my mouth to reply but a sixth sense told me it would be inappropriate to inform him in the present company that my father was teetotal. Instead I mumbled my thanks as a pint glass was thrust into my hand.

'Go on, knock it back man,' Mr O' Leary commanded loudly.

Feeling trapped I looked at him, then at the foaming beer as I raised it to my lips. I took a couple of mouthfuls, then lowered it and tried to edge away. But then I became aware that not only was he still looking at me, but so were Taff, Wilf and quite a substantial number of others.

'Come on, Nigel, let's see what the RAF taught you,' teased Taff in an infuriatingly loud voice. I glanced around and saw a circle of faces obviously expecting a performance. I had never sunk half a pint in one go, let alone a full one, but I could see no means of escape. I realised only too well what was expected of me. I looked again at the vast container in my hand which was still almost full.

'Get on with it, man,' bellowed Mr O'Leary.

I lifted the glass and gulped...and gulped...and gulped. I fixed my eyes on the surface of the liquid, going cross eyed in the process. I tilted it sharply towards me hoping desperately to swallow it more rapidly but only succeeded in spilling it down both sides of my chin. On and on I gulped until I felt my stomach would burst. Then, oh, bliss, I saw the bottom of the glass swill into view, then the brown tide levelled...sank...and at last was gone. Bent backwards with the glass inverted over my upturned face, I gasped for breath. Hurriedly I put it down and was engulfed in a mighty but ironic cheer. Mr O'Leary smiled benignly.

'That's better. Now you're on the books, lad. Thought for a moment you were going to be difficult. Can't have any behavioural problems here. Now come on, it will soon be time for dinner, gentlemen.'

I was about to stagger away to lose myself in the crush when Taff pushed me urgently. I looked at him and saw him nod his head towards the glass in my outstretched hand, then glance at Mike O'Leary. I saw I was still under scrutiny. Belatedly my brain started to function.again.

'Let me get you a drink, Mr O'Leary.' My voice revealed I'd just solved the trickiest question in an intelligence test.

'Oh, thank you so much, Mr Flaxton,' he boomed. Laughter enveloped me as a path opened up amid the crowd to the bar. I stepped along it to find a barman facing me expectantly.

'A pint for Mr O' Leary, please.' I leaned an elbow on the counter and looked around. Though there was plenty of noise in the room there was a noticeable silence in my vicinity. The barman-remained quite still as well. This time my brain swung into action rather more rapidly.

'Er, Taff, Wilf, are you ready for another?'

'Yes please, Nigel,' called two voices from a distance. 'And two more, please, barman,' I said importantly. This time he moved slowly towards the handles. I looked around again. There seemed still to be a certain atmosphere, an expectancy…

'Er, would anyone else care to join…'

A minor stampede rushed to the bar on to which hundreds of glasses crashed in overlapping salvoes. Actually, I got away with nine in the round. In that crowd it could have been far worse.

'Another one for yourself, sir?' The barman pointed accusingly at my glass which I had planted on the counter in front of me whilst I extracted the necessary small fortune from my wallet. Internally liquid sloshed around in the recesses of what had been my empty stomach. But I didn't dare contradict him in such company.

'Yes, yes, of course, er, thank you.'

I turned away into the crowd which now, mercifully, seemed to have lost interest in me. But Wilf and Taff suddenly were on my flanks. 'Dinner in five minutes, Nigel, so you'd better lose that quickly,' said Wilf. Inwardly I groaned, but outwardly I sipped with what I hoped looked like determination.

'Alright, you two, but I'm going to enjoy this one, so don't push me. Anyway, I'll take it into dinner with me.'

Taff looked at me in horror. 'Beer with dinner? Oh no, Nigel, there'll be wines and liqueurs, you can't spoil them with beer. You'd better drink up quickly.'

I eyed him suspiciously but he looked quite serious. After all, he had been here last year and obviously knew what he was talking about. So not wishing to offend protocol, I attacked my second pint. After a struggle I won.

'Gentlemen, take your seats for dinner,' called a voice across the jostling crowd. Immediately we were caught up in a surge which moved towards a pair of brown swing doors. Soon we were in a large room with tables placed in the traditional 'E'. Wilf and Taff steered me to our places which they had reconnoitred earlier. To my stomach's intense relief we were soon heartily tucking into a very satisfying meal.

Very soon I realised that Taff's assertions about wine was another example of his regular leg-pulling because waiters were flying to and fro with laden trays of drinks held on high, most of which were pints of beer. Neither did it surprise me when one man whisked three tankards in front of Wilf.

'Your drinks, sir.'

'Funny sort of wine, Taff,' I mumbled between mouthfuls.

'Nonsense, vintage hop, boyo. Cheers!'

'Up the Army,' challenged Wilf.

'Not if I can help it.' I grabbed my glass and emptied half of it enthusiastically. Somehow I felt more in the swing of things. The food was helping enormously and I began to imagine that I might, after all, be able to give a good account of myself in this competition. Beer in quantity didn't seem to be having the same effect upon me as cheap port.

The speeches which followed the meal were unremarkable. Mr O'Leary was praised by various minions and he duly praised everyone else. During his speech I became acutely conscious of the call of nature and hoped he wouldn't go on too long. Fortunately he announced that he had no intention of keeping us from the serious work of the evening, a sentiment which everyone cheered. He wished us all success with our teams in the remaining months of the season, thanked us all for the hard work we had put in and were going to put in, then sat down to thunderous applause. There was a brief moment of indecision after it had subsided; then we rose as one man and charged for the loo.

Having gained the desired relief, which occupied me longer than anyone else, I found my way back to the private room which was ours for the remainder of the evening. Mike O'Leary was holding court from a large winged brown leather armchair which contrived to accommodate his bulk with nothing whatsoever to spare. Ranged about him on low chairs and high stools were his courtiers, amongst whom were Taff and Wilf. The low, shiny-topped tables dotted amongst them were covered with a rash of pint tankards. I turned aside to the bar, bought three more and added them to those facing my opponents. As I pushed them on to the edge, putting some others in danger of being dislodged, I looked up and detected a flicker of alarm in Taff's eyes.

'Duw, that makes another three each here, already.'

'What, giving in on the wrong side of eight? I should have put some money on this.'

In truth and quite unaccountably I was feeling fitter by the minute. I seized my glass, swallowed a satisfying proportion and took great delight in the hint of qualm which flashed between the other two as they did the same.

Much of the remainder of the evening is not at all clear in my memory. I do remember feeling intensely happy and found everyone and everything vastly amusing, especially Mr O'Leary's jokes. At one point he leant forward and began beating the table in front of him forcefully and regularly and I tried to 'shush' everyone loudly because I thought he was going to make another speech. However, he broke into song.

'She'll be coming round the mountain, when she comes...' he intoned.

'She'll be coming round the mountain when she comes,' we all chorused. Soon the room echoed to innumerable vintage verses fresh in the minds of men not long returned from HM Forces. But it was intriguing to hear Mr O'Leary's personal contributions. I found to my surprise that, in addition to the varied and distinctly *risqué* excitement which I knew was in store for the girl, she was also going to experience a delightfully outrageous interview and worse in the headmaster's study. An impish vision of the pear-shaped. Mr O'Leary prancing around his desk chasing a scantily clad female floated before me and I collapsed in helpless laughter.

All the while glasses were emptied, and replenished, and emptied again...and I felt the RAF. would have been proud of my great courage and fortitude in the face of my unyielding enemies. But suddenly, to my intense surprise, they were unyielding no longer.

'You're a flamin' dark horse, Nigel. What would our revered Miss Rees think if she could see you now?' Wilf gesticulated none too accurately at the array of empty tankards. I looked around. There did seem to be a particularly large number and I became aware they were largely ownerless. The crowd had thinned considerably.

'We retire gracefully, boyo. Never let it be said the Welsh can't give in like gentlemen. Anyway, you're taller than us two. You've got more space to put it.' Taff rose to his feet, steadied himself, saluted beautifully and strode deliberately towards the door.

'Goodnight sir,' he called over his shoulder to Mr O'Leary. 'The Dayton Road contingent is falling out.'

'Watch him, Nigel,' urged Wilf. 'I've got to get him on the all-night bus. I'll get our coats. You keep your tabs on him.'

The admonition was timely for Taff was attempting to march along the corridor towards the front door. I trailed him as he burst through it, slithered down the steps, and continued marching as well as he could across the forecourt towards the pavement booming left, right, left, right to help keep his feet in order. Wilf brought up the rear with our coats and together we tried to wrestle Taff into his. But the tussle made him obstreperous

'Gerroff, I can put on my own uniform, damn you.'

We twisted him round as we forced his arms into his coat as best we could. Somehow my own arms were not responding too well and I felt Wilf was experiencing a similar problem. Taff looked up abruptly from the *melée*'

'Tis a fine night, men: Where are we going next?' His parade ground tones echoed down the deserted street with its rows of shops topped by windows behind which no doubt owners were asleep. One or two showed lighted curtains still and a few shops boasted refurbished neon signs which gleamed throughout the night. The harsh greenish glare of the large street lights illuminated our little group and I became worried lest Taff's noisy exuberance should attract complaint. I tried shushing him but my own voice was inclined to be unusually loud, I thought, and wasn't doing quite what I intended.

'You're coming home, with me,' said Wilf. Taff stopped in his tracks.

'No, man, no. I wanna go to… I wanna go to…'

We tried gently pushing him in the direction of the bus stop, but we might as well have tried moving a concrete pillar.

'I know what I want,' he yelled suddenly. Wilf and I stared at him, waiting tensely.

'CHIPS,' he roared.

'Oh jump in the canal, Taff,' I snapped. 'You can't get chips at this time of night.'

'Yes, I can – there.'

He pointed and moved off meanderingly behind his outstretched arm. I gazed in disbelief, but across the road an illuminated shop suggested it was indeed still open for business. To the best of our combined abilities, Wilf and I ran after him but he made the door and was in the shop before us.

'Chips, three times, corporal,' he commanded. Breathlessly, we expostulated.

'Duw, Taff, no, not for me, not after all that beer,' Wilf's voice bordered on panic.

'Nor me, old man,' I said, my stomach's had enough of a pasting for one night.'

'Nonsense. Army hasn't given up yet - chips now. Look, lovely stuff. Just what you need on a cold night.' He slapped some money on the counter. I watched without enthusiasm as the somnambulant shop assistant dredged a mass of chips from the bath of boiling fat and poured three large helpings on to three squares of newspaper. Taff seized the large vinegar bottle from the side of the counter and shook it vigorously. We got a shower bath and some reached the chips as well.

'Alright, if I've got to eat chips, I need salt.'

I seized the massive salt cellar and applied a very liberal covering to one helping, then passed it on. Dimly I had the notion that if salty things made you thirsty, then salty food might soak up liquid better even if it was already inside.

I cannot pretend I remember much more after that. We progressed slowly towards the road along which the bus ran to this part of the city in an all-night service. Taff made valiant efforts to continue vocal reports of the adventures of the female mountaineer in his rich baritone, but fearing the attentions of the police we kept stuffing chips into his mouth. In his turn he made sure Wilf and I kept eating ours.

Then, suddenly, I was waving to a departing bus as it headed for the city centre. I turned away and wandered off in the direction I knew my home to be. I believe innate knowledge came to my rescue for I have no recollection of walking along any of the roads between that bus stop and my home, nor indeed of getting into the house and into bed. Apparently the same instinct had come into play at the demob party which had been in the married quarters on the opposite of the airfield at St Athan. Friends told me they had guided me to the perimeter track then pushed me in the right direction. Whether I walked round it or took the direct route straight across the airfield I know not. Fortunately there was no night flying.

I realised I had made it home some hours later when I awoke abruptly. The room was dark, of course, but my mind was perfectly clear. I could feel the warm sheets enfolding me in their embrace, but a thought was being suggested to my mind almost at subconscious level. My brain grappled with the problem. There was something amiss, something I was going to have to do. Suddenly, I broke into a horrible, damp, hot and cold sweat. I leapt out of bed. I was going to be sick...and I was...horribly and shudderingly...on and on. The memory of it is quite ghastly.

Finally, when I felt I could, I staggered out of the loo, intending to clean myself up in the bathroom. On the landing I encountered my parents whom I had woken. I imagine I looked like death, warmed up a little.

'Er, I think I've got a chill in my stomach, or something.'

I was quite taken aback, knowing his views on such matters, when my father responded by laughing, though without much mirth.

'You'll learn,' he said. I did. I realised salt can be a powerful emetic.

Chapter 32

Every new teacher worries about keeping discipline. Yet, surprisingly perhaps, it is the one skill which cannot be taught. Students learn tricks and ploys from experienced colleagues during their practice sessions, but no one can be sure of his or her own ability to control children until the time when a class, your class for which you alone are responsible, sits staring at you for the very first time. Suddenly you are no longer a student with a teacher in the background to turn to if you find yourself in difficulties. This is your lot in front of you and they are weighing you up rapidly. How are you going to control them if they misbehave? Will you be able to quieten them if they talk too loudly, or shout at one another? What are you going to do if they start walking around, or throwing things, or wander out of the room.

I am sure every new teacher experiences a few nightmares in which he or she faces a class in uproar and screams ineffectually, whilst colleagues stand in a group looking in from the doorway. Above the din one catches disjointed comments.

'No, he hasn't got what it takes…if he's as bad as this now, what'll he be like in thirty years' time…poor devil…he'll be a nervous wreck before the term's out…'

Fortunately there is usually the honeymoon period when the class is comparatively quiet whilst contemplating the new teacher. It may be a few hours, or days, even weeks, or maybe just a couple of minutes. Its length depends upon many variables - the teacher's age, the hint of experience or lack of it, confidence of manner, tone of voice, the look in the eye.

I remember a forthright fourteen year old talking to me on this topic with the open assurance that precocious teenagers possess and use when they are sure of their audience. She described in detail the varied abilities of members of staff at the school in the matter of pupil control.

'...then there's Mr Seamarks. Now he's young, and good looking, and you'd think he'd be easy to fool around with. But there's just something in his voice. I can't quite describe it, but it makes you stop short of really messing about. It's funny, really, because he doesn't do much to keep you quiet, like giving out extra work or detentions - no, there's just something in his voice.'

Not surprisingly Mr Seamarks gained good promotion in the profession. That indefinable something in one's personality is what all young teachers yearn for. All hope they possess it and that in the practical situation it will grow and flourish quickly, so that soon it will be called experience. But its absence means disaster and if it doesn't issue from the root stock, then grafting from elsewhere is not likely to succeed.

Naturally, in trying to develop this quality, new teachers make mistakes, either under or over-exerting their authority. It's easy to be wise after the event, but much more difficult to handle every situation with precise judgment, especially when you have to decide on the spur of the moment how to react to an individual's misbehaviour. Usually this forms a challenge to your authority, which the group watches. Under-react, and as sure as night follows day more misbehaviour and more challenge will follow. Then, if you were easy-going the first time, how can you justify being harder for the second? If you are, you'll be thought unfair - a terrible fault in children's minds - and if not, you're weak and a pushover.

I remember Mrs S discussing the matter very forcefully with Taff Hughes. She was a very large woman, both in height and breadth, and had her own distinctive view about society which she advanced on every possible occasion. In a nutshell this was that the only authority that mattered in the world was her own. With her husband and a proportion of their family of ten children she ran a 'Rag and Bone' business, the central asset of which was the traditional cart. This plied up and down the city streets with house fronts echoing to her trumpeted commands, 'Bring out your RA-AAGS:' Such was the force of her personality that many householders felt it sensible to be compliant, with the result that as well as rags, all kinds of unwanted goods were given to the miniature minions who scurried to and fro between the houses and the family vehicle. This was pushed by Mr S who, whilst in no way such a physically well-furnished specimen as his wife, was nevertheless wiry and tough. With much going for it their business flourished, and on the occasions when Mrs S was summoned to appear at the city's courts for failing to send certain of her children to school with any kind of regularity, and was fined the regulation £5 with unfailing regularity, she always made great play of extracting a huge roll of notes from her handbag, peeling off five, plonking them firmly and without a trace of malice on the front of the dock.

'Five quid it is, me luv. 'Ere yar.'

The magistrate usually looked resigned at the inadequacy of his or her powers and the Attendance Officer, who reported these appearances to us, was furious and frustrated.

Mrs S was equally contemptuous of the authority of teachers. On this occasion Taff had kept Berny in for being disobedient and his release had brought his mother to the school in full cry five minutes later. She caught Taff coming down the stairs from the staffroom on his way home, barring his way with arms akimbo.

'Whad yow mean, young 'Ughes, keepin' our Berny in? 'E's work to do when 'e comes 'ome. I doan' want 'im westin' 'is time 'ere, so we'll 'ave no more o' that.'

'Well, now, Mrs S, I'm glad you've called.' From the staffroom I heard Taff's voice float upwards in tones of perfect reasonableness. 'He just doesn't like taking instructions, you see. All the class were told to be quiet whilst they were reading and Berny started to talk, I warned him once, but he carried on. So I had to do something. You see my problem.'

'Yers, but yow doan' 'ave to keep 'im in. Yow should jus' 'ollar at 'im, an' 'e'll shurrup.'

'But he didn't. Turned away, you see, very cheeky like, and two minutes later he was talking again.'

Mrs S snorted. 'But 'e din't take no notice o' yer because yow din't sound as if yow meant it, I'll bet. That's the trouble with all yow young teachers, kids doan' know where they are with yer. If I 'ad my way, yow wouldn' be let loose in the classroom afore yow was thirty.'

I remember being amused by this notion because Mrs S's philosophy of teacher training begged the question of inexperience at whatever age one began. True, a thirty year old might look more mature than someone of twenty-two, so the honeymoon period might be slightly extended. But thirty, forty or fifty, if the children spot you are inexperienced and weak into the bargain, they'll generally make your life hell. But Taff explained the situation beautifully.

'I see your point,, but you have to learn in the classroom no matter at what age you start. Alright, so I'm young and I make some mistakes, I don't mind admitting it. But I'll get better as time goes by and by the time I'm thirty, I hope I'll be a pretty experienced teacher.' There was a pause, but Mrs S was softening a little, so she missed the chance of the next comment. 'Put it like this,' - Taff was quick to pursue his advantage – 'when you had your first baby, I'll bet you made mistakes, but you got better as time went by. Now look where you are.'

Upstairs I dissolved into silent laughter. Inwardly I envied Taff the ready wit which produced this unanswerable *riposte*. Downstairs there was also silence as Mrs S pondered her reaction. But she had no choice, really, and soon she and Taff were talking like bosom pals.

'How's business these days, Mrs S?'

'Could be wuss, duck, could be wuss.'

Chapter 33

The immediate post-war years were ones of harsh austerity and schools as much as other institutions, or individual people, felt the full weight of the country's efforts to pull its economy back from the abyss of war debts. This meant that books were not renewed, materials were scarce and apparatus was old. We young teachers learnt to be both frugal and ingenious, as well as turning into first rate scroungers as we sought paper, paint, cardboard, wood and other materials for classroom models and displays. The rooms certainly needed enlivening. Their large size was an advantage, which many modern schools no longer possess, but they were drab. In Class Four's room there were glazed brown tiles on three walls to a height of about four feet; these were surmounted by a section bordered by wooden laths for display work. Above the walls soared to the ceiling, some eighteen feet high, which once had been painted cream. The room was light because the large window spread reached almost as high. But the decor was thoroughly uninspiring.

Every penny from official sources was spent on the absolute necessities of the curriculum - English, Arithmetic, Reading, Nature Study, Geograpy, History, Physical Training and Music. The last mentioned was singing taken once a week by every class; the teacher was Miss Rees, and how those children sang - they didn't dare do otherwise. But in each subject the amount of money available for new items each year was extremely small.

In September Miss Rees dispensed the requisite number of pencils, penholders and rubbers to each class with the admonition that in the following July she wanted the same number returned. Pencils, she accepted, would be stubs by then and rubbers (one between two children) would be worn down.

Penholders, however, were not subject to wear and tear so the full number would be returned. In this she was acting no differently to her colleagues in schools throughout the city and the country. Each class was allowed a gross box of pen nibs; three per child for the year.

Most teachers resorted to having blocks of wood with holes drilled (we had to supply these ourselves) for the appropriate number of pens and pencils; a tin for the rubbers which we counted out at the beginning of a lesson and counted in at the end. Some enterprising teachers took twelve pencils, cut them into four pieces each, sharpened the stubs and kept them locked away to be able to return a full quota of stubs. The remaining thirty-six were cut in half, forty-eight made available for lessons and twenty-four kept in reserve. Careful watch was kept on those heavy handed children inclined to break pencil points too often.

Most of us bought copies of magazines likely to be useful in providing pictures. Pictorial Education was popular because it offered large formats. Its pictures, of course, were ordinary black and whites as seen in newspapers. Colour in classrooms came largely from children's art work. Powder paint was cheap and therefore available in reasonable amounts. Six inch squares of shiny coloured paper with gummed backs were also in common use; I remembered these from my own junior school.

Large coloured sheets of sugar paper were available, fairly soft and useful for backing children's display work. Coloured manilla paper was altogether stronger and useful for model work. Various kinds of cardboard were also stocked for more enterprising model work and many other activities including scenery for plays. But the overriding consideration in using all such stock was to be as frugal as possible. Money was the greatest shortage; there was no extra to spend on anything remotely described as a luxury.

Football shirts and netball strip certainly came into that category. As I've mentioned the Dayton Road first teams had some very good players, often outstanding in skill. But as far as appearances went the teams comprised a motley crew. Financially pressed mothers put old shirts and blouses aside for matches and scrubbed them unmercifully afterwards to remove stains, then darned the tears and splits as best they could while the material precariously held together. When they looked too battered equally old pullovers of varying colours were pressed into service. The result was teams whose rough appearance hardly reflected credit upon themselves or their school. No one liked this and gradually everyone was saying that something ought to be done about it - teachers, Mr Brand, fathers (and some mothers) on the touchlines on Saturdays, and the boys and girls themselves.

But above all - Rocky. She released her pent-up feelings on the matter one day in the staffroom. We had just finished lunch and she was collecting the used dishes.

'I'm sick of taking our teams out looking like a bunch of scarecrows: It's so unfair. Some of them look really disreputable, as though they came from awful homes. Yet most of them are decent. Their parents just can't afford the strip.'

The pile of dishes grew as she slammed plate upon plate. It wobbled precariously as she picked it up and turned to the door. I leapt up and turned the knob.

'I'm going to see the Boss. We've just got to find the money from somewhere to dress them properly.'

I edged around her on the landing and held the kitchen door open. The pile of plates lived dangerously for a moment, then was deposited very firmly on the table to await collection. Rocky spun on her heels and made for the stairs.

'You're going to see the Boss now - this minute?' I called to the top of her head from the bannister rail. But with a clatter she was down the stairs and through the door to the playground.

School staff usually employed the soubriquets Boss or Old Man for headmasters but both were inappropriate for Mr Brand. We never met formally as a staff to discuss the school throughout my entire stay at Dayton Road, though he was usually with us in Miss Shenton's room at morning and afternoon breaks for coffee and tea. In the staffroom Miss Rees reigned, whilst Mr Brand sat in solitary state in his eyrie at the other end of the building. The exceptions were the rare occasions when he used his long desk in the hall, but even there he presided over empty space.

Then again, his physical prowess at stair climbing, for which he retained the staff speed record throughout my stay, would have made the Old Man label equally ridiculous. I never found out his age. Those gangling, flying legs and his seraphic beam as he floated along the corridor without a trace of breathlessness the instant he reached the top remained a sharp memory. I cherished an ambition to copy him well into my mature years, but when I pounded upwards, puffing and creaking I knew I was fighting a losing battle. So, on balance, the staff were right to choose Boss as less inappropriate. But that same afternoon as we stood drinking our tea, he almost called us to order.

'Um-ah, Miss Rockliffe has asked me whether we can find some money for football shirts and netball strip,' he announced to the tea cup he was holding. Then he looked up to find us all staring at him. Taff, Wilfred and I reacted to the trigger words money and football shirts, and the older women were surprised at the Boss actually addressing the assembled company. Miss Rees blinked rapidly. Rocky was the only who was ready for what was coming.

'Of course, there's no chance of our capitation money running to that sort of thing, but I feel that some parents might be willing to help us raise enough to purchase sets.'

'That's a great idea, sir.' Taff's quick enthusiasm erupted. Miss Rees glared; she took her First Officer role very seriously.

'You have Miss Rockliffe to thank for the notion, Mr Hughes. She mentioned the possibility to me at lunch time and I have been giving it some thought since. I believe I could ask certain parents to join with us. I am sure they could suggest various money raising projects.'

'Who would you ask, Mr Brand? enquired Miss Rees.

'Oh, Jeffrey Howard's mother, perhaps, he's such a good footballer, so he's likely to stay in the team. Then Mrs Jones, Peter's mother, and probably Mr and Mrs Ollerton. They're a very sensible couple, I find. I've met them two or three times.'

'Those sound alright. But there are some I wouldn't want to be asked, don't you agree?' Miss Rees turned to her two senior colleagues for support. Miss Rees's nature didn't brook argumentative parents.

Parent-Teacher Associations were plants of very tender growth in those days, if they sprouted at all. But absence didn't necessarily reveal stony ground. The propensity which many

Dayton Road parents had for walking into the building to tell us young teachers our job could be turned to our advantage as was about to be demonstrated. In due course Mr Brand informed us that he had written to his selected group asking them to help in the raising of some ready cash for the shirts and strip and that he had received their replies.

'There are two suggestions which have been put forward in each letter,' he informed us. 'These are organising a series of Whist Drives and a Grand Jumble Sale.'

I cannot think what else I imagined we might do, but my thoughts certainly were not enthused by these proposals. My only skill at cards lay in an ability not to finish too much out of pocket at Pontoon, a skill learnt in the traditional venue of the sixth form common room and perfected around numerous billet stoves in the RAF on cold winter nights. Whist I regarded as one of the pursuits of the card playing elite, like Poker, or even Bridge. I knew a few Whist players, of course. They played regularly, week in week out throughout the year and contrived to equip their kitchens and half furnish their houses with the prizes they brought home in triumph. Whist driving was a religion which demanded extraordinary skill on the part of its devotees and I knew I was not of their number.

But Jumble Sales were very different - quite at the opposite end of the social spectrum. A battered board with 'Jumble Sale TO-DAY' scrawled in chalk propped up outside the entrance to a sleazy looking hall in the more dilapidated areas of the city was a fairly common sight, but I had always hurried past. As a child the notion of wearing clothing bought in a jumble sale would have filled me with horror. The ultimate condemnation which mother could heap upon me whenever I looked particularly dishevelled was, 'You look as though you've been dressed at a jumble sale.' As a result I grew up regarding such things as events that took place in dens of iniquity, rather like billiard halls. Certainly I should have classified them alongside brothels had I known what they were. I was an obnoxious child.

But now it seemed that not only was I expected to know all about such things but, much worse, I was to be swept up in the organisation of one. The subsequent discussion in the staffroom next day worried me intensely.

'I shall duplicate letters to all parents informing them of the sale, asking them to send all their own jumble. Now you'll have to send two children to me each day with it. I can't have everyone bringing it to me direct or there'll be chaos. I'll clear extra space in the stockroom.- it'll take plenty as it's such a large room.'

Miss Rees had taken charge quickly. .I was surprised because I expected her to be opposed to the whole idea. But I hadn't taken into account her position as Number One. It would be intolerable if we all worked liked slaves and organised a highly successful event without her. Her position and credibility would take a dive and that was something she wouldn't endure. The only alternative was to lead and I soon found myself admiring her thoroughness.

Miss Shenton looked around the table. 'We must all go through our cupboards and garages and clear out anything we don't want. It will all be grist to the mill.'

'Duw, yes,' broke in Wilfred. 'It's amazing what gets sold at jumble sales in the Valleys. Looks the most broken down old junk you can imagine but someone finds use for most of it.'

'Three weeks on Saturday,' mused Miss Browning. 'By then we must have the hall planned, you know, where we shall have the tables and, we'll need a system for bringing out extra jumble as the first lots are bought. It's not a good idea to have everything out from the beginning; makes the customers stay longer and they buy more.'

'Don't worry, I'll see plans are drawn up well in advance,' said Miss Rees quickly. We'll need to organise something to put the cash in as we take it. If my experience is anything to go by, we'll need to keep a close watch on that. There are a few people around here who'll come looking for that kind of thing. Probably one or two of the children as well, I shouldn't wonder.'

'We had a sale at our church recently.' said Miss Shenton, 'and all the helpers wore aprons with large deep front pockets. They put the money in those. It looked marvellous - it was easy to find change yet no one could possibly steal it when they weren't looking.'

'What an excellent idea, Miss Shenton.'

Praise indeed, coming from Miss Rees. I was fascinated by the change which I was seeing in her. I knew she was an exceptionally hard working teacher who drove the children, too much occasionally I was inclined to think in my naïvety. But I had not yet seen her involved with any extra curricular activity. I was to learn that when she did it was pursued with the same relentless drive which characterised her teaching.

But the whole conversation was a new dimension to me. Everyone, it seemed, knew all about jumble sales except me. Taff wasn't present at the initial discussion because he was on duty but when he came up and changed with Miss Browning, he plunged into the conversation like an expert.

'We'll need plenty of time after school on the last few days to do the pricing. Takes a long time, that. I think the women are best at that, don't you agree, Nigel?'

'Oh, ah, yes, I'm sure they are.'

'And what are you best at Nigel, apart from drinking?' asked Rocky. She had been pulling my leg on that subject since Taff and Wilfred had regaled the staff with heavily embroidered accounts of my prowess at the football dinner. My protestations that I had never before tried out my capabilities in that direction had been laughed down by everyone, though Miss Rees hadn't shared in the amusement. She reacted with prim disgust that I was like all men. But I wasn't sure about Rocky. Was she secretly pleased that I had won the contest, or disappointed because it made me look a boozer? And now I couldn't use this opportunity to show a lead in this money raising venture which was so near to her heart because I felt completely useless. It was galling.

'I have to admit I don't know anything about jumble sales.' I decided the honest approach was best. 'You'll have to take me in hand and tell me what to do.'

'Oh, we'll find you plenty to do, Mr Flaxton, won't we ladies?' Miss Rees surveyed the table and naturally received three ready responses from the women.

'Watch it, Nigel - petticoat government they call it. You'll be run off your feet now,' said Taff.

'Don't be so rude, Mr Hughes.' Miss Rees attempted to crush him but he was made of sterner stuff and rarely suffered visibly under the verbal reprimands of the Chief Assistant. He certainly received quite a few because gently riling her amused him and she nearly always rose to his bait.

At this moment the bell monitor played his peal at the foot of the stairs. Unusually we had stayed throughout the entire lunch hour planning the Grand Jumble Sale.

'Do you really mean you've never helped run one of these?' Rocky asked me with an incredulous look on her face as walked across the playground.

'Too true - what's more I've never even been to one.'

'My lad, you haven't lived. This will certainly improve your education.'

Without elucidating further. she left me near my door and swept on to hers. I stood and watched her retreating figure, momentarily appreciating her attraction from both directions. As she turned towards her room she looked back fleetingly and inclined her head to the audience. My heart sang for the rest of the afternoon. But whilst cycling home afterwards I gave the matter deeper thought. I was sure now that Rocky didn't actually despise me for my football dinner behaviour but I needed to find something at which I could excel in her eyes. Now this jumble sale was looming I was going to appear merely an experienced idiot once again. Gloomily I decided I would become typecast in the role. All I could offer so far was reasonable skill with a camera but I'd soon found she hated being photographed. Very odd for someone who looked so sportively attractive.

The day after the handbills were sent out to homes I began to see what I was facing. As I surveyed the two rows of children waiting to come into the classroom I noticed some were carrying large bundles of rags, mostly tied with string.

'What on earth are you doing with this rubbish?' I asked no one in particular. I received shocked looks in reply.

'It's jumble, sir,' said Leslie reverently.

'Aaah…oh, I see. Yes, well, we must arrange for it all to be sent to Miss Rees. Right, girls, lead in.'

Whilst the children trooped in I took the chance to look more closely at the bundles. As far as I could see the contents were incredibly old and dirty. I called the register and then looked at the class. Some ten or twelve children were sitting expectantly with righteous expressions as they sat guarding their bundles on the desks in front of them.

'Right, we need two monitors to take this jumble each morning to Miss Rees. I'm going to appoint two boys who haven't yet got any particular job.' At the beginning of term I had intended to organise many specific tasks but my inexperienced imagination ran out after a day or so and I was left with a high rate of unemployment. So now about twenty boys' hands shot into the air.

'Sir, sir, me, please, oh, please, me sir.' The response wasn't so much a noise as an imitation of a snake pit. But as on other such occasions I revelled in their enthusiasm.

'Cyril, James, you'll do.' The snakes subsided with audible groans, leaving the two boys smiling happily but politely waiting further instructions. I had the sense to realise I should be in trouble if I sent anyone who would not meet Miss Rees's approval.

When I gave the word they began their task of carrying the jumble to the stockroom at the foot of the staffroom stairs. In the days that followed they made a number of well laden journeys. At break I sought Rocky. 'Ye gods, you should see the awful rubbish my class has brought so far: It's incredible; none of it'll sell, of course. I think it'll have to be thrown away immediately. It seems parents have taken this as a chance to get rid of extra rubbish.'

'Don't you believe it, Nigel. It may look like rubbish at present, but when it's sorted and priced, it'll look different. You'll be surprised at how much will sell. Don't forget, most people will wash or clean whatever they buy - and even if it has to be dry cleaned that's a lot cheaper than buying new clothes.'

Shortly afterwards I looked into the stock room. Miss Rees was in the middle of piles of clothing, some loose, some tied in bundles of varying sizes. Against a wall were other items - books, various ornaments, a rather elderly set of wooden steps heavily spattered with paint, some toys, two dolls forlornly propping up one another, and a large but very worn teddy bear. She was busily engaged in opening the bundles of clothing and sorting it into other piles of approximately similar garments. As soon as she saw me she pounced.

'You can do some of this at lunch time, Mr Flaxton. No real skill needed at this stage. Men's clothing on that side, women's on this. Shirts, pullovers, ties there, coats, trousers there, over here, dresses, skirts, tops - you know, blouses, cardigans, that sort of thing. Anything else, leave for me. You might get some petticoats or even some unmentionables but you'd better leave those alone. Now do you think you can manage that?'

Glad of some direction at last, I readily agreed. As the days passed it became quite a routine. Whenever any one of us had spare time at midday, or at the end of the afternoon, we continued sorting the jumble which continued to flow in a very steady stream. The motley collections of objects, as distinct from clothes, grew as well and one day we awarded Taff a metaphorical prize when his class produced a bicycle. Old and battered it certainly was, but it worked and could be refurbished.

'That's going to be priced at ten shillings, not a penny less,' he said. 'Bobby Carter brought it in - said it's his older brother's, who's been called up. Duw, I hope he doesn't want it when he comes home.'

'I should check with Mrs Carter, said Miss Browning, 'but they're a sensible family so I don't think Bobby would bring it without permission.'

Bobby's right to bring it was duly proved the next day and it became the star exhibit, as far as price was concerned. Everything else was much cheaper. The four women became the price fixing committee, with Taff and Wilfred being co-opted occasionally for tools, old wirelesses and such like. But what intrigued me most were the shoes. There were dozens of them, some in quite good repair. They ranged from reasonably fashionable through children's sandals to wellington boots. I couldn't imagine people would actually buy them; shoe selection and fitting was a matter of care and skill, I thought. Surely, people wouldn't give these a second look?

We stayed after school had finished on the Friday before the sale and were joined by some of the mothers who had volunteered to help. The dinner tables were pressed into service to make a long counter. It was ranged down the length of the hall and across the top end, with plenty of space on either side for sellers and buyers alike. The larger items were brought in and propped against the walls or on the heating pipes, which is where the bicycle stood resplendent with large white ticket on which Taff had inscribed '10/-: A BARGAIN'. The women roamed up and down the room laying out clothing and pinning notes to the front of the tables displaying prices, or pinning tickets to individual garments. As for me I slipped easily into the only job I could possibly undertake, that of errand boy.

By six o'clock the hall had taken on something of the appearance of a town market. It seemed to me there was an incredible amount of jumble, most of which I was sure would be rejected out of hand by the would-be purchasers. In fact when I looked around as we gradually came to the end of the final preparations, I wondered if any would even turn up. I said so to Rocky, quietly so that the parent-helpers couldn't hear.

'I think you're in for a surprise, Nigel. You see what it's like at ten o'clock tomorrow morning.'

We agreed to be at school just after nine so that any necessary final checks could be made. Because the timing was not all that precise I was rather later than I intended, so it was about half past nine on Saturday morning when I cycled into Dayton Road. At the far end I was surprised to see a knot of people near the school. I sped onwards with some urgency, feeling there had been an accident. But when I reached the place I realised the main door was locked and there was quite a substantial crowd waiting good humouredly outside it-. I decided to cycle on and use another door.

'There's Mr Flaxton - he's late.'

" 'Come on, young man - your pals have been here for ages.'

'Go and tell them to let us in, its cold waitin' out 'ere?

I grimaced, embarrassed, and prayed that the upper door was open. I jumped off my bike, pulled it on to the pavement and up the step to the door. It was firmly locked. I hammered on it hard with my fist. I knew that if everyone was in the hall they wouldn't hear me. After a lengthy pause it became obvious they couldn't. I beat a tattoo on the door, well aware that by now I had an audience. Some of the women had detached themselves from the group and were watching me closely.

'It's no good, you'll have to wait till they let us in,' called one. I smiled weakly not relishing the thought of meeting Miss Rees on Monday if I failed to get in before the rush. Then I heard Wilf's voice in the short corridor behind the door. I seized my chance and thumped the door wildly. A few seconds later I heard the bolts being pulled and it opened fractionally. As soon as he saw me he flung it wide, pulled me in and slammed the bolts home again.

'Hey, I know I'm late, but…' I began but was interrupted by more hammering on the door, punctuated by frustrated yells from outside.

;Come on, let us in, it's time you know.'

'You rotten lot, we wanna get in first.'

'Go on, Mr Flaxton, be a sport, open up.'

Wilfred grinned. 'Crowd of Amazons, that lot.' Then he shouted through the door. 'We won't open till ten and the only entrance is the other door.'

General moans greeted his remark but they sounded fairly good natured. I began to realise what was about to burst upon us. Hurriedly I put my bicycle into the stockroom, its normal hideaway, and rushed into the hall.

'Thought you'd overslept.' Rocky dashed past me, looking hot. I followed to where Miss Rees was talking to staff and parents in the final briefing session. She was also issuing uniforms, the aprons which Miss Shenton had suggested and which Miss Rees's class had made. They were yellow and each had a large deep pocket across the front. I must have registered my awkwardness as I tried to tie mine behind my back, watched by Taff and Wilf.

'Makes a lovely kangaroo, doesn't he? said Taff.

I grabbed something from a table and threw it at him. It was a woman's hat.

'Now you men, stop fooling about. Put that back, Mr Flaxton, quickly. Get to your places everyone.'

We moved behind the tables and dutifully took up our positions. She surveyed us like a Victorian store proprietor.

'Right, Mr Hughes. Open the door.'

Taff, who had been appointed to this duty, walked to the single door which was the entrance to the hall. He opened it fully, walked through, then I heard him pull back the bolts on the outside door which was close by. The hubbub of voices which we could hear through the closed windows rose in tone, then stopped suddenly. The outside door banged open and Taff sprinted in and dived under a table to reach his side of the counter. He was very closely followed by an army of charging women, supported by a sprinkling of men, a few teenagers and some of our own school children. I gasped as all hell broke loose in front of me. Within seconds the room was filled with people grabbing clothes, waving their arms to be served, fitting garments on to struggling children. I saw Taff's bike being lifted over the counter to outstretched arms and later he confirmed it had been sold within the first thirty seconds. I caught sight of Leslie's red hair weaving in and out waist high to women who completely ignored him in their efforts to snatch bargains. He had a left shoe in his hand and he seemed to be trying to find its partner.

'Have you lost the other one? I called.

'No sir,' he shouted back. 'This is me own one - I'm tryin' ter find a pair the same size. Ah, them'll do.'

He seized his prize and disappeared earthwards. I was sure he would be trampled underfoot. There was no hope of seeing him over the counter so I stooped to look underneath in the hope of glimpsing him among the struggling mass of legs. But my face stopped within inches of his; he was sitting underneath the table calmly trying on his shoes in comparative peace. He grinned as he saw my upturned face.

''Ow about them, sir, they fit me a treat! 'Ow much are they?'

I jumped up, looked at the counter, then bent down again. '2/6d - and cheap at the price.'

'Go, on, sir, lemme 'ave 'em for two bob.' I felt he knew me far too well.

'Alright, you rascal - but don't till Miss Rees.'

'Coo, ta, sir. Ta - ra - see yer Monday.'

The last I saw of him was the rapidly receding seat of his pants as he crawled agilely through the forest of legs. I stood up and put the single florin coin in the pocket of my apron. As I did so the extreme size of the pouch mocked me for I could see the other members of staff already with garments sagging under the weight of their takings. They were selling things and taking money at great speed, keeping up a flow of repartee, as though they had spent their lives on market stalls. By contrast I felt awkward and completely out of place. I looked hard at the front row of buyers to see if anyone needed help but everyone was intent upon the job in hand. For all the use I was, I felt I could walk out there and then and no one would notice.

I guessed it was only a matter of time before one of the others spotted my inactivity, so I decided to resort to cunning. I had learnt in the Forces that when I was in charge of a group of men in a situation which was quite beyond me the best ploy was to appear very busy. Then hardly anyone would ask me to do something or even ask me a question. They just used their own initiative which absolved me from having to make decisions about matters in which I had no experience.

I began tidying up the counters where grabbing hands had turned the neat rows of items into muddled piles. Then I dashed into the stock room to bring out more stuff to be sold. As I did so, the noise of the crowd rose excitedly as they realised there were new chances of bargains. I found it impossible to lay things out. As soon as I dumped the pile in my arms on to the counter it was pounced upon. Rocky and Miss. Rees watched carefully and called out prices as the goods were snatched up.

I could see Mr Brand sitting quietly in Miss Shenton's room beyond the crush, ready to receive cash, so I suggested relieving Rocky of some of hers.

'Sure, Nigel, this apron'll be round my ankles in a minute. Here you are.'

She grabbed a paper bag and stuffed it with a lot of coins. 'Go on, take that to the Boss, I'll keep the rest as change.'

In the classroom Mr Brand was sitting at a table near the teachers' desk with neat piles of new cash bags and bank account slips. The tranquility of the room and its occupant seemed worlds apart from the rampage in the hall.

'Ah, the first of the takings. Good, tip your bag out here, Mr Flaxton.' I complied and with practised swiftness Mr Brand swept the coins into piles which he arranged neatly at the front of the table. I retreated and collected more from each of the others in turn, realising that as a fetcher and carrier I had found a job which effectively kept me away from the task of selling, at which I was completely incompetent. I contrived to be quite efficient for once.

Then, suddenly, the hall emptied. It was quite remarkable. One minute the crowd was pushing and struggling as it had been since the beginning, then there was a great deal of space with only a few stragglers half-heartedly turning things over on the counter. Minutes later even these disappeared. I was puzzled, and looked at my watch. It was a quarter to eleven. I was wondering whether the scenes of the last three quarters of an hour represented a kind of first onslaught when Miss Browning said with obvious relief,

'Good, that didn't take too long. Come on Mr Flaxton, you've been a very good beast of burden, finish the job off, will you, and take what's left back to the stock room.'

'Isn't it rather early for that...I mean, won't there be more customers?'

'Good lord, no,' said Rocky. 'Everyone wants to get in at the beginning. It's no good coming later, anything worth having has gone by then. No, it's all over. We can clear up and go home.'

Although I felt relieved as I cycled up the long incline which took me towards my Saturday lunch, for which I now had a hefty appetite, nevertheless I brooded upon the next new experience which loomed. No doubt the sale had been very successful for the piles of cash had grown rapidly in front of Mr Brand and I felt sure we were well on the way to buying the strip. But the Whist Drives were still to come. Having planned these, six in all, we had to continue with them. I knew my knowledge of these events was also less than one degree above absolute zero and wondered what further surprises were lurking.

Chapter 34

In every way I found the first Whist Drive a complete contrast. To begin with, we teachers had nothing to prepare. One of the parents, Mr Ollerton, was a regular player and he organised the whole evening. He borrowed card tables and Mr Trenchard, the Caretaker, arranged for chairs to be borrowed from a local church because the school only had desks with fixed seats. Parents contributed prizes in response to a letter from Mr Ollerton and Mr Brand and when I returned to school on the Thursday evening when the first Drive was arranged, I found these set out on Mr Brand's desk in the hall. In front was a large placard showing a red diamond which I soon found was a visual aid for those people who had short memories about trumps. The hall had taken on a quite different atmosphere from daytime assemblies or the noise of indoor PT. The rows of green topped card tables each carrying a small, neat number and four chairs set around looked purposeful and, to me, rather mysterious. Packs of cards, scorecards and pencils were placed neatly on each. Having never been to a Whist Drive my appearance at this one was a matter of token support. Miss Browning and Miss Shenton were not coming, but the rest of the staff were and, like me, came simply to show willing. Mr Ollerton and his wife had matters thoroughly in hand. I was relieved to see that we had nothing to do this time.

The room began to fill. But this group of people was very orderly. They came in quietly, some nodding to Mr and Mrs Ollerton as they sat down. It was obvious that most knew one another and they were regular players. Soon most of the chairs were occupied, though I could see one or two tables where there were only three occupants.

I was propping up the wall at one end of the hall watching idly when Taff sidled up to me.

'Keeping out of the way, Nigel? I don't blame you.'

'Well, there's nothing to do, is there? I mean, this chap Ollerton has got things taped. He must be used to organising Whist Drives.'

'Sure, and all this crowd are regulars. I don't want to play with them if I can avoid it.'

An unseen hand punched my stomach. 'Play - you don't mean we might be roped in?'

'It's possible, boyo. They need four at each table see, two pairs at each. So some of us may have to make up the numbers.'

'Hell, no! I've never played proper Whist, only the knock-out kind. I wouldn't know what to do with a partner.'

'Mm, I'm not much better - and Melvin in my class said his Gran wants to play with me. She goes to all the drives around here and she's a terror. That's her over there by the door, facing this way.'

I followed his directions and saw a thin but very tough looking woman of immense age dressed entirely in black. Wisps of hair protruded untidily beneath a black hat with a battered brim. Round this faded flowers provided the one touch of colour in a portrait of gloom. She had the lifted chin and pouting, flat lips symptomatic of a marked absence of teeth. She was made of whippy spring steel forged in the social furnace of the city.

'She looks at least ninety,' I said. 'She couldn't do much to you: Why does she want to play with you particularly?'

'Melvin says she wants to get her own back on me because I kept him in last week when he should have been doing her shopping. When he got home the local shop was shut and she had to go without her cigarettes.'

'Oh, I see. No wonder you're in her bad books. Never mind, she's got someone opposite her, so she's got her partner for the evening.'

'Hey, but Nigel...'

'Good evening, ladies and gentlemen,' called Mr Ollerton above the discreet chatter, cutting short Taff's reply. I'm so pleased to see plenty of you here to support the school in raising money for our youngsters' team strips. Now it's time to begin. I see there are two spare places. Could we have these filled by two of the teachers?'

He looked up expectantly. Wilf at the other end of the hall actually turned away involuntarily. Taff looked at his feet and I felt myself colouring as faces turned towards me. Then I heard Miss Rees's voice.

'I'll make up one table and I'm sure Mr Brand will fill the other.'

I looked up sharply with both relief and surprise. 'Yes, I don't mind unless one of the younger men would prefer...' said Mr Brand in his mildest tone.

'No, no, sir, you carry on by all means,' said Taff quickly.

'Good, that's fine,' said Mr Ollerton.

At this point Rocky made an entrance. Her timing couldn't have been worse. All eyes swept to the door as she came in, obviously breathless from hurrying

'I do apologise, Mr Ollerton, I missed a bus.'

'Oh, don't worry at all. Actually you've come in the nick of time. You can now make up a table with the other three men teachers, then no one will be left out. Come on, take this table, will you?'

It wasn't really a question and none of us had the face to refuse in front of everyone, now poised to begin. We sat down quickly, glad at least to be out of the general gaze. Though intensely worried about making a fool of myself in another unknown pursuit, I consoled myself with the thought that at least we were all together at one table. Rocky had sat down opposite me so we would be partners. At least I shouldn't have to pretend with her; she was becoming well used to my incompetence.

Mr Ollerton offered a pack of cards to Miss Rees who had sat at a table near to him. Obviously she knew what to do because she cut the pack and showed him an upturned card.

'Spades are trumps", he announced, and flipped over his chart. At our table Rocky took the pack and dealt at speed.

'Good dealer, signs of a misspent youth,' said Wilf. She grinned.

'I'll take you on at this any day you like.'

I felt the punch again. 'Er, that means you've played before, I assume?'

'Good lord, yes'. She looked up with disbelief. 'Nigel, you don't mean you haven't played Whist before? What have you been doing all your life?'

I felt I had to defend myself. 'Ah, now if this were Pontoon it'd be a different matter.'

'Pooh - that's only an excuse for gambling. This needs intelligence.'

'That's what we're worried about,' quipped Taff.

Silence descended so suddenly that I couldn't avoid looking round expecting that something weird had occurred. But everywhere I saw only players intent upon their cards. I felt a sudden kick on my shin and swung round to see Rocky gesticulating at a card on the table. It was a four of hearts. I looked at my hand.- I had a three and an ace. After fractional hesitation I whipped out the ace, slapped it smartly on the table, and sat back. A twinge of confidence emerged in my brain and I looked at Rocky. Her expression extinguished it immediately. During the next few minutes the expression was repeated frequently. It began with a longish look at whatever card I played, rather as though she was seeing it for the first time in her life and wasn't sure what it was. Then she would look directly at me. Whenever I looked at her with what I hoped was a reasonably confident expression, she rolled her eyes to the ceiling. I remember thinking how attractively impish she looked. But I also got the impression she wasn't entirely happy with my play and this feeling was reinforced by the occasional giggle which bubbled to the surface from either Taff or Wilfred.

At the end of the hand we had four tricks, and they had nine. Suddenly the room relaxed, and a buzz of conversation rippled around the tables.

'Ah, well, could have been worse,' I said to Rocky.

'Worse? Nigel, you idiot! We could have had at least three more tricks. For heaven's sake watch what you're doing next time. If you ignore your partner some of these people will want to carve you into little pieces.'

'Oh, sorry.' I tried to look contrite. 'I'll try to do better next time. You'd better explain where I go wrong after each hand. I'll soon pick it up.'

'Me explain? We shan't meet again: You've got to move to another table. Partners change after each hand.'

This time my stomach was pummelled. I staggered to my feet and groped towards the chair Rocky indicated at a nearby table. I flopped down opposite a large woman with flaccid cheeks and an expression cast in concrete. Not a muscle moved as I slithered into my chair. My ancient loathing of Paul Jones dances rose from my subconscious and refused to go back again for the rest of the evening.

It was ghastly. Halfway through the next hand the woman who had to suffer me as partner gave vent to a high pitched squeak loud enough to make a number of heads turn disapprovingly. I glanced furtively over my fan of cards which I was deploying geisha-like to hide my face. But her expression never varied.

At the end of the hand I was on the losing side again and once again moved to another table. In fact that was the story of much of the evening. I suppose it was due to the law of averages that I was on the winning side occasionally. When this happened I tried to look nonchalant, as though everything that had happened earlier had been pure bad luck. But even my winning partners seemed to look at me with strange, wild expressions. But, incompetent though I was, no one criticised me openly, - for which I was truly grateful. I am sure it wasn't from deference to me as a teacher. Nor was it because the players were doing the whole thing in a good cause and therefore weren't taking the game too seriously. They were in earnest right enough. It was just that it seemed to be inviolate etiquette that no one spoke during play and after each hand there was no time for post-mortems. Mr Ollerton moved us all on too quickly for that, usually to my intense relief.

There was one moment which came as a notable and particularly memorable exception to the unwritten rule. Fate decreed that Melvin's Gran and Taff Hughes became partners half way through the evening. I caught his eye as he sat down and shrugged his shoulders helplessly. I smirked inwardly, selfishly pleased that he was in the hot seat, not me. Anyway I knew he had enough Welsh granite in his soul to withstand her.

Silence descended as usual, to be broken by the occasional flick of a card being laid, or the odd nervous cough. The colour rose in my cheeks with equal normality as I selected a card, then had second thoughts, put it back, changed my mind and brought it out. Then I held it up, poised, cogitating whether to let it go. My partner of the moment seemed to be turning slightly purple, so I did. I was pleased to see his colour drain away.

Suddenly across the hall steel struck on granite.

'You young bugger - you've trumped my bloody ace,' yelled Gran without the slightest hint of etiquette.

For a split second the silence continued as heads shot round to where Taff was facing his partner. Then the room erupted with helpless laughter. His bland expression seemed so incongruous as she half stood and brandished her cards over her head like Boudicca sweeping down on unsuspecting Romans. All she needed was a chariot.

After that the remainder of the evening went very well indeed. The tension evaporated and everyone treated the occasion much more as a bit of fun. Taff and I were humoured; I was even given some tips during play by opponents as well as partners. Everyone became very pleasant indeed…that is, everyone except Melvin's Gran who could be heard muttering to herself whenever there was lull in conversation.

'Can't see a bloody ace in front of his nose…'

When the evening reached its conclusion I found myself almost sorry, and was surprised to see we had been playing for two hours. Mr Ollerton quickly dealt with the prizes, calling out possible high numbers, so identifying the winner and the runner up.

'Finally, there is the booby prize", he said. 'I suppose someone might suggest that Mr Hughes ought to be awarded this outright.'

There was tremendous laughter at this in which Taff joined as cheerfully as anyone.

'No, no, I mustn't cheat the rightful winner,' he called out.

'It's probably you in any case,' called Miss Rees.

But she was wrong. It didn't surprise me at all to find that I had the lowest score and, amid further laughter, I was duly presented with a toilet roll.

We bought the football and netball strips and had money to spare to be put into the school fund for other activities. Soon I was able to photograph the first team looking resplendent in green shirts with white sleeves and collars, each with a number on the back, and wearing immaculate white shorts with green and white socks. The netball team looked positively angelic in their blouses and skirts and regulation position aprons. In fact there was a moment when we wondered whether they would be so concerned about their new appearance that their play might become low key.

We needn't have worried. If anything their play became even better. Now they were good and looked good, too.

Chapter 35

It was freezing cold in my bedroom. There was no heat in it at all and as usual I had my window open, a procedure insisted upon throughout my boyhood as absolutely necessary to the development of a truly healthy physique. My father was adamant upon this point. He had assimilated this from personal experience. Called up in 1916 he opted for the Royal Navy following an uncle, tales of whose exploits had coloured his childhood and after whom he was named. As a Petty Officer the uncle had led his battleship gun battery to winning feats in an annual big ships competition, on one occasion being the first to score eight hits in eight rounds. He won a number of medals, of which my father had one. Alas, the uncle didn't feature in the First World War, having died of cholera and been buried in a suitably commissioned tomb in Hong Kong.

My father's exploits were rather different. A few days after beginning training as a Signals Rating at the Crystal Palace he reported sick and was diagnosed with cerebrospinal meningitis. A doctor saw him on a Friday and pronounced he would be dead by Sunday. My brother and I were grateful for the diagnostic error. That my father finally recovered he ascribed to convalescence in a Navy institution where fresh air was regarded as the *sine qua non*. It worked for him. I remember him having nothing worse than the occasional cold throughout most of his subsequent life which lasted into his eighties.

I suppose the rigours of an icy bedroom had prepared me for interminable nights in freezing wooden billets in the RAF. These could give tolerable imitations of Siberia in winter when the stoves went out, just like our house which in those days did not have an all-night fire, let alone central heating, nor, of course, double glazing. It was also dark, though I knew it was time to get up.

I could hear my father shaving in the bathroom next to my room. I snuggled further down into the cylinder of warmth which my body had created during the night. I could never get the same experience when I got into bed at night because it always felt cold. As soon as it warmed up, I fell asleep. But it was different in the morning, so warm in its caressing embrace. I was loath to break out of its clasp on winter mornings.

Not that I minded getting up. Work held no worries for me. I lay there thinking about my bicycle ride to school which I so enjoyed; a quick steep slope up the hill to the top of our road, then a straight flat section between older houses, past the church orphanage. Here I would often see lines of rather quiet blue uniformed little girls walking crocodile-fashion to the church school at the bottom of the hill, near the park, which was in the opposite direction to my journey. Then I had a long downward glide, joining a busier road than ours, through some traffic lights and past another church which in years gone by had been set amidst open fields. It was still surrounded by yew trees and gravestones, but these were huddled behind a lych gate which had been moved too close to the church itself. Then there was another long free-wheel run past big houses on either side of the road, hidden by large and very mature trees set in long front gardens. In Victorian days this road had been the height of elegance. Now it was just a busy thoroughfare.

At the next traffic lights I turned left and dodged the tram lines alongside the popular terraces of the Rovers' ground. Then I had to negotiate a cobbled section of road especially treacherous to cyclists on wet or icy days. Here I turned across the wide convergence of five roads, then into the narrow streets which led to the school. I enjoyed that ride, usually with a rucksack on my back full of books, or bits and pieces for models to be made in craft lessons, or sometimes my camera.

'Nigel, you'll be late. Do get up, it's foggy again and you'll have to cycle slowly.' Mother broke my reverie. She sounded impatient. I slipped my arms out of the bed and under the eiderdown, from whence I extracted my underclothes and socks, which were beautifully warm. Then I half sat up, quickly slipped off my pyjama jacket and slipped on my vest, exposing as little of me as possible to the biting air. Then, with an almighty fling, I was out of ,bed and dressing with demoniac speed to keep as warm as I could until I was half dressed. Then I went into the bathroom, where there was an electric fire on the ceiling. Off came my shirt and vest, and I began to wash.

My father said it was ridiculous and why didn't I go straight into the bathroom, but it was a habit I'd got into in the RAF, where the ablutions were always miles from the billet. I had to admit the distance at home between bed and bathroom was much less, about fifteen feet I suppose.

'I don't know what you young men are coming to,' he would grumble. 'Can't face a bit of cold for a second.'

I always agreed. But I enjoyed the mornings once I was up. School was something to look forward to. Today the weather was indeed miserable with a wet glaze over the road surface that had me slithering dangerously round corners. I was relieved when I reached Dayton Road in one piece. I opened the outside door and pushed my bike inside. I unwound my scarf, slipped off my rucksack, pulled off the large sweater I wore over my normal clothes when bike riding and stooped to take off my trouser clips. Then I went into the classroom and shut the door.

From outside came the usual sounds of the playground. Shrill voices called cheerfully or angrily according to the seriousness of the game being played. There was the steady thump of a tennis ball being thrown against the classroom wall and caught - this would be a girl, usually. Occasionally there was a bang when a slip sent the projectile against a window pane. Whenever this happened I knew when I went outside no one would have seen anyone do such a thing.

The smell of the room was unmistakable but, for me, inviting. It was always beautifully warm; the coke boilers beneath were stoked up at five o'clock by Mr Trenchard. The age of the building contributed to the aroma and there was a faint whiff of the disinfectant impregnated sawdust spread daily by Mr and Mrs Trenchard as they swept out each classroom. It was strong but not unpleasant and its use over the years had left its mark in the atmosphere.

I looked round the room. It was getting near to the end of term and Christmas was approaching. There had been much talk of decorating rooms for the festive season and I knew I had to do something about mine. But I felt a little glow of pride as I surveyed it now. There was plenty of the children's work on display which had improved during the term. I had two sections devoted to handwriting, labelled 'THEN' and 'NOW'. The first contained an example from each child at the beginning of term. From half term onwards I had been adding to the 'NOW' section and giving marks for improvement. Most were distinctly better, which was rewarding to them and me.

There were plenty of pictures gleaned from magazines, with many examples of the children's paintings. At the side of the room was a model of a tournament ground with a host of decorated tents lining both sides each with a shield outside emblazoned with a coat of arms. Together they looked very realistic, though the individual designs would have shocked the College of Heralds. Two miniature knights on gaily caparizoned horses, borrowed from a friend's collection, charged each other in the lists.

I sat at my desk and looked at the empty room. Soon it would be full once again with those varied but engaging characters which comprised my class. Leslie would be in the front desk, second row, of course. Precocious and cheeky, he was forever looking for a chance to raise a laugh in the class. He thrived on an audience and I could imagine him in the future being the life and soul of whatever bar he chose to frequent. If I stood near his desk whilst taking a lesson, and he knew the answer to a question, he would hurl his hand upwards time and time again like a warrior shaking a spear.

'Sir...sir...SIR' he would yell and I would pretend not to notice.' I remember the lesson when words beginning with b-i had cropped up. The class gave me many examples to denote twosomes. Then I took them a stage further with t-r-i.

'That means three. Now, who can suggest words beginning with tri which show three parts?' I soon had triangle and tricycle, then James B suggested, 'What about that thing you fix your camera to, sir?'

'Good - that's a tripod. That means it has three feet, although to look at it three legs would seem better. Anymore...anymore words beginning with t-r-i you can think of...?'

For some minutes Leslie had been going crazy under my nose. He had accepted my instruction to remain sitting in his desk, but though he contrived to keep his bottom in contact with the seat he managed to gyrate every other part of his torso in a frenzied dance in his agonized appeal to add to the class's knowledge. All other hands became still as everyone gave their attention to his considerable performance. I gave in.

'Alright Leslie, what's your word?

He sat back triumphantly. 'Please sir, TRIPE.' He was well satisfied with the audience reaction.

I looked at the open space at the front of the room. It was a useful facility provided by the old classroom for although the desks could seat forty-eight children there was still plenty of room for movement. Better still, by pushing the front three desks of each row back into the gangways between the others, the space could be doubled and a spacious arena produced which the class used each week on Friday afternoons for Drama.

This was always thoroughly enjoyed. Though I did organise some formal acting with simple plays, even writing one or two myself, the children loved doing 'free drama'. This gave them opportunities to display their creative abilities, which often they did very well indeed for eight to nine year olds. I would depute someone to select a group, which, after a brief huddled conversation, would develop a 'play'. Completely unselfconsciously they would act parts, living them entirely, making up conversation as they went along. Naturally they couldn't sustain a particular theme for very long, but fertile imaginations did well, even if the girls dwelt too much on the lives of princesses and the boys lived permanently in the wild west and always finished rolling on the floor in mock fights.

These 'plays' produced revealing insights which taught me so much about the characters of the children. They also produced lovely touches of unconscious humour, like the occasion when

Angela, as the inevitable Princess, was discussing with Barry, her none-too-willing suitor, the fact that she wanted a baby. I had given Angela the job of cast selection so naturally she had taken the lead and Barry had been directed to become the Prince. Their respective social roles would have been very different had I appointed Barry as selector.

'My father, the King, says I must have a baby. He says he wants a grandson. The problem is…' she looked round the room and gave an exaggerated sigh, 'how will I get one?' The class gave Angela their undivided attention and there was no doubt she captured mine as well.

Barry shifted on his stool at the side of the stage and began to look uncomfortable. 'I dunno,' he ventured. Angela stamped her foot of authority.

'That's not good enough,' she said shrilly. 'You men are all the same, never any use when you're needed. Come here at once.' I wondered which adult in her life she was revealing.

Barry rose slowly and approached her, mid-stage. When he reached her she faced him, put both hands on his shoulders with careful deliberation and whispered conspiratorially,

'I'll show you how you can give me a baby.'

There was a dramatic pause which went on far too long for my composure but I refrained from interrupting. In the end Barry was forced to reply. 'Oh, ar, 'ow then?' He couldn't have sounded less enthusiastic, which niggled Angela.

'Not by just standin' there thinkin' about it anyway,' she snapped and pushed him away with such force that he nearly fell over. Then it transpired, to my relief, that her suitor was to travel the length and breadth of the kingdom enquiring for anyone to make a gift of a baby to the Princess. In those pre-TV days eight year olds were delightfully ingenuous.

As I sat at my own desk looking at those of the children I could feel the different personal links which were developing between me and their occupants, now waiting outside in the chill air to bring the room to life. I realised how vital those relationships were becoming to my success in teaching them. I knew I was going to be most successful with those who really liked and trusted me. It is a fact which became so much clearer during the ensuing years.

Much is said and written about schools today, what they should do and do not, and what they do achieve. Teachers learn about organisational theory, management theory, curriculum theory and much else besides, all of which have places in understanding the complexities of education in its widest sense as well as in research into what it actually accomplishes for the society it serves. But to achieve anything in teaching youngsters there is no substitute for the trusting, personal relationship. If anyone causes a child to disparage a teacher, whether parent, another child, TV programme, reporter, online blog or indeed the teacher him or herself, then he or she is bound to be less than adequate because the bond vital to success will be strained. The teacher needs much else besides, of course, but no matter who he or she is or at what level the teaching takes place, a trusting relationship has to be the beginning.

Hesitatingly, and with many mistakes, I was stumbling the first few steps along the path to this goal with Class Four. What was more, I was enjoying the experience hugely. You cannot ask for more in a job than that. This was what I had groped for when I struggled to answer the Principal's question at my college interview.

'Mr Flaxton, you're here: I thought you were absent. You haven't been to the staffroom to sign the attendance book and your class has been waiting outside for nearly five minutes. The bell rang ages ago, didn't you hear it?'

Miss Rees looked very cross. I hadn't even heard her open the door, having chosen a highly inopportune time to day dream. I apologised profusely and dashed outside to my class. But I don't believe she understood at all why I couldn't help smiling.

Chapter 36

'Nigel, just what are you up to?'

Rocky's voice accosted me from the door of the classroom which was open because the children had just gone home and I was clearing the table beside my desk. It was covered with papers, paint, glue and various oddments used during the last lesson, Art. The room was always in a mess after my Art lessons. Somehow my organisation of practical lessons went astray at the end and I finished up with a good imitation of an American tickertape procession after the crowds have left.

'I'm clearing up. We've just had Art…'

'I don't mean now. I want to know why half your class keep coming into my room at playtime asking me how I am going to decorate the room for Christmas, and what my frieze will be like. I get the message you've sent them to find out.' Rocky looked her best when she was on the attack. Not that she was really angry, just flushed at what she rightly assumed was my cheek.

'Oh, they weren't very subtle then. Pity.'

'I see…you want to fight to see who can produce the best classroom decorations. Right, you're on.'

I realised my tactical error at once. Putting Rocky on her mettle was bound to produce a result which would put my efforts so much in the shade they'd be invisible. I decided to throw myself on her mercy.

'To be honest, I'm no good at producing ideas. I can plan displays once I get a design, but I just can't seem to think them up. It sounds as though decorating the room for Christmas is part of religion here and I'd hate mine to look awful. So, can you help me with an idea?'

'You've got an almighty cheek.' She waggled her head in a show of annoyance as she stood hands on hips facing me. But there was the flicker of a smile about her mouth and her eyes were almost laughing.

'Worth an evening at the pictures, and meal afterwards?' I wheedled.

'Oh, I see, bribery as well. No morals, is it.' There was always a Welsh lilt to her voice when something aroused her.

'Frankly, yes, if you'll help.'

'Right. To-night, in town. There's a good film at the Odeon and we can go to the 'Cherry Grove' afterwards.'

'The Cherry Grove? Where on earth is that?'

'Don't you know your native heath? I'm surprised at you, Nigel. Well, you'll have to wait and see. I'll meet you outside the Odeon at half past seven. Bye.'

And she was gone. A delightful feeling of elation burst somewhere deep inside my chest and I whooped my excitement to the empty room. The door suddenly opened again.

'Did you call, Mr Flaxton?' Mrs Trenchard, mop in hand, wore a strange expression of surprise.

'Er, no…no, thanks, Mrs Trenchard. I was just, er, singing.'

'Oh, well, that's alright then, isn't it?'

She gave me a further strange look and withdrew. I leapt to a cupboard, opened it, ran back to the table, seized an armful of paper and stuffed it on the shelves. Paint pots, brushes, and glue followed indiscriminately. Then I slammed the door shut and locked it. Seconds later I was pedalling furiously, breaking all my previous records for cycling up the long incline home.

I came down to earth momentarily a couple of hours later upstairs on a bus travelling into the city. I was looking happily out of the window at the passing factories feeling so glad that my place of work was not alongside the impersonal assembly lines within them. Suddenly a hooter sounded its loud and mournful blast and shift workers poured out of the gates and sprinted towards bus stops.

'Damn,' I thought. 'I didn't sign out when I left.' But I consoled myself that the evening would make up for the wigging I should have to endure from Miss Rees the next day.

I was early and Rocky was late. I carved a rut in the pavement walking up and down in front of the imposing sweep of steps which befitted the Odeon's style of architecture. I was beginning to feel that the equally imposing commissionaire in his bright blue uniform with gold epaulettes and peaked cap peering down at me from the top was going to tell me to move on. Then she arrived. Of course I dared not mention she was late and she knew it. But apart from that she made no further attempt to rub in the bargain nature of the evening.

I forgot it within the first five minutes of the film. Not that I remember anything about that either. The evening was one of those delightfully exciting times when you are fully aware that the occasion could be a turning point in your life. No, we didn't spend it necking in the back row and nothing particular was said. But we both knew a relationship had been growing between us during the term which seemed likely to develop further. I felt a contented and warm glow inside. I confess I had schemed to contrive meetings with previous girlfriends, but suddenly I knew what writers meant when they described a new relationship as different. It was, but in a most undramatic way.

The only vague worry which nagged me slightly during the film was that perhaps this Cherry Grove place was an ultra swish restaurant which would set me back a month's salary for a meal. But I tried to brush it from my mind with the thought that Rocky had never given any hint of being that hard. I believe she guessed I was considering the possibility because she played up to my suspicions by walking us past a couple of sumptuous hotels after we left the cinema, saying, 'It's just a little way along this road', and pointing at their imposing façades.

But the Cherry Grove was an intimate little basement restaurant which I found absolutely delightful. To be truthful I was astounded at its existence because, not long after the war, my dear old home city had the reputation of having no night life whatsoever. So the Cherry Grove blossomed in the gloom unnoticed by a high proportion of the population…and on that night I was truly grateful it did so.

As we tucked into an excellent meal, Rocky gave me a gentle lecture on Art in the classroom.

'Save old Christmas cards, look at wrapping paper, watch shop windows - anything can give you an idea. Find a motif, make a template, get the kids to make one each, then paste them up on suitable backing which will give a contrast; the effect can be really striking. Or choose a scene where the kids can each make their own item from a group of similar things, say trees, or houses, or animals, then put them all up in groups, You can mix the good with the bad, but again the whole effect can be made to look super. What's more, each child makes something which is really his or her own this way. They love to be creative; you know that from your Drama.'

I began to get the message. 'Yes, I see. The trouble is, because I know I'm no good at Art myself, I feel at a loss to lead the kids.'

'So your classroom often looks lifeless. Oh, yes, I know you get plenty of stuff on the walls, but sometimes you need to make the whole room an experience of one particular thing. Occasions like Christmas, or Easter, or a special national event can be turned to very good use this way.'

'You ought to be a college lecturer. Why didn't they teach us this at St. Andrew's? Our junior craftwork course comprised mainly bookbinding.'

Rocky burst into laughter. 'I don't believe it.'

'Honestly - we did little else the first year. Wood, metal and plastics came in the second, the senior course.'

'Well, if they're still teaching that for juniors they need to come into the twentieth century. Anyway, I'll bring some old Christmas cards for you tomorrow. You can see if anything catches your eye amongst them.'

But from that moment all thought of the morrow drifted quite out of my consciousness. We finished the meal and made our way leisurely and very contentedly through the almost empty central streets to an all-night bus stop. When it came the bus was almost empty as well and we talked in subdued tones throughout the journey, oblivious of everyone and everything else.

After we left the vehicle there was a short distance to walk to Rocky's digs, past the athletics track which occasionally housed large noisy crowds, especially on speedway nights, but which tonight was as private as we were. I slipped my arm round her waist; she responded a second later with hers round mine. I looked at her; she turned her face upwards and smiled. We walked on slowly in complete silence.

We reached the entrance to her digs, an old house, one of a row which in Victorian days had been for the reasonably well-to-do. The gates had long disappeared and her landlord, a lorry driver, had parked his vehicle just inside where it occupied most of the short drive. A large green tarpaulin was tied neatly over the entire load, for the lorry was an open one.

Rocky stopped and leant back on the tarpaulin. I faced her, still saying nothing. Seconds later we were locked in a long and very satisfying kiss.

'It's been a super evening, Nigel. Thanks for taking me,' Rocky said eventually.

'Thanks for coming. I really have enjoyed myself; and thanks for being so helpful.'

We stood there, holding one another close, and kissing again. Then we stood side by side, arms around each other's waists, loath to part. Ahead of us, lights twinkled along the main road, as did hundreds of others away beyond us on the opposite side where a large industrial concern had factory buildings scattered across many acres of land. During the war they had made munitions there, a regular target in the blitz.

Suddenly Rocky sniffed, rather loudly.

'I say Nigel, your mac' smells a bit. I've just noticed.'

I was wearing a rubberised, light coloured trench coat with a bright red lining. I was very fond of it and it certainly didn't smell. I said so.

'Well, if it isn't that, something does pong around here. Can it be the factory?'

A suspicion crossed my mind and I tugged at the edge of the tarpaulin against which we had been leaning. I could just make out some letters stamped on the side of a box, one of hundreds stacked there.

The lorry was packed with kippers.

Chapter 37

Amongst Rocky's old Christmas cards I found one depicting a very cheerful snowman. He was chunky and wore a black top hat with snow on the brim and a red scarf round his neck. His eyes, nose and mouth were made from shaped pieces of coal, as were his buttons. He had round hands and feet and he appeared to be running, as much as a fat, cheerful snowman could be capable of such athletic activity.

I drew a large copy of his outline on a piece of card and made four templates. These were passed round the class and each child drew the outline on white paper. Then they added in their own ideas to complete his personality. The result was forty-eight individual snowmen with characters which would have kept a snowchiatrist at work until the following Christmas.

I surrounded the entire room including the door, the cupboards and the lower part of the windows with a belt of black paper, drew a wavy line near the bottom and commissioned an army of decorators to paint the frieze white up to this. Then I let one or two loose with some light blue paint to give it some shadows. We pasted up the snowmen, who then chased each other up little hills and down mini-dales in an unending line completely around the room. For good measure we interspersed some green Christmas trees and dabbed green holly leaves and red berries here and there. After school one day I kept a few faithful workers behind who handed up paper decorations whilst I balanced precariously on Mr Trenchard's huge step ladders. I cascaded these from above the large white globes which hung at the end of enormous chains which were the classroom lights.

Class Four were pleased with the whole effect. It was reasonably dramatic and the snowmen characters were a great hit. All the staff came to see them, as well as many children from other classes which did wonders for my ego. Since then I used the snowman template a few hundred times (why pass up a winner when you've got one?) and ,he was borrowed and redrawn interminably.

But my room didn't match Rocky's. Her frieze depicted a really lovely scene of Bethlehem, where individual houses with yellow windows were scattered along a plain and up a hill, canopied with a lovely dark blue night sky with hundreds of stars. One beauty stood directly above a cave. Occupying pride of place on another wall was a beautifully painted crib scene with the figures in glorious colours, especially the Wise Men, whose robes brushed the straw so vividly you could almost see them moving.

I slipped in alone to look at the room when I knew Rocky and her class had finished their preparations. It was lunchtime at the beginning of the last week of term. Suddenly I realised what she meant by making the room look alive. What an experience for the children, whose lives were passed in very uninspiring and drab surroundings: But that picture…

'Yes, Miss Rockliffe is very skilled with her paintbrush isn't she, Mr Flaxton?' As usual I hadn't heard Mr Brand come in. I spun round.

'You mean she painted those…?'

'Oh yes, they're her second. She did different ones last year equally as good. It's a wonderful gift but it must be very time consuming to paint such large scenes as well. What about you, are you going to try your hand at one next year?'

'Me, paint like that? No, I'm afraid not, never in a thousand years.'

'Well, never mind. Your room looks very lively as well, though quite different, of course.'

I was only too well aware of what he meant, now I'd seen Rocky's classroom. Yet another lesson.

The final one came home to me at the end of the week. I had a wonderfully rewarding time during those five days. There were the children's parties, games in the hall, and the staff had drinks in the staffroom one day after school. The children positively glowed and were on their best behaviour throughout the week.

Many gave me Christmas cards and in every way they could showed me they appreciated the time I spent preparing lessons, helping them to learn, encouraging them at sport and trying to make their classroom bright and cheerful.

I have since seen hundreds of teachers in their first year and many seem at their lowest ebb emotionally when they reach their first Christmas. Even Rocky told me she felt like packing the job in at that time the year before, a fact I found hard to believe seeing her as I did then. But I was on top of the world. True, Rocky herself had much to do with that…

On the last day of term, stupidly being too proud of my own room, I decided not to strip the decorations until the afternoon. I was about to start when the class implored me to leave the work until after playtime.

'Go on, sir,' said Berny. 'It won't take us long to get it all down.'

I fell into the trap. I organised a quiz, which they loved. Then, after the break I found them rather sluggish in doing the necessary jobs and, worse still, I realised I hadn't planned who should do what. Children may be naturally creative but clearing up seems positively unnatural as a few million parents will agree. I have never seen a neat, tidy, orderly room dissolve into utter chaos so quickly. Desks and floor became littered with torn paper, small bodies were mummified with large strips of frieze, arguments developed as to which snowman belonged to who because they all wanted to take one home. As I let the decorations down from the lights, perched on top of the step ladder, hands grabbed for the streamers and ridiculously early May Day dances began. When Mr Brand came in he was greeted by a scene from St. Trinian's.

'Er, we let the children go early on the last day, Mr Flaxton. You can send yours home as soon as you like.'

His voice just reached me above the din. The second the door closed my turret was besieged by a horde of dervishes.

'Can we go now, sir? Please, please, please…go on sir, you know it's Christmas.' They began to edge away towards the door. I knew the situation demanded great firmness but I hesitated…and was lost. The room emptied within ten seconds. Anyone outside the door at that moment would not have been a pretty sight. A few moments later I descended from my perch and continued the clearing up in complete silence and splendid isolation. Then Miss Browning came in.

'Just popped in to wish you a very happy Christmas. Have a really good holiday - you've worked very hard this term.'

'Oh, thank you. I hope you have a wonderful holiday as well. Thanks also for all the advice you've given me at various times.'

She looked round and pursed her lips. 'Well, here's the last piece. Next year start clearing up at nine o'clock in the morning!'

To-day the whole question of classroom displays would be dealt with by classroom assistants, which is why most primary school walls look so attractive. I wonder sometimes whether subconsciously this fact influences the choice of advertising as a career. Certainly modern primary classrooms provide excellent environments for children in marked contrast to the unadorned walls of my own experience, or those of many teachers I encountered early in my career. Rocky and her college partners were in a minority.

I was to see the phenomenon of a group taking charge of its behaviour on another, quite unexpected occasion. It was during an Annual Outing. Such events were long-standing features of life in the city's schools. In the thirties I had anticipated, and enjoyed, one each year from the age of seven until 1939. One in particular comes to mind – a visit to Hampton Court, inevitably getting lost in the maze, and a boat trip on the Thames.

Children paid a weekly amount towards the cost of these visits, so one of the chores on Monday mornings was to collect and record each payment. Each participant had a class-made card and each teacher had a master record which was completed so the payee could see the figure and date being entered.

We organised a visit to Liverpool docks and across the Mersey to New Brighton. We travelled on the now long gone overhead railway which enabled us to point clearly to the way ships entered, were unloaded, reloaded, and dispatched to sail the oceans of the world. Hopefully the avid interest shown by the children supplemented our classroom explanations and drawings of that part of the nation's maritime activity. A Significant Experience? I think it was.

Another year saw us at Conway Castle and Deganwy, with a return via some lovely Welsh countryside. Normally each visit included part of the time on a beach because living in central England sight of the sea was still a rare experience for many. But one year we visited London.

We went shortly after the Queen's Coronation to see the decorations in the Mall and to have a river boat trip along the Thames to view the famous buildings the children had seen in pictures, often taken by their teachers from magazines such as Picture Post or from Pictorial Education. The latter unfolded to a reasonable size for classroom display, but it had drawbacks. One was the frequent problem that you wanted two pictures which were back to back. It was only printed in black and white. It was also fairly expensive and was not supplied by the school. So it ate into my salary which to begin with was £300 pa. By the time of the Coronation I had earned three annual increments – only twelve more to go before I reached the full Assistant Teacher's salary.

On the Thames the captain of our boat explained that it was likely our journey would be interrupted because someone else was travelling the same path – the Queen and the Duke of Edinburgh. Their particular activities that day had revealed that the straightest line between two events was virtually along the river. If their timetable coincided with ours, we were told, the River Police would move us to the bank for an unspecified period.

We had not travelled far on the waterway when an officious looking boat aimed straight for us in a cloud of spray, turned neatly at the last moment and informed us via a loud hailer that we were to anchor near the bank immediately. Our boat duly chugged resignedly to obey. All teachers and children craned necks to see any likely flotilla coming past but there was nothing. We decided we were in for a lengthy wait.

But we were wrong. Suddenly a very neat craft appeared with a rear awning under which patently stood the Queen and the Duke. We were not the only other boat around with groups aboard, of course, but unfortunately we had been shooed to a point of some isolation, whilst the opposite bank was host to a small collection of parties who now cheered in the expected manner. The Queen, of course, responded by waving graciously to the nearby audience.

Absolute horror flashed across every child's face on our boat. As one they rushed to the side and leaned over dangerously as they screamed and shot hands and arms in the direction of the speeding Royals. Our boat tilted sharply in the same direction and the captain urged us to tell the children to step back. We tried but they were responding to an unseen group force.

Whether we were in serious danger I know not, but the situation was retrieved by the Duke of Edinburgh who, ever alert, turned towards the source of the dire screams and nudged the Queen to look in our direction. She did so and both gave an especial wave to our children. They knew that because there was no other boat beside us. The screams changed to wild cheers and, fortunately, a move backwards, the better to dance up and down. Amazed faces turned to their respective teachers as they shared the obvious fact that Royalty had responded to them personally.

Very shortly afterwards we were allowed to continue our chugging, but I doubt whether the children took the slightest notice of our explanations about the Tower of London or any other famous waterside building. The cliché is inevitable – their day had been made.

Frankly, I was puzzled by this. Certainly we had featured the Coronation in our classrooms. Occasionally special events were broadcast at times which fitted the school day; indeed Mr Brand had surprised us all by calling everyone into the hall to listen to the funeral service of King George VI – and surprised us even more by making everyone stand. True, this was for the religious part only, but inevitably one or two children fainted. He let Miss Rees and Taff Hughes carry them out.

So the children were fairly knowledgeable about the immediate members of the Royal Family and the Queen in particular. But in the emotion which swept through them on the Thames that day I saw the explanation of why people will wait for hours to see a Royal event, even crossing the globe to do so. I am sufficiently interested in them to spend hours in front of a television; I contrived to do so for the actual Coronation. I found a friend who had a set (black and white, of course) but was not at all interested to watch and was quite content to let Rocky and me look after the house for the day. But I have never been moved to watch them in the flesh.

There was an occasion when Princess Margaret visited the city and our school was allowed to stand on the pavement to watch her car. When she appeared the large black limousine sped past, spurred on of course by the children's cheers. But the overwhelming impression I had was of a small person quite dominated by the space around her. She was quite alone in the open back and the driver and one passenger by his side seemed to take no notice of her.

I did meet the Duke of Edinburgh many years later at a Gold Awards Ceremony for his Scheme at St James's Palace. Recipients were grouped into parties of about eighteen in the charge of one individual who was the official presenter. In fact he or she was told not to speak until addressed by the Duke, so I didn't have much to say until he asked who I was and then how many of the group came from my school. He was quite impressed when I answered 'twelve'. I wondered briefly whether to thank him for possibly averting a river tragedy some thirty five years before, but decided he might not remember.

Fifty years after our London visit the Queen celebrated her Golden Jubilee. I still had some battered photos of my classroom in Dayton Road at the time of the Coronation – images of St Edwards Crown were liberally spread across the walls – and forty plus well behaved children beamed at the camera from their desks, so I scanned it, cleaned it up and sent a copy to the school for interest. The head responded with a pleasant letter, explaining that probably I wouldn't notice much difference in the buildings. He enclosed a copy of the school's brochure with pictures of the current scholars in smart red uniforms. I certainly noticed the contrast in clothing which was very evident when my picture was placed side by side. Obviously there were no Jimmy Rs. There was also a greater cross section in the other kind of colour, a change which occurred in the mid fifties and which I noticed by being in a house in an area which became popular with immigrants. Having spent my life up to that time with the notion that all people, of whatever race, are equal, I was shocked to hear some of the comments of white people I knew whom I had thought were polite and pleasant. Dayton Road in the noughties seemed to be thoroughly integrated if the brochure was an accurate portrayal. That pleased me greatly. The buildings had been very well painted as well.

Chapter 38

My training, my contribution to the work of the Royal Air Force, and my first few years teaching at Dayton Road covered seven years. That brought me to that exceptionally noteworthy year, 1953. It seemed to be the year when the UK began to shake off the war years and the ensuing sharp austerity. The Queen celebrated it with her Coronation. Stanley Matthews celebrated it by getting an FA Cup Winners medal at last. Ed Hillary and Tenzing Norgay celebrated it by getting to the summit of Everest. Gordon Richards celebrated it by winning the Derby, also at last. But histories of the year have overlooked one other celebration.

Rocky and I were married.

The guest list was rather extended because six families were involved – Rocky's mother had died shortly after she was born and mine died when I was six. Both our fathers remarried – mine quite rapidly, Rocky's after eighteen years, so we both had step mothers. Both were delightful; Rocky was her father's bridesmaid. Mine was loving, affectionate and very sensible in dealing with me. She also gave me a half-brother who, though nearly nine years younger, has been a great friend over the years. A long time ago he emigrated to Canada, but not before he married a lovely Scots girl. I acceded to his request to be his Best Man

The staff and pupils of Dayton Road gave us a lovely dinner and tea service, the latter having gold tea and coffee pots. When the children were allowed to view this we were amused to hear one girl's hushed comment that we would be rich with all that real gold. If only...

We were married at the beginning of April, a popular time because you could claim married tax allowance back to the previous 5th April. The obvious Saturday was the 4th so we did quite well out of that arrangement. I had attended the church since a very young age because my father was very committed to it. Its members were keen on organising many activities which had slightly enlivened my teenage years which ran simultaneously with the war. In particular there was a very good amateur dramatic society which both of us joined. The inevitable friendships we built up meant that even more people were likely to expect invitations to our wedding. Rocky's father, bless him, accepted the well-over-a-hundred guest list with aplomb. Mine chipped in with payment for the room.

The service was at 12.00 noon. Its one unusual feature was the second hymn. Cwm Rhondda doesn't come to mind as the tune for a wedding hymn, but Rocky was adamant she wanted it. So I wrote some words which I hope were reasonably appropriate to the event.

We chose Ambleside for our honeymoon, so fairly late in the afternoon we were taken to the station and soon sped northwards, inevitably changing at Crewe. The line ended at Windermere, so Ambleside hotels had taxis waiting conveniently at the station entrance. Drivers waved small notices with their clients' names. Rocky and I were vaguely concerned when one elderly man with bloodshot eyes let it be known that he was for The Yewtree Hotel. As other taxis sped away we were slowly ushered into his, with another couple, obviously also just married. He installed the other man in the front seat and me between Rocky and the other young bride. Then he set off from the quiet and empty taxi rank.

Within a very short time he had passed every other Ambleside bound taxi. This was achieved by some ferocious driving which pitched me first into Rocky and then the other lady. By the time we reached the Yewtree, quite high up on a hillside, I had stopped apologising by mutual agreement. We then went inside at 11.00pm. The hotel had arranged a meal, but understandably the proprietor said he hoped we would come down for it quickly to enable the staff to go home. Accordingly we had the briefest of washes and descended to the dining room. Whilst eating, however, I realised I had left the room keys in our room and so shamefacedly had to ask for my oversight to be rectified. Rocky was not best pleased, though she moderated her glares when the other man plodded off to the proprietor for a duplicate key. At least I was first.

During the night there was a snowfall so in the sunshine next morning the countryside looked most attractive. The weather remained dry for the whole week so we enjoyed a mixture of hill walking (we had packed our heavy climbing boots) and coach trips. All too soon we prepared to return home and I paid the bill. I kept it as a reminder. The total, including a few drinks at the bar, was three guineas (three pounds three shillings). Certainly value for money!

Chapter 39

After one more term at Dayton Road Junior School I followed advice given me three years earlier by Mr Bartram to apply for a transfer to a secondary school. Because teachers were appointed to the city's Education Department rather than to individual schools they could be moved from one to another for various reasons. It was accepted that I wanted to make my career in the secondary sector. It was also the case that the post-war child population bulge had moved up as well so I was simply going with it.

It would be remarkably boring to recount all my experiences with secondary classes as I have with my early months at Dayton Road as I embarked on my learning curve in the profession. I spent six happy years at the Ashtree Secondary Modern School in a northern area of the city amongst a large housing estate built between the wars. The head gave me plenty of opportunity to experience breadth in teaching. So I spent a total of six months with groups taken for three weeks each to the city's camp schools. These were intended to give urban children experience of the country. Two were quite old with fairly Spartan accommodation, one for boys and one for girls. The head contrived to get Rocky to leave Dayton Road, which she did with some reluctance and take a one term residential appointment at the girls' camp school. A new group of secondary girls appeared every three weeks - some from inner city schools with varied behaviour problems, so Rocky gained much useful experience, such as when there was an altercation in the toilets which she investigated to find one girl threatening another with a knife.

'I'll have that, thank you,' she said, seizing the weapon.

The girl, surprised by such positive action by an adult, relinquished it immediately. There was a resident headteacher, as there was at the boys' camp school, but our experience was that they left discipline and control to their resident teachers - one at the girls' establishment.

After some negotiation with a local councillor the head of Ashtree School then contrived to get Rocky appointed to his staff, which had been his intention. Having met her with me at some functions he recognised what a good teacher she was, thus for a time we were officially professional colleagues again. So, when the powers-that-be at the Education Office bought a lovely Victorian mansion in the countryside and decided to allow a bold experiment - a group of both boys and girls from a mixed school to be residential for three weeks and the Ashtree was chosen for this, it was agreed that Rocky and I, as a married couple, both with camp school experience, should accompany the head.

The school then received quite astounding advice on control of a mixed group, the most idiotic of which was that we teachers should take it turns to hide in the bushes to spy on the youngsters in their free time and nip any sexual shenanigans in the bud! Of course the boys and girls behaved impeccably and we returned with other such groups. One occasion was near Christmas and we enjoyed special services in the local church. We also decorated the mansion in true 19th century style including a massive log fire in the equally massive grate in the main hall.

We also embarked on another new experience for schools in the mid fifties - holidays abroad. Europe was emerging from the trauma of war, so such visits were novel. Our first was to Versailles where we stayed in fairly Spartan accommodation in a school near the Palace. which gave us plenty of opportunities to visit the building and its grounds. There were also visits to Paris - the Louvre, the Science Museum, Montmartre (at midnight! - at the head's insistence), river trips on the Seine, being received by the Mayor's Secretary - with attendant photographers, whose work appeared in the papers back home.

Our next visit saw us staying in a hotel on top of a Swiss mountain, near Lucerne. This was spectacular and we enjoyed glorious weather. There were coach trips around valleys, glaciers, lake trips, museum visits - experiences which to-day would seem run-of-the-mill but which then were quite adventurous. The one unexpected snag was that the last funicular journey to the hotel was 6.00pm, so we had to call on all our ingenuity to keep fifty teenagers occupied each evening.

We saw a surprising phenomenon one morning when the mountain top was bathed in strong sunlight and the valley was filled with cloud. I knew of the Brocken Spectre from reading mountaineering books, so I was able to explain the shadow everyone could see projected on to the mist with a circular rainbow around the head. What intrigued us all was that although fifty or so individuals stood side by side each could see only one shadow - their own. You can sometimes see the feature from an aircraft window when the sun is on one side and clouds below on the other. I managed to film my shadow with the cine camera I took on this journey which, together with many still black and white shots, provided an interesting record for the parents' evening which followed our return.

My interest in photography supplemented my activities in all schools at which I taught throughout my career. Whilst at the Ashtree School I began to use colour, with two and a quarter inch square transparencies (from my second hand Rolleiflex camera) made up into substantial glass slides exhibited in a very large display case with internal illumination made in the school's woodwork department. The head thoroughly enjoyed the kudos he received from all visitors who saw this in the small space rather grandly referred to as the foyer.

A notable alteration to teachers' pay scales was introduced in 1956. Prior to that there were assistant teachers, a few posts of responsibility (£50 pa) chief assistants and heads. Given that there was one each of the last two at each school and many more of the first, promotion was not easy to come by. In the city it was policy to appoint from within, so, for example a chief assistant's post at a particular school would be advertised, people would send in applications to the Education Office and the headteacher would visit each one to see them teach. He or she would then draw up a short list to be interviewed by the Personnel Section of the Education Committee. No outsiders were allowed.

This engendered loyalty to the city. But in 1956 more posts of responsibility and heads of departments were created and chief assistants became deputy heads. Even heads of department were divided into posts worth £200 pa and £125 pa. Posts of responsibility were £75 pa. The first allocation of the new posts depended on the number of pupils on roll and were entirely at the behest of each headteacher, as had been the case of the few £50 posts. I had been given one of these, but it was not secure. In some schools they were rotated between all the staff to avoid favouritism! The difference with the new scales was their security and hence their inclusion in final pension calculations.

At the Ashtree I had been given a post of responsibility for oversight of History, so under the new arrangements the head gave me a £125 Head of Department (History) post, of which the school received an allocation of two. It also had two £200 posts, one he gave for English and the other for Geography. The second £125 post went to Maths. These allocations had little to do with his view of subject hierarchy, it was much more a reflection of his staff relations. He had taught with the Head of Maths years before; the light shone out of the eyes of the Head of Geography for him - a young teacher of my age but more favourable. The Head of English was a middle aged Scot with a degree in the subject who had spent years in a grammar school but had recognised where promotion lay in the post-war new order. Since being allocated to the school by the Education Office the head had held him in awe. He was, of course, the only graduate on the staff. The pupil roll numbered just over 600 and the assistant teacher roll was 20, a pupil/teacher ratio of 30 which was the norm for secondary schools.

Near the end of 1957 Rocky gave birth to our first son, followed fifteen months later by the second. Also in 1959 we left the city for good. For some time Rocky had advised me that I stood a better chance of promotion in other areas. Very doubtfully I applied for a £200 Head of English at a new school being formed by the amalgamation of two smaller ones in Nottingham. I was surprised to be called for interview, but when I met the other candidates I realised they were all local, so I imagined I had been called to preserve the notion that the short list was more widespread. Certainly I enjoyed the experience rather more than the one following my return from the RAF, but this time I was more prepared. The committee spent a long time deliberating and at one point the man who, to me, was the obvious choice and already Head of English at one of the closing schools, jumped up and muttered audibly,

'When they take this long it usually means an outsider is in the running.'

Slowly it dawned that he meant me, but finally his worries were swept side and he was invited to take the post. Before I left I was called aside by an official of the Education Department who thanked me for my application and said they would welcome another from me if I cared to submit one for another post. On my return home I told Rocky how right she had been. So next I applied for a post in Kent - and got it!

In this case the appointment was made entirely by the head, who had himself taught for many years in the city. Rocky contributed largely to the purchase of our first, and very old, car and I did a crash course in learning to drive and passing the test. I had, in fact, had a provisional licence for some time as friends and relatives nobly let me get experience in their cars. We had a friend who was an estate agent and our house was sold quite quickly. We bought a new one on the south side of a pleasant town in a former cherry orchard. The back garden contained one tree and next spring we vied with birds as to who got the most fruit.

At the school I found one teacher was an English graduate who had applied for the head of department post but had been passed over by the head! I had to call on all my interpersonal skills to keep good relationships in the department, especially so as he wasn't the only English graduate. I reminded myself that at college the March Hare told us that English (Advanced) was at least pass degree standard. My departmental colleagues had it at honours level, of course.

Despite my promotion we found two very young but well developed boys, a very old car and a very new house quite a drain on our finances. Neither of our families were in any sense well off so we looked for a way to solve the problem. We had made friends in surrounding houses, so we arranged for one lady to look after the boys each schoolday whilst Rocky went back full time to a primary school, which she enjoyed, and split her salary in two. This suited our friend whose husband was also a teacher.

We thoroughly enjoyed our years in Kent. We could reach the coast in about thirty five minutes, chugging sedately in our 1939 Standard Eight. True we had to fork out for a new engine but that did give it a very welcome new lease of life. We could reach a lovely arboretum in a short time as well as undertaking longer journeys, such as to Bournemouth where my parents had retired and further to Rocky's family in Newport, and back to our midland relatives. The last involved crossing London in pre-orbital or circular days so we chugged happily via Park Lane and Marble Arch, and Oxford Street on the return journey. We clocked sixty miles of urban landscape in each direction. I wonder what it is today.

We also chugged to Scotland for my brother's wedding, travelling along most of the Great North Road - the A1. Originally, of course, this had joined many towns together as needed in the days of stage coaches. Now by-passes were being built and we saw many signs indicating 'Road Works for the next X miles'. The highest value of X was 40! Nevertheless I was pleased to clock 80 miles over one two hour period.

Whilst at the Ashtree Secondary School I had investigated a course being offered at a Further Education College leading to an ordinary degree. This involved two evenings and one afternoon each week and was to last three years. For that I would have to get permission from the head, and felt that it could be arranged for all my 'free' periods to be on the one afternoon. His reaction was swift and devastating. I would be a disgrace to my colleagues by not teaching a full week. I would be implying that my existing qualifications were not good enough; he also had trained at St Andrew's. In short he demonstrated the class divide between graduates and certificated teachers. The former, very largely, were found in grammar and independent schools and were a race apart. I dropped the idea when, in his eyes, I committed another awful act by applying for a post outside the city - and even worse getting it. But in Kent I tried again with the B.Sc. (Econ) course

I mentioned earlier ('Legibility...the Eleventh Commandment'). But again I was successful in an application for promotion, this time a deputy headship, so another degree course slipped by.

Our move to Suffolk, found us in more wonderful countryside. Again we made an arrangement for the boys, though soon the elder one, Gareth, began attending an infants' school. Rocky then taught part time at my school. An unexpected cash gift came from the estate of a dear friend who had died from cancer, so we parted company with our old Standard and bought a much newer Hillman Minx - nevertheless also second hand. We also increased our dogs.

We had bought our first puppy just before leaving Kent. This was a Samoyed, one of which breed Rocky had possessed as a young child. Her father brought a young male home one day for her and it soon became an inseparable companion. I was not allowed to have a dog as a boy because my father doted on his immaculate garden, but walking to junior school I often passed a lady exercising a pair. Sometimes I contrived to get between them and rub their soft fur. So when Rocky and I decided to buy a dog we agreed immediately on the breed. We didn't realise how much a part of our lives they were to become.

Chapter 40

A survey of the main political events in education during the 20th century shows increasing involvement by central government. As is well known the main political tenet during much of the 19th was *laissez faire* and this included education. So much of it developed locally and only gradually did central government accept responsibility for funding. At the beginning of the 20th century it attempted to direct education centrally and established the Board of Education in 1900, then in 1904 School Regulations prescribed a subject based curriculum. Very quickly, however, responsibility for the curriculum passed to schools and an attempt to guide teachers was made through the publication of the book 'A Handbook of Suggestions for Teachers'. Further editions of this appeared from time to time and it was on the booklist I had to purchase prior to my enrolment at St Andrew's. However there was no reference to it in any lecture during my course there.

The century also saw a plethora of Reports as government sought to discover what actually was taking place in schools. I think this needs to be seen against the background of most Members of Parliament and certainly of the Civil Servants whose job it was to implement Acts of Parliament. They were products of the independent schools; in the most senior positions often they were from Eton. Their experience of schools and education was far removed from that of the great majority of the population and hence they had a need to learn about it.

An example was published in 1963 - 'Half Our Future', an investigation by the Central Advisory Council under the Chairmanship of Sir John Newsom into the 'Education of Children of Average Ability aged between 13 and 16'. The school leaving age was still 15 but, depending on date of birth, some pupils were near 16 on leaving. Average ability was a concept virtually unknown in the major public schools, though once I heard one of HM Inspectors report that at the well known public school where he had taught, a colleague had complained that their fourth stream was uneducable. Their intake comprised the top 4% of the ability range! What, I wonder, was his view of 96% of the population?

Reports usually carried recommendations. These could be for any and everyone involved in education at the local level. Whether LEAs took them on board usually depended upon finance, but there was also the intention that teachers should read them and adopt the ideas put forward. It was my experience that few did so. A common feeling was that government should leave them alone to get on with their job. At Dayton Road, for example, the two older women had schemes of work books they had first written in the early thirties; they continued to teach the same lessons in the same way twenty years later.

Throughout most of the 20th century schools were responsible for the curriculum. Obviously there was general agreement on the main content of English and Maths, though local inspectors, appointed for particular subjects, could exert significant influence, especially when a new school was constructed and an Inspector for Craft, for example, decided what wood and metalwork machinery was installed. But subjects such as History, Geography, Music, etc., were prescribed by schools - usually the head, but quite often by the subject specialist. Over the years there was much debate about the merits of this compared to countries that had a national curriculum, even national syllabi. It was jokingly said that at any time of the day the French Minister of Education would know what lesson all students were having throughout the country and at what level. Rocky's brother in Australia was infuriated that his children could not undertake further work when they had successfully completed that set down for each particular class. He was educated here, at Cambridge, and bridled at the restriction. But finally a National Curriculum was decreed for UK schools, described largely in terms of skills to be developed rather than prescribed subject syllabi, which some people had anticipated.

The most fundamental centrally directed change in the organisation of schools came in response to the famous Circular 10/65 - in 1965, of course. This required LEAs to draw up plans to make all secondary schools comprehensive and thus abolish schools that took selective entries after the 11+ examination. This had been hotly debated for years, now at last it was to be put into practice. Inevitably timetables for change differed between LEAs and often these were dictated by buildings. A large secondary modern school might be amalgamated with two much smaller grammar schools and find the joint roll increased from 600 to 1000+. Obviously there would be insufficient room so some new building would be needed, paid for, of course, by central government. To avoid being swamped by massive demands for such funds it was decreed that money would only be available for true increases in rolls, or 'roofs over heads'. The result was considerable variation in ages of pupils in schools as LEAs tried to fit all into existing buildings whilst constructing the absolute minimum of new ones. Various educational advantages were advanced to justify particular patterns, but the overall result was that somewhere in the country children could change schools at any age except 6 and 17. The mixture was further complicated by a few LEAs who refused to reorganise and managed to resist the strictures of central government, such as Buckinghamshire, Kent and Lincolnshire where to the present the 11+ examination sorts children for admission to a few grammar schools and rather more secondaries, albeit most without the 'modern' tag. Now, with many areas experiencing reduction in the child population, old divisions are being scrapped, once again to fit in with existing buildings.

In response to 10/65, Bedfordshire, where ten years later I was appointed head of an upper school, opted for the 'three tier' system of schools for 5-9, 9-13 and 13-18 ages. In fact for some years it was called the 'West Riding Scheme' as it was first developed in that part of Yorkshire. However Bedfordshire decided not to change on a single date, rather it divided the county into four areas, each to have a number of lower schools feeding into a smaller number of middle schools feeding in their turn to an upper school. Most middle schools were housed in existing secondary modern schools, but additional purpose built units were added on site as allowed for increased rolls. The rolling timetable for beginning comprehensive education was unusual, but it was achieved smoothly. Most upper schools were in new buildings.

Some LEAs have now reverted to junior schools for children up to the age of 11 and secondaries beyond that. Bedfordshire now faces the same possibility but understandably there is intense opposition to the loss of good and successful middle schools. There is a background problem with teachers, however. With very few three tier systems remaining teachers whose experiences lie solely in middle schools may face a problem when applying for promotion - have they sufficient relevant primary or secondary experience? There is much to commend teaching children in the middle years and much to be gained from transferring them at 13 - for example, a new start for new entrants to the teenage years and placing them as the youngest among many much older and more mature seniors. Inevitably, however, ultimate decisions will depend on finance, not educational considerations.

Over the years the school leaving age has been raised. In the 19th century, before education for all was dreamt of, children were workers and their lot in the mills that led much of the industrial revolution is well known. Forster's Education Act of 1870 first envisaged universal education, but only for children up to the age of 11 - and it wasn't fully enacted until 1878. Secondary education up to 13 years was started in 1902, then to 14 years by Fisher's Education Act in 1918. In 1936 the age was to be raised to 15 in 1939, but the start of the Second World War forced its postponement. As I completed my training at St Andrew's it was enacted in 1948. I remember buying a book of ideas entitled 'The Extra Year'. Another year was added in 1972 so that all children were then in school for eleven years, from 5 to 16. Recently, of course, provision has been made for the leaving age to be 18.

Not always has the alteration in the leaving age been entirely due to educational considerations; the needs of the labour market have provided influence to an extent. So the current change to 18 has some affinity with a high level of unemployment. Use of children as workers, or the opposite, is a matter of concern in most countries. The employment of young children in parts of India, for example, has recently been paraded on television. Families in southern India depend upon their children working in match factories to supplement income. The government tries to encourage children to be sent to school by the payment of subsidies to counteract the loss of income. For some years after officially retiring - and embarking on varied interesting kinds of part time educational work - I did some voluntary work for PLAN UK, formerly Foster Parents Plan, the first such organisation to link contributors to individual children in the countries in which they work. I was able to help link my former upper school in Bedfordshire with a village in southern India which wanted to provide a building to accommodate the children of an existing school that could only use quite inadequate rented premises. The building of a six classroom school with good toilet facilities was achieved with the local people providing voluntary labour and consequently keeping a large number of children away from the trials of their former sweated labour.

Earlier in the century, in 1944, when the war reached the stage when Allied victory was very likely, the famous Butler Education Act was passed. This provided for the three kinds of schools - grammar, secondary modern and secondary technical, with entries decided following the 11+ examination. The last group soon disappeared and effectively two types remained. Much has been written about the results of this Act, but I remember attending a function in London to honour its 40th anniversary. Sir Keith Joseph gave the keynote address, in which he explained how marvellous it is for a legislator to produce legislation which lasts so long. I felt this was an insight into politicians' motivation. Incidentally I met both Lord Butler and Sir Keith on other occasions - the former when he opened the Village College which was my first headship and the latter when he met a group of heads at his request and I was Convener of that group in the Secondary Heads' Association. Not surprisingly personal contact revealed different facets from their public personas.

One glaring inequality, never resolved, of the 11+ selection procedure was again due to buildings. Differing LEAs had different numbers of grammar schools as I explained earlier. The 'pass' rate, therefore, was different depending on where you lived. I have a friend who, as a boy, suffered the effect of that when he moved from a grammar school in one locality to another where he was directed into a secondary modern with no right of appeal.

Gradual pressure for change came from within secondary modern schools that had children of well above average ability. This emerged via the exams available to provide certificates with any value in the world of work. Before the war only grammar schools provided courses leading to School Certificate and Higher School Certificate. The former required passes in six subjects including English and Maths. The pass rate per subject was modest - 40%. Above 50% earned a Credit and above 70% a Distinction. A credit in a modern foreign language provided matriculation - minimum university entry requirement. Higher School Certificate could be achieved with either three 'main' subjects or two main and two 'subsidiary' subjects. The pass mark was 50%, above 60% was 'Good' and over 70% earned a Distinction.

In 1951 the General Certificate of Education was introduced to supplant School and Higher School Certificates. It was to be offered at Ordinary and Advanced levels, nominally at 16+ and 18 years of age. The great change it enshrined was that it was a single subject examination - how many passes were required depended on the organisation to which entry was sought, not on a number set down by the examining boards. Inevitably there were shrieks of 'dumbing down' from some sources, but these were ignored. What was not ignored was the prospect that bright secondary modern pupils might now enter for one or two subjects.

In 1955, at the Ashtree Secondary School I was given Class 1A as my form. There were four streams, labelled A, B, Inter and Remove. The head heard rumours that some of his colleagues were considering having courses leading to one or two 'O' levels and he wasn't the sort to be left behind. Nevertheless he blanched at the idea of publicly announcing the fact.

He came up with the idea that I, as class teacher, should invite 'my' children's parents to explain that we were considering a five year course leading to some 'O' levels and how much study that would mean for their youngsters. But to know what I said he insisted that I had the school's large tape recorder running for his later perusal! I couldn't hide it from the parents; I hoped my waffly explanation about its presence would satisfy them. I'm sure it did no such thing.

In time, of course, bright students were successful in many subjects at 'O' level, underlining the case for comprehensive education. Now politicians happily require 50% of students to achieve a Grade C (effectively a pass mark) in a number of subjects, often I feel nodding back to the days of six subjects for School Certificate, when only about 10% were expected to achieve that level.

Each year when results are published there are renewed criticisms about overall standards. These, I feel, stem from a confusion about the rationale of exams and their goals. They can be based on skills, such as the driving test. They can also be a means of restriction, for example entry into professions. In the case of the former ultimate success would be a 100% pass rate, but for the latter that would be useless. But a single exam system cannot deliver both goals, hence the confusion about results. Using the present system for restrictive purposes is usual, though it can be overdone as is seen with entry to veterinary courses. Few universities offer these and the number qualifying each year needs to be fairly small. So entry has been defined by requirement of the top A level grades in appropriate subjects because so many students would like to work with animals. A leading Professor of Veterinary Science once said to me that he would never make it to-day with his old results. Some good quality applicants must be lost by such stringent restrictions.

It is a pity that comprehensive education became a political football, though it is understandable given the basic views of the two main parties. Now it has been a feature of secondary schooling for over forty years it is salutary to realise that so much of the population experienced it - some 78% of people up to the age of sixty in 2013. Of the reminder only about 8% went to independent schools. Yet listening to people and plays on television one could easily imagine the proportions are 50-50. Often in plays one hears the disparaging phrase 'the local comprehensive' and the betting is that the writer is in the 8%

bracket. Indeed, if all politicians, programme makers, news readers, writers, seniors in businesses, bankers, officers in the Forces, senior policemen, in short all who lead in any way in society had to declare their educational background when speaking, the degree to which the 8% influence our lives would be very surprising to many of the 78%.

It is natural that people prefer to be with others of their own kind. What is not so natural is for some people to want to stratify society and so feel they are in the top echelon. In Sweden, with a group of heads, I saw equality in operation. At a university where I was to speak to a group of colleagues we went into the refectory for lunch and our friends wondered whether they could arrange for us all to sit together, so tentatively they put 'Reserved' notices on a few tables. These were immediately removed by various students, as though they were clearing litter. One evening I went to a fairly large dance-cum-party organised by students at the school to which I was attached. To check entry each person was ink stamped on the back of their hand and I was no exception. Later, as students wanted to quiz me about English education I sat on the floor with a group. Needless say on both occasions everyone's ability with the English language was excellent! Conversely, of course, I knew no Swedish.

On another visit I wanted to investigate their then new experiment in abolishing exams entirely. Obviously, however, they needed to apply restrictions to some areas of employment, yet achieve this without introducing inequality. Teachers were required to award grades regularly in subjects to students, then entry requirements to various professions, for example, were set out. Students who didn't achieve the required level could retake courses and most schools accommodated adult students, often in substantial numbers. It seemed that final decision about failure was left to the individual rather than being imposed by any organisation. However. schools' performances in total grades awarded were certainly published in the press and comparisons could be drawn even from differences of tenths of a point. This is a very brief outline of the system - understandably it was far more sophisticated. One difference in school organisation which intrigued us greatly was that departmental budgets were voted upon by all people in a school's locality. Such financial decisions were not a matter for heads!

I also went to Sweden on occasions when Rocky judged dogs, specifically Tibetan Spaniels. There was no objection to open competition in that activity; dogs were placed on merit according to the judge's view based on knowledge of the breed standard as laid down by the FCI - the International Dog Federation. Dog judging is the same activity the whole world over and we have been fortunate enough to engage in it in quite a few countries as well as for many years in the UK, including Crufts,

In recent years government has introduced more kinds of school to satisfy concerns about lack of competition. There has also been much development in the governance of schools. It so happened that I was fortunate enough to be a head for twenty-two years, each of my three schools being new. I would have thoroughly enjoyed the ability to have full financial control but that was given to schools just as I 'retired'. I experienced a taster, however, when the government introduced the Technical and Vocational Education Initiative (TVEI) in 1983. As was policy at the time a pilot project was funded centrally requiring the setting up of a local administrative framework, then after a few years withdrawing support in the hope that local benefits had been such that local finance would take over. The object of TVEI was to encourage schools to develop courses more relevant to the needs of industry and also embrace modern technology. Three LEAs were selected for this in which five schools were to be chosen for the funding which, most unusually, was made through the Department of Employment and not that of Education. Bedfordshire was one of the trial counties and, as soon as I heard of the proposals - and the finance that would be available - I volunteered my upper school. Unknown to me my Chairman of Governors had already decided that we would be one of the trialists. He was leader of the local Conservative party, then in a majority and this was a Conservative government initiative, so he carried the necessary weight.

Of course we collected a considerable amount of money which bypassed the LEA's officials, to their chagrin, so for a time I was not the most popular character around, nor with my colleagues.

Both teachers and students were called on to give talks and demonstrations and I found myself addressing some seventy Oxford University graduates who were on their Post Graduate Certificate course to give them qualified teacher status. In the question session I was quizzed closely as to how I accepted the unfairness the TVEI trial bestowed on my school, to which I answered that I was appointed to do the best I could for it alone; I had no responsibility for all schools in the LEA. I then countered by asking them how many really intended entering the teaching profession. The room erupted with laughter because, as I very well knew, they were using it as insurance against not being able to get better jobs and hold on to them throughout their active working lives.

We received a cross section of visitors, inspectors, education officials, employers from many parts of industry, other teachers and so on. The youngest students in the scheme were aged between fourteen and fifteen and we found they gained enormous experience in talking about their work on the new courses. It was fascinating to see a fourteen year old holding the floor and giving lucid explanations to some twenty very able and intelligent adults. Such students received more valuable skills beyond their new courses.

An unexpected downside was revealed at the end of the first year when the sixteen year olds reached their official leaving date. One intention of TVEI was that students would want to remain at school to gain further skills, but our leaving rate shot up. The reason came from the new use of computers in which the students rapidly became proficient. Part of the scheme required longer periods of work experience and a good number of local employers found their students very useful in developing computer use in their businesses, to the point where a number were offered jobs to be taken up the moment they left school, which naturally they did asap, much to their advantage and our dismay.

From the management point of view, however, there was much satisfaction in having real control of some finance. It was amusing to see the reaction of people given the job of alterations to the Science laboratories. An order was placed in July and we insisted on a penalty clause if the work was not completed by the 1st September. Shock and assurance that was impossible was met on our part by the assurance that we would place the work in other hands. The message got around that we were no longer the old soft touch of the LEA.

I had seen that attitude during the phased development of my school. We grew annually by a comprehensive year group taken from the former secondary moderns with additional buildings provided as the roll increased. Inevitably there had to be 'misuse' of what we already had, and for one year we suffered the absence of Science labs - the subject was temporarily housed as two rooms in what was to become a PE activities studio. There was a low temporary wall between the 'rooms' and water and drainage to and from temporary sinks was achieved via tubing around the walls. To avoid damaging the future high standard wooden floor this was omitted, leaving bare concrete to resound to any movement of metal framed chairs and tables. Lessons were a struggle for all concerned and a visit by the Chief Education Officer drew the comment that one really had to be dedicated to teach in such circumstances. It is a tribute to both Science staff and their students that examination results were very good.

But after three years phase two of the building was due to be ready to provide the necessary rooms and facilities for the new sixth form. Building began and the shell of a new block appeared. Suddenly, however, the builders disappeared. After some time my enquiries revealed that the firm had begun a new project elsewhere and I was left with the realisation that they guessed the LEA would do nothing about the delay in completing our building which they would do in their own good time. Angry at this ploy I talked with the Chair of Governors who said the LEA could end the contract and seek new builders but inevitably that would take time. Meanwhile we would have to accept temporary classrooms on site. Stubbornly I opted for the delay rather than submit to malpractice. I wasn't popular with the LEA officers who had to undertake additional paperwork.

At the beginning of term, as the first students entered the sixth form the temporary classrooms arrived. They were covered with large and disgusting graffiti. The school was on an attractive site on the edge of a popular village in the middle of the large rural area it served. These 'huts' would stand out like the sorest thumb. I got the impression this was a deliberate snub. I rang the Chair of Governors who instructed the appropriate people to have all the classrooms painted immediately. This was done and the students soon entered well decorated classrooms.

I was not surprised to receive an aggrieved telephone call from an LEA officer telling me that my request for painting should have been made through the 'usual channels'. I accepted the stricture but countered that the usual channels would have left the graffiti open to public gaze for some weeks at least. In time the second building phase was completed as quickly as possible by new builders. Since then, because the school has continued to grow year by year as its popularity has increased much more building has been undertaken by my successors who enjoy the power bestowed by the policy of school based financial control. I reached retirement age too soon!

Chapter 41

On the whole I enjoyed good relationships with LEA officials in the three counties in which my schools were, though lack of full control was always irksome. Because each school was new I was often engaged with builders and of my twenty-two headship years I spent eleven with them on site. I also learned much about plans and architectural briefing. The size of buildings was decided by a formula specifying the amount of space allocated to each child. The fact that I had the opportunity to open three schools says much about the expansion of the country's stockpile during those years but the concomitant reduction in space-per-pupil is a comment on the economy over that time.

My first school was the small Village College. Such institutions were the idea of Henry Morris who was Secretary to the Cambridgeshire Education Committee - the forerunner of the post of Chief Education Officer - in the twenties and thirties. His contention was that as the church was no longer the centre of the community the educational institution should become the social, recreational and educational centre instead. So it was to offer adult classes, opportunities for clubs and societies, contain a branch of the public library, offer clinics for young mothers and babies, sponsor exhibitions, etc. It would also contain a secondary school. Houses were to be built for the Warden, some teaching staff and the Caretaker. The buildings were to be attractive and well designed. In short it was to be truly a centre of village life.

Ten colleges were built before and after the war. Two areas were left, one on the east and one on the west of the county. The latter contained something of an anomaly - an all age primary school. Some five of these remained in the country. The Boundaries Commission was regularising odd county borders and it was expected that the western side would be altered and this school's area would be moved into neighbouring Bedfordshire. There was considerable local opposition to this because such a move would entail the loss of a projected Village College. So the border was left unaltered and a small but very attractive building was provided to house a one form entry secondary school by taking in the upper half of the existing 'primary' school.

The locality responded with delight and soon we had a wide ranging adult programme which, in two years, had the second highest adult enrolment in the county. Local houses were used for classes once the college was full. Local estate agents used the adult education brochure in their advertisements and a builder erected high standard houses on a small plot nearby with his brochures full of 'nearby facilities and activities'. But the interesting point for me was the fact that everything was completed so the first students could enter a lovely building on their first day. Indeed, so well prepared had it been that on the sports field the cricket square at first was not up to standard so there was time to dig it up and relay it! As I mentioned earlier the college was formally opened by Lord Butler, then Master of Trinity College and well known to senior members of the Education Committee.

In each college the three senior members of staff were the Warden (a title copied from some university colleges), the school's Deputy Head and the Adult Tutor - responsible for the adult education programme. Houses were provided for each of these. My first deputy had been at St Andrew's, though a year or two after me. He had taken posts abroad and had subsequently become head of a school in what was then Rhodesia. Concerned about the political changes he returned to the UK. After some time as a deputy he again got a headship. The first Adult Tutor also went on to headship where he served admirably for a long time and was subsequently rewarded with an OBE.

The second Adult Tutor was already a prolific author of sci-fi books under various pen names. He went on to an educational post in industry, then to a headship, then entered the Ministry of the Church of England. He has frequently appeared on television and still undertakes various lectureships. Recently I reviewed for Amazon two sci-fi books written by him and his wife.

It is satisfying to see how former staff members of my schools have gone on to greater things. All first deputies of my three schools became heads. One head of Physics from my upper school went on to be an inspector, then to the headship of an excellent school and has recently been knighted. I like to think that I influenced them slightly, if only perhaps demonstrating what not to do!

No doubt they and all teachers faced problems whenever cuts were made to educational budgets as happened all too frequently. These gave no chance of planning, they had to be accommodated more or less immediately. The school where I was deputy head had narrow corridors; the architect had faced a sudden reduction in his budget which he achieved simply by reducing the front to rear depth of the building. In July 1981 a sudden cut was announced and we had to face a 10% reduction in staff for September. This meant that planned additions for a further increase in the roll had to be scrapped with inevitable fudging which, understandably, was unpopular.

My second school, in Derbyshire, was in buildings of CLASP type. The acronym stands for Consortium of Local Authorities Special Purchase. This achieved greater value for money though also greater conformity and such buildings, not restricted to schools, are easily recognisable. For my school the architect brought into play a new concept, that of open planning, thus giving a reduction in building costs. Little heed was paid to what large groups of students would do in such areas and I was most concerned at open plan Science labs with the usual benches on which bottles of chemicals were to be stored. I remembered these from my grammar school where they were in lockable separate labs. He also provided separate Science lecture rooms with a main demonstration bench and tiered seating. The image in his mind of Science teaching in universities and colleges was very evident. Obviously he did not take into account the situation of hundreds of unoccupied teenagers loose in open plan buildings during wet lunch hours!

A better attempt was made with plans of the next projected upper school when I was in my final post, in Bedfordshire. These were laid before the group of existing heads and we were able to peruse them in detail. Looking at the dining hall and its entrance I asked ingenuously where the 'dinner queue' could stand. Outside the entrance door was a small area beyond which rooms were ranged but no corridor to the dining room. No account had been taken of the simple fact that on entry students needed to pass a desk where they handed in dinner tickets or had passes checked or paid, etc. Inevitably they had to form a queue, traditionally controlled by prefects and the teacher(s) on duty as was normal in those days. It was obvious the architect had never experienced such procedure. In the event the school was never built because the child population decreased.

That highlights the general problem of planning - how is accurate information to be obtained to inform future needs? There were formulae laid down centrally as to how LEAs were to estimate future child population numbers but local changes could occur quickly and render these useless. I met the intransigence of attitudes when the school was well established and popular but overall numbers of children in the county were falling. I was summoned to a Planning Committee meeting in County Hall to debate whether my school should be closed to lessen the overall projected spare capacity. I presented my figures of expected intake, based on careful research of numbers in all feeder schools and known local building projects and plans. The response was that these were hopelessly optimistic, as is 'always the case with headteachers!' However, I was sure they were conservative. I was proved correct as numbers on roll continued to grow. To-day the roll is 1850 with a sixth form of 600, far outstripping my modest figures.

The problem of planning is the impossibility of forecasting human activity and occasional sudden changes. For all of my teaching career schools had catchment areas from which intakes were drawn and not much notice was taken of individual anomalies. However as comprehensive education spread, far more active and politically astute parents had their children at such schools and these were keen to ensure the best for their youngsters. Choice of schools became a key requirement which elicited various changes of policy over the years as the main parties responded one way or another. I saw the beginnings of this process when, occasionally, I received a visitor who informed me that he or she lived outside my catchment area, even in a different county, but that they were determined to send their child to my school, so would I explain how they could do so? Of course I couldn't; I simply explained that I was only allowed to accept a child whose address was in the area. I confess to emphasizing the word address. Most got the message and in due course parents' cars made longer journeys than one would expect. My immediate successor enjoyed the removal of catchment areas as well as having school based management control. Soon intake numbers rose rapidly again. But none of this could have been built into wider planning procedures, the only arbiter was the school itself.

It is situated on a lovely site on the edge of a village which itself is centre to an extensive rural area. There is a large Research Establishment nearby and the Science Department enjoyed many useful links with it. One governor undertook some population research and came to the conclusion that the village had the greatest density of graduates in the country. There was competition for students, however, because there were four very well established independent schools which could cream off the most able children at age eleven because many parents could afford private education. Developing a successful alternative, therefore, was certainly a challenge and as we appointed the first members of staff I ensured we had a good cross section including some with grammar school experience and Oxbridge degrees. We also had excellent teachers of practical subjects and in many ways our leavers were welcomed in local industry.

Its location meant that the great majority of students travelled to it by coach. There is a long narrow drive up to and across the front of the building, at the end of which is an island. At the conclusion of the school day the coaches perforce have to line up, collect their passengers and then, when the first moves all have to follow along, round the island and away. There is no time to waste; anyone left behind has to be taken home or collected. The downside to this is the difficulty of organising after-school activities. Occasionally I used to amuse visitors in my room as the end of session bell sounded and we stood by the window to witness the disappearance of nearly a thousand students in ten minutes flat. By the time I left there were about eighteen coaches. A friend has told me that this year there are thirty-six! Some are privately contracted by parents' groups. No doubt there is no formula which could have predicted that.

I mentioned the narrow drive. The architect informed me this was deliberately so to prevent access being made part way along it to fields on either side which could have been targets for housing development. Later someone, somewhere, altered the appropriate regulations and the fields are now covered with houses. Another example of planning going awry.

The phased development of the school meant appointing a significant number of new teachers each year, so I spent many hours reading application forms and interviewing. I well remember my own interview, or rather interviews, for the Village College. Some of the applicants were called to have individual interviews with three senior LEA officers, including the Chief. Then we were taken to view the partly completed buildings, though I had already done this. Three weeks later a smaller number was called and again interviewed individually by officers. We were told that in the afternoon we would be interviewed by them sitting with the full governing body, which had declined to appoint representatives for the purpose. Left to our own devices at lunchtime we candidates walked into central Cambridge, found the well-known Blue Boar, and enjoyed a good lunch with a decent red wine. This was not on expenses, however. It must have put me on good form when facing the twenty-six interviewers ranged around a very large oval table. Later, after some deliberation I was called back and offered the post.

I tried to make the process as stress free as possible for our candidates. As they arrived I took them to the staff room and gave them coffee or tea. I was well used to this process because I had long since decided that I would not have such items brought to me in my room - I would make my coffee, etc., in the small adjunct to the staffroom amusingly referred to as the kitchen. It had a sink, a refrigerator and an electric socket and plenty of cupboard space for everyone's mugs and cups for guests. I would then take the group on a tour of the school during which, when lessons changed, they could see and judge the students at close quarters. If, as was usually the case, the post they were applying for was in a department I left them with the head of department so he or she and the other staff could assess how well individuals might fit in - and vice versa.

I always said, and meant it, that the interview was a two-way process; it was as much a matter of applicants assessing whether they really wanted to join our staff as us choosing one of them. Not everyone liked my style, which they could readily see as the day progressed. I assured them that if anyone wanted to drop out at any point they were free to do so without loss of expenses. At lunchtime they were taken to the dining hall where staff always ate and sat with the students at tables each with eight places. I did reserve a table for the candidates so they could talk together. The one privilege I always reserved for staff was as and when they went for lunch they went to the top of the queue to be served - they had work to do or needed some leisure time during the lunch break, and we were not in Sweden!

In the afternoon individual interviews took place with the Chair of Governors, the appropriate County Inspector or the Area Education Officer, the head of the appropriate department, and me. When it came to the point of making a decision it was most usual that a unanimous decision came easily. Occasionally, of course, there were two first rate candidates and I would have welcomed an opportunity to select both. For me the worst part of the day always came when the post had been offered and accepted and I returned to the staffroom to thank the other candidates for their applications and wish them success in other applications. Often there was sincere regret on both sides.

Probably the occasion when this process was quite a bore was after the suddenly imposed 10% reduction in staffing in 1981. Rapidly application numbers shot up as more teachers chased fewer jobs. We had advertised for two basic posts, suitable for candidates who had just qualified by taking PGCEs after gaining their degrees. One was for Geography, the other for History. I received just over three hundred for the first and just under two hundred and fifty for the second. Reducing those to two lists of six took a very long time.

The phased growth of the school affected both parents and students. The former faced the problem of committing their youngsters to a completely unknown future or, if they could afford to do so and their children were bright enough, sending them to one of the independent schools at age eleven. For the students the majority knew they were special because they had been told so since they were in the lower schools; then they transferred to the middle schools knowing their stay would be just two years. At the various meetings I had with parent groups before the opening they listened intently as I described the curriculum, the intended staffing and the buildings together with the ethos I hoped to develop.

The children finally arrived, dressed in their new uniforms - the second such outfit parents had bought in two years. I stress finally. Upper schools in the previous phases had been accommodated temporarily on middle school sites awaiting building completion. In our case, I was informed, building was well advanced and we could open properly housed. As the intended opening day approached it was obvious the building would not be safe so local radio was invoked to announce the children would have an extra week's holiday. Then at 9.00pm on the day before they were to arrive the builders cut through the main electricity supply cable! They assured me they would have a generator and temporary lights in the hall well before opening time. This was essential because the hall-cum-theatre had no windows. Of course the students arrived first, so we had to usher them into the tiered seating with only reflected light from the open door. The upside of this was that they were absolutely silent, though I don't recommend it as a method of class control. I began by welcoming them and assuring everyone that none of us would forget the school's opening. Suddenly I was interrupted by the noise of a generator starting close at hand and a harsh yellow light illuminating the hall by shining directly into the students' eyes.

When I had introduced the form tutors - or class teachers if you prefer - each read out the list of names of his or her charges and then led them away to their classroom. This entailed a neat balancing act as everyone walked in single file across raised planks as the builders continued to lay floor tiles. As the days passed the building was brought into full readiness, though a hidden problem wasn't revealed immediately and had yet to manifest itself.

In the surrounding area was a large airfield used to train pilots of large airliners. It had long been a possible venue for London's third airport. The architect's brief, therefore, was to provide as much sound reduction as possible. He achieved this by having no opening windows in most rooms but with an air conditioning-cum-heating system throughout the building - even with humidity control in the Music rooms. The roof space above all the blocks was generous and the equipment impressive, with trunking snaking for many metres. During the first warm September days there were some complaints that rooms were rather warm and I asked for thermometers to be available and read regularly. Then the weather turned colder and I received the opposite complaint. Matters got worse as the term proceeded and temperature graphs showed many classrooms below the required 64 degrees fahrenheit at the beginning of each day. I persuaded the Caretaker to start the heating boilers even earlier than his official instructions, but the problem remained. Without full managerial control I could only keep passing on my concern to the LEA. Finally, as the weather turned really cold, I said I would have to send the students home if the minimum required temperature could not be achieved. It was a hollow threat because as they and I knew I had no control over the provision of coaches, but, of course, someone might mention the problem to local radio or television…

Finally a full investigation was undertaken and the air conditioning trunking was opened. The problem was immediately apparent. All internal equipment lay in pieces, never having been fitted. Subsequent enquiries revealed there had been a dispute between the builders and the air conditioning specialists, so their workers had simply put down their equipment and left. No one had checked inside the trunking afterwards! In a short time we enjoyed well conditioned air, cooler in summer and warmer in winter - not the reverse.

In stark contrast to the readiness of my first school work on the sports field of the upper school was not begun for some months after it opened. Then suddenly the contractors brought some impressive heavy machinery on site and appeared to be undertaking levelling. Having no responsibility for this work neither I nor any Games staff took close interest. Then someone pointed out that piles of soil were stacked into mini-hills well away from the buildings alongside an isolated lane that skirted the site. On the field surface many stones were revealed and we were asked to organise lines of students to pick these up. This we did, thinking how sensible it was to ensure no stones could surface through the soil when it was redistributed. However it gradually disappeared from the site. Stones having been removed by unpaid labour the field was then sown with grass seed. Many more months passed before it was ready for use. Even then it required plenty of fertilizer.

We were able to appoint an excellent Head of Environmental Studies, Tom M. The site had a small copse which had been untouched for many years so this provided opportunities for studying both flora and fauna - the latter being mainly birds. Tom was very knowledgeable about both, as well as a number of rare breeds, so when he developed a small farm such rarities as Soay and Jacob sheep and Silky chickens were bred. Tom also ensured students had experience of the financial side of small holding as well as using all necessary skills, such as sheep shearing.

We decided to use a particular area of land for the farm. On the overall plans a small building appeared on this area. After the school had been open for some weeks bricklayers arrived and started laying courses of bricks. They did so most enthusiastically and the walls rose...and rose...and rose. Soon it took on the appearance of a mini-skyscraper devoid of windows. Many eyebrows were raised as well, so I called the Adviser for Environmental Studies. He arrived to see for himself; immediately he contacted the building firm. In their turn they contacted the bricklayers and told them to look closely at the plans. Very shortly the height of the walls was reduced by half. We crossed giraffes off the list of potential rare breeds.

The first year group thoroughly enjoyed their special status. With a comparatively small number of teachers close relations soon developed and we enjoyed the good points of a small school, as I knew from the experience of my first headship. The buddy feeling has remained within the group over the years as I discovered on two much later occasions. When a purpose built Sixth Form Centre was commissioned by my successor, previous students were invited to the opening. The first year group, who obviously were the first sixth formers, decided to have their own celebration and so booked the building for a party a few days before the official event. With some of the original staff I was invited - and on arrival found myself kissed by a large number of beautiful young ladies!

Years later when I queued in the local surgery for the annual flu jab, I glanced at the notice board and saw a note headed, 'Were you in the first group at the Upper School in 1975?' There followed details of a get-together at a nearby restaurant. I sent an email saying I was around on the first day and received a delighted reply inviting me to join them. The organiser, I remembered, had left to join an airline; later she told me she had spent twenty years as cabin crew with another one. Again I was welcomed with many kisses, this time by ladies I knew were forty-six years old. I had privileged information!

Before the opening, when I spoke to groups of parents at various meetings, I carried around a site model made by the architect to establish site lines from various angles. All the blocks were fixed in place except one - a projected swimming pool. With full financial control my successor invited me to join a committee investigating additions to the building. So we looked at swimming pools. There is no doubt one would have been a very popular facility for the school and the area. We visited a number, but enquiries about finance revealed that each operated at a loss. It would have been rash to recommend such a situation. What was built later was an excellent addition to the sports hall with fully equipped exercise rooms. It was opened by a well-known athlete who was a former student and often appears on television as a commentator of athletic events. Now it carries her name.

The cosy relationship between staff and students was cemented at the end of the first autumn term with a 'concert' at which both engaged in plenty of leg pulling. I dressed as a zombie cleric and sang epitaphs revealing greater knowledge of their activities than they might have imagined. Some students produced an excellent spoof of Play School in which the staff were obviously children. So, when the next academic year began the first year group were shocked to find a large number of new students thoroughly enjoying their new surroundings with a new cohort of teachers they didn't know. Naturally they felt ostracized. It was some time before they adjusted fully to the changes and relationships. The one strange feature they experienced which could never be altered was the fact that they had no senior, more mature, students above them. In due course they assumed that mantle which they did very well, but their experience in the school was unique.

There is no doubt that some bright students from the age group in the locality went to independent schools, so when the first sixth formers left there was only a modest number that went on to university. However one student went to Cambridge, an event which I know greatly bolstered the school's image. In a couple of years university entrance was twice the national rate. Following one girl who insisted on leaving an independent school to enter our sixth form a steady stream followed and continued annually - without any loss of prospects for the individuals. As Convenor of the area branch of the then Secondary Heads' Association I knew my independent colleagues well because all were members. My Chair of Governors was also an independent school governor, so relationships between the schools were friendly. This meant that parental choice of education for their children was perfectly open. The total number of students in the sixth form has continued to rise so the change to 18 of the official leaving age may not make a great difference. Perhaps, however, the nomenclature of Years 12 and 13 will at last take over from the 'Sixth Form'.

Chapter 42

A Convenor? Really a Secretary. I seemed to collect jobs like this as a matter of course. Shortly after being appointed to the Village College the group of wardens appointed me their secretary, to the surprise of the Chief Education Officer who rang me to enquire what my duties were. He seemed concerned that the newest and youngest warden should be so quickly elevated to a position of wider responsibility. I assured him I would be just a lowly scribe. Nevertheless I soon found myself organising a conference of all community college heads as LEAs slowly accepted that school facilities should be available for use by all people in their localities.

As students our first introduction to teachers' unions came at college when we were addressed by representatives of the two main ones - the National Union of Teachers and the National Association of Schoolmasters. As we saw it the great difference between them was that the former admitted both men and women but the latter did not. No doubt there were other matters of policy they were concerned with, but the great majority of our year group decided we preferred to be with both men and women, so we joined the NUT. As far as we knew every teacher was in a union so it seemed sensible to follow suit.

The first occasion to evince a show of militancy came in the mid-fifties when the government decreed that teachers' superannuation payments would rise from 5 to 6% of salary. Large meetings were held and everyone became strongly opposed to the change. I felt that it would be much better to campaign for better pay all round rather than threaten to strike over what everyone really knew was a *fait accompli*. So at the meeting I attended I voted against strike action over the raised superannuation payment. It so happened that I was sitting in the front row. After I raised my almost solitary arm a loud voice behind me yelled,

'Make that man stand up and show himself to his colleagues - he's a blackleg!'

I recognised the voice as that of a headteacher of a school near to the Ashtree. I certainly did not stand up, though I would have welcomed the opportunity to point out the true meaning of the word 'blackleg'. But the NUT in those days was dominated by headteachers. Nevertheless the incident made me question whether I would ever go on strike. I decided that probably I would not. Over another matter I did write a letter of resignation, as requested by the city's branch of the NUT, as did all its members, to threaten our employers. The gesture was useless, however, as both sides knew it would not be acted upon.

Subsequently I left the NUT and joined the NAS, but only because they offered their members an excellent home insurance deal. Later still I joined the National Association of Head Teachers (NAHT), but found secondary heads were in a minority, so I joined the Head Masters Association. There was an equivalent organisation for Head Mistresses so I didn't feel too bad about joining an all-male affair. Not long afterwards the men and women decided to get together so the Secondary Heads Association (SHA) came into being. I collected the job of Convenor for the county one day when my colleagues were dividing up various jobs. It was in no sense because they felt I was particularly a 'union' man. SHA is now ASCL - the Association of School and College Leaders. I am now a Life Member, an honour given by virtue of age only!

A group of SHA members decided there was an opportunity to visit the European Parliament in Strasbourg. We qualified for a grant which reduced our travel and accommodation costs. Most wives accompanied us, as did Rocky. We enjoyed an excellent explanatory talk by one of the officials but our visit to the Chamber was badly timed because members were just voting electronically upon a range of issues which had been debated. The procedure was very protracted and I was left wondering how much previous debate there had been. We also learnt that because there had been no agreement about a permanent location for the

Parliament it met in rotation, the other bases being Luxembourg and Brussels. Because it was necessary to keep all officials in each base thoroughly informed, verbatim typed records of every meeting were taken daily by road to the other two sites. We were each required to write an answer to a question they supplied. These perforce were handwritten; I wondered who read them and whether they were typed and triplicated immediately for dispatch.

A very recent news item carries the information that possibly Strasbourg will be dropped as a venue for the Parliament, thus reducing costs very considerably. No doubt a final decision will not be made quickly; France will not enjoy the loss of its location in the triple base.

We also visited an excellent vineyard in the Mosel Valley and bought some of its produce. Unusually I kept two bottles for a considerable period and was delighted when finally they were opened.

A couple of years later the group decided to arrange another visit, this time to Brussels. We were surprised, and rather embarrassed, when the official detailed to speak to us about the workings of the European Parliament appeared. He was the person who had performed the same duty in Strasbourg! He gave no indication of recognition and we were unable to decide whether he had forgotten us or was a good actor.

My personal decision about striking or not was tested occasionally when as a member of SHA I found most of my staff taking such action. Was I prepared to counteract their action in any way, or should I join them? Usually I fell back on the advice given by SHA that members should not lessen the effects of other union strikes. On one occasion that proved impossible, however, due to the fact that so many of the school students travelled by coach. A politician irritatingly disparaged teachers by saying they worked for only five hours a day. Unions responded by instructing members to do just that, which meant afternoon sessions were considerably shortened - our school day always began at 8.30. In towns students could be sent home early. I had no power to call our coaches early, so I faced having many hundreds of students unoccupied in buildings without teachers. Obviously there were safety considerations. I compromised by sending them all to the large playground which doubled as tennis courts and supervising them personally, praying for fine weather and no emergencies. Fortunately I received a favourable answer. Finally the LEA agreed to alter the transport timetable and the firms involved were happy to agree because most coaches were free in the early afternoons. Gradually the action stopped as the cause of it withdrew his comments. I did not feel my staff relationship was damaged, but I did feel that my view of strike action was strengthened. In most walks of life a large number of people are inconvenienced through no fault of their own. Surely intelligent people can invent better ways of hitting those who really cause the problem? Of course that is likely to take more effort to achieve and so calls for more time and ingenuity to put into operation. However I am more inclined to go along with such ideas rather than just walking out.

I collected another job in the share-out organised by my colleagues - that of Chair of the Leavers' Service Committee. .The idea of the annual event came from the Chief Education Officer and I was happy to be involved. The Service was held in the central church in the town; choirs were trained by a head of Music and various fairly well known individuals invited each year as guest speakers. Probably the best known was Terry Waite who was an excellent conversationalist at dinner the night before the Service. This was before he was taken hostage and therefore so often in the news headlines. Each year we selected a particular theme, once choosing 'To Boldly Go'. I suppose concern over the split infinitive was inevitable!

The Service didn't survive long after the Chief and I retired. No doubt its demise was due to the expenditure involved.

Chapter 43

I am eternally grateful to Rocky and our two sons, Gareth and David, for accepting so willingly our various changes of locality as I gained promotion. They were absolutely brilliant. They also accepted the time I spent studying for a degree which, at last, I undertook whilst I was Warden of the Village College. Again Rocky sparked this off because she spotted a news item in the 'Telegraph' that a course in the Sociology of Education was being developed at Enfield College of Technology under the auspices of the Council for National Academic Awards (CNAA). I applied, was interviewed and accepted with exactly the same time commitment as announced for the BA Ordinary course so many years earlier - one afternoon and two evenings a week. On this occasion my request for release for the afternoon session was willingly granted by the Chief Education Officer and my deputy was happy to be in charge - he had been a head as I mentioned erlier. It began in February and was due to last a further two and a half years. I found it very stimulating, further enhanced when I was granted a reader's admission to Cambridge University Library. This meant I could access any book or periodical on any reading list.

I soon became acquainted with a lecturer from a College of Education who was also on the course. In the July following its inception the organisers decided to rearrange it to run for three years from that date - two for Part One and one for Part Two. My friend and I were not keen on the extra time this entailed, so we quietly undertook a strategy to circumvent this. Four lectures were held each week for two parallel groups reading for Part One, so she went to two and I went to the others. We took full notes with carbon sheets in our notebooks, exchanged these weekly and attended lectures in turn, so we each attended fortnightly. Neither of us could have managed this without our easy availability of books. The Chief also gave me a term's sabbatical to write a thesis as required for one of the sections of the honours course.

One hidden difficulty was manifested when the CNAA validated each course. Concerned to maintain high standards the tutors tended to overdo things and a friend who had a London University Psychology degree said our course was nearly as full as his total course! But my companion and I had to admit to our ploy after successfully sitting finals. We got away with paying an extra fee. Now, of course, the CNAA does not exist and all such colleges and polytechnics are universities and award their own degrees. Enfield College is now Middlesex University.

Having completed one I wondered about a Master's degree and enrolled with Nottingham University for an M.Phil. I decided to research problems newly qualified teachers faced in their probationary year as I mentioned in a previous chapter and interviewed a hundred teachers and their headteachers. Nearly everyone allowed me to tape record the interviews so I had plenty of evidence. I also sent out follow up questionnaires. I then faced the work of turning what I had into data and drawing conclusions. However, as seemed to be a pattern in my life, before I could set about my thesis I was appointed to my upper school and faced the work of developing it from scratch. Naively I thought I would have some spare time before things got very busy. I didn't. Reluctantly, after a while, I had to withdraw my registration; My tutor kindly said he regretted that because he felt I would have been successful.

I suppose that comment stuck in my mind when, years later, I heard that a one-off one year course leading to an M.Phil. was being offered by Cambridge University. Tentatively I applied and enjoyed a highly stimulating interview with two possible tutors. I was accepted by a college because internal membership was required. Then two events occurred which sabotaged this attempt. The first was that the CEO would not release me for a full year until the following year. Then my father died and I was taken up with the unavoidable problems that produced. So I gave up thoughts of a second degree. It would, of course, have been entirely for personal interest.

After twelve years in my third headship I reached the fortieth year since qualification. I had assumed I would follow the usual practice of retiring but undertaking some part time teaching because I felt well able to do so. But as I mentioned earlier other opportunities presented themselves as education changed in many ways. At first it was arrangements for GRIST (Grant Related In-Service Training, another wonderful acronym), but then I joined SIMS (Schools Information Management Systems). Here I was to spend eleven years but only on three, later two, days per week. I gave telephone help to schools using timetable software. Calls were logged as they came in and once I saw a very surprising juxtaposition - one from my former grammar school followed by one from the school whose premises we shared in Stroud at the beginning of the wartime evacuation period.

I was well looked after by many young people who were brilliant with computers which I most certainly am not. For my part, though, I could offer some knowledge of schools, staffing and timetables so there was a happy partnership. But as my birthdays came round at seemingly greater speed I decided it was time to bid farewell. I had been involved with education of one kind or another for fifty-eight years.

Noble Sir? I hardly think so! Fortunate? Most certainly. I once listened to a Professor of Education telling us that people of my generation in teaching had everything going for them during the years of expansion, so much so that provided we did nothing foolish if we wanted promotion we were 'hoovered up into senior posts'. I can accept that. I am sure that is why I found my whole career very satisfying and enjoyable. Very rarely did I get out of bed dreading the day ahead.

But I know there are teachers who find the work very stressful indeed. One source of such a problem lies in the deceptively simple task of keeping control of a class. I can give two examples of lack of control. Near the church I frequented in my home city were two secondary schools, one for boys and the other for girls. The buildings were some two hundred metres apart, the space between occupied by quite large houses. If I was at church for any reason during a schoolday the non-stop noise from the boys' school was loud and insistent. The girls' school, however, was very quiet. Working in the former would have been awful, I feel,

One of the activities I first took up in my semi-retirement state was to help schools monitor real learning time in classes, so I shadowed certain students during part of each day. In one class in one school I sat incognito at the back of a class that called out, shouted to one another, walked around and generally made themselves total nuisances. The young teacher ignored the mayhem and spoke quietly to one or two students who gave her some attention in the first row of desks. This continued for the forty minutes of the lesson, at the end of which the students rushed out, then walked normally along the corridor behaving quite properly. Usually I would not mention what I had seen in a class to the headteacher, because I wanted anonymity for the exercise, but on this occasion I broke my rule. I was relieved to hear that the young lady had already decided to give up teaching and was leaving shortly.

That begs the question as to why she had trained in the first place. A single job interview cannot easily recognise which candidates will have good class control and which will not. Today there is more opportunity for some people to enter the profession by completely training in schools. This certainly gives both the school and the prospective teacher every opportunity to assess ability to exercise control. The skill is one of those hard to define and even harder to teach, but if you don't possess the ability to bring a noisy class under control very quickly, you will not enjoy teaching.

Of course classes are often noisy for very good reasons. Practical lessons in workshops, Drama lessons, discussion groups, PE lessons, etc., and many others, will all result in noise but it should be purposeful and able to be silenced when necessary for further teaching and explanation. The mistake often made is for the teacher to talk too quickly over declining noise and discussion. The trick is to wait for silence before you start speaking again. But that requires you to get silence quickly in the first instance.

Occasionally I taught Drama. If you are encouraging youngsters to perform actions creatively they will be noisy!

Once I attended a course on Drama in the Secondary School at Swansea University where, in addition to the section on Dance I described earlier, a very personable lecturer gave us many insights into Drama teaching, In the matter of control she used the concept of the freeze signal which she said needed to be loud enough for everyone to hear and for everyone to be trained to respond accordingly. She then, in my opinion, ruined the idea by suggesting hitting a tambourine. I decided not to emulate excellent members of the Salvation Army and looked for an alternative. Surprisingly I found I could clap my hands very loudly in a particular way. On the rare occasions my decibels were insufficient I could yell 'Oi' at the top of my voice both loudly and unusually. Used sparingly it was effective. Mentally I thanked my efforts on the RAF Sergeants' Course. We had used the signal with a whistle on playground duty so many years before at Dayton Road; the first sound meant 'everyone stand still, in silence' and a second blast indicated everyone should move into lines for classrooms with no talking.

I enjoyed acting as well as teaching Drama. Rocky joined me in the amateur society I had been in since I was in my late teens and she really excelled. The society produced two plays each year, usually comedies, though once we staged 'Duet for Two Hands' by Mary Hayley Bell. The character I played, Stephen Cass, has to play two pieces of music on a baby grand piano, one of which accompanies another character singing in Norwegian. At one point a 'ghostly' piano is heard off stage and off-key. Our stage was small, so if I was to mime playing a third piano, correctly tuned, would be necessary. So I wondered whether I could play for real. Years before, aged six, I had given in to my father's exhortations to have piano lessons. He did not play himself but, a stickler for punctuality and regularity he insisted I did half an hour's practice each evening - not the best way to encourage enjoyment of learning. I was not taught any interesting modern tunes, only pieces I had never heard as well as hymn tunes. So when I was evacuated I was able to drop the lessons.

I asked a head of Music to annotate the 'Duet' scores with fingering and then I practised with far greater enthusiasm until I mastered playing, despite the fact that Stephen Cass wears gloves.

Friends who were pianists said I performed competently, so we managed with two instruments. After the final performance, of course, I stopped playing, then, after about a year, someone asked whether I could still play the pieces. I then realised I had no residual knowledge whatsoever. The skill had completely disappeared.

Later, in another society, Rocky played the central character in 'Arsenic and Old Lace'. This also requires on-stage piano playing - something she had never done. We used a piano with a dummy keyboard, angled so this was not visible to the audience, and Rocky mimed to a record. I was in the audience with the County Adviser for Drama next to me. Well into her performance he whispered that it was refreshing to see someone actually playing rather than miming. Praise indeed!

Near Christmas one year the group put on a medley of items, including me acting as Scrooge facing a projection of Marley's ghost. I recorded Marley's words, so on stage I was effectively taking both parts. I was dressed with the appropriate nightcap and made up to look pinched and miserly. The local paper took shots of various performances and I appeared on the front page alongside a smiling Father Christmas from a department store under the headline, 'The Faces of Christmas'.

I suppose the joint performance Rocky and I enjoyed most was in 'The Happiest Days of Your Life'. We had both acted in a previous production, but this time we were Godfrey Pond, Headmaster of a Boys' School and Miss Whitchurch, Headmistress of a Girls' School inadvertently sent to share premises. In the film of the play the roles were acted by the unforgettable Alistair Sim and Margaret Rutherford.

The first head of Music at the upper school produced an operetta entitled 'Newcomer' written and composed by her husband. Both were excellent musicians. The theme is the life of the individual and there were many parts for students with good voices. I was asked to take one part that was less appropriate for teenagers - that of 'War'. I performed dressed in modern camouflage uniform with miniature sergeant's chevrons and a black beret, suitably angled and replete with cap badges. My experience of an RAF version obviously came in useful as

I barked orders at characters miming a bayonet charge, One of the ladies who served school meals saw me at a rehearsal and suggested I should appear in my role and supervise the returned plate trolley in the dining hall. This was always a problem as students rushed out without stacking plates carefully. So I did - and really hammed the stentorious sergeant. Apparently I was so successful many students were frightened to bring their plates to the trolley at all! For my part I had expected much leg pulling because I was so obviously overplaying.

In 'A Century of Education' by Richard Aldrich et al. the point is made that during the hundred years the emphasis in education moved from teaching to learning. At nearly the halfway mark our Psychology course at St Andrew's certainly homed in on child-centred learning. But much of the whole course was devoted to the practice of teaching - hence our weekly visits to schools and our periods of block practice underscored by our precious record books. The greatest catalyst for the change undoubtedly was the computer and allied technology. A classroom to-day is so different from my earliest ones by virtue of the learning equipment used by all individuals. The teacher now is far more a manager of learning resources than a didactic source of knowledge. The 'Ole Country Boy behind the Norfolk reeds' with his room full of Mac computers was in the vanguard, of course.

The shift in emphasis was not welcomed by some teachers who felt the role in which they were safe was being undermined. I was not one of them. Whatever I know about the new technology I have learned from people often young enough to be my grandchildren. I am quite content to be treated by a young doctor provided he or she is a success. I enjoyed some golf lessons from a young professional who was a former student. Teaching and learning roles depend on where the skills and knowledge lie that are to be transmitted. Age and or position should not affect the interchange.

I can reminisce about my own schooldays and how I got information on any topic. The school library had many empty shelves but there were the complete volumes of the fourteenth edition of the 'Encyclopaedia Britannica' I mentioned earlier.

These we used very extensively. However if we needed to read a particular book a visit to the local branch of the city's library was necessary entailing a short walk from school or a cycle ride from home. If the book was not there a bus ride was required to visit the central library which was far more extensive. Either way the exercise took some hours, maybe days if a request had to be put in. Now I have a Kindle and can download a book in a matter of minutes.

I am sufficiently enthusiastic to revel in that. It shows how firmly education is in the hands of the learner today.

About the Author

Nigel Flaxton (pen name) opened three new schools as a headteacher, then retired to part time work in various ways, concluding with eleven years helping schools with a Windows based timetable program. He and his wife bred, showed and judged dogs; he judged twice at Crufts and overseas from Finland to New Zealand.

He has also written books in different genres. *Sammy the Samoyed* is a novel about the life of a dog that has a variety of experiences, some amusing and some serious. It is available on Amazon, as is *Moltation*, a short sci-fi story about the discovery of an amazing means of self-protection. The website www.roadfork. co.uk offers *Roadfork in the Valley* as a free download which is a novel based on the revelations of Emanuel Swedenborg, the 18th century Swedish scientist, nobleman, theologian and seer, in which six disparate characters begin the exploration of their surprising continued existence after death.